Sir Edward Coke and
"The Grievances of the Commonwealth,"
1621–1628

STUDIES IN LEGAL HISTORY

Published by The University of North Carolina Press
in association with the
American Society for Legal History

Sir Edward Coke
and
"The Grievances of the Commonwealth,"
1621–1628

by Stephen D. White

THE UNIVERSITY OF NORTH CAROLINA PRESS
CHAPEL HILL

© 1979 The University of North Carolina Press
All rights reserved
Manufactured in the United States of America
ISBN 0-8078-1335-4
Library of Congress Catalog Card Number 78-16418

Library of Congress Cataloging in Publication Data

White, Stephen D., 1945–
  Sir Edward Coke and "the grievances of the
Commonwealth," 1621–1628.

  (Studies in legal history)
  Bibliography: p.
  Includes index.
    1. Law—Great Britain—History and criticism.
2. Coke, Edward, Sir, 1552–1634. 3. Great
Britain—Politics and government—1603–1649.
I. Title. II. Series.
KD612.W47   328.41′092′4 [B]   78-16418
ISBN 0-8078-1335-4

For My Parents

Contents

Acknowledgments

I began my work on the parliamentary career of Sir Edward Coke in 1968 and would never have completed it without the advice and encouragement that I continually received from Samuel E. Thorne, who first suggested that I work on Coke and who suffered through this project with me from beginning to end. I am also deeply indebted to Wallace MacCaffrey, who read several drafts of this book, as well as the doctoral thesis on which the book is partly based, and whose help and support have been invaluable to me over the past seven years. I also wish to give special thanks to Charles M. Gray, whose comments on successive drafts of the book have invariably been most helpful; to Morton J. Horwitz, whose penetrating criticisms of the book were always useful; to Morris S. Arnold, who gave me valuable help and encouragement in my work; and to David S. Berkowitz, who allowed me to use and quote from his forthcoming book on John Selden and who made many valuable suggestions about my work on Coke. In addition, I received very helpful comments on the thesis on which this book is partly based from Elizabeth Read Foster and Thomas A. Green and from Theodore K. Rabb, who was also kind enough to show me a chapter from his forthcoming book on Sir Edwin Sandys. I also profited greatly from my conversations about Coke with Harold Berman, G. R. Elton, Harold Garrett-Goodyear, George S. Kuehn, Peter Lubin, Barbara C. Malament, and Howard Nenner.

My research on Coke's parliamentary career during the 1620s could not have been carried out had it not been for the work of the following scholars who have been associated with the Yale Center for Parliamentary History: J. H. Hexter, Mary Frear Keeler, Robert C. Johnson, Maija Jansson Cole, William B. Bidwell, Norah M. Fuidge, Elizabeth Read Foster, and Robert E. Ruigh. Almost all of the unpublished parliamentary sources that are noted in the bibliography were consulted in the form of annotated (or occasionally unannotated) transcripts that were made available to me at the center. Work on these materials was begun long ago by the late Wallace M. Notestein, Frances H. Relf, and Hartley Simpson, and it has been carried on by the scholars noted above. I am very grateful to J. H. Hexter, the director of the center, for allowing me to use and quote from these materials and for advising me about my work on Coke. I also wish to thank William B. Bidwell for answering so many of my questions about the parliament of 1628 and giving me such helpful criticisms of my chapter on Coke and the Petition of Right. Finally, I owe particular thanks to Maija Jansson Cole, not only for having commented on the same chapter, but also for having helped me in my work on Coke on countless occasions during the past eight years.

My work on Coke has also been greatly facilitated by the cooperation that I received from the librarians and library staff members of the following institutions: Harvard University; the Institute for Historical Research, London University; Wesleyan University; Yale University; the British Museum Library; and the House of Lords Record Office. I am also grateful to the Society of Fellows, Harvard University; to the Harvard Law School; and to Wesleyan University for having provided me with financial assistance while I worked on this book. I also wish to thank the American Society for Legal History for its support of my work and the editors of The University of North Carolina Press for their assistance. I am also grateful to Elizabeth Bouché, Amanda J. Katz, Edna Haran, and Jane Tosto for their secretarial help.

Abbreviations

APC	*Acts of the Privy Council of England* (1542–1604), ed. John Roche Dasent; and *Acts of the Privy Council of England* (1613–1631).
Berkowitz, *Selden*	David S. Berkowitz, *Scholar in Politics* (a forthcoming work, the tenth chapter of which is entitled "Selden and the Petition of Right").
CD *1621*	*Commons Debates, 1621*, ed. Wallace Notestein, Frances Helen Relf, and Hartley Simpson.
CD *1625*	*Debates in the House of Commons in 1625 . . .*, ed. S. R. Gardiner.
CD *1628*	*Commons Debates, 1628*, ed. Robert C. Johnson, Mary Frear Keeler, Maija Jansson Cole, and William B. Bidwell.
CD *1629*	*Commons Debates for 1629*, ed. Wallace Notestein and Frances H. Relf.
CJ	*Journals of the House of Commons, 1547–1714.*
CSPD	*Calendars of State Papers, Domestic Series.*
CSPVen	*Calendars of State Papers* (Venetian).
Chamberlain, *Letters*	*The Letters of John Chamberlain*, ed. N. E. McClure.
Cobbett, *PH*	[William Cobbett], *The Parliamentary History of England . . .*
D'Ewes, *1624*	Sir Simonds D'Ewes, Proceedings in the House of Commons, 19 February–29 May 1624.
Erle, *1624*	Sir Walter Erle, Proceedings in the House of Commons, 19 February–29 May 1624.
Eliot, *Negotium*	Sir John Eliot, *Negotium Posterorum.*
Elton, *TC*	G. R. Elton, *The Tudor Constitution.*
Foster, *1610*	*Proceedings in Parliament, 1610*, ed. Elizabeth Read Foster.
Gardiner, *History*	Samuel R. Gardiner, *History of England . . . 1603–1642.*

HMC	Historical Manuscripts Commission
Holdsworth, History	Sir William Holdsworth, A History of English Law.
Holland, 1624, I	Sir Thomas Holland, Proceedings in the House of Commons, 25 February–9 April 1624.
Holland, 1624, II	Sir Thomas Holland, Proceedings in the House of Commons, 10 April–15 May 1624.
Holles, 1624	John Holles, Proceedings in the House of Commons, 23 February–19 May 1624.
Howell, ST	A Complete Collection of State Trials . . . Edited by [W. Cobbett and] T. B. Howell.
Institutes	Sir Edward Coke, Institutes of the Laws of England.
Jervoise, 1624	Sir Thomas Jervoise, Proceedings in the House of Commons, 23 February–28 April 1624.
Kenyon, SC	J. P. Kenyon, The Stuart Constitution, 1603–1688.
LD 1621	Notes of the Debates in the House of Lords . . . 1621, ed. S. R. Gardiner.
LD 1621–1628	Notes of the Debates in the House of Lords . . . 1621, 1625, 1628, ed. S. R. Gardiner.
LD 1624–1626	Notes of the Debates in the House of Lords . . . 1624 and 1626, ed. S. R. Gardiner.
LJ	Journals of the House of Lords, 1578–1714.
Nicholas, 1624	Edward Nicholas, Proceedings in the House of Commons, 19 February–29 May 1624.
Notestein, 1604–1610	Wallace Notestein, The House of Commons, 1604–1610
P & D	[Edward Nicholas], Proceedings and Debates of the House of Commons in 1620 and 1621, ed. T. Tyrwhitt.
Pym, 1624	John Pym, Proceedings in the House of Commons, 19 February–7 May 1624.
Pym, 1624a	John Pym, Proceedings in the House of Commons, 13 April–10 May 1624.
Pym, 1625	John Pym, Proceedings in the House of Commons, 1625.
RP	Rotuli Parliamentorum.
Return	Return of the Name of Every Member of the Lower House of Parliament . . . (part 1, Parliaments of England, 1213–1702).
Reports	Sir Edward Coke, The Reports of Sir Edward Coke . . .

Rich, 1624	Sir Nathaniel Rich, Proceedings in the House of Commons, 23 February–6 March 1624.
Ruigh, *1624*	Robert E. Ruigh, *The Parliament of 1624*.
Spedding, *Bacon*	Francis Bacon, *The Works of Sir Francis Bacon*, ed. James Spedding, R. L. Ellis, and D. D. Heath.
Spring, 1624	Sir William Spring, Proceedings in the House of Commons, 19 February–27 May 1624.
SR	*The Statutes of the Realm.*
TED	*Tudor Economic Documents*, ed. Richard H. Tawney and Eileen Power.
Tanner, *CD*	J. R. Tanner, *Constitutional Documents of the Reign of James I, 1603–1625.*
White, "Coke"	Stephen D. White, "Sir Edward Coke in the Parliaments of 1621 and 1624."
Zaller, *1621*	Robert Zaller, *The Parliament of 1621.*

Author's Note

Spelling and Capitalization: Spelling and most capitalization have been normalized in quotations from source materials.

Dates: Dates are given in the Old Style, but the beginning of the year is taken to be January 1.

Citation of Sources for Coke's Parliamentary Speeches: Many passages in this book consist of abbreviated reconstructions of speeches that Sir Edward Coke made in the parliaments of the 1620s. In these reconstructions, some of which run over several paragraphs or even several pages, I try to give a clear, accurate picture of what Coke said in Parliament by weaving together quotations and paraphrases from the fragmentary and sometimes somewhat unreliable reports that were made of his speeches by his contemporaries. I have also attempted, in some cases, to clarify Coke's meaning by inserting my own comments into my reconstructions of his speeches. The sources on which I have based these reconstructions are cited at the end of each reconstructed speech. When a particular passage from a particular speech calls for special comments, I make these comments immediately in footnotes that precede my main citation for the entire speech in question.

Sir Edward Coke and
"The Grievances of the Commonwealth,"
1621–1628

One

Introduction

Sir Edward Coke (1552–1634) was a prominent member of the English ruling elite for about four decades, and for two centuries after his death, his writings exerted a profound influence on English and American law. At no point in his career did he dominate English politics; but he still stands out from the other leading figures of the late Elizabethan and early Stuart periods because of his versatility, his singular capacity for survival, and his powerful influence on his contemporaries and on posthumous generations. Coke was active in the law courts for almost forty years, first as a private practitioner, then as a legal officer of the crown, and finally as a royal judge. He served in every parliament held between 1589 and 1628 as either a member of the Commons or an advisor to the Lords. He also worked with the Privy Council for over thirty years, initially as an occasional assistant, and later as a full-fledged member. At the same time, he participated in the factional political struggles of the later Elizabethan and early Stuart periods while accumulating a fortune that became the envy of his contemporaries. Finally, in Elizabeth's last years, he began to publish various legal works that revealed a wide knowledge of earlier English legal sources and an unparalleled ability to integrate the diverse elements of English common law into a coherent whole; and, coupled with his many years of practical legal experience and his politically influential position, they eventually established him as the leading legal authority of his era. In none of these spheres of activity was Coke without rivals, nor was he preeminent in all of them. He wielded far less political power than men like Salisbury or Buckingham, and his parliamentary experience and influence did not exceed that of such men as Sir Edwin Sandys. Bacon and Ellesmere rivaled him in legal expertise, whereas younger antiquarians like Selden and Prynne were better read in earlier legal sources. Nevertheless, none of Coke's rivals and contemporaries— with the obvious exception of Bacon—succeeded in as wide a range of legal, political, administrative, and literary activities. None was as politically prominent and influential for so long a period of time. And none exercised such a profound influence on the subsequent development of English law.

Coke was born on 1 February 1552 at Mileham in the county of

Norfolk.[1] His father, Robert Coke (d. 1561), was a London lawyer who came from a well established but not prominent gentry family from Norfolk, as did his mother, the former Winifred Knightley. After attending the Norwich Free Grammar School and Trinity College, Cambridge, Edward entered Clifford's Inn in 1571 and moved on to the Inner Temple in the following year. Called to the bar in 1578, he quickly acquired not only a large legal practice but also a formidable reputation within the legal profession. He was made a reader at Lyon's Inn when he was only twenty-seven and was called to the Bench of the Inner Temple at the age of thirty-two, and in 1592 he gave well-attended readings at the latter institution on the Statute of Uses.[2] Meanwhile, his marriage in 1582 to Briget Paston linked him to an old and important Suffolk family and is said to have brought him £30,000.[3] By the later 1580s, moreover, he had become tied to Lord Burghley, the queen's leading councilor and the head of the Cecil faction, and his professional and political standing at court enabled him to become a successful candidate for a series of increasingly important official appointments.[4] Having served as recorder of Norwich (1586), justice of the peace for Norfolk, and recorder of London (1591), he became solicitor general in 1592 and began to assist the Privy Council,[5] and in 1593 Elizabeth made him Speaker of the House of Commons, even though his only previous parliamentary ex-

1. Much of the following biographical material can be found in Catherine Drinker Bowen, *The Lion and the Throne*; Holdsworth, *History*, 5:425–56; and *Dictionary of National Biography*, s.v. "Coke, Sir Edward"; and in the other biographical works cited in fnn. 47 and 48.

2. See "Sir Edward Coke's 'Vade Mecum'," pp. 111–15. (For notes on this work of Coke's, see J. H. Baker, "Coke's Note-books and the Sources of his Reports.") Coke's Norfolk connections may have contributed to his rapid professional advancement. Norfolk men were particularly prominent in the legal profession of this period and held a large number of high legal offices under Elizabeth and James I (see A. Hassell Smith, *County and Court*, pp. 63–64; and Wilfrid Prest, *The Inns of Court under Elizabeth and the Early Stuarts, 1590–1640*, pp. 32–36).

3. Holdsworth, *History*, 5:426 n. 6.

4. Precisely when Coke established his connection with the Cecils has not yet been determined, but by 1587 he had become acquainted with Burghley (see Conyers Read, *Lord Burghley and Queen Elizabeth*, p. 496 n. 6; and R. Hindry Mason, *The History of Norfolk*, p. 385).

5. For notes on the offices that Coke held in this period, see his "Vade Mecum." Coke first served on the Norfolk commission of the peace in 1584 (see J. H. Gleason, *The Justice of the Peace in England, 1558 to 1640*, p. 149). He was also a Norfolk justice of the peace in 1586, 1588, and 1591 and served on all sixteen commissions appointed between 1593 and 1603. He was ranked forty-seventh in 1586 and thirty-fifth two years later, but although he rose to twentieth in 1593, he never stood higher than seventeenth under Elizabeth (see Smith, *County and Court*, p. 352). On his early association with the Privy Council, see *APC, 1592–93*, passim.

perience had been as a burgess for an obscure Suffolk borough in the parliament of 1589.[6] His progress continued in 1594 as the queen made him attorney general in preference to Sir Francis Bacon, whom the earl of Essex was actively promoting for the same office.[7] Upon succeeding to this position, Coke began to investigate and prosecute traitors, recusants, and dissenters while also appearing in the central courts in many more routine cases;[8] and in 1601 he appeared in a highly prominent role as chief prosecutor of the earl of Essex and his followers.[9] Meanwhile, he continued to assist the council and serve on various commissions, and in the parliaments of 1597 and 1601 he acted as an advisor to the House of Lords.[10] In 1598, moreover, after the death of his first wife, Briget, he had solidified his connection with the Cecil family and further increased his fortune by marrying Lady Elizabeth Hatton, who was the grand-daughter of the late Lord Burghley, the niece of Sir Robert Cecil, and the widow of the nephew and heir of the late lord chancellor, Sir Christopher Hatton.[11] In 1601, the favor that Coke enjoyed with the aging queen was given public expression when he entertained her lavishly at one of his estates and gave her presents worth over a thousand pounds.[12]

Elizabeth's death in March 1603 and the succession of James I did nothing initially to damage Coke's political interests, perhaps because he was so closely connected with the king's principal advisor, Sir Robert

6. On Coke's participation in the parliament of 1589, see *Return*, p. 425; and J. E. Neale, *Elizabeth I and her Parliaments, 1584–1601*, pp. 211–13. On his participation in the parliament of 1593, see Neale, *Elizabeth I and her Parliaments, 1584–1601*, pp. 241–323 passim; J. E. Neale, *The Elizabethan House of Commons*, pp. 290, 324, 343, 344, 345, 362, 365, 382; and Smith, *County and Court*, pp. 273–74, 324.

7. Read finds "no evidence" that Burghley favored Coke over Bacon for this position and suggests that Coke may have owed his promotion to the queen herself (*Lord Burghley*, p. 496 and n. 26). On Bacon's efforts to become queen's attorney, see Jonathon Marwil, *The Trials of Counsel*, pp. 76–78.

8. For some of Coke's activities as attorney, see John Hawarde, *Les Reports del Cases in Camera Stellata*, pp. 22–158 passim; and the volumes of *APC* and *CSPD* that cover the period 1593–1606. On his involvement in economic administration in this period, see Appendix B.

9. See Bowen, *Lion and the Throne*, pp. 136–59; G. B. Harrison, *The Life and Death of Robert Devereux, Earl of Essex*; and Louis A. Knafla, *Law and Politics in Jacobean England*, pp. 19–20.

10. His main official function was to advise the Lords on proposed legislation (see *LJ*, 2:191–225 passim (1597); and 2:226–59 passim (1601)). On these two parliaments, see Neale, *Elizabeth I and her Parliaments, 1584–1601*, pp. 325–432.

11. John Chamberlain, *The Letters of John Chamberlain*, 1:54.

12. Ibid., 1:131; cf. Lawrence Stone, *The Crisis of the Aristocracy, 1558–1641*, pp. 452–53. Shortly thereafter. Coke gave his daughter Anne in marriage to Sir Thomas Sadler's son, along with a dowry of £3,000 (see Chamberlain, *Letters*, 1:131). For contemporary

Cecil, later earl of Salisbury.[13] He was reappointed as attorney in April 1603 and in May was elevated to the dignity of knighthood. While continuing to work with the Privy Council and advise the upper house in Parliament,[14] he also counseled the king on financial and legal affairs and attained great notoriety by prosecuting Sir Walter Raleigh[15] and those who were implicated in the Gunpowder Plot.[16] Meanwhile, his rise to power had continued in 1606, when James I made him chief justice of the Court of Common Pleas; but within several years, he began to lose favor at court and with the king. His difficulties had initially arisen at least partly because he had angered James by some of his judicial decisions, particularly those concerning ecclesiastical jurisdiction.[17] But his loss of favor at court was probably due not solely to his ideological differences with the king and may have had political causes as well. It is clear at least that after Salisbury's death in 1612, Coke had no powerful protector at court and became more vulnerable to the political intrigues both of the Howard faction and of his old rival, Bacon. In 1613, on Bacon's advice, James removed Coke from the Common Pleas and made him chief justice of the Court of King's Bench. This change in office was clearly a demotion, and Coke protested against it. But it was not a major blow to his political career, and he retained considerable influence at court. He received a place on the Privy Council,[18] where he helped to

comments on Coke's wealth in this period, see William Harrison, *The Description of England*, p. 173; and Thomas Wilson, "The State of England, Anno. Dom. 1600," p. 25 and n. 2. For a note on Coke's fortune, see W. J. Jones, *Politics and the Bench*, p. 37.

13. Evidence of Coke's close connection with Robert Cecil can be found in their extensive correspondance. Some of this correspondance is printed or calendared in *HMC, Cecil/Salisbury*, vols. 4–19; *HMC, Third Report*; *HMC, Fifth Report*; *HMC, Sixth Report*; *HMC, Seventh Report*. Some of their letters are also printed in *CSPD*.

14. On Coke's activities in the parliament of 1604–10, see Notestein, *1604–1610*, pp. 119, 227, 256, 379, 396. See also *LJ*, 2:263–686 passim; Foster, *1610*, 1:64–65, 212–14; and Robert Bowyer, *The Parliamentary Diary of Robert Bowyer, 1606–1607*, esp. pp. 102–34, 139, 146, 210, 295, 327.

15. On Raleigh's first trial, which was held in 1603, see Gardiner, *History*, 1:123–36; H. L. Stephen, "The Trial of Sir Walter Ralegh"; Willard M. Wallace, *Sir Walter Raleigh*, pp. 202–16; and Robert Lacey, *Sir Walter Ralegh*, pp. 295–307. Coke was also involved in the proceedings that led to Raleigh's execution in 1618. See Gardiner, *History*, 3:141–48; Wallace, *Raleigh*, pp. 302–7; and Lacey, *Ralegh*, pp. 369–74.

16. See H. R. Williamson, *The Gunpowder Plot*; and Philip Caraman, *Henry Garnet, 1555–1606, and the Gunpowder Plot*.

17. See Holdsworth, *History*, 5:428–32; Roland G. Usher, *The Rise and Fall of the High Commission*; Roland G. Usher, *The Reconstruction of the English Church*; Christopher Hill, *Economic Problems of the Church*; and Knafla, *Law and Politics*, pp. 134–45, 297–302. Charles Gray of the University of Chicago is currently working on a comprehensive study of the ways in which Coke and other judges used writs of prohibition to stop suits in ecclesiastical and other courts.

18. *APC, 1613–14*, p. 255; *CSPD, 1611–18*, p. 205.

prepare for the parliament of 1614[19] and to plan the Cockayne Project;[20] and he was given an important role in investigating the sordid and politically delicate Overbury affair.[21] There was even talk of making him treasurer. He also enjoyed other, minor successes during this period. In 1614 he was elected high steward of Cambridge University; and in the previous year, his oldest son Robert had made a brilliant marriage with Lady Theophilia Berkeley.[22]

In 1616, however, Coke's political fortunes took a disastrous turn. After being summoned before the council in June, he was forbidden to go on circuit and ordered to revise his *Reports*. Four months later he was dismissed from his judicial and conciliar offices. Officially, his dismissal was ascribed to the allegedly anti-Royalist positions that he had expressed in his *Reports* and on the bench. He had alienated James I by denying the king's right to ask the judges for separate opinions or to stop common-law proceedings by royal writ of *de non procedendo rege inconsulto*, and he had repeatedly clashed with Lord Chancellor Ellesmere about the scope of Chancery jurisdiction.[23] His published case reports were also criticized for containing numerous errors.[24] Nevertheless, his judicial philosophy was hardly the sole cause of his political troubles. By 1616 the duke of Buckingham had acquired great power at court, and Coke had angered him by disposing of a lucrative clerkship without consulting him. In addition to that, Coke may have alienated other influential court figures by inquiring too deeply into the Overbury case, and he was still vulnerable to the attacks of his old rival Bacon.[25]

During the rest of James I's reign, Coke's political fortunes fluctuated

19. On Coke's role in this parliament, see Thomas L. Moir, *The Addled Parliament of 1614*, pp. 120–21; and *LJ*, 2:687–717 passim.

20. See Appendix B.

21. See *CSPD, 1611–18*, pp. 307–62 passim. See also Knafla, *Law and Politics*, p. 127 and the works cited at p. 127, n. 4.

22. See "Vade Mecum," pp. 118–19; and Lawrence Stone, *Family and Fortune*, p. 255 and n. 2. In 1615 Coke was made lord high steward of Gloucester, which was a post that had been held by Sir Robert Cecil in 1604 (see William Bradford Willcox, *Gloucestershire*, p. 207, n. 2).

23. See John P. Dawson, "Coke and Ellesmere Disinterred"; Samuel E. Thorne, "Praemunire and Sir Edward Coke"; J. H. Baker, "The Common Lawyers and the Chancery"; and Knafla, *Law and Politics*, esp. pp. 155–80.

24. *APC, 1615–16*, p. 649; and Knafla, *Law and Politics*, pp. 123–54. For the text of Lord Chancellor Ellesmere's critique of Coke's *Reports*, see Knafla *Law and Politics*, pp. 297–318.

25. For contemporary documents and comments concerning Coke's fall, see *CSPD, 1611–18*, pp. 372–411 passim and p. 443; *APC, 1615–16*, pp. 644–50; *CSPVen, 1616–17*, p. 245; *HMC, Third Report*, p. 596; *HMC, Ninth Report*, 2:387a; *HMC, Tenth Report*, 1:97 and 4:18; *HMC, Eleventh Report*, 7:245 and 302; *HMC, Twelfth Report*, 9:125;

greatly, and his changing relationship with the court is therefore difficult to trace, let alone explain. Nevertheless, a few tentative generalizations can still be made about his political position between his fall in June 1616 and James I's death in March 1625. First, although he failed to regain great influence at court, he never abandoned hope of doing so and was ready to curry favor with leading courtiers in order to further his political ambitions. Second, his hope of regaining royal favor was not entirely unrealistic, nor were his efforts to ingratiate himself at court completely ineffectual. Third, although James I and Buckingham certainly mistrusted him, they also feared and respected him and probably believed that the proper combination of royal inducements and threats (which frequently worked in other cases) could neutralize him politically and prevent him from becoming a martyr and might even make him a useful member of the governing circle. Finally, although Coke sided with parliamentary critics of the court in the parliaments of 1621 and 1624, he did not lead whatever parliamentary "opposition" may have existed during James's last years.[26]

As his political position was deteriorating, Coke made a blatant attempt in December 1616 to regain his standing by securing Buckingham's support. Despite the vehement protests of his second wife, the influential Lady Hatton, Coke planned to make their youngest daughter Frances marry the duke's older brother, Sir John Villiers. Negotiations for the match dragged on for months, while both Bacon and Lady Hatton tried to prevent it, and, in the meantime, Coke became embroiled in various legal difficulties. Ultimately, however, his ploy met with at least limited success. The marriage finally took place in September of 1617,[27] and within two months Coke was miraculously restored to his place on

---

HMC, *Le Fleming*, p. 15; HMC, *Supplementary Report . . . Mar & Kellie*, p. 63; HMC, *Montagu*, 1:248, 250; Roger Wilbraham, "The Journal of Roger Wilbraham," pp. 116–17. For modern discussions of Coke's fall, see Cuthbert William Johnson, *The Life of Sir Edward Coke*, 1:318–27; Gardiner, *History*, 3:23, 24, 84; Holdsworth, *History*, 5:353 and n. 3; Bowen, *Lion and the Throne*, pp. 378–95; David Harris Willson, *James VI and I*, p. 382; Stone, *Crisis of the Aristocracy*, pp. 444–45; W. J. Jones, "Ellesmere and Politics, 1603–1617," pp. 53–57; and Knafla, *Law and Politics*, esp. pp. 176–77. On the clerkship over which the dispute between Coke and Buckingham may have arisen, see Walter Yonge, *Diary of Walter Yonge*, p. 29; Sir James Whitelocke, *Liber Familicus of Sir James Whitelocke*, p. 59; and H. R. Trevor-Roper, *The Gentry, 1540–1640*, pp. 11–12 and p. 11 n. 1. W. J. Jones's *Politics and the Bench* and Louis A. Knafla's *Law and Politics* present clear pictures of the political role of early Stuart judges and thus render Coke's fall much more comprehensible than previous historical works have done.

26. On the question of whether a real parliamentary opposition to the crown existed between 1604 and 1629, see chap. 2, fn. 1.

27. On this celebrated and sordid episode in Coke's life, see Bowen, *Lion and the Throne*, pp. 393–411.

the council.[28] During the next three years it was rumored that he would secure higher office, and although no such appointment was forthcoming he remained on the council, served on several important royal commissions, and played conspicuous parts in the trials of Suffolk[29] and Yelverton.[30] In the fall of 1620, he helped Bacon and others plan for a new parliament, and early in 1621[31] he was returned to the Commons for the first time since 1593 as a royal nominee from the Cornish borough of Liskeard.[32] As the session progressed, however, he acted more and more independently of the court, and in the fall he openly challenged the king's positions on foreign affairs and on Parliament's right to discuss them. After Parliament's adjournment in late December, he was dismissed from the council and imprisoned in the Tower. His books and papers were seized by the king's agents. He was examined by the council and accused of treason, and he was prosecuted in the Court of Wards for the recovery of an old debt to the crown of £30,000.[33]

Once again, however, Coke was able to avert political ruin. He was released from the Tower in August 1622 and was instead confined to one of his country estates. By November, after the treason charges against him had been dropped, along with the case against him in the wards, he was granted full freedom.[34] A year later, when the court was preparing for a new parliament, a plan was formed to prevent him from sitting in the Commons by sending him on a commission to Ireland,[35] but it was canceled at the last minute, perhaps through Prince Charles's intervention on his behalf.[36] In February 1624, Coke took his seat in the lower house as a burgess for Coventry.[37] Throughout this parliament he fully supported the policies of Buckingham and the prince, avoided serious constitutional clashes with the king, and seemed on the point of regaining favor at court.

Shortly after Charles I's accession, however, Coke turned against Buckingham and the new king for reasons that are obscure, and he finally

---

28. *CSPD, 1611–18*, p. 485; Willson, *James*, pp. 387–88; and Stone, *Crisis of the Aristocracy*, p. 596.

29. See *CSPD, 1619–23*, p. 94; and Menna Prestwich, *Cranfield*, p. 164 and n. 1.

30. See *CSPD, 1619–23*, pp. 191, 192–93.

31. See Spedding, *Bacon*, 7:114; and Zaller, *1621*, p. 18.

32. *Return*, p. 450; David Harris Willson, *The Privy Councillors in the House of Commons, 1604–1629*, p. 78 and nn. 45 and 49.

33. See *CSPD, 1619–23*, pp. 242, 283, 316, 319, 332, 333, 347, 349, 418. On the aftermath of the parliament of 1621, see Conrad Russell, "The Examination of Mr. Mallory after the Parliament of 1621."

34. *CSPD, 1619–23*, pp. 439–40, 461.

35. Ibid., pp. 134, 144, 150, 151, 156; *CSPVen, 1623–25*, pp. 183, 192, 196.

36. *CSPVen, 1623–25*, p. 217.

37. *Return*, p. 460; Ruigh, *1624*, pp. 63, 109.

became irreconciliably opposed to the policies of the royal court. In the parliament of 1625, he sat in the Commons for Norfolk and lost whatever credit he might still have had with the king's favorite or the king by attacking royal foreign policy, criticizing the government's management of finance, and making only slightly veiled attacks on the duke himself. Charles I therefore excluded him from the parliament of 1626 (along with five others) by picking him sheriff of Buckinghamshire.[38] Coke's protests against this maneuver were in vain, but two years later he was again returned to the Commons, and this time he took his seat without incident. In the parliament of 1628 he played a leading part in promoting the Petition of Right and attacking Buckingham, and he repeatedly rejected compromises with the king of a sort that he might have accepted only a few years earlier. For reasons that are as yet unknown, he did not return to Parliament for the 1629 session.[39] Instead, he finally withdrew from active political life at the age of seventy-six and spent his last years in the country finishing the final volumes of his *Institutes*. Nevertheless, although he was no longer politically active, Charles I was so worried about the possible political impact of his writings that royal agents seized his papers soon after his death.[40]

Coke died in 1634, but his writings remained as fundamental legal authorities for the next two centuries. He had published eleven volumes of case reports between 1600 and 1615, and two more volumes appeared posthumously in the late 1650s.[41] He had also published a *Book of Entries* in 1614[42] and the first part of his *Institutes* in 1628.[43] The last three parts of his *Institutes*, which had been confiscated by the crown, were published in 1644 by order of the Long Parliament.[44] Down through

---

38. For a contemporary comment on this incident, see *Wentworth Papers, 1597–1628*, p. 240.

39. On Coke's absence from the parliament of 1629, see *CD 1629*, pp. 58, 138, 191 and 191 n. e; *CJ*, 1:921; and *CD 1628*, 1:19–20.

40. See *CSPD, 1634–35*, pp. 165, 340, 348, 351; Holdsworth, *History*, 5:454–55 and nn. 4 and 5; and Baker, "Coke's Note-Books," pp. 78–80.

41. *Les Reports de Edward Coke*, 13 vols. (London, 1600–1615, 1656, 1659). In the present work, all citations are to *The Reports of Sir Edward Coke, Knt. in English, in Thirteen Parts Complete . . .* (Dublin, 1793). On these works, see Holdsworth, *History*, 5:461–66; Baker, "Coke's Note-Books"; T. F. T. Plucknett, "The Genesis of Coke's Reports"; Charles Marshall Gest, "The Writings of Sir Edward Coke"; L. W. Abbott, *Law Reporting in England, 1485–1585*; and Knafla, *Law and Politics*, pp. 123–26.

42. *A Booke of Entries* (London, 1614).

43. *Institutes of the Laws of England*, part 1 (London, 1628). In the present work, all citations are to *The First Part of the Institutes of the Laws of England; or A Commentary upon Littleton . . .* 19th ed. 2 vols. (London, 1832).

44. *Institutes of the Laws of England . . .* , parts 2–4 (London, 1644). In this work, all citations to the *Second, Third* and *Fourth Institutes* are to the London edition of 1797. On the efforts made in the Long Parliament to find Coke's writings and have them published,

the early nineteenth century his *Reports* and *Institutes* were frequently reprinted, along with several other minor works,[45] and they were avidly studied and reverentially cited by generations of English and American judges and lawyers. During the same period, writers on politics and government from Lilburne and Hobbes to Jefferson looked to Coke's writings as sources either of wisdom or of views worthy of serious criticism.[46]

As Coke's influence on Anglo-American law and political thought was waning in the nineteenth century, historians began to study his career and thought and his posthumous influence; and down to the present day they have almost invariably viewed him as a vitally important figure both in the history of his own age and in the general history of English public and private law. Although no scholarly biography of him has ever appeared,[47] he is the subject of several informative essays and biographical sketches;[48] and important episodes from his life and aspects of his career are treated in narrative histories,[49] in biographies of his contemporaries,[50]

---

see Sir Simonds D'Ewes, *The Journal of Sir Simonds D'Ewes*, p. 108 and nn. 109 and 110, and pp. 118, 174, 330, 358.

45. His other works include *The Complete Copy-Holder* (London, 1641); and *A Little Treatise of Bail and Mainprize* (London, 1635).

46. On the Levellers' use of Coke's writings to support their positions, see Joseph Frank, *The Levellers*, pp. 58–59; H. N. Brailsford, *The Levellers and the English Revolution*, pp. 122, 124, 128, 535, 584, 618; and Christopher Hill, "Recent Interpretations of the English Civil War," p. 28. For Hobbes's attack on Coke, see Thomas Hobbes, *A Dialogue between a Philosopher and a Student of the Common Laws of England*; D. E. C. Yale, "Hobbes and Hale on Law, Legislation, and the Sovereign"; and Holdsworth, *History*, 5:480–82. For a defense of Coke's views by Matthew Hale, see Holdsworth, *History*, 5:499–513. On Coke's influence on colonial Americans, especially John Adams, James Wilson, and Thomas Jefferson, see H. Trevor Colbourn, *The Lamp of Experience*; and Charles F. Mullett, "Coke and the American Revolution."

47. Bowen's *Lion and the Throne* is a useful popular biography. See also Humphrey W. Woolrych, *The Life of the Right Honourable Sir Edward Coke Knt.*; Johnson, *Life of Sir Edward Coke*; Charles Warburton James, *Chief Justice Coke*; Hastings Lyon and Herman Block, *Edward Coke*. For early biographical sketches, see John Aubrey, *Aubrey's Brief Lives*, pp. 67–8; Thomas Fuller, *The History of the Worthies of England*, 2:451–53; Lord John Campbell, *Lives of the Chief Justices of England*, 1:245–357; and Edward Foss, *The Judges of England*, 6:108–28.

48. See Sir William Holdsworth, "Sir Edward Coke"; Holdsworth, *History*, 5:423–93; *Dictionary of National Biography*, s.v. "Coke, Sir Edward"; Samuel E. Thorne, *Sir Edward Coke, 1552–1952*; Roland Greene Usher, "Sir Edward Coke"; and Roland Greene Usher, "James I and Sir Edward Coke." See also Francis Robert Aumann, "Lord Coke"; Burch, "The Rivals"; and Jesse Turner, "Concerning Divers Notable Stirs between Sir Edward Coke and his Lady."

49. See Gardiner, *History*, vols. 1–6; and Edward P. Cheyney, *History of England*.

50. See Spedding, *Bacon*; Willson, *James*; Prestwich, *Cranfield*; Marwil, *Trials of Counsel*; Knafla, *Law and Politics*; Jones, "Ellesmere and Politics"; John Forster, *Sir John Eliot*; Harold Hulme, *The Life of Sir John Eliot, 1592–1632*; Wallace, *Raleigh*; Lacey,

and in works on Parliament,[51] the courts,[52] and other subjects.[53] Similarly, although no general study of Coke's legal thought has ever been published, his legal ideas are the subject of several brief studies[54] and are given considerable attention in most general histories of English private and public law.[55] His constitutional thought has attracted the interest of

---

Ralegh; and R. H. Tawney, *Business and Politics under James I*. See also Vernon F. Snow, *Essex the Rebel*; Dorothea Coke, *The Last Elizabethan*; Michael Van Cleave Alexander, *Charles I's Lord Treasurer*; A. F. Upton, *Sir Arthur Ingram, c. 1565–1642*; and The Rt. Hon. Sir Jocelyn Simon, "Dr. Cowell." Important information on Coke will also be found in forthcoming works on John Selden by David Berkowitz and on Sir Edwin Sandys by Theodore K. Rabb.

51. In addition to the works cited above in fnn. 6, 10, 14, and 19, see Elizabeth Read Foster, *The Painful Labor of Mrs. Elsyng*; Williams M. Mitchell, *The Rise of the Revolutionary Party in the English House of Commons, 1603–1629*; Frances Helen Relf, *The Petition of Right*; Clayton Roberts, *The Growth of Responsible Government in Stuart England*; Ruigh, *1624*; Colin G. C. Tite, *Impeachment and Parliamentary Judicature in Early Stuart England*; Willson, *Privy Councillors in the House of Commons*; and Zaller, *1621*. In addition, see David S. Berkowitz, "Reason of State in England and the Petition of Right"; J. Stoddart Flemion, "Slow Process, Due Process, and the High Court of Parliament"; J. Stoddart Flemion, "The Struggle for the Petition of Right in the House of Lords"; Elizabeth Read Foster, "Petitions and the Petition of Right"; Elizabeth Read Foster, "The Procedure against Patents and Monopolies, 1621–1624"; J. H. Hexter, "Power Struggle, Parliament and Liberty in Early Stuart England"; Wallace Notestein, "The Winning of the Initiative by the House of Commons"; Conrad Russell, "The Foreign Policy Debate in the House of Commons in 1621"; Conrad Russell, "Parliament and the King's Finances"; Conrad Russell, "Parliamentary History in Perspective, 1604–1629"; and Christopher Thompson, "The Origins of the Parliamentary Middle Group, 1625–1629." See also J. N. Ball, "The Parliamentary Career of Sir John Eliot, 1624–1629"; and D. C. Spielman, "Impeachments and the Parliamentary Opposition in England, 1621–1641."

52. In addition to the works cited above in fnn. 17 and 23, see H. E. Bell, *An Introduction to the History and Records of the Court of Wards and Liveries*; J. S. Cockburn, *A History of the English Assizes, 1558–1714*; John P. Dawson, *A History of Lay Judges*; Charles M. Gray, "The Boundaries of the Equitable Function"; Douglas G. Greene, "The Court of the Marshalsea in Late Tudor and Stuart England"; Joel Hurstfield, *The Queen's Wards*; W. J. Jones, *The Elizabethan Court of Chancery*; Jones, *Politics and the Bench*; Rachel R. Reid, *The King's Council in the North*.

53. See, in particular, Marvin Arthur Breslow, *A Mirror of England*; Astrid Friis, *Alderman Cockayne's Project and the Cloth Trade*; Brian P. Levack, *The Civil Lawyers in England*; Prest, *Inns of Court*; and Smith, *County and Court*.

54. In addition to the works cited above in fnn. 17, 23, 41, 48, and 51–53, see William S. Holdsworth, "The Influence of Coke on the Development of English Law"; Sir William Holdsworth, "Sir Edward Coke"; Frank Douglas Mackinnon, "Sir Edward Coke"; and John Underwood Lewis, "Coke's Theory of Artificial Reason"; Garrard Glen, "Edward Coke and Law Restatement"; George W. Kuehn, "Coke's Cawdrey *Treatise* 'of the King's Ecclesiastical Laws' and Persons' *Answer*, 1605–1609"; and Charles M. Gray, "Reason, Authority, and Imagination." On Coke's views on copyhold tenure, see Charles M. Gray, *Copyhold, Equity, and the Common Law*; and Eric Kerridge, *Agrarian Problems in the Sixteenth Century and After*. For notes on his views about parliamentary representation, see Milicent Barton Rex, *University Representation in England, 1604–1690*; and Derek Hirst, *The Representative of the People?*

55. For comments on Coke's role in the history of English private law, see Holdsworth, *History*, vols. 1–13; T. F. T. Plucknett, *A Concise History of the Common Law*; Alan Harding, *A Social History of English Law*; S. F. C. Milsom, *Historical Foundations of the*

many writers, who have studied several aspects of it,[56] and legal historians have discussed the impact on later law of some of the cases that he reported and/or decided.[57] The contents of his library[58] and the composition of his *Reports* have been analyzed;[59] and historians have become increasingly interested in his views about economic regulation,[60] law reform,[61] and the early history of England and English law.[62]

Common Law; and J. H. Baker, *An Introduction to English Legal History*. Coke's place in the history of English public law is discussed in Frederic W. Maitland, *The Constitutional History of England*; Thomas P. Taswell-Langmead, *English Constitutional History from the Teutonic Conquest to the Present Time*; J. R. Tanner, *English Constitutional Conflicts of the Seventeenth Century, 1603–1689*; David L. Keir, *Constitutional History of Modern Britain since 1485*; Frederick G. Marcham, *A Constitutional History of Modern England, 1485 to the Present*; Elton, *TC*; Kenyon, *SC*; and G. E. Aylmer, *The Struggle for the Constitution, 1603–1689*.

56. For more detailed discussions of certain aspects of Coke's constitutional views, see Raoul Berger, "*Doctor Bonham's Case*"; J. W. Gough, *Fundamental Law in English Constitutional History*; Charles M. Gray, "Bonham's Case Revisited"; Donald W. Hanson, *From Kingdom to Commonwealth*; Margaret Judson, *The Crisis of the Constitution*; Kenyon, *SC*; R. A. MacKay, "Coke—Parliamentary Sovereignty or the Supremacy of Law?"; Charles Howard McIlwain, *Constitutionalism, Ancient and Modern*; Charles Howard McIlwain, *The High Court of Parliament and Its Supremacy*; George L. Mosse, *The Struggle for Sovereignty in England*; Charles Ogilvie, *The King's Government and the Common Law, 1471–1641*; Samuel E. Thorne, "The Constitution and the Courts"; Samuel E. Thorne, "Courts of Record and Sir Edward Coke"; Samuel E. Thorne, "Introduction"; Samuel E. Thorne, "The Equity of a Statute and Heydon's Case"; and F. D. Wormuth, *The Royal Prerogative, 1603–1649*.

57. See, for example, A. W. B. Simpson, "The Place of Slade's Case in the History of Contract"; H. K. Lucke, "Slade's Case and the Origin of the Common Counts"; J. H. Baker, "New Light on Slade's Case"; and A. W. B. Simpson, *A History of the Common Law of Contract*, pp. 281–315 and 485–509. See also Edith G. Henderson, *Foundations of English Administrative Law*; L. B. Boudin, "Lord Coke and the American Doctrine of Judicial Power"; and Charles H. Randall, Jr., "Sir Edward Coke and the Privilege against Self-Incrimination."

58. W. O. Hassall, *A Catalogue of the Library of Sir Edward Coke*. See also Stone, *Crisis of the Aristocracy*, pp. 705–7.

59. See fn. 41, above.

60. See Donald O. Wagner, "Coke and the Rise of Economic Liberalism"; Donald O. Wagner, "The Common Law and Free Enterprise"; Christopher Hill, "Recent Interpretations of the English Civil War," p. 28; Christopher Hill, *Intellectual Origins of the English Revolution*, pp. 225–65; Barbara Malament, "The 'Economic Liberalism' of Sir Edward Coke"; and David Little, *Religion, Order, and Law*, pp. 167–217 and 238–45. For briefer discussions of Coke's views on economic organization, see John U. Nef, *Industry and Government in France and England, 1540–1640*, pp. 42, 92, 112, 154; Eli Heckscher, *Mercantilism*, esp. 1:272, 277, 280ff., 290ff., and 317; Penelope Corfield, "Economic Issues and Ideologies"; J. P. Cooper, "Economic Regulation and the Cloth Industry in Seventeenth-Century England," esp. pp. 80–81; and Knafla, *Law and Politics*, pp. 97–98, 103, 126–27, 150–53.

61. Donald Veal, *The Popular Movement for Law Reform, 1640–1660*, esp. pp. 65–69; Hill, *Intellectual Origins*, esp. pp. 227–30 and 256–57; Thorne, "Coke"; Samuel E. Thorne, "Tudor Social Transformation and Legal Change"; and Knafla, *Law and Politics*, esp. pp. 107, 121, 128.

62. See J. G. A. Pocock, *The Ancient Constitution and the Feudal Law*, esp. pp.

Valuable and informative as these studies are, the current state of historical scholarship on Coke is unsatisfactory in several respects. First, historians have simply failed to treat too many important aspects of his life and thought. Almost no detailed, systematic research has been done on his career, and, as a result, very little is now known about anything but the most dramatic and celebrated incidents in his life. Historians have yet to investigate such subjects as his private law practice, his private fortune, or his more routine conduct in the many offices that he held. Nor have they learned very much about his political, financial, familial, or personal connections at court, in London, in the country, in Parliament, or within the legal profession. Research on his legal thought has been much more extensive than work on his career, but relatively few of his ideas and concerns have been studied closely. Most historians have focused their attention solely on his abstract views about "fundamental law," parliamentary power, court jurisdiction, and the general problem of sovereignty. Writers who have discussed his economic views have dealt mainly with his ideas about monopolies and guilds and have hardly considered the economic implications of his views on other legal topics. The writers who have noted his interest in legal reform have discussed a few of his explicit proposals for changing the law but have given little attention to his less overt efforts to reshape the law through his legal decisions and writings. Several historians have analyzed his view of the English past, but no one has systematically studied his use of legal and historical sources, or analyzed his relationships with other legal antiquarians of his era. His connection with such figures as William Perkins[63] and Roger Williams[64] have been duly noted, but his religious views have never been investigated.[65]

30–69; Christopher Hill, "The Norman Yoke"; F. Smith Fussner, *The Historical Revolution*; and Charles M. Gray, "Introduction." See also M. I. Finley, "The Ancestral Constitution," pp. 40–42; Donald R. Kelley, "History, English Law, and the Renaissance"; Christopher Brook and Keven Sharp, "History, English Law, and the Renaissance"; and Donald R. Kelley, "A Rejoinder."

63. On the sermon that Perkins dedicated to Coke, see Christopher Hill, "William Perkins and the Poor," p. 216. On another sermon dedicated to Coke, see Louis B. Wright, *Middle-Class Culture in Elizabethan England*, p. 334.

64. See O. E. Winslow, *Master Roger Williams*, pp. 43–45; and John Dykstra Eusden, *Puritans, Lawyers, and Politics in Early Seventeenth-Century England*, p. viii.

65. For a note on this subject, see Malament, "Coke," p. 1323 n. 13. For extracts from "The Foundation of the faith of Sir Edward Coke, all written with his own hands in the extremity of his last sickness, IX June, 1634" (Add. MS. 29, f. 591, British Museum, London), see James, *Coke*, p. 47. Fuller's sketch of Coke's life contains brief notes on his appointment of worthy ministers to the livings that he controlled, his devotion to the cathedral of Norwich, his support of Sutton's hospital and a free school at Thetford, and his founding of a school at Godwick (*Worthies*, 2:451–53). On his successful protest against the practice of making sheriffs swear that they would help to put down "heresies"

The failure of historians to study Coke's career more closely is related to another set of deficiencies in modern Coke scholarship. Because they have not studied his legal views in conjunction with his political career, they have been particularly prone to view him exclusively as a legal or constitutional theorist and to devote more attention to tracing his posthumous influence than to analyzing the significance of his views for his own era. Their propensity to view him in this way has led them to exaggerate the clarity, coherence, and consistency of his constitutional views, to take little account of the more subtle changes that his positions underwent during his long career, and to underestimate the degree to which his statements on certain constitutional questions were shaped by the precise political context in which they were made.[66] It has also induced them to underestimate his strong interest in attaining certain highly specific, substantive objectives, such as the enactment of particular bills; the resolution of particular cases in favor of particular parties; the implementation of certain economic, religious, or foreign policies; or the advancement of his own political fortunes. They have assumed, in other words, that Coke was far more interested in implementing his own general interpretation of the constitution than in achieving specific, practical results. And by making such an assumption, they are able to avoid the question of how Coke's more abstract constitutional views were related to his more pragmatic concerns.

A third problem with modern work on Coke is that historians have not succeeded in reaching any clear consensus about those few aspects of his thought that have been studied in at least some detail: his ideas about "fundamental law" and the role of judges in interpreting parliamentary enactments, his views about the proper role of the state in regulating economic activity, his attitude towards law reform, and his use of precedents from England's medieval past to support his own statements of the law of his day. Some constitutional historians have argued that he came close to equating "the fundamental law" with certain immutable legal principles that neither Parliament nor any other body could override and that judges were to use as standards for determining the legality of parlia-

---

and "lollaries" [*sic*] and aid the church ordinaries and commissioners, see *APC, 1625–1626*, pp. 255–56. For a brief discussion of his role in the Commons's attack on the bishop of Norwich in 1624, see chap. 5.

66. Historians often divide Coke's life, like Beethoven's, into three distinct parts: a youthful, royalist period, which was characterized by ambition and excess and which lasted until 1606; a more mature but still combative judicial period, which continued until 1616 or perhaps as late as 1620; and a final, serene parliamentary period, which lasted down to his death in 1634 and perhaps beyond. More subtle changes in his outlook and behavior have rarely been successfully integrated into this conventional tripartite picture of his career.

mentary legislation; and they claim that he thereby anticipated modern American ideas of judicial review.[67] Others suggest that he gradually moved towards the view that Parliament was a sovereign legislature.[68] Still others maintain that his views about the nature of statute law were essentially the same as those of later medieval judges.[69] Similarly sharp disagreements divide writers on Coke's economic thought. Some have asserted that he espoused liberal views about economic regulation, or at least contributed to the incorporation of such ideas into English common law.[70] But it has also been argued that his economic views were highly traditional[71] or at least contained many traditional elements.[72] Writers on Coke's views about law reform have also had difficulty in reaching any consensus about his attitude towards the condition of English law during his lifetime. While some have asserted that he worked to reform, modernize, or rationalize English law,[73] others have characterized him as an intransigent defender of the legal status quo.[74] Finally, while all historians agree that Coke used earlier legal sources in ways that now seem blatantly inaccurate and anachronistic, they explain this fact in different ways and attach different kinds of significance to it. Some suggest that he deliberately distorted medieval precedents in order to lend legitimacy to his own private interpretations of the law, but others attribute his alleged misuse of precedent to his lack of historical awareness. While some believe that his use of ancient authorities to support his own legal opinions reveals his conservatism, others regard his skillful manipulation of these authorities for his own purposes as an index of his radicalism.

The failure of historians to reach any consensus about these particular aspects of Coke's thought is only partly attributable to their relatively straightforward disagreements about the substance of his views on subjects like economic regulation, legal reform, or parliamentary and judicial power. This failure is also due to the confusion that results from their occasional tendency to conflate several distinct types of historical inquiry: the reconstruction of Coke's views on particular subjects and the attempt to relate them to the immediate historical context in which they were developed; the study of his influence on many successive generations of English and American judges; and the analysis of his role in, or contribu-

67. See Gray, "Bonham's Case"; and Berger, "*Doctor Bonham's Case.*"
68. See Mosse, *Struggle for Sovereignty.*
69. See Thorne, "The Constitution and the Courts."
70. See Wagner, "Coke and the Rise of Economic Liberalism"; Wagner, "Common Law and Free Enterprise"; and Hill, *Intellectual Origins,* esp. p. 256.
71. See Malament, "Coke."
72. See Little, *Religion, Order, and Law,* pp. 167–217.
73. See Hill, *Intellectual Origins,* p. 256; and Little, *Religion, Order, and Law.*
74. See chap. 3, fn. 1.

tion to, certain long-term historical processes like the modernization or rationalization of English law, the development of the doctrine of parliamentary sovereignty, the growth of modern historical consciousness, the liberalization of the common law, and the adaptation of the law to the economic "needs" of a specific class or a particular form of economic organization. The confusions resulting from a failure to distinguish between these different types of historical inquiry are compounded by the fact that so many theoretical or methodological problems are involved in any attempt to relate Coke's thought and career to any of the various processes of modernization noted above. Not only is it difficult to construct any clear definition or model of these processes; it is also very hard in particular cases to identify Coke's role in them.

A final defect in the view of Coke that emerges from the historical literature concerning him has arisen because of changes in the orientation of current scholarship on the early Stuart period and on the English Revolution.[75] When historians viewed this conflict as a clash between two parties over constitutional principles, Coke had a secure and easily identifiable place in discussions of its origins or causes. He was seen as the main theorist of the self-conscious opponents of the early Stuarts, and his entrance into Parliament was thought to have cemented that alliance between the common lawyers and the parliamentarians that made the revolution inevitable. Now that historians have developed various competing interpretations of the revolution, however, it is less easy to decide how to fit Coke into discussions designed to explain the outbreak of this conflict. Did he propound constitutional theories legitimating the increasing political power of gentry and merchants and adapt the common law to the needs of a new economic order? Did he belong to a political faction that gradually became estranged from the court and turned into a distinct, country party possessing its own distinctive ideology but having material interests similar to those of so-called courtiers? Was he a pragmatic, opportunistic politician and administrator whose alienation from

75. On the changes that have taken place during the past century in the historiography of the English Revolution, see Lawrence Stone, *The Causes of the English Revolution, 1529–1642*. For works that reflect very recent trends in the study of the causes of the Revolution, see Paul Christianson, "The Causes of the English Revolution: A Reappraisal"; Russell, "Parliamentary History in Perspective"; John K. Gruenfelder, "The Electoral Patronage of Sir Thomas Wentworth, Earl of Strafford, 1614–1640"; Paul Christianson, "The Peers, the People, and Parliamentary Management in the First Six Months of the Long Parliament"; Clayton Roberts, "The Earl of Bedford and the Coming of the English Revolution"; Mark Kishlansky, "The Emergence of Adversary Politics in the Long Parliament"; and James E. Farnell, "The Social and Intellectual Basis of London's Role in the English Civil Wars." For some critical comments on these recent trends in the study of the Revolution, see Hexter, "Power Struggle, Parliament, and Liberty"; and Derek Hirst, "Unanimity in the Commons, Aristocratic Intrigues, and the Origins of the English Civil War."

the royal court resulted simply from a series of accidents? Was he a Tudor statesman whose traditional views led him to embrace reactionary alternatives to Stuart policies? To answer only one of these questions affirmatively seems inadequate. But to give mild assent to all of them would be evasive.

In this book I analyze Coke's activities in the parliaments of the 1620s and am primarily concerned with his place in the history of pre-revolutionary England. My general purpose is to begin the process of constructing a more satisfactory picture of his career and thought than is found in previous writings about him. His parliamentary career between 1621 and 1628 constitutes an important and relatively self-contained chapter in his life and can be viewed as the climactic phase of his lengthy political career. Although he had participated in the six parliaments held between 1589 and 1614, his parliamentary actions take on particular importance during the 1620s. In this decade Parliament became the only institution through which he could significantly influence English government and wield the kind of power that he had not previously exercised in other offices. As a prominent member of Parliament in 1621, 1624, 1625 and 1628, he attacked many existing practices, policies and laws and tried to eliminate these abuses through parliamentary action. Like other members of Parliament, he often referred to these abuses as "the grievances of the commonwealth." When he used this ominous and ideo-logically-laden catch-word, he was expressing the view that these abuses harmed not just the limited, private interests of particular groups or classes, but the collective well-being of all English subjects; and when he urged Parliament to implement what were called "remedies" for such grievances, he was claiming to speak for the good of English society as a whole. His efforts of the 1620s to promote parliamentary remedies for the grievances of the commonwealth can therefore be treated as his final attempt to control and rule English society in a way that accorded with his own conception of the public good.[76]

Historians have long recognized the importance of Coke's parliamentary activities during these years and have discussed some of the more dramatic incidents from this phase of his career.[77] But because they have not presented a full picture of his role in Parliament between 1621 and 1628, a full-scale study of this subject is clearly called for. Such a study, moreover, seems well suited to serve as a starting point for a

76. For further comments on the use of the term "grievances" in the parliaments of the 1620s, see pp. 31–33.

77. Coke's parliamentary activities are at least touched on in many of the works cited above in fnn. 50–56.

reexamination of Coke's entire career. Between his call to the bar in 1578 and his death in 1634, his fortunes and political position underwent many changes, as did his views on many different topics. As a result, one cannot regard any period in his life as typical or confidently apply to his whole career generalizations based upon his actions and utterances during a brief span of years. Nevertheless, the sources for the parliaments of the 1620s have certain distinct advantages over other evidence bearing on Coke's life and thought.[78] First, they reveal more clearly than most other sources the range of his concerns, because they record his speeches on a great variety of legal and economic issues as well as his remarks about parliamentary privilege and judicature. Second, these speeches contain material that is highly relevant to current controversies over his ideas about economic regulation, his attitude towards law reform and his conception of Parliament's constitutional role. Third, Parliament's debates during these years reveal with unusual clarity the similarities and differences between his views on various issues and the views of other parliamentary members; and they illuminate the process by which he so strongly influenced the ideas and actions of his contemporaries. Fourth, Coke's parliamentary speeches of the 1620s are sometimes more explicit than his published writings about the relationships that he perceived between particular legal rules, procedures, and institutions on the one hand, and the general condition of the commonwealth on the other. They also indicate quite clearly the specific uses to which he wished to put Parliament's various privileges and powers and the role that he assigned to Parliament in promoting the public good as he defined it. In his *Reports* he frequently stated that particular common-law rules, as he interpreted them, benefited the commonwealth, and that the adoption of other rules would vex the realm with many "mischiefs" and "inconveniencies." In these works, however, he was far more concerned with proving that his statements of common-law rules were correct than with demonstrating the "conveniency" for the commonwealth of particular legal rules. In his parliamentary speeches, by contrast, he often made some effort to show not only that his interpretations of the law were correct, but also that they were "reasonable" and promoted the "public good."[79]

A study of Coke's parliamentary activities during the 1620s therefore can illuminate both the final phase of his career and his life as a whole and thereby make a start at remedying the deficiencies in Coke scholarship

---

78. For a fairly full list of these sources, see Robert C. Johnson, "Parliamentary Diaries of the Early Stuart Period." The best discussion of these sources in to be found in *CD 1628*, 1:1–35.

79. On Coke's use of the terms "mischiefs," "inconveniencies," and "reasonable," see p. 80.

that I have noted above. These general objectives can be best achieved not by chronicling his parliamentary actions during this decade, but rather by studying his answers to a set of questions that he and his fellow members repeatedly posed during these years. What were the grievances of the commonwealth? What were their causes and their actual or potential effects? And how could they best be remedied? An analysis of Coke's changing answers to these questions during the 1620s leads to several different kinds of results. It demonstrates that a significant change in his political outlook and parliamentary priorities took place during this decade and that this change was closely related to a complex process by which later Elizabethan disputes over specific, substantive issues were transformed by the later 1620s into sharp conflicts over general court policies and broad constitutional issues.[80] This study also clarifies Coke's general beliefs about how the English commonwealth should be ordered by exploring what he meant by such crucial phrases as "certainty in law," "quietness of possession," "freedom of trade," and "the liberties of the subject."[81] Such an analysis, moreover, can lead to a clearer understanding of his views during this period about the nature, function, and powers of Parliament by showing what sort of role he thought Parliament should and could play in remedying the grievances of the commonwealth. Finally, it can serve to raise questions about whose interests Coke was trying to promote through parliamentary action and about the means he employed to promote them.

During the early 1620s, Coke actively supported parliamentary remedies for abuses that he and his fellow members called grievances of the commonwealth. But despite the intensity of his concern about these grievances, his attitude towards them was not that of an opposition leader, a constitutional theorist, or a proponent of an antitraditional ideology. Rather, it reflected his previous experience as a politician, judge, and administrator; his training as a common lawyer; and his position as a well-regarded, if not always well-favored, member of an elite governing circle. In the parliaments of 1621 and 1624, Coke generally blamed the grievances of the commonwealth on the malevolent actions of particular private individuals whose presence in any community he regarded as the inevitable result of man's corrupted and corruptable nature. He also blamed some abuses on certain courtiers and thought that specific insti-

80. This view of the course of English political history between c.1590 and c.1630 differs substantially from the one that is set forth, explicitly or implicitly, in the works cited above in fn. 85 by Christianson, Gruenfelder, Russell, Kishlansky, Farnell, and Roberts. For a further note on current controversies concerning early Stuart politics, see chap. 2, fn. 1.

81. On Coke's use of the terms "certainty in law" and "quietness of possession," see chap. 3. On his use of the phrase "freedom of trade," see chap. 4. His use of the phrase "the liberties of the subject" is discussed in chap 7.

tutional flaws in English government and law had provided opportunities for evil people to vex honest subjects and the commonwealth as a whole. He was particularly critical of certain aspects of English legal administration, and he also attacked restraints on free trade as being corrupt, inconvenient, and often illegal. Although he was obviously concerned about the actual and potential "effects" of grievances and believed that these grievances seriously damaged the public good, he did not regard them as dire threats to the commonwealth and did not believe that they demanded immediate remedy. His critique of English society in this period was thus a moderate one, even though it may have implied somewhat less traditional criticisms of English institutions. His basically moralistic, traditional, and yet pragmatic attitude towards grievances shaped his parliamentary activities in 1621 and 1624 in four important ways. First, while it allowed him to criticize particular courtiers and a few court policies and to propose moderate institutional reforms, it did not impel him to attack the court as a whole; and it made him amenable to compromises with courtiers and other parliamentary members in the interests of remedying particular grievances through parliamentary action. Second, it did not predispose him to make novel claims about Parliament's authority or responsibility, to engage in disruptive constitutional controversies about the subject's liberties, royal authority, or Parliament's privileges and powers, or to develop a coherent constitutional ideology. It required only that he discuss such matters when their proper resolution was essential to the implementation of particular parliamentary remedies.

Third, because of his continuing faith in English institutions and his failure to develop a coherent critique of them, he was not inclined to propose fundamental reforms in English law, constitutional structure, or economic organization. Instead, while he tried to promote general values like certainty in law, quietness of possession, and freedom of trade, and to defend the liberties of the subject, he generally did so by attacking the more obvious threats to these interests that were posed either by specific individuals or by institutional arrangements that were obviously defective, corrupt, or corruptable. Insofar as he saw the need for changes in existing substantive legal doctrine, he still thought that they could be best carried out by judges ruling on individual cases and did not conceive of such changes as real alterations in legal doctrine. Instead, he saw them as restatements or clarifications of ancient common-law rules that had been either misunderstood or foolishly abandoned, as true interpretations of previously misunderstood statutes, or as applications to new situations of well established common-law rules and principles. As a result, while the remedies for grievances that he supported in Parliament generally advanced the interests of the landholders and merchants for whom he primarily spoke, they did not necessarily do so in the most efficient or rational way, and they may also have benefited other members of the commonwealth for whom Coke sometimes expressed a paternalistic concern. These remedies were thus shaped by his conception of the public good and of the interests that he hoped to promote and by his notions about what constituted legitimate parliamentary action. Moreover, they reflect relatively simple and traditional values and concerns. By "freedom of trade" Coke often meant either "fair trade" or else trade that was free from unreasonable interference by corrupt men or from legal restraints that served the interests of only a few private individuals. By "quietness of possession" he meant merely the peaceful enjoyment of property rights without fear of losing them by some obvious form of legalistic chicanery. And when he spoke of "certainty in law," he was usually referring only to a feeling of confidence that one had access to inexpensive, uncorrupted, and definitive legal remedies. Although he frequently referred to "the liberties of the subject," he made few efforts to expand or even define them and rarely, if ever, suggested that they were seriously threatened by royal action.

Finally, Coke's attitude towards the grievances of the commonwealth during the early 1620s was not such as to make him propose general reforms in the law, the constitution, or the prevailing system of economic organization. Instead, it induced him to support many specific, moderate remedies for particular grievances. While these remedies probably benefited landholders, merchants, and perhaps others as well, they did not do so very dramatically. They did not erect any strong legal barriers that protected these groups against the demands of an absolutist state. Nor did they greatly facilitate the "improvement" of landed estates or of industrial or commercial enterprises. Instead, they were designed to provide some English subjects with easier and more inexpensive access to uncorrupted legal processes and remedies and to protect them from harrassment and vexation by those whom he called the "caterpillars of the commonwealth."[82]

During the later 1620s, Coke's views about the grievances of the commonwealth changed significantly, but not in such a way as to lead him to a much more coherent institutional critique of English society. He became increasingly prone to blame all grievances on the royal court and to regard them as ultimate threats to the liberties of the subject and to the very life of the commonwealth. While his critique of English society thus assumed a more political and constitutional character, it still did not imply the need for systematic reforms in English law or economic organ-

82. On Coke's use of this phrase, see pp. 50, 51, 73.

ization. Nevertheless, his recently developed conviction that the court was to blame for the grievances of the commonwealth led to important changes in his parliamentary actions. He now directly attacked the king's leading minister, the duke of Buckingham, and portrayed Parliament as an independent political and constitutional counterweight to the court. He virtually abandoned his earlier efforts to implement piecemeal remedies for grievances through parliamentary compromise and instead attacked general policies of the royal court. At the same time, he became more interested in developing a consistent, coherent constitutional position, and devoted more energy than before to promoting a parliamentary declaration of the subject's liberties that would establish clear limits on the exercise of royal power. By the end of the parliament of 1628, therefore, Coke had abandoned the relatively accommodating political and constitutional stance that he had taken in the two last parliaments of James I. He had finally become a true political opponent of the Stuart court and had at last developed a more coherent and uncompromising constitutional position that was in direct conflict with the one espoused by Charles I and his supporters. Thus, while Coke never reached the point of supporting systematic parliamentary efforts to adapt English law to new social and economic conditions, he had developed at the end of his life constitutional positions that might facilitate such a process of adaptation in the future.

©︎ Part One

The Early 1620s

Two

Coke in the Parliaments
of 1621 and 1624

In both 1621 and 1624, Coke played an extraordinarily prominent role in Parliament's proceedings. In terms of sheer activity, he must be reckoned the leading member of the lower house in these years, because he delivered more speeches and committee reports in both years than any other member and ranked first in 1621 and second in 1624 in the number of committees on which he served. He was not, however, merely an active member of these parliaments. He was also a highly influential leader who proposed many remedies for the commonwealth's grievances and who frequently bore the main burden of justifying or legitimating the Commons's actions. In spite of his prominence in these two parliaments, he lacked the power to direct or control their proceedings. He was rarely in a position to initiate a whole new line of parliamentary inquiry or action; and he usually responded to events over which he had little control and acted in accordance with the Commons's collective decisions. As a result, his parliamentary speeches from these years cannot be viewed as self-contained, self-explanatory statements of his views on particular subjects. Rather, they must be regarded as public remarks that were profoundly influenced by the political and procedural context in which they were made. It is therefore impossible to understand his parliamentary behavior in 1621 and 1624 (or, indeed, during the entire 1620s) without considering some of the more general features of the parliamentary sessions in which he participated.

A striking feature of James I's last two parliaments was their ambiguous and transitional character. Like earlier, Tudor parliaments, they served largely as occasions for transacting important but limited governmental business and acted as integral, albeit occasional, parts of the English central government. In both of these years, however, the Commons sometimes tended to assume greater responsibility for formulating general policies, to become a center of opposition to acts and policies of the court, and to serve as a forum for abstract constitutional debates. When these tendencies became more fully developed under Charles I, Parliament became a new kind of body that either could not act or else acted in novel and ultimately revolutionary ways; but in James I's last years, Parliament still functioned in a relatively traditional manner.[1] In 1621 and 1624, the Commons, the Lords, and the king still regarded parliamentary meetings primarily as occasions on which they could remedy the grievances of the commonwealth by making slight adjustments in the governance of the kingdom. Many of the grievances that were discussed in these two years were ones that had been attacked in previous, Tudor parliaments; and they were generally treated as isolated defects in an otherwise sound social system and as discrete violations of generally accepted principles of law, government, and policy. Members of Parliament usually blamed these grievances on individual evildoers and expected to eliminate them by providing for proper legal enforcement, or else by slightly modifying the law so as to cover new ways of committing old offenses. Almost all remedies for grievances considered in 1621 and 1624 reflected this traditional view of abuses and of Parliament's role in eliminating them. They were usually very specific and presupposed the existence of a general consensus among the governing classes about basic legal and social values and about how Parliament should use its power to defend or promote these values. These remedies were also designed to mesh with the preexisting policies and procedures of other governmental bodies. Parliamentary members often argued about what the real grievances of the commonwealth were, about how generally accepted norms should be defended or applied in particular cases, and about whether particular parliamentary remedies were appropriate or lawful in particular cases. They knew, however, that they had to settle some of these differences if Parliament was to carry out its appointed governmental function, and in 1621 and 1624 they were able to resolve their disagreements much more frequently than is commonly supposed.

Nevertheless, in these two years, some members of the Commons were beginning to talk about their grievances in ways that were relatively

1. For works that stress the more traditional aspects of early Stuart parliaments, see G. R. Elton, "A High Road to Civil War?"; G. R. Elton, "Studying the History of Parliament"; Russell, "Parliamentary History in Perspective"; Russell, "Foreign Policy Debate"; and Kishlansky, "Emergence of Adversary Politics," pp. 618–28. Although these writers do not express identical views about early Stuart parliamentary history, they all minimize the role of conflict in Parliament's proceedings between 1604 and 1629 and deny that a real opposition party existed in Parliament in this period. In addition, they all insist that the arguments that sometimes broke out in the parliaments of this era did not foreshadow and did not culminate in the revolutionary actions of the Long Parliament. Finally, both Elton and Kishlansky insist that members of both houses strongly believed in the need to cooperate with the crown, reach consensuses, and transact governmental business under royal direction; and they thus interpret early Stuart parliamentary history in a way that builds upon Elton's view of Tudor parliamentary history (see G. R. Elton, "The Body of the Whole Realm"; and G. R. Elton, "Tudor Government"). For vigorous attacks on this revisionist view of early Stuart parliamentary history, see J. H. Hexter, "Parliament under the Lens";

new and that threatened Parliament's ability to function.[2] They were more ready to claim that these different grievances were interconnected and to treat them not just as sporadic violations of fundamental legal and social principles but as serious threats to these norms. They were also more prone to blame them on the court. This new perception of grievances led them to support new kinds of parliamentary action and, ultimately, to develop a new view of English constitutional structure. Some members were increasingly inclined to propose their own general remedies for what they saw as general grievances,[3] to reassert and redefine abstract principles of law and governmental policy, and to interpret their own privileges and powers more broadly and take a narrower view of the king's authority. They came closer to seeing themselves as a distinct body having a unique responsibility to govern the commonwealth and a duty to oversee and sometimes oppose the actions of the court. As the Commons became more aware of the range of their grievances and more ready to propose general remedies for them, as they became more anxious to assert and define the rights of subjects and their own privileges, and as they expressed more general opposition to the court, Parliament had more and more difficulty in reaching the kinds of compromises that were necessary if it was to function in traditional ways or at all.

In spite of these forward-looking tendencies, the main outlines of Parliament's activities in 1621 and 1624 still conformed generally to the model set by previous parliaments. These two parliaments differed markedly not only from the Long Parliament but also from the parliaments of the later 1620s. In 1621 and 1624, members of the Commons did not mount a full-scale assault on a favored royal minister, nor did they issue a scathing indictment of court policy. They adopted no statement of constitutional principle comparable to the Petition of Right; and they never suggested, as they did in the later 1620s, that Parliament should join with the king to reform the realm. In 1621 and 1624, even outspoken members of the lower house did not yet express fears of "the civil tyranny of an arbitrary, unlimited, confused government," controlled by a "wicked and malignant party" of "jesuited papists," bishops and "corrupt" clergy, and

---

Hexter, "Power Struggle, Parliament, and Liberty"; and Hirst, "Unanimity in the Commons." Hexter in particular, insists that serious conflicts broke out in the parliaments held between 1604 and 1629 and that the willingness of certain prominent members of Parliament to express opposition to certain royal actions is an important feature of Parliament's proceedings during this quarter century. For other general comments on early Stuart parliamentary history, see Theodore K. Rabb, "Parliament and Society in Early Stuart England"; and David S. Berkowitz, "Parliamentary History, American Style."

2. This new point of view, may, of course, have been anticipated to some degree in Elizabeth's last parliaments and in the first two Parliaments of James I.

3. This point has been made by Notestein in "The Winning of the Initiative."

certain "councillors and courtiers," who had "a malignant and pernicious design of subverting the fundamental laws and principles of government, upon which the religion and justice of this kingdom are firmly established."[4] They did not attempt to abolish important governmental institutions. They made few attempts to state formally either their own privileges or the liberties of the subject, and they rarely tried to implement general policies that differed from those of the crown. Above all, they were generally willing to compromise on substantive, procedural, and constitutional issues so that they could remedy at least some of their grievances.

Two issues dominated Parliament's proceedings in 1621 and 1624: the so-called cause of religion abroad and at home, and the many grievances of the commonwealth. Late in 1620 the deepening religious and political crisis on the continent had induced James I to call a parliament for the first time in almost seven years.[5] He now needed money to aid his son-in-law, the elector Frederick V, against the recent Spanish invasion of the Palatinate. But although the king wished to aid the Protestant husband of his daughter Elizabeth, he still intended to follow a conciliatory policy towards both Catholic powers on the continent and domestic English recusants. He wanted Parliament to supply him for a limited war against Spain in the Palatinate, but he still planned to marry his son Charles to a Catholic Spanish princess and was determined to resist any parliamentary pressure for a more aggressively anti-Spanish policy. The king also wished to continue his mild policy towards domestic Catholics and would not listen to those pressing for a more repressive one.

James I asked the parliament of 1621 to trust in his "care and piety and forwardness in religion."[6] But many of its members—especially in the Commons—lacked faith in his policy of negotiation abroad and persuasion at home, and their concern about the "cause of religion" was so intense that they came close to expressing this lack of faith publicly. They were determined to deal with the recusant threat at home and the Spanish threat abroad; and they were particularly intent upon doing so because they were convinced that these two threats to the commonwealth were closely connected. In both 1621 and 1624 the Commons angered the king by urging him to enforce existing laws against recusants and by proposing the enactment of even more repressive measures.[7] They were

4. These phrases are taken from John Pym's speech of 25 November, 1640 on Strafford (Kenyon, SC, p. 206) and the Grand Remonstrance of 1641 (Kenyon, SC, pp. 230–32).
5. On the background to the calling of the parliament of 1621, see Zaller, 1621, pp. 9–26.
6. CD 1621, 2:7.
7. On the Commons's attacks on recusants in 1621, see Zaller, 1621, esp. pp. 41–45,

even more aggressive in 1621 in voicing their dissatisfaction with the king's foreign policy. Many members of the lower house opposed the proposed marriage of Prince Charles to a Spanish princess and preferred a sea war with Spain to military intervention in the Palatinate. In the fall of 1621 they expressed these views about war and foreign policy, first in a formal petition and later in a declaration. Their actions led to a constitutional confrontation with the king over their privilege of free speech, and when they adopted an extreme "Protestation" of their liberties in December 1621, James adjourned and then dissolved Parliament.[8] By 1624, however, royal foreign policy had changed in such a way as to make James I's last parliament a relatively "happy" one.[9] The court had abandoned the Spanish match, and it was now willing to allow the Commons far greater freedom than before to discuss war and foreign policy. Throughout this session some possibility remained that the king would again dissolve Parliament if its actions displeased him.[10] But the Parliament of 1624 concluded with the passage of many notable statutes and a subsidy bill in which Parliament formally expressed its views on foreign policy and war.[11]

Although James I's last two parliaments were marked by tensions and disagreements, they were not dominated by constitutional or political conflicts. Their members reached numerous compromises on both substantive and constitutional issues and successfully remedied at least as many grievances as any Elizabethan parliament. The term "grievance" was a very vague one—and conveniently so. Members could apply it to any practice, institution, law, policy, or procedure that they disliked with-

---

130–33. On similar attacks made in the parliament of 1624, see Ruigh, *1624*, esp. pp. 238–40, 243–44. On English attitudes towards domestic and/or foreign Catholics in this period, see Breslow, *A Mirror of England*; K. S. Van Eerde, "The Spanish Match through an English Protestant's Eyes"; Carol Z. Wiener, "The Beleaguered Isle"; Carol Z. Wiener, "Popular Anti-Catholicism in England, 1559–1618"; Robin Clifton, "The Popular Fear of Catholics during the English Revolution" and the works cited at p. 23, n. 2; and Robin Clifton, "Fear of Popery."

8. On the Commons's debates on foreign policy and free speech in the fall of 1621, see Harold Hulme, "The Winning of Freedom of Speech by the House of Commons"; Zaller, *1621*, pp. 142–87; Russell, "Foreign Policy Debate"; and Hexter, "Power Struggle, Parliament, and Liberty," pp. 42–43. On the question of whether these debates show that a real constitutional conflict took place in Parliament during the fall of 1621, see chap. 5, fn. 142.

9. Coke later referred to the parliament of 1624 as "Foelix Parliamentum" (*Institutes*, 3:2). According to Ruigh, "[t]he entire session was so frought with mutual suspicion that it belied Coke's ascription" (*1624*, p. 1). But if the mood of this parliament was not truly happy, the session still produced results about which Coke and some of his fellow-members could be pleased.

10. See Ruigh, *1624*, pp. 393–94.

11. For a discussion of some of the statutes that were passed in 1624, see chaps. 3 and 4. On the subsidy act of 1624, see Ruigh, *1624*, pp. 245–55.

out having to demonstrate its illegality.[12] It was generally assumed that "grievances" damaged "the public good," but members did not always explain precisely how they did so and usually attacked "grievances" that were of relatively little concern to most English men and women. Some grievances were said to harm farmers, apprentices, or the poor.[13] But whereas such claims may well have been accurate, it seems unlikely that a list of grievances drawn up by these subjects would have closely resembled the list of grievances considered by the Commons in 1621 and 1624. Although the Commons's efforts to remedy grievances in these two years did not constitute a crass attempt to use parliamentary power to promote class interest, and although these efforts may have brought some benefit to groups for whom members had relatively little concern, the rhetoric used by the spokesman of the House cannot be taken at face value. It did not simply describe what the Commons were doing; it also served to explain and justify the House's actions. One of the ways in which members tried to lend greater legitimacy to their proposals for remedies for grievances was to claim that in calling for such remedies they were speaking for the whole commonwealth. But even though these members were elected by a relatively large number of English subjects, their parliamentary speeches did not necessarily express the views of all commonwealth members, or even of the people who voted for them.[14] Among the specific abuses most frequently discussed in the lower house in 1621 and 1624 were particular patents of monopoly, specific practices of trading companies, corruption in the customs system, problems in the organization of the wool and cloth trades, excessive legal and court fees, the corrupt practices of court officials, delays in justice, the characters of juries, and the use of legal procedures for the purposes of harassment and avoidance of legal obligations.[15] The Commons sometimes organized these grievances under the two main headings of abuses in law and abuses in trade, but they did so largely for procedural reasons and developed no coherent

12. For examples of the Commons's use of this term in 1621, see CD 1621, 2:21, 22, 56–57, 84–85, 89, 149, 162, 192, 198, 206.

13. See ibid., 2:90, 91, 137, 178, 184, 186.

14. For a discussion of the claims of members to speak for the English nation, see Judson, Crisis of the Constitution, pp. 244–310. In his recent study of early Stuart voters and voting, Hirst argues that "there was some justification for Parliament's claims to be representative" (The Representative of the People?, p. 193). But although he has shown that the early Stuart electorate was considerably larger than historians had previously supposed and that "genuine consultations" took place between parliamentary members and "large numbers of ordinary people" (The Representative of the People?, p. 193), he has not demonstrated that members actually expressed the concerns of ordinary people in parliamentary speeches or that these members proposed parliamentary actions that actually benefited or would have benefited these ordinary people in any very significant way.

15. For a useful list of the main grievances attacked in 1621 and 1624, see CD 1621, "Introduction," 1:3–5.

program for legal or economic reform. Although they frequently claimed that trade should be free and that the subject's liberties should be maintained intact, they rarely explained what they meant by "free trade" or "the liberties of the subject," or expressed consistent views about how law or government should be reformed so as to promote the public good. Instead, they simply attacked impediments to free trade and alleged violations of the subject's liberties.

In attempting to remedy grievances in these ways, the Commons were doing nothing very new in 1621 or 1624, but they were particularly eager in these years to seize the opportunity afforded by a parliament to remedy certain grievances of the commonwealth. Their eagerness to do so was mainly due to three facts. First, no new statutes had been enacted in almost a decade; and although later Elizabethan and Jacobean parliaments had made numerous new laws, they had not passed many bills that had been well supported in the Commons. In 1621 and 1624 members therefore hoped to pass many bills whose enactment they regarded as long overdue.[16] Second, the king's recent grants of monopoly patents and the duke of Buckingham's use of his increasing powers of patronage had exacerbated a concern about governmental corruption that had probably been mounting since the 1590s.[17] A meeting of Parliament gave members a chance to voice this concern and to convert it into parliamentary action. Third, members were particularly concerned about economic grievances in 1621 and 1624, because they were meeting during a severe trade depression that they hoped to alleviate partly by parliamentary action. Their inquiries into its causes, moreover, led them to discover new grievances and provided them with a pretext for attacking other long-standing abuses.[18]

For these reasons the Commons gave particularly close attention to specific grievances in 1621 and 1624. In each of these years they established a Committee for Courts to investigate legal abuses, a Committee of Trade to inquire into the depression and other economic problems, and a Committee of Grievances to investigate monopolies and other

16. On the unenacted legislation of later Elizabethan and early Jacobean parliaments, see Notestein, *1604–1610*, pp. 47–54. On Lord Chancellor Ellesmere's efforts to promote the passage of legislation in early Jacobean parliaments, see Knafla, *Law and Politics*, pp. 91–122.

17. On corruption in later Elizabethan and early Stuart England, see Robert Ashton, *The Crown and the Money Market, 1603–1640*, esp. pp. 67–78; J. P. Cooper, "The Fortune of Thomas Wentworth, Earl of Strafford"; Joel Hurstfield, "Political Corruption in Modern England"; Joel Hurstfield, "The Political Morality of Early Stuart Statesmen"; Wallace T. MacCaffrey, "Place and Patronage in Elizabethan Politics"; J. E. Neale, "The Elizabethan Political Scene"; Stone, *Causes of the English Revolution*, pp. 85–88; Stone, *Crisis of the Aristocracy*, esp. pp. 67–68, 193; and Lawrence Stone, "The Fruits of Office."

18. See chap. 4.

miscellaneous abuses. They also discussed grievances in the full house, in committees of the whole, and in many different select committees. They hoped to remedy grievances in three different ways: by petitioning the king, by passing bills, and by using Parliament's newly revived power of judicature to pass sentence on offenders against the commonwealth. In the winter and spring of 1621 they found many patents of monopoly to be grievances and petitioned for their cancellation. Their petitions were generally granted.[19] At the end of the parliament of 1624 they presented the king with a petition of grievances; and although it was not answered by James I, Charles I responded to it in 1625.[20] Sometimes, instead of merely petitioning the king against existing abuses, the Commons considered bills to outlaw them and prevent similar ones from arising "in time to come." They deliberated on bills introduced in previous parliaments, bills brought in by various members, and bills drafted during the session in response to their various investigations. They also considered the king's so-called bills of grace, although they often amended them.[21] The sudden dissolution of the parliament of 1621 checked the Commons's legislative endeavors only briefly because most of the bills considered in that year were reintroduced in the parliament of 1624.[22] Most of these measures never became law, but over a hundred were considered and the parliament concluded with the passage of over thirty-two public acts.[23] The most celebrated legislative product of this parliament was the Statute of Monopolies, but many other noteworthy bills were passed: the act against concealments, which limited the royal prerogative of *nullum tempus occurrit regi*; an act against informers that markedly diminished the number of informations brought in the central courts on penal statutes; a statute of limitations for personal actions at common law; various acts regulating court procedure and local justice; and an act for the continuance and repeal of statutes that was far more comprehensive than previous acts of this kind. The parliament of 1624 also effected an important change in English economic policy by weakening the Merchant Adventurers' control over the cloth trade[24] and passed several bills concerning clothing, a new usury act, and a bankruptcy statute. The Commons also

19. See Foster, "Procedure against Patents and Monopolies."

20. For the petition of 1624, see Cobbett, *PH*, 1, cols. 1489–1497. For comments on it, see Foster, "Petitions." On Charles I's answers to this petition in 1625, see chap. 6.

21. On the king's bills of grace, see Zaller, *1621*, pp. 21, 52, 97, and below, pp. 63–64.

22. On the continuity in the legislative work of early Stuart parliaments, see Notestein, "Winning of the Initiative," pp. 40–41.

23. Not counting the subsidies or the general pardon. See 21 *Jac.* I, *cc.* 1–32 (*SR*, 4, pt. 2, pp. 1209–46).

24. See B. E. Supple, *Commercial Crisis and Change in England, 1600–1642*, p. 68.

tried to remedy grievances in 1621 and 1624 by initiating parliamentary trials of those whom they held responsible for certain specific abuses. In 1621 they began judicial proceedings against Sir Francis Michell, Sir Giles Mompesson, Sir Henry Yelverton, Sir Francis Bacon, Sir John Bennet, Edward Floyd, and Bishop Theophilus Field; and although the Lords took no action against the last three men, they found the other four guilty and sentenced them. In 1624 the Commons initiated similar proceedings against Lord Treasurer Middlesex, Bishop Samuel Harsnett, and Dr. Thomas Anyan; and although neither Harsnett nor Anyan were ever judged, the Lords found Middlesex guilty and gave him a harsh sentence. By means of these judicial proceedings, parliamentary members hoped to purge the government of certain corrupt officials, punish other offenders against the commonwealth, and set examples to deter still others from wrongdoing.[25]

Although many members of the Commons wished to remedy grievances in the three ways noted above, they knew that they could not act effectively on their own. Bills required the consent of both houses and of the king, as did most judicial proceedings. The Commons's petitions could accomplish nothing without favorable royal responses. The king, moreover, could always frustrate their attempts to remedy grievances by dissolving Parliament and could try to avoid calling another one for many years. The Commons were aware of these facts and knew that the only productive parliaments were "happy" ones in which "contestation" was avoided and "good correspondency" maintained between the Commons, the Lords, and the king. They were therefore prepared to compromise and to avoid all unnecessary clashes about substantive, procedural, or constitutional issues. Compared with parliaments of the later 1620s, or with the short-lived Parliament of 1614, those of 1621 and 1624 were both relatively happy, for although the Commons sometimes "hunted" after grievances, contrary to the king's command,[26] and considered a few proposals for significant changes in governmental policy,[27] they were still generally successful at preserving that "good correspondancy" without which effective parliamentary action could not take place.[28]

They were able to do so at least partly because of the king's receptivity

25. See chaps. 3 and 5.

26. *CD 1621*, 4:5–6. James made this command in his opening speech to the parliament of 1621.

27. See, for example, the proposal made in 1624 to throw open the cloth trade. On this proposal, see pp. 107–10.

28. On the importance that parliamentary members attached to achieving compromises that would enable them to transact legislative and other parliamentary business, see Kishlansky, "The Emergence of Adversary Politics," pp. 618–24; and Elton, "Studying the History of Parliament," p. 9.

to moderate reform proposals. In his opening speech to the parliament of 1621, James I conceded that he might have been deceived into doing things harmful to his people and expressed his willingness to withdraw monopoly patents that he had granted previously. He said that a "fit" king should take care to have "just and faithful" judges under him and promised not to spare any judge whom Parliament found "faulty." The king also declared that the "many new crimes and abuses that do daily creep into this kingdom" could be best remedied by laws made in Parliament.[29] In response to James's speech, the Commons proposed reforms that were rarely controversial.[30] Few of the patents that they attacked had determined defenders, and most were quickly withdrawn by the council after their condemnation in the Commons. Most of the bills that the Commons promoted were old measures. Many had the king's support, and some had actually been drafted by royal ministers. The Commons's judicial proceedings were rarely controversial, because they were not directed against men whom the Lords or the king were determined to defend, and when the Commons met strong opposition to a particular remedy, they usually modified or abandoned it. They accepted most of the Lords' proposed amendments to the bills against monopolies, informers, and concealers. They failed to protest strongly when most of their proposals for court reform died in the upper house, or when those whom they had accused of wrongdoing went unpunished.

The Commons were also willing to compromise on constitutional questions concerning their own privileges and powers; and they rarely tried to develop highly consistent constitutional positions on these matters. They naturally wished to maintain, and perhaps extend, their privilege of free speech. But they avoided clashes with the king over this issue until very late in 1621, and in 1624 they were more concerned with actually influencing foreign policy than with establishing their right to do so.[31] They also accepted numerous compromises concerning their role in parliamentary trials; and when faced with a choice between getting a particular offender punished and maintaining a consistent theory of parliamentary judicature, they almost never chose the latter.[32] Some mem-

29. For this speech, see *CD 1621*, 2:13 and the other versions cited in the notes therein. See also Zaller, *1621*, pp. 31–5.

30. The following points are discussed and documented in chaps. 3–5.

31. Russell warns against overestimating the Commons's concern about questions of privilege (see "Parliamentary History in Perspective," pp. 23–4; and "Foreign Policy Debate"), and Hirst issues a somewhat similar warning (see Derek Hirst, "Elections and the Privileges of the House of Commons in the Early Seventeenth Century," esp. pp. 861–62). Hexter, however, places much greater stress on conflicts over this issue (see "Parliament under the Lens"; and "Power Struggle, Parliament, and Liberty," pp. 42–3).

32. On the flexibility with which the Commons conducted their parts in parliamentary trials, see Tite, *Impeachment*, esp. pp. 141–48 and pp. 218–20.

bers insisted strongly on their right to legislate on almost any subject, but very few of their bills raised any questions about the extent of Parliament's legislative power. Although their debates on disputed elections sometimes led them to discuss the nature of parliamentary representation, such discussions never led them to question the constitutional status quo.

The willingness of the Commons to compromise on most issues helps to explain Parliament's relative success at remedying grievances in 1621 and 1624. But their willingness to do so was itself the product of conditions that prevailed during the early 1620s. Parliament's ability to compromise on proposed remedies for grievances naturally depended upon what types of remedies were proposed and upon how they were promoted. The decisions of parliamentary members to support particular remedies in particular ways depended in turn upon how these members conceived of their own grievances. The view of grievances that generally prevailed in the Commons during the early 1620s was conducive to compromise for several different reasons. First, although members bitterly complained about grievances like monopolies, they did not regard them as ultimate threats to their own interests or to the commonwealth. They were therefore unlikely to make nonnegotiable demands that these grievances be remedied, to impute evil intentions to anyone who opposed their proposals, or to regard as catastrophic Parliament's failure to remedy any particular grievance. They were prepared to bargain. Second, the Commons did not generally regard their grievances as being interrelated. As a result, their proposed remedies for grievances tended to be highly specific and did not raise fundamental and controversial questions about English governmental, legal, and social institutions. Third, the Commons usually explained the existence of grievances by referring to the corrupt acts of particular individuals and to the malfunctioning of particular institutions. They did not blame grievances on the king or the court, or suggest that they arose because of basic flaws in the commonwealth. Their attempts to remedy grievances, therefore, did not provoke confrontations with the king, his advisors, or the Lords. Nor did they presuppose any fundamental distinction between a beneficent Parliament and a corrupt and untrustworthy court. Fourth, the Commons generally portrayed their grievances as violations of legal, social, and moral norms that were accepted by all responsible members of the English ruling elite. As a result, they saw little need for Parliament to restate these norms and provoke the kind of intense controversy that such an attempt at restatement would have necessarily entailed. Parliament could thus act without all of its members having to agree on the rationale for its actions. Finally, given their view of grievances outlined above, the Commons were not likely to propose parliamentary remedies for them that would raise fundamental questions about Parliament's privileges and powers. By and large, members thought that they could remedy the commonwealth's grievances simply by enforcing existing laws and by employing well established and uncontroversial parliamentary powers whose exact scope and legal bases they were willing to leave undefined.

For these reasons, compromises could be and were achieved in James I's last two parliaments. But in these same two years, Parliament's ability to compromise and function in traditional ways was in jeopardy, primarily because certain subtle changes were taking place in the attitudes of members of the lower house. These changes in attitude did not reflect clear-cut changes in self-interest. Nor were they simply reactions to the new threats to their interests posed by the policies of the Stuart court. The Commons's way of perceiving grievances was changing in such a way as to make them less willing to accept the kinds of compromises that were necessary to effective parliamentary action. They were coming to regard even seemingly trivial abuses as fundamental threats to the commonwealth, or as symptoms of serious diseases in the body of the realm. They were also more prone to regard them as interrelated parts of a network and to blame them on the court. Instead of suggesting that abuses grew out of a failure to enforce the law, they began to suggest that they arose because of basic disagreements about what the law was. Finally, they were making closer and closer associations between grievances, causes of grievances, and actual and potential effects of grievances and occasionally talked as if the court were undermining the public good and threatening the realm with destruction.

Central to these changes in the Commons's perception of their grievances were the processes that led them to believe that seemingly disparate abuses were actually related to one another. This belief of theirs sometimes served to transform their expressions of concern about particular grievances into more general critiques of English governmental institutions. Although members usually attributed particular grievances to the corrupt actions of specific individuals, they also believed that corruption, like sin, heresy, or witchcraft, had a natural tendency to spread from one part of the commonwealth to another, and that it would ultimately infect the whole realm if it were not rooted out. As a result, their discussions of particular, corrupt acts often turned into more general debates on the actual or potential impact on the commonwealth of particular forms of corruption.[33] The Commons's concern with the progressive workings of

33. On 15 March, 1621, Sir Robert Phelips reported the charges of corruption that had been made against Bacon (CD 1621, 2:224–26) and asked on the following day, "If the fountains be muddy what will the streams be [?]" (CD 1621, 2:269). The same belief in the capacity of corruption to spread is illustrated by several of Coke's speeches that are

corruption, moreover, was probably intensified, and in their eyes justified, by religious problems at home and abroad. Some members believed that popery posed the most serious of all threats to the commonwealth, and that it grew not only through the political successes of continental Catholic states, but also through the corruption of the souls of individual English subjects. They believed that continual vigilance in maintaining true religion was necessary if religious corruption were to be prevented from infecting the whole commonwealth, and this belief may have both reflected and reinforced their general propensity to see great threats in small grievances.[34] Finally, their tendency to believe that the macrocosm could be seen in microcosmic events may have reinforced their anxieties about seemingly minor social ills.[35]

The trade depression of the early 1620s also induced members of the Commons to look beyond specific abuses and to consider the relationship between these grievances and the workings of their society as a whole. It encouraged them to see the commonwealth as a system composed of interconnected parts, to inquire into the relationships between seemingly disparate grievances, and to look for connections between manifest grievances and other social institutions. One of the most recurrent themes in their economic debates in 1621 and 1624 was the search for the causes and effects of grievances. In an effort to understand the depression and find a cure for it, members frequently tried to uncover the latent causal connections between specific grievances and the general state of the realm and between blatant abuses and seemingly innocuous practices, laws, and institutions.[36] Some of their ideas about the depression were confused and inconsistent, while others were carefully calculated to provide a pseudoeconomic rationale for favoring particular interest groups. But the concern of the Commons about the so-called stop in trade, like their anxiety about the state of religion and the workings of corruption, en-

---

discussed below in chap. 3. It was also common for speakers to compare the commonwealth to "the natural body" and to claim that an illness affecting one part of it would ultimately damage the whole. See, for example, *CD 1621*, 2:19 (Calvert's speech); and *CD 1621*, 2:180 (Digges's speech). On Coke's use of such analogies, see pp. 51, 54–55, 68.

34. In 1621, for example, the Commons's first petition against recusants called on the king "to command that [Jesuits and popish priests] may be kept close prisoners, *lest the contagion of their corrupt religion do yet run further*, which we find to have spread too far already to the diverting of the good subject's hearts of this realm from their due obedience both to God and the king" (*CD 1621*, 5:459; my italics). Coke also compared recusants to "locusts" (*CD 1621*, 2:456) and to the embryo "asleep *in vagina*" (*CD 1621*, 2:26). For a full discussion of this conventional imagery, see Wiener, "The Beleaguered Isle," esp. pp. 43, 46–49.

35. On this characteristic feature of Elizabethan and early Stuart thought, see E. M. W. Tillyard, *The Elizabethan World Picture*, passim; and Keith Thomas, *Religion and the Decline of Magic*, pp. 265, 394.

36. See, for example, *CD 1621*, 2:29, 73, 75–78, 115, 137–40, 178, 212–17.

couraged them to see great significance in the smallest grievances, to organize discrete social phenomena into patterns, and to view small abuses as dire threats to the commonwealth.

The exigencies of the Commons's legal arguments also had similar effects. In order to demonstrate that a particular abuse required a parliamentary remedy, members sometimes tried to show that it did not harm only narrow private interests. To do this, they had to explain its actual or potential effects. Sometimes, as in their debates on the depression, they had only to construct causal chains connecting particular with general grievances.[37] On other occasions, however, their efforts to demonstrate the general social effects of specific abuses were aided by their increasing propensity to view the law itself as a system made up of interdependent parts. They could argue that the mere toleration of a particular abuse could overthrow general legal principles that were essential to the maintenance of many different social interests, to the preservation of basic social institutions, and to the proper functioning of the commonwealth as a whole.[38] Prevailing theories of parliamentary representation, moreover, lent further credence to their claims that particular abuses truly harmed the whole commonwealth. Every Englishman was deemed to be present either in person or by representation in Parliament, and while the Lords represented only themselves, the Commons were thought of as representing "great multitudes."[39] This legal fiction made it easier for members to equate their own concerns with those of the commonwealth, because it partially relieved them of the burden of demonstrating that they actually spoke for public and not private interests.

Finally, the lower house's own procedural machinery may have reinforced the tendency of its members to see their grievances as parts of a pattern, to note the interrelationships between different grievances, and to regard specific abuses as particular manifestations of general social ills. The recurrent processes of referring complaints about grievances to committees, of subsuming particular grievances under more general headings, and of debating the same grievances over and over again could lead to such results, particularly since similar abuses had been debated in Parliament for more than a generation. A specific monopoly patent, for example, could be seen as only one example of the general grievance of monopoly patents, which could be viewed in turn as only an illustration

37. On Coke's views about the actual and potential effects of certain legal abuses, see chap. 3.

38. This was also one of Coke's favorite lines of argument. For his most extensive use of it, see pp. 238–41.

39. For instances in which Coke expressed these views, see *Institutes*, 4:12; and three of his parliamentary speeches from the early 1620s: (1) *CD 1621*, 4:36; 5:252; *CJ*, 1:516; (2) *CD 1621*, 2:527; 6:240; and (3) Erle, 1624, f. 142v.

of monopolies established by any means. Monopolies in general could then be regarded only as examples of general impediments to free trade (a category that also included impositions), and impediments to free trade could then be viewed as one of several general causes of the depression. A particular monopoly patent, moreover, could be discussed simultaneously in various different substantive and procedural contexts and could then be seen as part of an even larger and more complex network of interrelated grievances, particularly if its causes, effects, and incidents were considered. It could be seen as only one of the abuses attributable to defendants in parliamentary trials, and it could then be associated with the other illegal acts of these same offenders. It could be seen as the work of monopolists, who could then be classed together with informers, promoters, and concealers as "caterpillars of the commonwealth." It could also be viewed as an example, cause, or effect of many other legal abuses and grievances such as the pursuit of private gain at public expense, the creation of disaffection between a king and his people, the use of royal authority to advance private ends, the illegal use of proclamations, the sale of "flowers of the crown," the granting of offices to ignorant and corrupt men, the imprisonment of honest men contrary to Magna Charta, the taking away of a man's inheritance by preventing him from exercising his lawful trade, the deception of the king by his councilors, the overthrow of established trades and mysteries, the taking away of the general liberty of the subject, or a tax on all the inhabitants of England levied without parliamentary consent. All of these issues could be and were raised in debates on particular monopoly patents. The longer these debates continued, the easier it was for the Commons to make such associations, the more intimate these associations seemed, and the more odious and threatening such individual patents seemed to them.[40]

This transformation in the Commons's perception of the grievances of the commonwealth took place very slowly. It was far from being completed in the early 1620s, and its full effects were not felt in Parliament until the late 1620s, or perhaps even the early 1640s. Nevertheless, it was underway in 1621 and 1624 and was beginning to affect the Commons's proceedings in several different ways. First, it led them to consider several general remedies for grievances and to assume more general responsibility for the governance of the realm. Second, because so many of their grievances seemed to demand parliamentary remedies, members attached increasing importance to Parliament's privileges and powers and began to regard slight attacks on them as threats to the commonwealth. Third, because threats to Parliament's privileges and to

40. For a discussion of the debates in which many of these points were raised, see chap. 4.

the liberties of subjects seemed to emanate from the court, the Commons became more interested in identifying and maintaining the legal boundaries of royal authority. Fourth, as members began to attack court policies and to formulate their own (sometimes in collaboration with their allies in court or in the Lords) and as they tried to limit the king's power and expand their own, Parliament gradually became more of a center of political and constitutional opposition to the king and court. Fifth, all of these changes were leading towards a subtle shift in the character of parliamentary debate and argument. Previous parliamentary discussions of grievances often resembled arguments in common-law courts about cases between party and party. Participants in these debates usually had a highly specific objective: they wished to win their case. Their purpose was not to secure parliamentary support for some general legal principle but to persuade Parliament to take a particular course of action. They therefore showed relatively little interest in constructing arguments that were consistent from debate to debate, and instead they focused their attention on presenting legal justifications for the specific parliamentary courses that they favored. As the 1620s progressed, however, parliamentary debates on grievances took on a different character. Discussions of particular abuses became occasions for debates on general court policies or broad constitutional issues, and members became more interested in establishing the validity of broad legal and governmental principles than in persuading Parliament to take any specific, substantive action.

The ultimate effect of these changes in Parliament's proceedings would be to render compromises impossible, and when its members could no longer compromise, Parliament could no longer act at all. Moreover, if Parliament could no longer act, the grievances of the commonwealth would go unremedied, and Parliament's inability to remedy them would itself become a major grievance that the Commons could blame on the king and the court. It was Charles I, however, and not his father, who was accused of trying to destroy Parliament. James I's difficulties in dealing with Parliament were considerable, but they should not be exaggerated. The fact that the constitutional and political conflicts of the reign of Charles I were clearly foreshadowed in the parliaments of James should not obscure the fact that the last two parliaments of the first Stuart were relatively productive and still outwardly resembled Elizabethan parliaments in many important respects.

Coke's speeches and activities in the parliaments of 1621 and 1624 were marked by the same ambiguous tendencies as the proceedings of the Commons as a whole. On the one hand, he favored limited measures to eliminate specific grievances, shrank from formulating dogmatic positions on general constitutional questions, and skillfully avoided direct confrontations with the king or the court. On the other hand, his occasional tendency to see even small grievances as threats to the commonwealth sometimes brought him close to supporting general remedies for grievances, to attacking court policies, and to adopting doctrinaire positions on central constitutional issues. His speeches of these years expressed not only his dissatisfaction with the state of the realm, but also his uncertainty about what the commonwealth's real grievances were and about how they could be explained and remedied. He, like many of his fellow members, was often inclined to blame England's ills on a few corrupt individuals such as Bacon, Bennet, Cranfield, and Mompesson. This diagnosis of England's afflictions led him to suggest very simple cures for them, like the dismissal and punishment of corrupt judges and monopolists and the cancellation of monopoly patents and illegally created offices. He also realized, however, that the existing system of legal administration and economic regulation was itself defective and allowed—if it did not encourage—corruption to flourish. If this sort of corruption were to be rooted out, Coke realized, law and government would have to be reformed so that they could no longer be exploited by the lewd, the unworthy, and the litigious.

In calling for a crackdown on corruption and for reforms in legal procedure, Coke was merely repeating proposals made in earlier Jacobean and Elizabethan parliaments. Belief in the adequacy of such measures depended upon the assumption that the grievances of the commonwealth were not caused by any fundamental flaws in the realm's institutions or political leadership. As the 1620s progressed, however, Coke was coming to believe that some abuses were caused by the active malevolence of certain prominent courtiers, while others continued to exist because of the court's inability or unwillingness to check them. Unlike abuses caused by corrupt individuals and/or corruptable institutions, grievances attributable to royal action or inaction called for new sorts of remedies. But what sorts of remedies? Coke never confronted this question directly until the later 1620s, and even then he failed to answer it satisfactorily. But throughout this decade, he sensed that failures of royal policy and illegal royal actions were the true causes of grievances that Parliament had a duty to remedy and that it could remedy only through the use of certain broad powers. His strong interest in maintaining or even expanding Parliament's power to remedy grievances is shown by the fact that his most dogmatic and uncompromising speeches of 1621 concerned parliamentary privilege and not some other constitutional topic. When he took a strong stand with respect to this issue, he did so not to defend ethereal legal principles for their own sake, but because he saw an indissoluble connection between the maintenance of specific parliamentary privileges and the remedy of specific, substantive grievances.

The specificity of Coke's concerns during the early 1620s can be easily revealed in a summary of his parliamentary activities during this period. As chairman of the Commitee of Grievances in both 1621 and 1624, he led and coordinated the Commons's attacks on particular monopoly patents and other miscellaneous abuses. He also took part in many highly technical debates on legal abuses and the trade depression and helped to draft the Petition of Grievances of 1624. He also chaired or served on numerous legislative committees and debated many bills in the full House, and he drafted or promoted some of the most important legislation considered in these years, including the bills against monopolies, informers, and concealers; bills aimed at reforming the central courts; and proposals for modifications in the organization of the wool and cloth trades. Finally, he did more than any other member of either house to promote the revival of Parliament's judicial powers and to insure the success of the Commons's proceedings against particular offenders. In 1621 he led the Commons's attacks on Michell and Mompesson and played an important, if less spectacular, role in the cases of Bennet and Bacon; and in the case of Floyd, he succeeded in maintaining the lower house's claim to be a court of record while averting a clash with the upper house. In 1624 he again led the Commons in their attempts to use the judicial powers of Parliament, this time in the cases of Middlesex and Harsnett.

Coke's great influence both in the Commons and in Parliament as a whole is easily explained. His extensive governmental experience both in and out of Parliament and his formidable legal reputation naturally brought him respect from other members. He had held many high offices in both central and local government and in 1621 at least was a member of the council. He had participated in every meeting of Parliament since 1589, had served as Speaker of the Commons in 1593, and was an expert on parliamentary precedents and procedure. And his published writings and his years as a judge and legal officer of the crown had established his reputation as the most eminent legal authority of his era. Coke, moreover, was highly knowledgeable about many of the specific issues that arose in these two parliaments. His decades of work with the council and his participation in its investigations of the trade depression had acquainted him with most economic issues debated in the early 1620s. His work on a council subcommittee charged with preparing for the parliament of 1621 had given him firsthand knowledge about the crown's so-called bills of grace; and, as a participant in six previous parliaments, he knew about the past history of many bills that the Commons hoped to enact. Finally, he seems to have taken considerable pains sometime prior to the opening of parliament in 1621 to collect, organize, and interpret parliamentary precedents that would support the revival of Parliament's powers of judicature.

A third factor contributing to Coke's influential position in these two parliaments was his ability to speak with authority on a very wide range of subjects. Some members of the lower house were particularly well informed about economic issues. Others were legal experts. Still others were well versed in parliamentary precedents and procedure. Coke, however, could debate all of these matters with supreme confidence and was thus unusually well equipped to explain intricate relationships between economic, legal, and constitutional issues and to work out compromise positions that would satisfy the Commons without alienating the Lords or the king. Finally, he seems to have had a unique ability to translate complex and abstract legal questions into simple, concrete terms. Not only could he find convincing legal precedents for the positions that he adopted, he was also able to construct analogies that enabled his listeners to see resemblances between novel issues and more familiar ones and to apply traditional wisdom to complex and seemingly unprecedented problems. Thus, he was generally able to convince his fellow members that his views were fully supported both by authority and by reason. On some occasions he may have wearied the House or aroused the amusement of some of its members; and some of his speeches may show symptoms of slight senility. But his ability to persuade Parliament and justify its actions was matched by no other member.

Coke's political role in these parliaments is less easily explained or characterized than the extent of his influence. He was obviously not a faithful supporter of the king, but he did not hold an unambiguous position as a leader of an opposition party. Nor did he seem to act as the spokesman for any particular region or interest group. Historians have described him as the leader of a coalition of lawyers and parliamentarians who opposed James I. But the very existence of such a party is difficult to demonstrate, and even if a parliamentary opposition did exist, Coke's relationship to it must have been exceedingly complex. His imprisonment at the king's command after the close of the parliament of 1621 is an unambiguous index of his loss of royal favor. But why he lost his position at court is not entirely clear. What is clear is that Coke did not become a consistent, dogmatic opponent of court policies until the reign of Charles I, and that in 1621 and 1624 his primary objective was to promote parliamentary remedies for particular grievances in law and in trade.

ℭ *Three*

"Grievances in Law"

Nothing could be more misleadng than to characterize Coke as an obdurate defender of the legal status quo, as a spokesman only for the narrow interests of common lawyers, or as a principled opponent of legislative changes in the English legal system.[1] Although he praised the common law lavishly and preferred it to all rival legal traditions,[2] he sometimes criticized the existing system of legal administration; and while he often warned against changing basic common-law principles,[3] he favored the modification of certain legal procedures and the reestablishment of sound legal doctrines that had been previously overthrown. He owed his own rapid rise to fortune and power at least partly to his professional success in the law and had probably made more money from his legal skills than anyone else of his generation.[4] But he still favored certain legal reforms that ran counter to at least the short-term interests of the legal profession and occasionally blamed its lower orders, like the attorneys, for creating certain legal abuses.[5] While he reserved some of his most scathing attacks on English legal administration for courts that did not administer the common law, he did not make them the scapegoats for all of the commonwealth's grievances in law.[6] He denounced several

1. The views expressed here differ markedly from those of historians who emphasize Coke's firm opposition to legal change. Gardiner says that Coke was by nature "a bigoted adversary of all reform" (*History*, 4:40). Holdsworth stresses his "conservative prejudices" (*History*, 5:445). Prestwich likens him to Lord Eldon (*Cranfield*, p. 148). Niehaus claims that he "symbolized the corrupt and inefficient legal system of his day" (Charles R. Niehaus, "The Issue of Law Reform during the Puritan Revolution," p. 20). And H. R. Trevor-Roper characterizes him as "the cracked, pedantic, unimaginative idolator of the existing common law, with all its abuses" (H. R. Trevor-Roper, "Three Foreigners," p. 244). For works that take account of Coke's support for various types of legal change, see Thorne, "Tudor Social Transformation," p. 22; Thorne, *Coke*; Hill, *Intellectual Origins*, pp. 225–65; and Veall, *Law Reform*, pp. 65–69.
2. See, for example, *Reports*, 2, Preface; *Institutes*, 3, the epilogue (at p. 243).
3. See fn. 7, below.
4. See pp. 4–5 and n. 12.
5. As a barrister, moreover, Coke may have had little sense of solidarity with solicitors and attorneys, and he definitely regarded the increase in the size of the latter group as a cause of the "multiplication of suits" (*Institutes*, 4:76). On the distinction between barristers and lesser members of the legal profession in this period, see Prest, *Inns of Court*, pp. 47–70; J. H. Baker, "The Status of Barristers"; J. H. Baker, "Counsellors and Barristers"; and Veall, *Law Reform*, pp. 44–51.
6. See pp. 59–63.

statutes, like Westminster II and Henry VIII's Statutes of Wills, but only because they overturned fundamental common-law rules;[7] and he enthusiastically praised other acts, like the Statute of Uses, for having greatly benefited the commonwealth.[8] He also criticized previous parliaments for having enacted bills so "ill-penned" as to introduce "uncertainties" and "mischiefs" into the law;[9] but he had no doubts about the professional legal competence of Parliament's leading members during the 1620s. He naturally believed in his own skill as a legal draftsman and also respected the legal talents of some of his colleagues in the lower house like John Glanville, William Noy, and John Selden. Coke's support for changes in English law may seem inconsistent with his conviction that the common law was perfect. It is not. Coke believed that the common law consisted not only of specific substantive and procedural rules, but also of certain general principles, and that existing law might have to be modified in such a way as to make it conform to these general norms.

In both 1621 and 1624 Coke often criticized the legal status quo and called on Parliament to help reform it. He complained about numerous abuses, supported many statutory changes in the law,[10] and joined in Parliament's campaign against corrupt judicial practices.[11] These actions demonstrate his strong belief in the need for certain legal changes. But to describe him simply as an advocate of parliamentary law reform is inadequate, if not inaccurate. To do so would not distinguish him from a host of others who called for legal change during the Tudor-Stuart era.[12] Moreover, by assimilating his calls for legal change into a fictive tradition of legal reform, it would obscure the deep-seated conflicts that existed in premodern England as to the direction that legal change should take. The crucial question, therefore, is not whether Coke supported parliamentary

7. See pp. 71, 72, 79 n., 194.

8. See *Sir Anthony Mildmay's Case* (*Reports*, 6:40–43, at 43). Not surprisingly, Coke also praised the statutes whose enactment he had helped to promote during the early 1620s (see *Institutes*, 3:181–94; and 4:76–77). In addition, in the epilogue to his *Third Insitutes*, he not only admitted the deficiencies of English "preventing [i.e., preventitive] justice" but also wrote that "the consideration of this preventing justice were worthy of the wisdom of a Parliament" (*Institutes*, 3:243). In the preface to his *Fourth Reports*, moreover, he claimed that the reduction of the penal statutes into "method and order" could only be done by Parliament and would be an honorable, profitable and commendable work for the whole commonwealth."

9. See p. 79 and fn. 190, below.

10. Although writers like Niehaus and Judson dismiss early Stuart legislation as being of little importance (see Niehaus, "Law Reform," p. 49; and Judson, *Crisis of the Constitution*, p. 89) Coke expressed a different view of it in the upper house on 31 May, when he said, "Your lordships see more good bills [now] than this hundred years" (*CD 1621*, 3:378).

11. See pp. 53–57.

12. On prerevolutionary legal reform and/or expressions of support for it, see G. R.

law reform. In some sense, he clearly did. What one must determine is how and why he wished the law to be changed and what role he assigned to Parliament in this enterprise. Satisfactory answers to these questions are difficult to come by. Any attempt to reconstruct Coke's views about legal change from his parliamentary speeches of 1621 and 1624 involves at least five major difficulties. First, because his complaints about legal abuses often concerned complex, obscure, and as yet unstudied aspects of legal administration, it is often hard to know precisely what they were about let alone to assess their accuracy or to determine how they were shaped by his own distinctive outlook on the commonwealth's legal grievances. Second, given the obscure character of many legal abuses that he attacked, it is difficult to calculate the actual effects of his proposed parliamentary remedies for them or to determine precisely which segment or segments of English society derived the greatest benefit from these remedies. Third, his repeated claims that these remedies would promote the public good are difficult to interpret. Although they cannot be accepted at face value, they cannot be regarded simply as calculated attempts to legitimate and obscure his use of parliamentary power to promote the interests of certain groups within English society.[13] Fourth, the fact that his parliamentary speeches present no clear program for legal change is in itself significant; but it makes it hard to reconstruct his ideas on this subject without rendering them more coherent than they really were. Finally, because these speeches hardly ever mention the substantive legal problems with which his *Reports* were primarily concerned, they cannot

---

Elton, *Reform and Renewal*, pp. 129–57; G. R. Elton, "Reform by Statute"; Arthur B. Ferguson, *The Articulate Citizen and the English Renaissance*; Hill, *Intellectual Origins*, esp. pp. 225–65; Whitney R. D. Jones, *The Tudor Commonwealth, 1529–1559*; Knafla, *Law and Politics*, pp. 105–22; Marwil, *Trials of Counsel*, esp. p. 65; Theodore K. Rabb, "Francis Bacon and the Reform of Society"; Barbara Shapiro, "Codification of the Laws in Seventeenth-Century England"; Barbara Shapiro, "Law Reform in Seventeenth-Century England," esp. pp. 281–88; Robert Tittler, "Nicholas Bacon and the Reform of the Elizabethan Chancery"; Veall, *Law Reform*, esp. pp. 65–74; and Gordon Zeeveld, *Foundations of Tudor Policy*. Although these works all touch on important issues concerning legal change and support for legal change in the Tudor and early Stuart periods, a reading of these studies suggests that the phrase "law reform" may not be a very useful one for categorizing or analyzing the legal history of this era, because historians have not yet developed satisfactory criteria for distinguishing between the different types of legal changes that were made or proposed between ca. 1500 and ca. 1640. On the legal changes proposed during the English Revolution, see Mary Cotterell, "Interregnum Law Reform"; Niehaus, "Law Reform"; G. B. Nourse, "Law Reform under the Commonwealth and Protectorate"; Stuart E. Prall, *The Agitation for Law Reform during the Puritan Revolution*; Stuart E. Prall, "Chancery Reform and the Puritan Revolution, 1640–1660"; Shapiro, "Codification"; Shapiro, "Law Reform," esp. pp. 288–97; Goldwin Smith, "The Reform of the Laws of England, 1604–1660"; and Veall, *Law Reform*.

13. See pp. 76–85.

be used as the sole basis for a reconstruction of his views about legal change.[14]

This discrepancy between the subject matter of Coke's *Reports* and that of his parliamentary speeches strongly suggests that he assigned Parliament only a limited role in the process of amending the law. Although he did not openly acknowledge any definite legal limits on Parliament's power to legislate, he apparently believed that it should not meddle with every abuse in the legal system and should leave certain tasks, like clarifying common-law doctrine, to the judges. Moreover, his strong belief in the necessity of legitimating the use of parliamentary power to effect legal change may have constituted an effective limit on his ability to use this power for such purposes. However, because he never directly discussed the norms that should govern attempts to make statutory changes in the law, his ideas on this subject remain unclear and can be only tentatively reconstructed from his statements about particular remedies for specific legal abuses. In spite of these difficulties, one can arrive at certain conclusions about Coke's views about legal change during the early 1620s by noting the legal grievances that he attacked in Parliament, by analyzing his views about their causes and effects, and by examining the remedies that he proposed for them. It will then be possible to take up more basic questions about the sorts of legal changes that he favored and about the ways in which he wanted these changes to be brought about.

The principal legal abuses that Coke attacked in 1621 and 1624 were judicial corruption; the use of various legal procedures to harass some men and defraud others of their rights; the absence of clear jurisdictional boundaries between courts; the excessively high cost of litigation; the dilatoriness of many legal proceedings; the inadequacy of existing statutes of limitation; the illegal delegation of judicial and quasi-judicial powers; and a burdensome, crippling increase in the caseload of most English courts. This list includes numerous abuses attacked by other seventeenth-century critics of the legal system, but it still serves to distinguish Coke's critique of the law from theirs. It indicates his lack of support for debt reform, land registration, or legal codification and suggests that he did not attach the highest priority to reviving local courts. It also shows that his critical attitude towards some parts of the legal profession did not lead him to support reductions in the authority of judges or in the privileges of lawyers. Finally, this inventory also reveals Coke's failure to support parliamentary solutions for the great problems relating to property law and statutory construction that he had repeatedly

14. See pp. 78–81.

discussed in his *Reports*; and it shows that he wanted Parliament to deal almost exclusively with defects in existing legal procedure.

Further insights into Coke's attitude towards legal change emerge from a consideration of his ideas about the direct and indirect effects of those legal abuses that he wanted Parliament to eliminate. In the absence of any comprehensive historical study of Elizabethan and early Stuart court administration, it is difficult to understand these abuses fully, or to calculate the burden that they imposed on particular groups within English society. It is nevertheless clear that Coke's attacks on them were based upon his detailed knowledge of the English court system, and that his concern about them was shared by other members of Parliament. Like his colleagues, he wanted to remedy grievances in law partly because he believed that they directly damaged the material interests of certain subjects. In his opinion, the corruption of judges and juries caused some subjects to lose just causes and drove others to bribery. He also believed that excessive court fees imposed significant costs on all litigants[15] and thought that an excessive number of costly lawsuits resulted from the lack of clear boundaries between different jurisdictions and from a lack of effective statutes of limitation. He also believed that honest men were directly harmed by the many complex rackets that had grown up in the interstices of the legal system and that served only the interests of the "caterpillars of the commonwealth."

For Coke, however, such direct costs were not the most significant or troubling effects of legal abuses. He believed that costly, capricious, and corruptible legal procedures seriously threatened certainty in law and quietness of possession, and that they thereby damaged not only those whom they harmed directly but other members of the commonwealth as well.[16] According to Coke, many men lived in fear that they might be compelled at any moment to go to London and defend themselves against unjust informations brought by common informers. Many landholders could not sleep at night for fear that technical flaws in their titles might jeopardize their entire inheritances. Litigants who had won their cases in one court could not be sure that they would not be drawn into fresh lawsuits in another. Honest men could never be sure of getting

---

15. G. E. Aylmer notes that Coke once supported high fees in the central courts and that he did so by arguing that "those that will put themselves to so much trouble as to come to London when they may have justice in the country deserve well to pay the counsellors' and officers' fees" (G. E. Aylmer, *The King's Servants*, p. 190, quoting *CD 1621*, 4:374). What Aylmer fails to note, however, is that the bill that Coke was supporting in this speech was designed to discourage the bringing of suits to Westminster. On Coke's efforts to check the flow of suits to the central courts, see pp. 65–69, below.

16. On the importance that Coke attached to these values and on the meaning that he seems to have ascribed to them, see pp. 22, 79–80.

justice when they needed it, because their cases might be heard before corrupt judges or juries. Such uncertainty and insecurity, Coke thought, severely damaged the interests of all English subjects.

He also believed that many legal abuses had particularly serious effects because they existed in a highly integrated social and legal system. Although he developed no theory to explain how the costs of legal abuses were passed on from one subject to another until they constituted a burden on the whole commonwealth, his concern about this process is clearly expressed by his repeated use of certain dynamic metaphors for the legal system and/or its constituent parts. He sometimes pictured courts as clocks and claimed that the malfunctioning of even their smallest wheels would cause entire mechanisms to break down.[17] He thought of the jurisdiction of courts as a network of streams and foretold terrible results if the streams were to lose their channels.[18] He imagined a court as a circle, no part of which could be altered without breaking the symmetry of the whole.[19] He likened the commonwealth to a garden about to be overrun by weeds or devoured by a plague of caterpillars; or else he pictured judicial corruption as a living, growing plant.[20] He saw justice as a body of water emanating from a fountain and believed that corruption at the source would ultimately infect everything.[21] He also compared the court system to a human body in which every member had to play its proper part.[22]

These traditional but powerful figures express Coke's anxiety about the potential threats to the realm that were posed by grievances in law. But because he attributed these grievances primarily to the corrupt acts of a few individuals, and not to the court's malevolence or to fundamental flaws in the commonwealth's political or constitutional structure, he was inclined to believe that Parliament could remedy them by traditional means. His remarks about legal abuses generally reflect his assumption that English society was neatly divided into two groups: honest men, whose simple enjoyment of their rights was conducive to the public good; and those lewd and unworthy people who would stop at nothing in their ruthless, unscrupulous pursuit of private gain. Coke's search for the causes of legal abuses was often a search for scapegoats; and at the end of his quest, he usually found disreputable men who had no recog-

17. *Institutes*, 4:2.
18. See fn. 96, below.
19. See p. 59.
20. See p. 57.
21. See p. 54.
22. *Institutes*, 4, Proeme. In the epilogue to this work, he also pictured the jurisdiction of courts as a "high and honorable building" that might lack windows or "sufficient lights" or have other architectural deficiencies.

nized place in traditional social models and whose actions he could portray as some foreign, cancerous growth within the commonwealth.[23] At the same time he recognized that structural defects in the legal system provided such men with far too many opportunities to harm honest subjects and the commonwealth as a whole. The givers and takers of bribes were going unpunished. Laws against the sale of offices were insufficiently strict and went unenforced. Rules governing court procedures had many back doors through which professional parasites, like concealers and informers, could enter and harass honest men; and Parliament's failure to repeal obsolete statutes or eliminate inconsistencies between different regulatory acts had provided informers with further opportunities to damage the public good. Parliament's further failure to define court jurisdictions or to pass effective statutes of limitations had enabled other unscrupulous litigants and racketeers to vex men who wanted nothing more than the quiet enjoyment of their rights.

Although Coke realized that legal abuses were partly caused by the malfunctioning of certain governmental institutions, he constructed no coherent critique of the English legal system and developed no clear program for reforming it. His failure to do so can be seen from an analysis of his promotion of parliamentary remedies for legal abuses in 1621 and 1624. He wanted Parliament to use its judicial powers against corrupt judges and believed that by doing so it could cut off diseased members of the commonwealth and provide examples for potential offenders in the future. He called for new, statutory qualifications for jury service to insure that men would be tried by "sufficient" and impartial jurors. He advocated parliamentary reform of legal procedures and laws that were being exploited by informers, concealers, and other malicious litigants. He wanted to regulate court fees so as to reduce the cost of justice and to prevent court officials from enriching themselves at the expense of honest litigants. These remedies were almost identical with those proposed by earlier advocates of legal change,[24] and although they reflected Coke's desire to protect certain basic social and legal values, they hardly constituted a self-conscious program to modernize English law. Moreover, because they did not arise out of any conviction of Coke's that the commonwealth was in immediate peril, he was not willing to fight vigorously for their adoption and implementation. He supported these remedies far more forcefully than is generally supposed and attached more importance to securing their adoption than to settling more cosmic constitutional questions. But he worked for their implementation through

23. For Coke's fullest statements on bribery in his writings, see *Institutes*, 3:145–49, 223–26.

24. See the literature cited in fn. 12, above; and Notestein, *1604–1610*, pp. 47–54.

compromise, not confrontation, and often acquiesced in their modification or even in their rejection. Many of his proposals for court reform died in the Commons, while others were put to sleep in the Lords. He failed to secure Bennet's conviction for bribery and ultimately accepted substantial amendments to his most favored legislature proposals like the bills against informers, concealers, and monopolists. These efforts to promote piecemeal legal change mark the culmination of earlier efforts to remedy grievances in law in traditional ways, and they cannot be equated with later attempts to adapt English law to the needs of an emergent capitalist order. Nevertheless, they arose out of a sense of dissatisfaction with the condition of the commonwealth, and this dissatisfaction ultimately became transformed in such a way as to lead to significant constitutional and political conflicts within the English state.

The grievances in law that Coke attacked in the early 1620s can be conveniently, if somewhat arbitrarily, broken down into four main groups of interrelated abuses: the corruption of the judicial system, abusive practices in the courts at Westminster, problems concerning the relationship between central and local jurisdictions, and various other abuses that threatened legal certainty and security of property and caused "multiplication" and "multiplicity" of suits.[25] His sharpest and fullest parliamentary attack on judicial corruption occurred in a speech to the Lords about the case of Sir John Bennet, a judge of the prerogative court of Canterbury who had also served on the High Commission and as a master in Chancery and chancellor to Queen Anne. Bennet was accused in 1621 of taking bribes in numerous probate cases, and his offenses prompted Coke to warn the Lords about the dangers to the commonwealth posed by judicial corruption.[26] In order to appreciate the force of his remarks, one must remember not only that corruption of various sorts had been the subject of mounting complaint for over a generation,[27] but also that the parliaments of the early 1620s saw several attacks on corrupt judges and legal officers besides Bennet. In these years, the Commons prosecuted Lord Chancellor Bacon; former Attorney General Yelverton; and the earl of Middlesex, who was not only lord treasurer but also master of the wards.[28] They also investigated charges of corruption against Sir John Craddock, commissary of the diocese of Durham and a member of the High Commission; and Dr. John Lambe, the chan-

25. On Coke's use of these phrases, see pp. 66, 78, below.
26. On Bennet's case, see pp. 54–55, and chap. 5.
27. For references to works on Elizabethan and early Stuart corruption, see chap. 2, fn. 17, above.
28. On Bacon's and Middlesex's cases, see chap. 5. On Yelverton's case, see Zaller, *1621*, pp. 118–24; and Tite, *Impeachment*. pp. 118–22.

cellor of the bishop of Peterborough.[29] In addition, the Commons's investigations of monopolies led them to complain about royal grants to monopolists and others of certain administrative and quasi-judicial powers, like the power to prosecute, pardon, or compound for certain offenses.[30] Meanwhile, the Commons were also attacking the corruption of the customs farmers,[31] the venality of many court officials,[32] and the many devious practices by which informers had made a racket out of the enforcement of economic regulations that were supposed to promote and maintain the public good.[33]

Like other members of the Commons, Coke saw these individual abuses as parts of a pattern; and his increasing awareness of the institutional context in which bribes were given and received profoundly affected the way in which he perceived and portrayed Bennet's illegal acts. It made him see this judge's offenses as not simply illustrations of man's corruptable nature, but as symptoms of more general social grievances; and it led him to use the Commons's debates on these specific offenses as not only an occasion for proposing exemplary punishments for this offendor, but as an opportunity for suggesting more general remedies for judicial and administrative corruption. After terming Bennet's case "a weighty cause," Coke expressed his hatred of bribery and declared that those who kept their hands from it were "blessed." But after having thus portrayed Bennet as an individual sinner, he went on to consider the social consequences of this sinner's acts. He asserted that a corrupt judge was the greatest of all grievances and harmed the commonwealth more than anyone else, because he made every subject a tenant at will for his rights. Bennet, moreover, had taken bribes in testamentary cases, and Coke therefore called him an "eater of the dead and of the goods of the dead"[34] and then compared him both to the Pope and to the ravenous sheep of the Cotswolds. He also insisted that Bennet's offenses not only harmed those directly involved in the cases before him, but also concerned "the whole land." "If the fountains be corrupted," he said, "look for no health from anything that comes from them." "Corrupt the ground," he told the Lords, "and all derivatives will be corrupt." He warned them, however, that they could not eliminate judicial corruption simply by judging and sentencing Bennet, even though he pointedly reminded them

29. On the cases of Craddock and Lambe, see Tite, *Impeachment*, p. 138.
30. *CD 1621*, 2:6.
31. See chap. 4, p. 98.
32. See p. 58.
33. See pp. 67–69.
34. Coke later wrote that the word "bribery" came from "the French word *briber*, which signifieth to devour, or eat greedily, applied to the devouring of a corrupt judge" (*Institutes*, 3:144).

of the hanging of corrupt Anglo-Saxon judges and compared such judgements with the purging of the Augean stables. "By punishing a corrupt judge," he told them, "we do well, but it cuts but off a rotten branch, it takes but away the effect. But to take away the root and cause of corruption, order must be taken that offices be not saleable. Make what law you will, inflict what punishment you will, little good will come of it if offices be bought and sold. He that buys must sell."[35] This speech and Coke's subsequent proposal of a law "in futurum" against the buying and selling of offices reflect his realization that corruption had deep-seated institutional causes, as well as personal and moral ones; but his failure to work for the enactment of any such bill during the 1620s indicates the weakness of his institutional critique of English legal administration, his propensity to fall back on moralistic explanations for legal abuses, and his belief that these abuses did not pose an immediate threat to the realm.

Further indications of Coke's concern about legal corruption can be found in his remarks about the "insufficiency" of jurors. Like some later reformers, he believed that juries should be reformed by purging them of men of mean condition.[36] In 1621, he strongly supported the bill "for avoiding of insufficient jurors" by arguing that because "[a]ll under the degree of barons" were to be tried by juries of their "peers," it was "fitting" to insure that jury members would be "sufficient . . . in estate and understanding," and that they would be "most near the place" of those on trial and not be "suspicious" of them. Although he was certain that too many poor men were serving on juries, he was not too clear about what effects their presence had on the outcome of the cases they heard. Although he suggested that it made trial by jury to be like a game of chance, he also implied that it resulted in a clear pattern in jury verdicts when he stated that because of it, rich men feared jury trials, whereas beggars were fearless. Nevertheless, he was sure that juries could best be reformed by restricting jury service to men of some worth, because "it had always been thought fit to prescribe [by statutes] a value of estate to such as should be empannelled in juries."[37]

Coke did not get the jury bill enacted and thus failed to purge juries of men who he thought were particularly corruptable, but he was more successful in attacking what he regarded as another form of legal corrup-

35. For his speech, see CD 1621, 3:75–77; 5:95–96; 6:392–93.
36. See Veall's discussion of the views of William Sheppard, John Marsh, and William Leach (Law Reform, pp. 114, 117, and 118 respectively). On proposals made for jury reform during the Revolution, see Veall, Law Reform, esp. pp. 98, 156–59; and Prall, Law Reform, pp. 54–60.
37. For Coke's speech, see CD 1621, 2:300–01; 3:21; 4:237; and 5:337. For abstracts of the bill, see CD 1621, 3:19; and 5:80. And for arguments on the bill's behalf, see CD 1621, 7:187–90.

tion: the crown's practice of granting quasi-public powers to private persons. He believed that many such grants were patently illegal, but he was particularly inclined to oppose them because they were often made to men whose "mean" condition made them unfit, in his opinion, to exercise power.[38] Debates on this abusive practice also provided him with further opportunities to show how corruption damaged the commonwealth. In 1621, he described to the House in the most minute detail the workings of the patent held by Sparrow and Sparrow for concealed tithes and, after charging that the patent was a threat to "all the nobility, gentry, and commonalty of England," he expressed his horror at the fact that so "mean" a man as Sparrow had been "so saucy" as to vex a privy councillor under the color of his patent.[39] He also complained about the concealments patent of Typper and Typper,[40] which another member, Sir Thomas Edmondes, attacked as "a great grievance to gentlemen" because it called men's lands into question on the slightest pretext.[41] Coke expressed even greater opposition in 1621 to Ferrar's General Remembrancer patent and to Lepton's patent for drafting documents for the Council of the North.[42] He explained to the Committee of Grievances that Ferrar would keep "a register of all fines, recoveries, judgment[s] etc., in all the King's courts of record in England and Wales and a calendar of all men's wills." He then insisted that such men should not have access to records of this sort, because they might "alter them and corrupt them, and so overthrow all our estates";[43] and he later emphasized how dangerous the patent was by noting that it concerned "all men living and dead."[44] Coke was equally horrifed by the patent granting Sir John Lepton the exclusive right to draft all formal documents concerning matters before the Council of the North. Among Coke's many objections to this patent was that the rights of litigants in that court would be prejudiced if they were "tied to one man who must see their evidence, and, if there be a cross bill, the evidence of both sides."[45]

38. Most of the patents that he attacked were withdrawn by the council. See Foster, "Patents and Monopolies."

39. CD 1621, 2:243–44; 5:49, 308; 6:73; CJ, 1:562. On the patent, see CD 1621, 7:344–45. On concealments generally, see pp. 72–79, below.

40. For his speeches on this patent, see: (1) CJ, 1:532; (2) CD 1621, 4:180; 6:79; CJ, 1:567; (3) CD 1621, 4:180; 5:61–62; CJ, 1:567. On the commission established by this patent (on which Coke had thrice served), see CD 1621, 7:350–55.

41. CD 1621, 2:149; 4:116; 5:264; 6:19. On Coke's attacks on Townshend's concealments patent (for which see CD 1621, 7:344), see White, "Coke," pp. 715–17.

42. For these two patents, see CD 1621, 7:362 and 394 respectively. The first of these two patents had not yet been put into execution.

43. Ibid., 2:134; 4:100; 6:9; P&D, 1:90.

44. CD 1621, 6:271.

45. See Ibid., 2:363–64; 3:244; 4:336–37; 5:374–75; 6:154; CJ, 1:620; P&D, 2:64–65.

Not surprisingly, some of Coke's most florid attacks on corruption are found in his speeches on the inns and alehouse patents and on Sir Giles Mompesson,[46] the great monopolist who controlled them. He charged that the alehouse patentees had overthrown the beneficent rule of the justices of the peace and made them servants of projectors, and that they had vexed "poor men" and forced subjects to travel to London to answer suits.[47] Among his many complaints about the patent for inns were that it was "an offence against the general justices of the realm"; that it caused "the grievous vexation and oppression of the subject, not only the innholders but all travellers and so all the subjects"; that it vexed the poor "with multiplicity of outlawries"; and that it burdened the people "by oppression, plague, and vexation," and thereby caused depopulation.[48] Serious as these charges were, it was only in a later speech to the Lords about Mompesson's offenses that Coke identified the general evil of which the monopolist's actions were merely a symptom. After telling the Lords that yearly parliaments had once been accounted necessary "for the redress of many mischiefs and grievances which daily increase in the commonwealth," he asked rhetorically if there were "not the same necessity still." He then declared:

The kingdom and commonwealth may be likened to a fair field and a pleasant garden, but if the field be not tilled and the garden often weeded, infaelix lolium et steriles nascuntur avenae. And all humors increase in the body if they be not purged, humores moti non remoti corpus laedunt. So likewise abuses and corruptions increase in the commonwealth. Therefore often parliaments are necessary that good laws may be made to prevent and punish them, ut poena ad paucos metus ad omnes perveniat.[49]

Coke ultimately secured the enactment of a penal statute against monopolists, but he never followed through on his proposals to root out judicial corruption. Instead, he and other leaders of the Commons turned their attention to other grievances in law, like various abusive practices in the central courts. In 1621 and 1624, members of the Commons frequently equated legal reform with remedies for court abuses. When Sir Lionel Cranfield cited grievances in law as one of the three principal grievances of the subject in 1621, he proposed as a remedy for it "that all courts be rectified and kept within their bounds, that so the subject may not be tossed to and fro; and that fees be ordered in every court."[50]

46. On the Mompesson trial in 1621, see chap. 5.
47. CD 1621, 2:118–19; 4:89; 5:484; 6:284; P&D, 1:79.
48. CD 1621, 2:145–46; 4:110; 5:260, 522–23; 6:14, 301; CJ, 1:530; P&D, 1:102–3.
49. CD 1621, 2:197–98. On the earlier part of this speech, see chap. 5, p. 151.
50. CD 1621, 2:89; 4:58. On Cranfield's support for changes in the law in 1621, see Zaller, 1621, pp. 38, 50, 62; and Prestwich, *Cranfield*, pp. 286–329 passim.

Cranfield's plan for coordinated court reform was never realized in the early 1620s, and its supporters instead focused their attention on abuses in particular courts. Nevertheless, in 1621 at least, the Commons debated a few abortive proposals to regulate abuses in several courts at once. Cranfield's proposal was never presented to the House as a bill, but it found favor with many members, including Coke,[51] and a committee was appointed to consider it.[52] In addition, Edward Hoby brought in a bill "for the more indifferent hearing of all causes and counsel towards the same in all courts,"[53] while Sir William Cope called for an act against bribery in all courts.[54] William Noy wished to legislate against the buying and selling of judicial offices,[55] and Coke advocated the enactment of statutes of limitation for suits in central courts and in ecclesiastical courts as well.[56]

Nevertheless, although Sir Dudley Digges told the Lords in late May that the Commons wished to pass bills "for the regulating of courts and abuses of all courts,"[57] only one such proposal was debated at length in 1621 or 1624—the bill against undue fees and new offices in all courts of justice. This bill, which had been drawn by Coke and six other lawyers,[58] alluded in its preamble to two main court abuses: the "increasing of fees ... beyond that which anciently has been used and allowed," and the "erecting of new offices in courts of justice." The former abuse it termed "an unjust extortion and unsufferable exaction upon the subject," and the latter "an unnecessary and unjust burthen upon the commonwealth." It then voided all grants of court offices made since James I's accession, prohibited all grants of new offices, and barred all court officers from taking fees greater than those allowed to them before 1598.[59] The bill's second reading on 3 May provoked a debate in which Coke took a leading part.[60] After maintaining that the king could not even grant new offices at his own charge,[61] he responded to those members, like Attorney General Heath, who had argued that Parliament should not regulate the

51. See *CD 1621*, 3:327; 6:174.
52. See Ibid., 4:212–14; 2:282–83; 4:232; 2:295–96; 5:72, 330–31.
53. Ibid., 5:380.
54. Ibid., 2:328; 3:100–101; 4:267; 5:104–5, 352.
55. Ibid., 3:151; 2:341; 4:295; 5:137; 6:131; *CJ*, 1:606.
56. See *CD 1621*, 2:64–65; 4:431; 5:452; *CJ*, 1:519; *P&D*, 1:35.
57. *CD 1621*, 3:364.
58. Ibid., 5:317; *CJ*, 1:569.
59. *CD 1621*, 7:211. The bill may have been designed to supplement 1 *Jac.* I, *c.* 10 (*SR*, 4, pt. 2, p. 1027), which outlawed certain court fees and which was later cited in the attacks on the new fees of the Chancery masters (see pp. 61–62, below).
60. For the debate, see *CD 1621*, 3:149–51; 2:341; 4:294–95; 5:136–37, 364; *CJ*, 1:606.
61. Coke made this point in reply to Cranfield, who wanted the bill to allow the king to do this (*CD 1621*, 3:139; 4:294). According to Coke, a royal grant of a new office

internal workings of courts.[62] He claimed that Parliament "always" had had the power to question new court fees and had exercised it "without dishonor to the King." For Parliament to have this power was fitting, he continued, for it could then scrutinize all "innovations" in court procedure. Such innovations, he thought, were always dangerous, for every court was "like a circle, you cannot add anything unto it but you mar it. If you put new unto old it will never agree." After citing precedents for his position, he successfully moved to have the bill committed for minor amendments.[63] It was never reported back to the Commons, however, and he made no attempt to revive it in 1624. No other bills reforming several courts at once were considered in the early 1620s, as advocates of court reform instead tried to eliminate particular abuses in particular central courts, like the Chancery, the Exchequer, and the Court of Wards.

Coke was one of the leaders of an attack on Chancery abuses that was launched in the parliament of 1621. His eagerness to criticize that court was obviously intensified by his long-standing antagonism towards Bacon and his hostility to courts that encroached on common law jurisdiction.[64] But his conviction that Chancery was in need of reform was shared by many of his contemporaries, including Bacon himself,[65] and by later advocates of legal reform.[66] Coke may have promoted Chancery

---

without a fee was void. For the precedent that he cited for this position, see CD *1621*, 3:150, n. 121.

62. On 28 February, in the Committee for Courts, Noy tried to distinguish between court abuses that should be regulated by statute and court abuses that should be controlled by "admonition" (CD *1621*, 6:293–94; cf. 6:21, 275; 5:265, 532); and on 2 March, Sackville reported to the House that the committee had accepted this distinction (CD *1621*, 2:154; 5:20; 6:24). At the same committee meeting on the twenty-eighth, Heath had claimed that one of the cases under discussion was "not worthy of the consideration of this high court" (CD *1621*, 6:274). After Sackville had reported Noy's views to the House on 2 March, Cranfield said, "The lower house of parliament has not authority to determine jurisdiction of courts, it belongs to the prerogative of [the] king. We may inquire and complain, but reformation only can be by the king." To this, Edward Alford replied, "Jurisdiction[s] of courts are to be limited by parliament, [for] parliamentum omnia potest except altering the right line of the crown" (CD *1621*, 6:205). In a conference with the Lords about the informers bill Coke strongly asserted Parliament's power to regulate court jurisdiction (see p. 68, below), but on other occasions he took pains to show that the proposals that he supported did not limit the authority of courts and simply established procedures for litigants to follow (see. pp. 66–67, below).

63. CD *1621*, 2:341; 3:150; 4:295; 5:137; 6:131; *CJ*, 1:606.

64. On Coke's attacks on Chancery prior to 1621, see the works cited above in chap. 1, fn. 23.

65. See Veall, *Law Reform*, pp. 34–35; Ogilvie, *The King's Government*, pp. 95–96; and Zaller, *1621*, p. 95. On Ellesmere's support for Chancery reform, see Knafla, *Law and Politics*, pp. 155–60.

66. On the attacks made on Chancery during the revolutionary period, see Holdsworth, *History*, 1:428–34; Veall, *Law Reform*, esp. pp. 178–93; Prall, "Chancery Reform"; Prall, *Law Reform*, esp. pp. 81–90. See also the other works cited in fn. 12, above, on proposals for legal change during the Revolution.

reform with particular vehemence, but he actually assigned a lower priority to it than to the remedy of other grievances in law; and his criticisms of this court constituted only one aspect of his critique of English legal administration. Coke's contemporaries found the same general defects in Chancery as in other English courts: excessive litigation, inordinate delay, lack of certainty and finality in judicial decisions, excessive costs, and corruption. Several thousand suits were begun in Chancery every year. They often dragged on for years or even decades. And even after a judgment had been given in them, they could be easily reopened. Such lengthy and complex litigation was costly as well as unpredictable in outcome and provided many opportunities for corrupt officials to enrich themselves at the expense of litigants.[67]

Previous parliaments had tried to remedy some of these abuses,[68] but only in 1621 did the Commons systematically attack them.[69] This attack consisted of two main parts, and Coke was closely involved in both of them. First, in the Committees for Courts and Grievances, members protested against Chancery's protection of debtors and their sureties and criticized the court for exceeding its jurisdiction in certain cases. They also investigated the activities and the fees of the Chancery masters and registrars and began judicial proceedings against Lord Chancellor Bacon that culminated in his conviction of bribery by the Lords. Second, these committee debates and investigations led to the proposal of various bills to define and limit Chancery's jurisdiction, to subordinate it to common-law courts, and to reduce the fees taken by its officials. Throughout these debates, Coke repeatedly maintained that Chancery could not meddle in matters determinable at common law, that it was not a court of record and could not set fines, and that it ought to be strictly subordinated to the common-law courts. His actions show that he perceived abuses in the Chancery and wished to eliminate some of them by bill. But they do not indicate, as some writers have suggested, that his attacks on this court arose merely out of jurisdictional jealousy, common-law chauvinism, or enmity to Bacon; or that he placed the highest priority on eliminating abuses in this court.[70]

The first Chancery abuse debated in 1621 was the issuance of bills of conformity. These bills ordered creditors to accept less than they were owed in repayment for debts and to refrain from suing debtors or their

---

67. Veall, *Law Reform*, pp. 32–36; Holdsworth, *History*, 1:423–28.
68. Zaller, *1621*, pp. 90–91.
69. On attacks on Chancery in the parliaments of 1621 and 1624, see Gardiner, *History*, 4:109; Holdsworth, *History*, 5:445; Niehaus, "Law Reform," p. 48; Zaller, *1621*, pp. 90–97; and Veall, *Law Reform*, p. 35.
70. Niehaus ("Law Reform," p. 48) is simply mistaken when he writes that in 1621 "all other matters of legal reform were virtually submerged in the assault on Chancery."

sureties at common law.[71] Only a detailed study of the recipients of these bills would reveal what sort of people were actually hurt by them; but whoever they were, they were obviously powerful or had had powerful friends.[72] The City of London petitioned the king against bills of conformity in the summer of 1620,[73] and the Commons later cited them as a cause of the current trade depression.[74] In the Commons's first major discussion of them on 14 March,[75] Coke asserted that their issuance was a "detestable and new project" and was illegal for two reasons. First, the chancellor had the power "to help a man upon a bond . . . only in three causes, (1) of covin, (2) of misaccident, as fire or robbing, (3) of breach of confidence"; and because the chancellor had issued bills in cases that fell into none of these three categories, he argued, their issuance was unlawful. Second, Coke observed that it was a "high point of injustice" for the bills to have been issued before creditors had had time to answer. He went on to endorse the view that their issuance was a cause of the depression, and he concluded by suggesting that Chancery's abusive proceedings in this particular instance showed that it was in need of general reform.[76]

Although the king quickly issued a proclamation against bills of conformity,[77] the Commons continued to investigate Chancery and soon discovered another abuse to attack—the fees taken by the Chancery masters.[78] In 1618 these officials had successfully petitioned the king for an increase in fees, but because a statute of 1604 had restricted the payments that court officers could receive, the masters felt the need to have their new fees ratified by Parliament in 1621. By petitioning the

71. See *CD 1621*, 2:222; 4:153–54; 5:49–50; 6:63. See also Prestwich, *Cranfield*, p. 299; Jones, *Politics and the Bench*, pp. 64, 66, 114; and Zaller, *1621*, pp. 75, 86, 90.

72. The issuance of bills of conformity could easily lead to the defrauding of creditors and was therefore particularly suspect during a depression that saw many business failures—or pseudo-failures (see Supple, *Commercial Crisis*, pp. 10–11, 49 n. 2, 55, 56, 174).

73. *CD 1621*, 2:222; 4:67; 5:297. According to the solicitor, the king had replied to the City that the bills "should be taken as a persuasion not a compulsion" and were not intended to protect sureties as well as principals (*CD 1621*, 4:67; 2:101).

74. See *CD 1621*, 4:150; 5:297; 6:63. On the Commons's debates on the causes of the depression, see chap. 4.

75. *CD 1621*, 2:221–23; 4:153–54; 5:39–40, 296–97; 6:63; *P&D*, 1:156–60. For earlier debates on these bills, see *CJ*, 1:525 (17 February) and *CD 1621*, 4:117; 6:21, 274, 293; 5:265, 531 (28 February).

76. *CD 1621*, 2:222–23; 4:154–55; 5:297; 6:63; *P&D*, 1:159.

77. *CD 1621*, 7:581, 590 and nn. 10–11, 620.

78. Chancery fees were frequently attacked both in and out of Parliament (see Veall, *Law Reform*, p. 34), and while other courts were attacked on the same grounds (see Zaller, *1621*, pp. 93–94 and n. 39), Chancery may have been particularly vulnerable to criticism on this point (see Holdsworth, *History*, 1:425–26; Zaller, *1621*, p. 94). On the Chancery masters, see Holdsworth, *History*, 1:416–28; and on the Commons's attack on them in 1621, see Zaller, *1621*, pp. 94–95.

Commons to approve them,[79] however, they only provided Chancery's critics there with another target and with a further justification for proposing general reforms of that court. After charging on 23 April that the statute of 1604 made the new fees illegal Coke quickly moved on to a more general attack on the masters. He claimed that their exercise of quasi-judicial power was illegal, because no judge could make a deputy, and because they dealt with cases falling outside of Chancery's jurisdiction.[80] Several days later he reported that the Committee of Grievances had found the new fees to be a "grievance" and added several new arguments for this position. He claimed that approval for the fees had been obtained through bribery, that the judges had never approved them, and that the order for them had been passed illegally. After expanding on his earlier remarks about the masters' illegal exercise of judicial power,[81] he again suggested that such abusive practices demonstrated the need for statutory regulation of Chancery.[82]

Although Coke often supported legislation to reform Chancery, he actively promoted only two of the seven bills that the Commons considered in 1621 and 1624.[83] The first of them was one that he had drafted himself. Early in 1621 he called for the passage of a statute of limitations for certain suits in Chancery. In an attempt to conciliate opponents of parliamentary regulation of the courts, he insisted that his purpose was "not to restrain the Court's jurisdiction, but the parties in prosecution." He also emphasized that he was not now proposing time limits for royal actions in Chancery, although he hinted that such limits would actually benefit the king.[84] He merely proposed "to limit a time, within which all suits shall be commenced, which were to be proved by testimony of witnesses." After claiming that this proposal would be "plausible to the subject and acceptable to the judges who for want of this limitation are many times perplexed," he gave two arguments in its favor. First, if real actions at common law could be limited to a certain time by 32 Henry VIII, c. 2, then suits in Chancery could be similarly limited. Second, if such time limits were reasonable for common-law

79. See CD 1621, 7:519–21; 1 Jac. I, c. 10 (SR, 4, pt. 2, p. 1027); and Zaller, 1621, p. 94.

80. CD 1621, 3:62–63, 2:316.

81. Ibid., 3:97; 2:327; 4:266; 5:103, 352; 6:104; P&D, 1:333–34; CJ, 1:594.

82. CD 1621, 3:98; 5:104–5. These remarks were made in a speech given in a debate following his report from the committee. On Coke's motion, the Commons then condemned the new fees as a grievance in the creation and in the execution (CD 1621, 3:90; on these terms, see p. 120) and the king later revoked them by proclamation (CD 1621, 7:411–12).

83. On these bills, see Zaller, 1621, pp. 90–97; and White, "Coke," p. 154.

84. CD 1621, 2:65: "My meaning is not to . . . limit the king, for nullum tempus occurrit regi." Coke nevertheless supported a bill that limited this royal prerogative (see pp. 72–76, below).

actions, which were based upon matters "of record," they would be even more reasonable for Chancery suits that turned on testimony, which was "ever best" when it was "greenest," especially when a man could lose his whole estate through the testimony of his adversary's witness.[85] Nothing ever came of this proposal, however. His bill never received a third reading in 1621 and does not seem to have been revived in 1624.[86] Another proposal that he made in 1621 to repress "the overflowing" of the Chancery's jurisdiction seems never even to have been put into the form of a bill. Coke had originally suggested this measure to eliminate the Chancery abuses uncovered by the Committee of Courts' investigations into Fuller's case. This complex dispute over the lease of a rectory had given rise to an even more tangled jurisdictional battle between Chancery and the Court of Wards,[87] and the latter, in Coke's opinion, had demonstrated the need for clarifying the jurisdictional boundaries of all courts, especially Chancery. He charged that the court's proceedings in the case were "against law and fit to be helped by Parliament," but although he promised to draft a bill checking the illegal expansion of Chancery jurisdiction,[88] his plan came to nothing.[89]

Another court frequently attacked in the parliaments of 1621 and 1624 was the Exchequer.[90] Early in 1621, Solicitor Heath told the Committee of Courts about various abuses in it and said that they could be eliminated by three royal "bills of grace," which would outlaw levying debts in the king's name, excessive charges for passing sheriff's accounts, and excessive fees for licenses for alienations.[91] The third of Heath's bills became the subject of a major debate on 26 March when a Mr. Taylor

---

85. *CD 1621*, 2:64–65; 4:431; 5:452; *CJ*, 1:519; *P&D*, 1:34–35.

86. Edward Alford tried and failed to revive it, along with other legislation on Chancery. See Holles, 1624, f. 101; Nicholas, 1624, f. 80v; Erle, 1624, f. 86v; *CJ*, 1:686, 737.

87. For abstracts of this case, see *CD 1621*, 6:292–93, 294–95; 2:153–54; 4:164.

88. Ibid., 5:305; *CJ*, 1:559.

89. Although a committee debated Coke's proposal during the spring recess, it apparently accomplished nothing (see *CD 1621*, 2:295; 5:330–31; 4:232; *P&D*, 1:261; *CJ*, 1:578). On 17 April, Coke again stressed the importance of his proposal (*CD 1621*, 2:295–96; 4:232; *CJ*, 1:578). He was later appointed to a new committee ordered to draft a bill "to regulate the Court of Chancery" (*CJ*, 1:590–91; *CD 1621*, 3:79–80 and nn. 14 and 19), but this committee seems never to have reported back to the House. In 1624 Coke spoke on only one bill concerning Chancery: the bill for reversing Chancery decrees. This bill provided that such decrees could be challenged within a year of issue and be reexamined by the two chief justices, the chief baron, and the chancellor (see *P&D*, 1:274; Gardiner, *History*, 4:109; and Zaller, *1621*, p. 96). When this bill was reported to the House on 26 April, Coke criticized it because he believed that procedures already existed for reversing Chancery decrees (see *CJ*, 1:775; Pym, 1624a, f. 19v; Nicholas, 1624, f. 177; Erle, 1624, f. 162v; Holland, 1624, I, f. 49).

90. See Zaller, *1621*, p. 97; and Aylmer, *The King' Servants*, pp. 188–91.

91. *CD 1621*, 5:16, 265, 352; 6:21. On the first two of these bills, see White, "Coke," pp. 160–62 and nn. 2–14.

complained about "the great rate upon fines and recoveries" and called it "a burden to the subject and a diminishment of the King's revenue."[92] Coke then raised suspicions about these new rates by noting that Bacon had had a hand in raising them and complained that since their establishment the crown's total revenue from them had declined.[93] Noy then made a significant point by adding that the increased cost of levying fines and recoveries had induced many men to find other, less secure means of transferring real property.[94] Further debates on the bill in 1621 and 1624 were marked by Coke's obstinate refusal to let the exchequermen testify against it; but although he successfully squelched opposition to it in the Commons, it never passed the Lords.[95]

The Court of Wards was no more immune to Coke's attacks in 1621 and 1624 than was the Chancery or the Exchequer. Early in 1621 members of the Commitee for Courts criticized this court for its role in Fuller's case,[96] for its grants of protections to wards and their sureties against actions of debt,[97] and for its procedures in inquisitions post mortem. These criticisms led to only one legislative proposal: the bill against secret offices and inquisitions. Its main purpose was to prevent heirs of deceased tenants from being vexed by false claims that all or part of their ancestors' lands had been held in chief of the crown and were therefore liable to fall into the king's hands. It required that heirs be given both reasonable notice of all inquisitions post mortem and full opportunity to challenge the findings of inquisitions (or "traverse and office") without having to obtain a special license.[98] On the bill's second reading in 1621, Coke called it "one of the best bills come into this House" and criticized it only for its lack of stringency. He charged that the refusal of the Court of Wards to allow a traverse of an office without license was illegal and

---

92. CD 1621, 4:199. For the text of the bill see CD 1621, 7:185–87.

93. Ibid., 4:199.

94. Ibid., 4:199; 6:323; P&D, 1:227–28; CJ, 1:575.

95. On the later history of the bill in 1621 and 1624, see White, "Coke," pp. 162–64 and nn. 20–32.

96. For references to abstracts of this case, see fn. 87, above. Coke regarded the case as not just an illustration of the unlawful expansion of Chancery jurisdiction, but also as an indication of the need for defining the jurisdiction of all courts. "If a fair river overflow," he said, "it will in the end lose his channels. So if courts know not or keep not their jurisdictions, they lose it [sic]." Such a danger now existed, he indicated, for courts were "clashing" and "interfering" with one another; and he therefore moved for a bill that would establish the jurisdictional limits of all courts (CD 1621, 5:12). For his later remarks on Hall v. Fuller, see CJ, 1:559.

97. After others had attacked this abuse (CD 1621, 2:100; 5:473), Coke moved to have "a bill drawn which should give the creditor his debt and damages and [provide that] the sureties should be secured only of the lands of the heir." He also asked to be placed on the committee to draft this bill (CD 1621, 2:100; CJ, 1:525).

98. For the text, see CD 1621, 7:193–97. On the early stage of the bill's legislative history, see White, "Coke," pp. 167–68 and nn. 18–24.

wished that the bill had said so explicitly. He also complained that the bill might not prevent inquisitions from being held secretly and moved for an amendment requiring that notice of an impending inquisition be brought to the heir's dwelling place.[99] His proposed amendments seem never to have been made, however, and the bill did not pass in the Commons in either 1621 or 1624.[100]

Some of the bills that Coke supported in 1621 and 1624 were directed not at abuses in particular courts but at various procedures by which cases could be transferred from local courts to Westminster. He believed that English justice was becoming increasingly expensive and dilatory at least partly because too many suits were being brought from local to central courts. He also thought that unscrupulous litigants were exploiting the procedures by which this could be accomplished, because they realized that the long delays and the high costs of justice at Westminster could be turned to their own private advantage whether they were plaintiffs or defendants. They knew that they could sometimes acquire effective immunity from prosecution if a suit against them fell—or could be made to fall—under the jurisdiction of one of the central courts. They also realized that the mere threat of a suit in Westminster often induced men with good cases to settle out of court. In Coke's opinion, private informers probably constituted the most important group of people who were manipulating the legal system in these ways. Who the others were and what they were actually doing is not clear. Nor is it certain that there were any objective criteria by which their activities could be distinguished from those of subjects whom Coke regarded as honest. Nevertheless, he and his fellow members believed in the existence of a class of unscrupulous litigants who were maliciously exploiting lawful procedures in order to serve their own nefarious purposes. In order to check at least some of their activities, Coke supported three separate bills aimed at reducing the number of occasions in which local suits could be brought to Westminster: the inferior courts bill, the bill concerning process of peace and good behavior, and the bill against informers.[101]

The preamble to the inferior courts bill stated that the removal to Westminster of suits initiated in the courts of cities, liberties, and corporate towns was causing "intolerable delay of justice and great expenses of money and loss and trouble to those which justly and honestly . . . have

99. *CD 1621*, 5:114.
100. On the later history of the bill in 1621 and 1624, see White, "Coke," p. 169 and nn. 28–32. On Coke's remarks about it in the parliament of 1625, see p. 193, below.
101. In addition, by supporting the bill for continuance and repeal of statutes, Coke hoped to diminish the number of informations brought on penal statutes. See p. 69, below.

sought only to recover or get satisfaction for debts, duties or wrongs owing, due or done to them." The bill then provided that certain actions begun in these courts could not be removed to London if the debt, damages, or things demanded did not exceed £5 in value and if the case did not concern freehold property. It further provided that certain cases remanded to these local courts could not be stayed before judgment, and it also established stricter conditions for the removal of suits to Westminster by writs of habeas corpus or certiorari.[102] Coke never presented an explanation of the abuses against which the bill was directed and the House never asked for one. In 1624 he easily guided it through the Commons,[103] and after its enactment he cited it in his *Fourth Institutes* as a bill that had helped to check "the multiplication of suits."[104]

The bill for process of peace and good behavior had a much more difficult passage; but Coke successfully defended it against attack in both 1621 and 1624 and ultimately secured its enactment. The grievances that it was supposed to remedy are as obscure as the abuses attacked by the inferior courts bill, but they were of obvious concern to Coke and other members of the Commons. The preamble to the bill stated that the corruption or negligence of officers of the King's Bench and Chancery enabled "divers turbulent and contentious persons" both to exempt themselves effectively from local jurisdiction in certain kinds of cases and to threaten their enemies in the country with prosecution at Westminster. To repress their activities, the bill provided that processes of peace and good behavior and writs of certiorari and supersedeas be issued in open court.[105] Like other bills Coke supported, it blamed legal abuses on both a class of evil private men and loopholes in court procedure; and by reforming the latter it aimed at denying the former opportunities to injure honest subjects. Such procedural reforms, however, could be regarded as encroachments on the power of Chancery and King's Bench. Thus, Edward Alford attacked the bill in 1621 for taking "too much from higher . . . courts" and giving "too much to the justices of [the] peace."[106] In reply, Coke said that although the bill concerned two of the realm's "highest courts," it merely placed them under restrictions already established for

---

102. *CD 1621*, 7:191–92. The draft bill differs only slightly from the final act, 21 *Jac.* I, *c.* 23 (*SR*, 4, pt. 2, pp. 1232–33), except that the latter was specifically restricted to suits "not concerning freehold or inheritance or title of land, lease or rent."

103. See White, "Coke," pp. 172–73 and nn. 7–11.

104. *Institutes*, 4:76–77.

105. 21 *Jac.* I, *c.* 8 (*SR*, 4, pt. 2, pp. 1217–18). For an abstract of the bill, see *CD 1621*, 4:42. On the abuses that the act was supposed to check, see its preamble and Edward Jenks, "The Prerogative Writs," p. 529 and n. 29. On Ellesmere's earlier expressions of concern about the misuse of writs of certiorari, see Knafla, *Law and Politics*, pp. 113–14.

106. *CD 1621*, 5:17. For other criticisms of the bill, see *CD 1621*, 4:117–18.

other courts and had the laudable objective of limiting judicial discretion. He also argued that the bill would promote local justice and that it had the same objectives as the statute that established the system of *Nisi Prius*.[107] Several months later Coke had to answer similar objections to the bill at a conference with the Lords. One of the judges had complained that it "absolutely restrained" both Chancery and King's Bench in several ways and abridged their jurisdiction by restricting their power to issue writs of certiorari to remove actions out of the quarter sessions. Coke met these objections just as he had countered Alford's the previous March. He first insisted that the bill did not "restrain" either the King's Bench or Chancery but merely established certain procedures that litigants in these two courts had to follow. He then maintained that the bill was "agreeable to the wisdom of Parliament," which had made many other laws for the furtherance of local justice.[108] His defense of the bill apparently satisfied the Lords, who passed it with only minor amendments;[109] and although it again encountered opposition in 1624, it was ultimately enacted.[110]

Of the three bills that Coke hoped would promote local justice and check the flood of cases to London, the informers bill was by far the most significant and provoked the greatest debate. Common informers (who were also known as "relators" or "promoters") were repeatedly vilified during the century prior to the Revolution.[111] Although Parliament regularly gave private persons an incentive to enforce regulatory legislation by granting them part of the fines imposed for the violation of penal statutes, many subjects thought that private informers were turning the enforcement of statutes into a racket; and they probably had good grounds for thinking so. Under Elizabeth and James I, several parliaments attempted to check the abusive practices of informers;[112] and the Privy

107. Ibid., 5:16–17; 4:118. Coke cited 27 *Edw.* I, *c.* 4.
108. For this conference, see *CD 1621*, 4:374–76; 5:384. For Coke's report of it, see *CD 1621*, 3:324–25; 2:397–98; 4:382; 5:180, 387; 6:172–73; *CJ*, 1:628–29; *P&D*, 1:109–10.
109. See *CD 1621*, 3:340–42; 6:388–89; 2:404; 6:177.
110. Before assenting to the bill, James I made some critical remarks about it. See D'Ewes, 1624, ff. 128v–129.
111. On informers generally, see G. R. Elton, "Informing for Profit." Very useful discussions of informers and informations on penal statutes can be found in Maurice W. Beresford, "The Common Informer, the Penal Statutes, and Economic Regulation"; Maurice W. Beresford, "Habitation versus Improvement"; Peter J. Bowden, *The Wool Trade in Tudor and Stuart England*; and Margaret Gay Davies, *The Enforcement of English Apprenticeship*. For an example of late Elizabethan complaints against informers, see Harrison, *Description of England*, pp. 175, 438. It is important to bear in mind that complaints about informers were generally bound up with complaints about the confused state of the penal statutes on which informers laid their informations.
112. On earlier proposals to amend methods of enforcing penal statutes, see T. F. T. Plucknett, "Some Proposed Legislation of Henry VIII"; Jones, *Tudor Commonwealth*, p. 212; and Elton, *Reform and Renewal*, pp. 129–57 passim. Three Elizabethan statutes dealt

Council sometimes responded to complaints about them by staying their informations.[113] These measures obviously seemed inadequate to members of the Commons in 1621, and they quickly began work on a new bill against informers.[114] In its final form it provided that an offense against a penal statute had to be prosecuted in the county in which it had occurred, and it required the informer to swear that the alleged offense had occurred in the county in which he had brought the information within one year of the commencement of his suit. The bill also allowed defendants in informations to plead the general issue and provided for their acquittal not only if the offense against them went unproved, but also if the informer failed to show that he had brought the information in the proper county.[115] On 6 February, Coke praised this bill for closing the "back door" left open by the last Elizabethan statute against informers.[116] Two days later he stated that no other bill in the House was "more easeful for the subject" and explained in great detail how its wording might be improved.[117] When the Lords strongly objected to certain parts of it after its passage by the Commons, Coke defended it and ultimately persuaded the Upper House to expedite it. The Lords' exceptions against it closely resembled their objections to the bill for process of peace and good behavior. Some charged that it took away the "liberty of the Star Chamber" and abridged the power of "other courts extremely,"[118] but at two lengthy conferences Coke rebutted these charges successfully. At the second of the conferences he again insisted that Parliament could regulate court jurisdiction and procedure and then argued that informers should not have the "election to go to Westminster Hall" whenever they chose, for terrible results would ensue "if all [cases] were brought up to London." London was the "head" of the body politic, he said, and if all blood were to run to it, the body would then "die of an apoplexy."[119] The Lords

---

with informers: 18 *Eliz.*, *c.* 5 (*SR*, 4, pt. 1, pp. 615–16); 27 *Eliz.*, *c.* 10 (*SR*, 4, pt. 1, p. 717); and 31 *Eliz.*, *c.* 5 (*SR*, 4, pt. 2, pp. 801–2). For a discussion of these three acts, see Davies, *Apprenticeship*, pp. 27–28, 64–67; and for Coke's comments on the last of them, see *Institutes*, 3:191–95. On proposals made in early Jacobean parliaments to modify existing methods of enforcing penal laws, see Davies, *Apprenticeship*, p. 71; and Notestein, *1604–1610*, p. 51.

113. See Davies, *Apprenticeship*, pp. 63–72; and Bowden, *Wool Trade*, pp. 171–72.

114. The bill was preferred and read the first working day of the Parliament. See *CJ*, 1:510–11.

115. 21 *Jac.* I, *c.* 4 (*SR*, 4, pt. 2, pp. 1214–15). The editors of *CD 1621* print no draft version of this bill, which was drastically altered before its enactment in 1624.

116. *CJ*, 1:511; *CD 1621*, 2:31.

117. *CD 1621*, 2:43; 4:30; *CJ*, 1:514. On later discussions of the bill in the Commons and on the king's views about this legislative measure, see White, "Coke," pp. 198–200 and nn. 47–69.

118. See *CD 1621*, 3:20; 2:300.

119. For reports of the first of these conferences, see *CD 1621*, 2:317–18; 3:36–40;

ultimately passed the bill,[120] and when it was revived in 1624 it was easily enacted.[121]

While supporting reforms in the central courts and attempts to check the overcentralization of English justice, Coke also promoted other bills designed to stop the multiplication of suits, promote certainty in law, and preserve quietness of possession. This group of bills included minor measures like a bill "to enable judges and justices of the peace to give restitution," a bill to enable Prince Charles to lease lands in the duchy of Cornwall, a jeofails bill, and two more significant legislative measures: the bill for the limitation of personal actions at common law and the bill against pretences of concealments. In addition, although Coke did little to promote the passage of the great bill for continuance and repeal of statutes, he clearly supported it and later praised it in his *Institutes*.[122] The restitution bill gave nonfreeholders a relatively speedy remedy against forcible entries and provided that if they had been in possession for more than three years, they could not be sued under 8 Henry VI, *c.* 9 for reentering on those who had entered on them.[123] It was described in 1621 as a "good bill for staying of suits,"[124] and its enactment in 1624 probably owed something to Coke's support.[125] His role in promoting the bills for Cornish leases and jeofails was more considerable. In 1621 he actively sponsored the former bill and explained to the Commons how it would promote "certainty in law." It was easily enacted.[126] He also spoke at length on behalf of the jeofails bill, which he later described in the *Fourth Institutes* as "a good law for ending of suits."[127] In May of 1621 he explained its content and rationale in this way. Two earlier statutes had been "helpful" in preventing judgments from being over-

---

4:241–43; *CJ*, 1:545; *P&D*, 1:290. For reports of the second conference, see *CD 1621*, 2:324; 3:84–86; 4:260; 5:350; 6:102; *CJ*, 1:593; *P&D*, 1:328. For Coke's remark, see *CD 1621*, 3:84. Coke made this remark at the second conference. For his use of this same image in a speech about English trade, see p. 106, below.

120. *CJ*, 1:663; *CD 1621*, 2:521.

121. See White, "Coke," p. 206 and nn. 145–63.

122. For his later comments on this act (21 *Jac.* I, *c.* 28), see *Institutes*, 3:192; and *Institutes*, 4:76–77. On his earlier views on the state of the penal statutes, see p. 78, below.

123. For a note on this statute (21 *Jac.* I, *c.* 15), which extended to nonfreeholders the rights previously granted to freeholders by 31 *Eliz.*, *c.* 11, see Holdsworth, *History*, 4:487–88. For the text of the bill introduced in 1621, see *CD 1621*, 7:39–40. For the final act, see *SR*, 4, pt. 2, p. 1222.

124. *CD 1621*, 4:190; *CJ*, 1:572.

125. For his speech on the bill in 1624, see Pym, *1624*, f. 52.

126. For his speeches on the jeofails bill, see *CD 1621*, 5:592 n. 3; *P&D*, 1:108; *CJ*, 1:537. For the final act (21 *Jac.* I, *c.* 29), see *SR*, 4, pt. 2, p. 1240. For earlier comments of Coke's about the issues dealt with in this bill, see *The Prince Case* (*Reports*, 8:1–62, at 27).

127. *Institutes*, 4:72.

turned or delayed because of technical errors, but even after their enact-ment such errors as "not writing the juror[']s name rightly" could still delay judgments. The present bill, he claimed, would take away "all these rubs and give a speedy way to trials and judgement," and he opposed any delay in its passage.[128] The Commons quickly approved it, and in 1624 it was enacted with only minor changes.[129]

Like the bills for jeofails and Cornwall and the restitution bill, the statute of limitations for personal actions at common law was drafted "[f]or quieting of men's estates and avoiding of suits";[130] but it was far more significant than these other measures and provoked much more controversy. The statute 32 Henry VIII *c.* 2 had set time limits for real actions,[131] but as Coke had pointed out in his *Reports*, the vast majority of real property cases were now being brought by personal actions.[132] Since no statutes of limitation for the latter were in force, people could sue for property rights that had allegedly accrued to them in the very distant past, and men who could trace back their titles for centuries might suddenly lose their inheritances. Moreover, one group of real ac-tions, *formedons*, had been held to be out of the statute of 1541.[133] The limitation of actions bill of 1621 therefore set time limits for actions of *formedon* and all personal actions.[134]

Coke's support of this bill not only reveals his wish to check the multiplication of suits and promote quietness of possession and certainty in law; it also reflects both his long-standing hostility to entailed estates (which could be sued for by *formedons*)[135] and his willingness to work against the interests of at least a certain segment of the legal profession. Although he did not draft the bill, which had been introduced in the

---

128. *CD 1621*, 3:295; 2:384; 4:365; 5:175; *CJ*, 1:625. The two statutes to which Coke was referring were 32 *Hen.* VIII, *c.* 30 and 18 *Eliz., c.* 14. For his earlier comments on these acts, see *Playter's Case* (*Reports*, 5:36); *Walcot's Case* (*Reports*, 5:36); *Baynham's Case* (*Reports*, 5:37); *Rowland's Case* (*Reports*, 5:42); and *Sir John Heydon's Case* (*Reports*, 11:5–8).

129. See *CJ*, 1:688, 738; *LJ*, 3:274; *CJ*, 1:746.

130. This passage is taken from the preamble to the draft bill (*CD 1621*, 7:3).

131. On this act, see Holdsworth, *History*, 4:484–85; 6:20, 51, 344, 351; and Pluck-nett, *Concise History*, p. 719.

132. See *Alden's Case* (*Reports*, 5:105–6). In the preface to his *Eighth Reports*, Coke lamented the decline of the real actions. On the rise of the action of ejectment as the principal mechanism for trying cases involving title to real property, see Holdsworth, *History*, 7:4–23; Plucknett, *Concise History*, p. 574; and A. W. B. Simpson, *An Introduction to the History of the Land Law*, pp. 135–45.

133. *CD 1621*, 4:21; 5:4.

134. In the original bill, time limits ranged from twenty years for actions of *formedon* to one year for actions on the case for slander. Most actions were limited to six years (see *CD 1621*, 7:3–6). For the time limits finally agreed upon, see 21 *Jac.* I, *c.* 16 (*SR*, 4, pt. 2, pp. 1222–23).

135. See the prefaces to the *Third* and *Fourth Reports*. See also p. 72, below.

parliament of 1614,[136] he sponsored it in both 1621 and 1624.[137] On its third reading in the Commons in 1621, three objections were made against it. Merchants claimed that "[t]he accounts of factors and debts betwixt merchants cannot be determined within the time limited by the act, because they are often times long beyond the sea." Sir Henry Poole charged that the bill would deprive some subjects of "their right and true inheritance[s]." and William Noy, who actually favored the bill, observed that it would be "very prejudicial to lawyers."[138] Coke sympathized with only the first of these objections and later proposed an amendment to meet it; and he easily dismissed Noy's warning with one of his favorite aphorisms: "Expedit reipublicae, ut sit finis litium." Poole's objection, however, required a more elaborate answer. According to Coke, it reflected Poole's failure to realize that the present bill would undo the mischiefs introduced into the common law by two medieval statutes, Westminster II and 34 Edward III, *c.* 16. He maintained that the bill would simply reestablish two important common-law principles that these two acts had taken away: that all land should be fee simple, and that "a man should make his entry within one year after the right accrued." After stating that under the statute of Edward III a man who had had land for two hundred years might be sued for it and lose it, Coke illustrated the kind of excessive litigation that the present bill would check by noting that at one of the recent Norfolk Assizes, there had been "17 score nisi priusses" and "not the 5th part" of them had been "worth 20s." He also said that there was "no better" bill in the House, and that counties like Norfolk would give the king a yearly subsidy in return for its passage.[139]

When debate on the bill resumed almost two months later, the three objections previously made to it were raised again. One lawyer observed that although it was "[p]rejudicious to contentious persons and lawyers," it was "a very good bill for the commonwealth"; but another member noted that "[a]s lawyers will lose in one way by this bill, they will gain in another way, by purchasing." Merchants continued to insist that six years was too short a time limit for their actions of account,[140] and Coke therefore moved for an amendment that would meet this objection without altering the bill's main substance.[141] Once again, however, Poole's objections provoked great debate. He now asserted that the bill was

136. See *CD 1621*, 7:15 n. 4; and Moir, *The Addled Parliament*, p. 204.

137. On the bill's second reading in 1621, Coke carefully explained its purpose to the House and also expressed one small reservation about it (*CD 1621*, 2:32; 4:21; 5:4).

138. Ibid., 4:169; *CJ*, 1:562. Of the "exceptions" listed in *CD 1621*, 4:169, numbers (1) and (3)–(6) are Poole's. Noy said that he "would not, as a lawyer, assent" to the bill.

139. *CD 1621*, 4:169–70; 5:50; *P&D*, 1:193; *CJ*, 1:562.

140. *P&D*, 2:101; *CJ*, 1:626–27; *CD 1621*, 3:303–4; 2:389.

141. *P&D*, 2:102.

"fruitless and idle, unjust and injurious," and that it would not accomplish "what it promiseth; which is to prevent multiplicity of suits." Moroever, he insisted that even if it were to "procure peace," "[e]vil is not to be done that good may come thereof." The effect of the bill, he claimed, was to "give one man's right to another" and was therefore *malum in se*. His objection, therefore, was that if rights to bring *formedons* were limited, some people would be unable to sue for estate tails that were rightfully theirs.[142] In reply, Coke expanded upon his remarks of the previous March. He stated that estate tails were "prejudicial things" that had been established by Westminster II against the maxim of the common law that "land should be fee simple." After the passage of this statute, he claimed, "no tenant, nor farmer, or purchaser was sure of his estate." Coke may have argued therefore that it was not *malum in se* for Parliament to take away rights whose existence was antithetical to basic common-law principles.[143] Once Poole's objections to the bill had been answered and it had been amended in accordance with Coke's motion, the Commons finally passed it.[144] It failed to get through the Lords[145] but was speedily enacted in 1624.[146]

Like the limitation of actions bill, the bill against pretences of concealments was designed to promote "peace" and "quietness of possession" and to check "the multiplication of suits," but it was directed at a somewhat more complex and obscure set of legal and administrative abuses. As Coke later explained in his *Third Institutes*, these problems arose from the fact that prior to the enactment of the concealments bill in 1624, "in respect of that ancient prerogative of the crown that *nullum tempus occurrit regi*, the titles of the king were not restrained to any limitation of time: for that no statute of limitation that ever was made did ever limit the title of the king to any manors, lands, tenements, or hereditaments, to any certain time."[147] Thus, the crown could never lose its right to sue for the recovery of what were known as "concealed lands," that is, property rights that a subject enjoyed while "concealing" them from their true owner, the king. Conversely, property holders lived under the continual threat of being sued by the crown for all or part of their landed inheritances. Coke regarded this state of affairs as grievously vexing to secular and ecclesiastical property holders and to the commonwealth as a whole. His reasons for taking this position were probably the

142. *CD 1621*, 4:370; *P&D*, 2:100–1; *CJ*, 1:626.
143. *CD 1621*, 2:388; 4:37; 5:383.
144. *CJ*, 1:627. For the amendments, see *P&D*, 2:102; *CJ*, 1:627; *CD 1621*, 4:371; 4:3–4 and n. 8.
145. *LJ*, 3:172.
146. As 21 *Jac.* I, *c.* 16 (*SR*, 4, pt. 2, pp. 1222–23).
147. *Institutes*, 3:188.

following ones. In the first place, even when royal actions for concealments had merit, Coke apparently thought it unjust that subjects should
lose property rights that they, their ancestors, or their predecessors had
enjoyed for a long period of time. Secondly, he recognized that even when
the crown had little or no basis for a concealments suit against a subject,
the defendant in such a case might face two great and perhaps insuperable
difficulties. First, he might be left defenceless in a case where "records and
other muniments, making good [his] estate and interest . . . were not
to be found."[148] Moreover, because many "questions and doubts" still
existed about what property rights had passed to the crown from the
monasteries and chantries, further questions and doubts naturally arose
about the titles of subjects who now had legal interests in what had
formerly been monastic or chantry property; and if such subjects were
sued for concealed lands, they might have great difficulty in defending
their rights. The third and most significant reason for Coke's concern
about the concealments issue was that Elizabeth and James I had issued
patents to private persons granting them either the right to concealed
lands, or else the power to compound with subjects for them. Whether
these monarchs had adopted this practice as a device for raising revenue,
as a way of settling the concealments issue, or as a means of providing
courtiers with a lucrative and legitimate source of funds is not clear.
What is clear is that the recipients of concealments patents acquired very
valuable powers. These "concealers," as they were called, were in a position to sue many landholders for concealed lands, or in some cases for
concealed tithes. Moreover, because such suits were apparently easy to
initiate but difficult and expensive to contest, the concealers seem to have
been in a position to use the threat of litigation as a means of inducing
landholders to compound for their allegedly concealed lands, and/or to
pay off the concealers. Needless to say, landholders saw little or no
distinction between such inducements to compound and simple extortion;
and it was no accident that Coke referred to concealers as "viperous
vermin" and "caterpillars of the commonwealth."[149] He believed, moreover, that their activities and, indeed, all the abuses associated with pretences of concealments did actual harm even to those landholders who
were never sued for concealments or approached by concealers, for in his
opinion these abusive practices disturbed "the quietness of possession"
of every English landholder.

148. Ibid., 3:188.
149. Ibid., 4:76. See also *Institutes*, 3:188; *Arthur Legat's Case* (*Reports*, 10:110–14);
and *The Case of the Dean and Chapter of Norwich* (*Reports*, 3:73–76). On concealments,
see C. J. Kitching, "The Quest for Concealed Lands in the Reign of Elizabeth" and the
literature cited at p. 63, n. 1.

Coke commenced his attack on the concealments rackets on 19 February 1621. In a debate on monopoly patents held in the Committee of Grievances, he singled out royal grants of concealments for special condemnation and noted that while subjects could not sell their claims to land—for that would constitute champerty—the king could lawfully do so; and he maintained that special legislation was necessary to remedy this abuse.[150] Such legislation, he said, had been considered by Parliament in 1614, when "[t]here was a bill drawn that if the crown have been out of possession sixty years without profit, the King would shut his hands"; and he moved that a similar bill now be considered.[151] His motion carried, and on 1 March he brought in his own draft bill "for the general quiet of the subjects against all pretences of concealments."[152] After observing that concealers should be condemned along with alchemists, monopolists, promoters, depopulators, and projectors, he stated that his bill would check their evil activities by barring the king from suing for lands unless he or his predecessors had been "in possession or answered rents or put in charge or stood *in supra* upon record within a space of 60 years."[153] By proposing a sixty-year time limit on royal actions for concealments, Coke was clearly trying to bar royal suits for concealed lands that had passed to the crown from the monasteries and chantries more than sixty years before and had later been granted to subjects. On the bill's second reading the following day, exceptions were taken to parts of it by those who believed that it did not sufficiently limit the rights of the crown;[154] and after Coke had responded to these exceptions,[155] the bill was committed.[156] During the rest of the session and in 1624, however, the bill was attacked primarily for limiting the crown's rights too severely. In 1621, Sir Henry Poole claimed that it threatened the king's rights in wastes, forests, and liberties; and although Glanville answered his objections effectively,[157] similar ones were made when the bill was reintroduced in the parliament of 1624. On 23 February Coke successfully moved that the bill "march first," along with the monopolies and informers bills;[158] but he had to answer a serious attack on the bill the following day. After the bill's second reading, Mr. Wentworth charged that although its inten-

---

150. For a discussion of the main part of this speech, see pp. 119–21, below.

151. *CD 1621*, 4:79 and n. 8; 6:251. On the consideration of this bill in the parliament of 1614, see *CJ*, 1:474–75.

152. *CD 1621*, 5:16, 226. For abstracts of the bill, see *CD 1621*, 5:18, 266; 4:250.

153. Ibid., 5:17, 266; 2:151; 6:22; *CJ*, 1:533; *P&D*, 1:112–13.

154. *CD 1621*, 5:18; *CJ*, 1:534.

155. *CD 1621*, 5:19; 2:152; *CJ*, 1:534.

156. *CJ*, 1:534.

158. *CD 1621*, 3:65; 4:250; *CJ*, 1:588. The bill later passed the Commons (*CJ*, 1:588) but not the Lords (*CD 1621*, 3:354).

158. Holles, 1624, f. 81; Spring, 1624, f. 9.

tion was merely "to confirm the title of the subject against old titles of the king if the possession had gone with them sixty years," it actually abridged "the reasonable and due rights of the king beyond the meaning of the House," and it therefore required amendment.[159] In reply, Coke said that subjects would rather give the king "a continual subsidy" than be vexed by concealers. He went on to assert that few men in the House had not received tickets alleging defects in their land titles, and that anyone who received such a ticket could not sleep at night, knowing that "all his living" had been "called into question." Coke then brushed aside all of Wentworth's objections and insisted that because the bill was "exceedingly beneficial" to the king's subjects, it would benefit the king; for if his subjects were rich, he could not be poor. According to Coke, the king gained nothing from pretences of concealments; they only benefited the patentees, who exploited legal technicalities so as to enrich themselves at the commonwealth's expense.[160]

The Commons, however, were "not satisfied" with Coke's responses and referred the bill to the committee,[161] which later amended it so as to meet Wentworth's objections.[162] When Coke reported it to the House on 18 March, it contained a new clause explicitly reserving the king's rights in several cases; but, according to Mr. Whistler, it still threatened certain royal rights. Coke again defended it,[163] but again failed to convince the House, which had it recommitted for further amendments.[164] On 7 April, the Commons finally passed the bill,[165] and Coke took it up to the Lords, to whom he "especially recommended" it "as a bill concerning the general good and quiet of all the ecclesiastical and temporal estates of the whole kingdom."[166] On three separate occasions, Coke urged the Lords to proceed quickly with the bill, which he referred to as "the great peacemaker of the church and commonwealth,"[167] and on the twentieth the Lords sent it back to the Commons with several amendments, which were then referred to a committee.[168] These amendments apparently limited the bill in some way, for on the twenty-fourth Coke reported to the House that the committee had agreed to them, "choosing rather to

---

159. Pym, 1624, f. 5v; Spring, 1624, f. 18; Nicholas, 1624, ff. 7v–8.
160. Braye, 1624, f. 8; Spring, 1624, f. 19; D'Ewes, 1624, f. 69; Nicholas, 1624, f. 8; Pym, 1624, f. 5v; CJ, 1:673, 717.
161. Pym, 1624, f. 5v; CJ, 1:673, 717.
162. Pym, 1624, ff. 7–7v.
163. Pym, 1624, f. 31v; Holland, 1624, I, f. 59v; CJ, 1:739.
164. CJ, 1:752; Pym, 1624, f. 45.
165. CJ, 1:757.
166. LJ, 3:293.
167. Ibid., 3:386. See also CJ, 1:701, 704, 786, 789.
168. LJ, 3:397, 398; CJ, 1:708.

take what we have now [by the bill] than to lose all."[169] The bill passed the Commons and on the twenty-ninth[170] it received the king's assent.[171]

The preceding discussion of Coke's efforts to remedy grievances in law through parliamentary action during the early 1620s suggests several sorts of conclusions about his attitude towards English law and legal change during this period. It reveals some of the distinctive features of his critique of the existing legal system and indicates what role he assigned to Parliament in amending the law. It also facilitates the identification of the interests and values that he wanted Parliament to promote and defend and may also help to explain his failure to promote those interests and values more forcefully and effectively. Finally, it clarifies the relationship between his critique of the legal status quo on the one hand and his political and constitutional stances on the other. A straightforward survey of his parliamentary activities in 1621 and 1624 conclusively demonstrates that he was highly critical of the English legal system, and it suggests that he placed a higher priority on remedying certain legal abuses than on effecting significant constitutional changes. While he often blamed grievances in law on corrupt individuals, he also attributed them to structural defects in established judicial procedures. Moreover, he wanted to eliminate these defects by enacting statutes that some members of Parliament regarded as encroachments on the powers of the king's courts and legal officers and even on the rights of the crown itself. He also wanted to repress the corruption of judges and court officials and to reduce the cost of justice; and he favored measures that might have reduced the income that lawyers derived from fees. Nevertheless, he failed notably to endorse many legal changes that received support from other seventeenth-century critics of English law or to anticipate many later efforts to adapt the law to the changing needs of more affluent landholders and merchants. As a member of Parliament during the early 1620s, he never supported debt reform, land registration, or legal codification. He made only moderate criticisms of the court system and the legal profession. He did not support legal changes that would have shifted the costs of economic change from one class to another. And needless to say, he never favored either the abolition of private property or the replacement of the common law by a legal system based upon either civil law or the law of God.

169. *CJ*, 1:710. Although the bill had obviously run into trouble in the Lords, Prince Charles apparently helped to secure its passage there (see Stowe Ms. 366, f. 38v; quoted in Notes to the Yale Transcript of Erle, 1624).

170. *CJ*, 1:710, 793.

171. D'Ewes, 1624, f. 128v. For the final act (21 *Jac.* I, *c.* 2), see *SR*, 4, pt. 2, pp. 1210–11.

Coke's failure to call for debt reform clearly distinguishes his critique of the English legal system from that of some other proponents of legal change.[172] In his *Reports*, he had tried to resolve certain important questions that arose in this branch of the law[173] and had contributed to the development of bankruptcy laws.[174] But he never called for the abolition of imprisonment for debt, and he sometimes engaged in traditional vilification of debtors and bankrupts.[175] Although he wished to promote quietness of possession and certainty in law, he never expressed interest in establishing a system of land registration that might have made the titles of landholders more certain and secure.[176] He believed, as many others did, that it should be made easier for English subjects to acquire knowledge and understanding of the law; but he wanted to attain this goal not through statutory codification of the law, but through the publication and dissemination of works like his *Institutes*, which he wrote in English rather than Law French so that they might reach a wider, nonprofessional audience.[177] Like other seventeenth-century advocates of legal change, he thought that too many cases were being heard in central instead of in local courts, but he lacked any nostalgic attachment to local justice and expressed no strong desire to strengthen local community ties.[178] He sometimes blamed the increasing cost of justice on venal court officials and even on lower orders of the legal profession, and he strongly attacked legal corruption. He had no wish, however, to limit judicial discretion or to curtail significantly the privileges of lawyers.[179] While he recognized the need for changes in the existing legal system, he insisted that the common law itself was free from any imperfections, and he never considered replacing it with another type of law. He never proposed to change the law by means of statutes that directly promoted the interests of one class at the expense of another and never expressed support for parliamentary efforts to clarify important parts of common-law doctrine.

172. On proposals that were made between 1640 and 1660 to amend the law of debt, see Veall, *Law Reform*; Prall, *Law Reform*; Niehaus, "Law Reform"; and Shapiro, "Law Reform."

173. Cases on the law of debt can be found in almost every volume of Coke's *Reports*.

174. See *The Case of the Bankrupts* (*Reports*, 2:25–26), which discusses the Elizabethan bankruptcy statute 13 *Eliz., c. 7*. On Coke's support of a bankruptcy bill in 1621 and 1624, see Appendix C.

175. See Appendix C.

176. On seventeenth-century proposals for a land registry, see Hill, *Intellectual Origins*, p. 166; and Shapiro, "Law Reform," pp. 295–96.

177. See the prefaces to *Institutes*, 1–4.

178. On the desire of some later advocates of legal change to return to a system of local, communal justice, see Veall, *Law Reform*, pp. 168–78; and Shapiro, "Law Reform," pp. 293–94.

179. Coke's views on these matters can be contrasted with those of later figures whose ideas are discussed in Veall, *Law Reform*, chaps. 8–9.

The limited scope of Coke's parliamentary proposals for legal change can be partially explained through a consideration of his views about Parliament's proper function in amending the law. A comparison of his parliamentary speeches on legal abuses with his *Reports* shows that he actually favored many legal changes that he failed to promote in Parliament, and that he wanted to effect them not by statute but by judicial decisions that might sometimes require guidance from legal writers like himself. In fact, his parliamentary speeches never dealt directly with the legal abuses that had most concerned him in his *Reports*. Some of the abuses that he had noted in these writings, to be sure, were ones that he later attacked in Parliament. He had complained in his *Reports* about the "multiplicity" of lawsuits,[180] judicial corruption,[181] dilatory legal proceedings,[182] the confused state of the penal statutes,[183] and the excessive cost of litigation;[184] and he had repeatedly noted that the speedy and definitive termination of disputes invariably benefited the commonwealth.[185] Nevertheless, these abuses were not the ones that he had discussed most frequently in his writings or the ones that these works were primarily designed to remedy. His eleven volumes of case reports, which he had published before 1616, had alluded to defects that he barely mentioned in the parliaments of the 1620s such as the continuing existence of numerous doubts, questions, uncertainties, and diversities of opinion among judges and lawyers about the most important questions of private law;[186] as well as the extraordinary currency of "absurd and strange

180. He said that this "inconvenience" was one of the results of "[t]he neglect of the assises and real actions" (*Reports*, 8, Preface; cf. *Higgen's Case* [*Reports.* 6:46]). He also praised many judicial rulings on the grounds that they would help to terminate disputes (see fn. 185, below). On the similarity between Coke's views on the increase in suits and the views of his contemporaries, see Thorne, "Tudor Social Transformation," p. 22; and Hill, *Intellectual Origins*, p. 231. For some Elizabethan comments on the increase of suits, see Harrison, *Description*, p. 170; and Lambarde, *Archeion*, p. 18.

181. *Reports*, 4, preface.

182. Ibid., 10, preface.

183. Ibid., 4, preface.

184. Ibid., 8, preface; 9, preface; 10, preface.

185. One of his favorite aphorisms was, "Expedit Reipublicae ut finis sit litium." For his use of it, see, for example, *Ferrer's Case* (*Reports*, 6:9); *Henry Peytoe's Case* (*Reports*, 9:79b); and *Baspole's Case* (*Reports*, 8:98b). For other remarks of his about the importance of terminating suits quickly, see *Boueston's Case* (*Reports*, 5:105); *Higgen's Case* (*Reports*, 6:45); *Brediman's Case* (*Reports*, 6:59); *Reports*, 8, preface; *Lampet's Case* (*Reports*, 10:48, 52); and *Institutes*, 1:56a.

186. See, for example, *Reports*, 1, preface; 2, preface; 3, preface; 4, preface; *Goodall's Case* (*Reports*, 5:97); *The Countess of Rutland's Case* (*Reports*, 5:98); *Foliamb's Case* (*Reports*, 5:116); *Whelpdale's Case* (*Reports*, 5:120); *Palmer's Case* (*Reports*, 5:128); *Spencer's Case* (*Reports*, 6:10); *Sir George Garson's Case* (*Reports*, 6:77); *Reports*, 7, preface; *Hensloe's Case* (*Reports*, 9:41b); *The Case of Sutton's Hospital* (*Reports*, 10:35); *The Case of the Marshalsea* (*Reports*, 10:77).

opinions" about the answers to such questions.[187] While he did not regard these problems as being inherent in the common law itself, he nevertheless explained them in a way that was foreign to the style of his parliamentary speeches. He attributed them partly to the failure of lawyers to follow Plowden's example in reporting cases,[188] to "late inventions" in conveyancing, and to simple errors and crudities in many legal instruments drafted by both laymen and lawyers.[189] He thought that they were also due to the poor drafting of certain statutes;[190] and to the failure of lawyers and judges to grasp the "true reasons" of earlier cases, to reconcile apparent differences between old authorities, or to settle doubts about important points of common-law doctrine and statutory construction.[191] Later in life, but not in Parliament, he came close to suggesting that defects in the law were also caused by the increasing prosperity of landholders and by increased activity in the land market, which were phenomena that he saw as resulting from the dissolution of the monasteries and the dispersal of monastic lands into "so many several hands."[192] Early in life he had developed the view that by publishing his own highly idiosyncratic and tendentious reports of important judicial decisions he could reconcile seemingly contradictory authorities,[193] explain the true construction of important statutes,[194] and promote true understanding of important common-law rules. And in his eagerness to achieve these goals he had been prepared to shape and even distort the judicial opinions that he professed to be reporting.[195] He also seems to have thought that by attaining these more specific goals, he could accomplish the more general purpose of promoting legal "certainty"[196] and

187. *Reports*, 1, preface.

188. Ibid., 1, preface.

189. Ibid., 1, preface; 2, preface; 10, preface; *Sir Anthony Mildmay's Case* (*Reports*, 6:43). For Coke's advice on how to avoid the first of these problems, see *Institutes*, 1:212a; and *The Lord Mountjoy's Case* (*Reports*, 5:7).

190. *Reports*, 1, preface.

191. Coke did not make a point of noting that previous lawyers and judges had failed to perform these tasks, but he clearly suggested that his own performance of them, in case after case, was a novel achievement.

192. *Institutes*, 4:76–77.

193. See, for example, *The Lord Buckhurst's Case* (*Reports*, 1:2a); *Bothy's Case* (*Reports*, 6:32); *Green's Case* (*Reports*, 6:30); *Ughtred's Case* (*Reports*, 7:74); *Crogate's Case* (*Reports*, 8:67a); *The Six Carpenters' Case* (*Reports*, 8:147b).

194. *Reports*, 3, preface. In the preface to his *Tenth Reports*, for example, Coke noted that five of the cases included in earlier volumes of this work dealt with the interpretation of 32 *Hen*. VIII, *c*. 1 and 34 *Hen*. VIII, *c*. 5.

195. For an illustration of Coke's methods of reporting cases, see Gray, "Bonham's Case." On Coke's work as a law reporter, see also the works cited above in chap. 1, fn. 41.

196. For evidence of the value that Coke placed on "certainty in law" and of his desire to avoid "uncertainty," "doubt," and "confusion," see, for example, *Clayton's Case* (*Reports*, 5:1–2); *Long's Case* (*Reports*, 5:121); *The Lord Mountjoy's Case* (*Reports*, 5:6);

"quietness of possession"[197] and that he could thereby render a great and general service to the commonwealth. In his *Reports*, therefore, he had tried to lay down rules that were "reasonable"[198] and consonant with authority, that would avoid "mischiefs" and "inconveniences,"[199] and that would be certain and conducive to the quietness and repose of property holders.

His proposed parliamentary remedies for legal abuses had the same general objectives as his *Reports*, but their scope was much more limited.

Slingsby's Case (Reports, 5:19); *Coulter's Case (Reports,* 5:31); *Fitzwilliam's Case (Reports,* 6:34); *Sir Anthony Mildmay's Case (Reports,* 6:42–43); and *Blackamore's Case* (*Reports,* 8:158b). See also *Institutes,* 1:152b.

197. See, for example, *Reports,* 1, preface; 4, preface; 6, preface; 9, preface; 10, preface. In his *First Institutes,* he asserted that "certainty" was "the mother of quietness and repose" (p. 34b), and in his report of *Clayton's Case,* he wrote that "uncertainty" was "always the mother of confusion and contention" (*Reports,* 5:2).

198. Appeals to "reason" and/or "reasonableness" are numerous in Coke's writings. See, for example, *The Lord Buckhurst's Case (Reports,* 1:1a); *Albany's Case (Reports,* 1:113); *The Lord Mountjoy's Case (Reports,* 5:6); *Spencer's Case (Reports.* 5:17, 18); *Higgenbottom's Case (Reports,* 5:20); *Foster's Case (Reports,* 5:60); *Gooch's Case (Reports,* 5:61); *Perryman's Case (Reports,* 5:84, 85); *Garnon's Case (Reports,* 5:88); *Penruddock's Case (Reports,* 5:102); *Hungate's Case (Reports,* 5:103–4); *Ferrer's Case (Reports,* 6:8); *Bothy's Case (Reports,* 6:31); *Thetford School Case (Reports,* 8:131a); *Richard Godfrey's Case (Reports,* 11:44); *Institutes,* 1:56b, 59b, 62a, 97b, 140a, 141a, 178a, 183b. In his *First Institutes,* Coke made it clear that he was referring not to "every unlearned man's reason" (p. 62a) or to "every man's natural reason" (p. 97b), but to "artificial and legal reason warranted by authority of law" (p. 62a), which was "an artificial perfection of reason, gotten by long study, observation, and experience" and was "summa ratio" (p. 97b). In none of his writings, however, did he clearly state the criteria by which rules, customs, policies or institutions could be found to be reasonable or unreasonable.

199. Coke used the first of these terms to refer to a "private loss" ("privatum damnum") and the second to refer to a "public evil" ("publicum malum"). He maintained that the law would sooner tolerate the former than the latter ("Lex citius tolerare vult privatum damnum, quam publicum malum."), and, to explain the workings of this principle, he wrote, "it is to be observed, that it is holden for an inconvenience, that any of the maxims of the law should be broken, though a private man suffer loss; for that by infringing of a maxim, not only a general prejudice to many, but in the end a public uncertainty and confusion to all would follow" (*Institutes,* 1:152b; cf. 97a–97b, 246a). In his *Reports,* Coke frequently argued for the validity of his own interpretations of the law on the grounds that they would avoid "mischief(s)" or on the grounds that they would avoid "inconvenience(s)." For examples of the first type of argument, see *Sir William Pelham's Case (Reports,* 1:15); *Henstead's Case (Reports,* 5:11); *Agnes Gore's Case (Reports,* 9:82a); *Robert Mary's Case* (*Reports,* 9:112b); *Magdalen College Case (Reports,* 11:71). For examples of the second type of argument, see *The Case of Alden Woods (Reports,* 1:52); *Capel's Case (Reports,* 1:62); *Corbet's Case (Reports,* 1:87); *The Countess of Rutland's Case (Reports,* 5:26); *Jeffrey's Case (Reports,* 5:68); *Fitzherbert's Case (Reports,* 5:81); *Hoe's Case (Reports,* 5:90); *Semayne's Case (Reports,* 5:92, 93); *Wade's Case (Reports,* 5:115); *Wyat Wyld's Case (Reports,* 8:79b); *Dowman's Case (Reports,* 9:11a); *Mackalley's Case (Reports,* 9:66a); *The Case of the Isle of Ely (Reports,* 10:142); *Richard Liford's Case (Reports,* 11:50). Like Coke's arguments from "reason," these arguments from "mischief" or "inconvenience" rarely include statements of the criteria by which one could determine that a mischief or inconvenience would result from the application of a particular legal rule.

They were concerned almost exclusively with legal administration and procedure. They were meant to protect subjects from costly, endless lawsuits; from the rackets of informers, concealers, and other "lewd" men; and from the decisions of corrupt judges and insufficient jurors. They were also designed to make legal remedies cheaper and to enable subjects to get definitive, conclusive judgments. But Coke's parliamentary remedies for legal abuses had almost nothing to do with the substantive legal rules by which a subject's case would be decided once he got to court. Coke's failure to support the use of parliamentary authority to establish sound, substantive common-law rules clearly reveals something important about his views on legal reforms and requires explanation. He certainly did not deny Parliament's power to declare and/or enact the rules that he had laid down in his *Reports*, even though he may have attributed to the judges great latitude in construing such parliamentary declarations or enactments.[200] He could not have been certain, moreover, that his own legal opinions had gained complete acceptance, particularly after the attacks on his *Reports* associated with his fall in 1616. Finally, it is hard to believe that he attached a higher priority to the remedy of procedural and administrative abuses than to the final resolution of vexing questions about the most central points of the law of real property and obligations. If the foregoing assumptions are correct, then Coke's failure to continue in Parliament the work he had begun in his *Reports* can probably be attributed to three main convictions of his: that statutory codification of English law was neither practicable nor desirable; that questions and doubts about substantive common-law issues could generally be better resolved by the judges than by Parliament;[201] and that however corrupt and inefficient the Stuart court might be, it was still staffed by men who were sufficiently competent and honest to reach sound judicial decisions and thus to continue the work that he himself had begun as a judge and reporter.

Coke's abiding faith in the judges and his conviction that Parliament should not meddle with substantive legal issues imposed certain limits on the sorts of parliamentary legal changes that he could support. But the limited scope of these changes cannot be explained solely by reference to these two beliefs of his. In order to account for his willingness to support

200. In fact, by supporting the monopolies and concealments bills, Coke had, in effect, upheld Parliament's power to make declarations and enactments on highly significant legal issues. There is no comprehensive study of his views on statutory interpretation, but this aspect of his legal thought is touched on in many of the works cited above in chap. 1, fn. 56.

201. Just before expressing his support for attempts to reform the penal statutes, he indicated that he saw no advantages to be gained from "bringing ... the common laws into a better method" (*Reports*, 4, preface). On proposals made during this period for codifying the law, see Shapiro, "Codification."

certain legal changes and not others, one must also consider the identity of his primary constituents; his perception of their interests and of the primary threats to those interests; his common-law training and position within the legal profession, and, perhaps most importantly, his belief in the necessity of legitimating whatever changes he supported in the legal system. His failure to work for certain legal changes that received strong support during the English Revolution was probably due to two facts. These changes would not have benefited and might well have harmed his primary constituents. Moreover, they reflected an ideology that was entirely foreign to him and to those for whom he spoke. Abolition of imprisonment for debt, the revival of communal justice, and the replacement of the common law by a legal system based on scripture were generally supported by social groups for which Coke expressed nothing more than an occasional paternalistic concern. His own critique of the law, by contrast, reflected the concerns of substantial landholders and merchants, even though it may have sometimes resembled the attacks of "meaner" men on the legal system.[202] Coke claimed, of course, to be attacking the grievances of the entire commonwealth and not the private vexations of any particular class of subjects. But while he may have made this claim with the utmost sincerity, there is no reason to suppose that it was objectively true. It still seems reasonable to conclude, with several eminent authorities, that Coke generally equated "the grievances of the commonwealth" with abuses that were "obnoxious to country gentlemen,"[203] with the added proviso that his proposed remedies for these grievances may have sometimes benefited other groups as well. This conclusion is, of course, speculative and can be validated only by a meticulous quantitative analysis of the economic costs of the abuses that he attacked. But in the absence of any such study, the burden of proof should lie with those who would argue that bills designed to reform some abuses in court procedure significantly benefited subjects who were

202. In his study on law reform between 1640 and 1660, Veall divides reformers into five main groups: the Levellers; the Diggers; supporters of the civil law; "moderate reformers" like William Sheppard and Matthew Hale: and others who supported only the most minimal legal reforms (*Law Reform*, pp. 98–99). He then states that "[a]ll these groups except the third were "continuing the tradition of Coke; they all grew out of [*sic*] Coke's innovations and adaptations" (*Law Reform*, p. 99). Although Veall is correct in stressing the similarity between Coke's views on legal change and the views of later "moderate reformers" like Hale, and although the Levellers often appealed to Coke's writings for support (see chap. 1, fn. 46), Coke's views on legal change have little to do with those of either the Diggers or the Levellers. A more satisfactory interpretation of proposals for legal change during the revolutionary period is given by Shapiro, who repeatedly stresses the sharp cleavage between radical and moderate proposals for legal change (see "Law Reform," esp. p. 297).

203. *CD 1621*, "Introduction," 1:3.

never likely to be involved in litigation at Westminster. Even though it is difficult to identify the groups that benefited from such legislation and to specify their distinguishing characteristics, there is no reason to suppose that all subjects profited from these parliamentary remedies equally or at all.

Nevertheless, one cannot simply equate Coke's support for parliamentary legal change with an effort to use parliamentary power to promote certain limited class interests, or with an attempt to modernize or rationalize the law and adapt it to the needs of a particular economic order. For his attitude towards the law was shaped not only by class interest, but also by other factors that served to limit even further the kinds of legal changes that he was willing to bring about by parliamentary action. First of all, Coke spoke not only for more substantial landholders and merchants, but also for common lawyers. Even though the interests of these groups often coincided, they may not always have done so; and it seems likely that Coke showed more tenderness for the interests of the legal profession than other upper-class critics of the legal system. In particular, he was unsympathetic to the view that greater legal certainty could be achieved through the adoption of a formal legal code and a reduction in judicial discretion. In addition, the scope of the legal changes that he supported in Parliament may also have been limited by the need that he felt to establish their legitimacy, particularly because he apparently believed that only a small number of arguments could justify modifications of existing law. When he called for a statutory change in the legal status quo during the 1620s, he was invariably prepared to justify it in only a few ways. He would suggest that his proposal would benefit the commonwealth. And he might further state that it would protect and foster the established rights of subjects, restore the preexisting legal order, leave other legitimate legal interests and powers intact, repress evil, or protect such basic comon-law values as "certainty" and/or "quietness of possession." No legal rule compelled Coke to make any of these claims. Nor would the legal force of his proposal—if it were enacted—depend on their validity. The question arises, therefore, as to what status or function these claims had for Coke. Were they all-purpose rationalizations that he could have used to justify any legal change that he happened to favor? Or did they articulate the standards that he thought should be met by all legal changes? In other words, did the need to justify proposed legislation by making these sorts of claims constitute a significant, if self-imposed, check on Coke's use of parliamentary power to effect legal change? No definitive answer to this question can possibly be given, but several observations about it can be made. To begin with, one must not underestimate Coke's ability to show that the legal changes that he favored would restore the ancient common law and promote the public good. Nor should one assume that because he recognized only a limited number of justifications for legal change, and because these justifications were all highly traditional in character, he was unable to manipulate the law in such a way as to achieve certain social, economic, or political goals. Coke's ability to manipulate the law while covering his tracks is quite well attested. Nevertheless, his exclusive reliance on conventional methods of legitimating legal change may still have served to limit the sorts of legal change that he could endorse. For it necessarily prevented him from using arguments that were later employed to justify more blatant forms of legal modernization or rationalization. Coke was in no position to argue for the destruction of certain preexisting rights or institutions on the grounds that it would promote economic growth or the more efficient use of community resources. Nor was he entirely free from the burden of demonstrating that the legal changes that he supported were morally defensible. As a result, he probably had a harder time promoting parliamentary legal change than his successors in the lower house during the next two centuries.[204]

There were thus certain inherent limits on the sorts of legal changes that Coke could support or conceive of supporting as a member of Parliament during the early 1620s. His efforts to remedy grievances in law had a markedly traditional character and did not constitute straightforward attempts to modernize the law, to maximize the material interests of his constituents, or to adapt the law to the needs of an emergent capitalist order.[205] They grew out of a basically moralistic critique of the English legal system, and this critique did not imply the need for fundamental institutional change. Like many of his contemporaries, Coke shared James I's belief that some members of the commonwealth inevitably grew ever more "crafty in sin" and continually found out new ways of harming their fellows, and that the governors of the kingdom were therefore obliged to be constantly vigilant in purging the realm

204. In *The Transformation of American Law, 1780–1860*, Morton J. Horwitz maintains that it was only in the very late eighteenth century that American lawyers "can be found with some regularity to reason about the social consequences of particular legal rules" (p. 2) and to reassess established legal rules "from a functional or purposive perspective" (p. 3). Although the present study suggests that Coke looked at legal rules in this way with some regularity, it also indicates that he was far less free than later lawyers, judges or legislators to manipulate the law in such a way as to make it an instrument for promoting social and economic change.

205. This study thus attempts to qualify but not reject Christopher Hill's thesis that Coke's actions as a judge, legal writer and member of Parliament continued and extended the process of "adapting" English law "to the needs of a commercial society" (*Intellectual Origins*, p. 256).

of new corruptions and abuses.[206] Nevertheless, while Coke's attitude towards grievances in law remained generally conservative throughout the early 1620s, it had the potentiality to become more innovative, at least politically and constitutionally. All that was required for such a transformation to take place was for him to discover that sin and corruption were not only endemic in the commonwealth as a whole, but that they also pervaded the royal court.

206. In his opening speech to the parliament of 1621, James I said, "[I]t is the king's office to care and procure the making of good laws, for as in corruptissima republica there may be plurimae leges, so it is true [that] ex malis moribus bonae leges oriuntur; and the world, the older it grows, the more sinful it grows and more crafty in sin; and therefore wise princes had need upon all occasions to make new laws because of so many new crimes and abuses that do daily creep into this kingdom which cannot be so well redressed without the calling of a parliament" (CD 1621, 2:5–6). A generation earlier, William Lambarde had also expressed the view that legal problems inevitably arose as the world grew older and more iniquitous (see Lambarde, *Archeion*, p. 18).

Four

"Grievances in Trade"

Legal abuses were not the only grievances of the commonwealth for which Coke hoped to find parliamentary remedies during the early 1620s. He also believed that English economic organization was seriously flawed and that Parliament should play an important role in reforming it, since in his view the promotion of trade was essential to the public good.[1] Although the ongoing trade depression intensified his concern about economic issues in these years, he regarded this crisis as only a symptom of more basic economic problems. While calling for a return to economic principles that he portrayed as traditional parts of the common law, he tried not only to remedy abuses that he blamed on the Jacobean Court, but also to make significant changes in English economic organization. Although he never called for the dismantling of all existing trade regulations, his parliamentary speeches on economic issues during the early 1620s still constitute a sharp, if unsystematic, critique of prevailing English economic organization. And while he ultimately subordinated the concerns voiced in these speeches to more abstract constitutional issues, they nevertheless constitute an important element in his social thought.

In 1620, England had plunged into a severe depression that continued on into 1624 with little improvement. The depression brought with it numerous business failures, much unemployment, many riots of the unemployed, and the serious threat of yet more social disorders.[2] It naturally stimulated intensive debate about its causes and about possible ways of restoring prosperity;[3] and it also provided various interest groups with both a new framework for the discussion of old grievances and a pretext for attacking unfavorable governmental policies and the privileges

1. For references to works that deal with Coke's views on economic organization, see chap. 1, fn. 60.
2. On the depression of the early 1620s, see Friis, *Alderman Cockayne's Project*; Supple, *Commercial Crisis*, esp. pp. 52–72; R. W. K. Hinton, *The Eastland Trade and the Common Weal in the Seventeenth Century*, pp. 12–32; and J. D. Gould, "The Trade Depression of the early 1620s."
3. Supple, *Commercial Crisis*, p. 58. On contemporary responses to the trade crisis, see, in addition to the works cited above in fn. 2, J. D. Gould, "The Trade Crisis of the Early 1620s and English Economic Thought"; J. D. Gould, "The Date of *England's Treasure by Forraign Trade*"; and B. E. Supple, "Thomas Mun and the Commercial Crisis, 1623." For examples of such responses, see Joan Thirsk and J. P. Cooper, eds., *Seventeenth-Century Economic Documents*, pp. 1–32, 210–16, 474–79.

of business rivals.[4] Although the trade crisis did not spark the development of truly novel economic theories, it may have stimulated greater awareness of the close connections between different economic sectors and different geographical régions and more sensitivity to the impact on the commonwealth as a whole of particular economic institutions and governmental actions. In this way it may have facilitated the development of more systematic critiques of English society and government.

One of the principle forums for the discussion of the depression was the House of Commons. Although the Privy Council was actively investigating the crisis throughout this period and considering ways of alleviating it,[5] members of the Commons still wished to inquire into its causes themselves and to consider their own parliamentary remedies for it. They never suggested that Parliament assume sole responsibility for managing the economy, and they did not attach the highest priority to economic issues, but they nevertheless devoted considerable attention to grievances in trade. Members complained about a great variety of economic abuses that they cited as at least indirect causes of the depression. But the longer they debated these abuses, the more ready they were to subsume them under a few general headings and to organize their discussions around three interrelated but separable issues: the general causes of the trade depression, the organization of the wool and cloth trades, and monopolistic trading practices. In 1621, members usually argued that the depression resulted from what they called the "decay of money," the "want of money," or the "loss of treasure," but by 1624 they claimed that it also resulted from the unfavorable "balance of trade," the "overburdening of trade," and the "monopolizing of trade." While their causal analysis of the depression led to many proposals for ending or alleviating it, they gave particular attention to plans to improve the wool and cloth trades, because they believed that England's prosperity depended upon the proper functioning of these economic sectors. In both 1621 and 1624, the Commons also made increasingly coherent complaints about the so-called monopolizing of trade, which they came to regard as a general cause of the depression. In 1621 they generally directed their attacks against royal grants of monopoly rights over the making of certain commodities, but by 1624 they had moved on to condemn a whole range of monopolistic privileges that had diverse legal origins and concerned various types of economic activity.

The Commons's debates on economic issues were thus fairly straightforward, but they expressed conflicts that were less clear-cut than did de-

4. See, for example, the debates discussed below on pp. 105–10 about the privileges of the Merchant Adventurers Company.
5. See Supple, *Commercial Crisis*, pp. 53–54, 66.

bates on legal abuses or constitutional questions. Discussions of economic abuses did not pose simple questions that divided court from country, royalists from parliamentarians, free traders from mercantilists, or representatives of one region from those of another. Instead, they expressed a variety of intricately intertwined conflicts of political interest, regional affiliation, and economic ideology. Moreover, these interconnected conflicts were at least partially masked, because members usually employed the same conventional rhetoric even when they disagreed violently about matters of substantive policy. They mouthed the same platitudes about the virtues of tillage and trade, the evils of monopoly, the virtues of free trade, and the obligation of Parliament to promote the public good and to repress the ruthless pursuit of private gain. Since members could draw very different conclusions from these same bits of traditional wisdom, their substantive positions must be analyzed along with the justifications that they presented for them. It is not enough to know that a particular member supported freedom of trade and/or government of trade. One must also note the context in which he used these terms and try to grasp the sense in which he used them.

Coke was less prominent in debates on economic affairs than in discussion of legal abuses, but his extensive legal, governmental, and administrative experience enabled him to offer informed opinions on important economic issues.[6] He had participated in the council's initial inquiries into the trade crisis[7] and was conversant with the ideas of contemporary economic analysts like Misselden, Malynes, and Mun;[8] and, like others of his generation, he had developed an appreciation for sta-

6. This study confirms Holdsworth's view that Coke was quite knowledgeable about practical economic problems (see *History*, 5:457), rather than the view of Friis, who claims that he tended to "consider all things from the narrow legal point of view" (*Alderman Cockayne's Project*, p. 204). On his experience in dealing with economic problems prior to 1621, see Appendix B.

7. In May 1620 he was appointed to a commission ordered by the council to undertake a general investigation of the decay of the cloth trade (*APC, 1619–21*, pp. 197–98).

8. Misselden's principal works are *Free Trade* (1622) and *The Circle of Commerce* (1623). For a discussion of his views, see Supple, *Commercial Crisis*, pp. 199–201. Malynes wrote two pamphlets during the early 1620s: an answer to Misselden's *Free Trade*, entitled *The Maintenance of Free Trade* (1622); and an answer to Misselden's *Circle of Commerce*, entitled *The Center of the Circle of Commerce* (1623). He had, however, worked out his views on the economy in a treatise published two decades before, entitled *A Treatise of the Canker of England's Commonwealth* (1602). For a discussion of Malynes's views, see Supple, *Commercial Crisis*, pp. 201–11. Mun's views are presented in two pamphlets: *A Discourse of Trade* (1621); and *England's Treasure by Forraign Trade* (1664). For discussions of his views and writings, see Supple, *Commercial Crisis*, pp. 211–19; Supple, "Thomas Mun"; and Gould, "The Date of *England's Treasure*." Parallels between the views of these three writers and the views expressed by Coke in 1621 and 1624 will be mentioned in subsequent notes.

tistical indexes of the economic workings of the commonwealth.[9] Ever since 1593, moreover, he had often joined in the council's investigations of economic issues,[10] and between 1613 and 1621 he had given close attention to three topics that were central to the Commons's debates on trade during the early 1620s: local trade and manufacturing; foreign trade; and wool production, cloth production and cloth exports. Finally, he had been involved in debates on the legality and convenience of monopoly patents for almost three decades, and he was knowledgeable about the organization of trading companies and London livery companies.[11]

Coke's parliamentary speeches reflect his prior experience with economic affairs and contain very full statements about many important economic issues; and they can be used as the basis for reconstructing his views about economic organization and regulation. Nevertheless, they are difficult to interpret partly because of the conventionalized style of the debates in which they were delivered. Coke's more general statements about economic affairs were expressed in such traditional and even hackneyed terms that they often seem indistinguishable from the remarks of those with whom he obviously disagreed. Moreover, they contain no explanation of the crucial distinction that he made between restraints on free trade, which he believed to be illegal and inconvenient, and government of trade, which he regarded as both lawful and beneficial to the commonwealth.[12] Furthermore, his speeches on the economy are also difficult to interpret because, like the writings of Jacobean pamphleteers, they do not express ideas that seem to have been deduced from general principles about economic organization; instead, they contain what often seem like isolated, ad hoc responses to specific economic problems created by the depression.[13] Finally, Coke's ideas about how the economy should be organized are difficult to reconstruct because even his broadest parliamentary statements about economic organization cannot be treated as unambiguous expressions of his views about general economic policy. Like many dicta set forth in common-law arguments and decisions, they were not simple statements of abstract principle from which definite

9. On this intellectual trend, see Lawrence Stone, "Elizabethan Overseas Trade," pp. 30–31. Coke was well acquainted with Burghley and Sir John Popham, two of the men whom Stone identifies as leaders of this trend.

10. On the role played by the Elizabethan Privy Council in economic administration, see Vincent Ponko, Jr., *The Privy Council and the Spirit of Elizabethan Economic Management, 1558–1603*. On the role played by the Jacobean council in managing economic affairs, see Friis, *Alderman Cockayne's Project*; and Supple, *Commercial Crisis*.

11. See Appendix B.

12. See pp. 136–41, below.

13. Supple, *Commercial Crisis*, p. 197.

conclusions could be automatically deduced, but general propositions whose scope, while not precisely demarcated, was often a bit narrower than it seemed. As a result, the significance of these remarks becomes apparent only when they are analyzed in the precise argumentative context in which they were made. In spite of these difficulties, however, an analysis similar to the one made in the previous chapter can lead to certain general conclusions about Coke's views on economic organization. By identifying the economic grievances that he attacked, by analyzing his views about their causes and effects, and by examining the remedies that he proposed for them, one can arrive at some understanding of how he thought the economy should be organized and of what role he wished to assign to different governmental institutions in regulating it.

The grievances in trade that Coke wanted Parliament to remedy in 1621 and 1624 were as numerous as the legal abuses that he was attacking at the same time. The most general grievances that he discussed were the depression itself, England's loss of treasure, excessive taxation on commerce and the monopolization of trade. But his critique of the English economy went beyond these generalities and was focused on many more specific matters that were not merely incidental to the trade crisis but independent subjects of complaint. Among the economic abuses that Coke attacked were specific monopolies on the making, selling, importing, or exporting of various commodities; the corruption of the customs farmers; the engrossing of trade by London at the expense of the outports; the low price of wool; the undervaluation of silver; the recently introduced staple system for internal wool distribution; the harassment of the Cinque Ports by the Merchant Adventurers; the export of specie to Ireland, Scotland, the continent, and the Indies; the monopolistic control of the Welsh cloth trade by the Shrewsbury Drapers; excessive importation, particularly of luxury items like French wines; specific taxes imposed by the crown and the Merchant Adventurers; the exportation of English wool; and the unemployment of "the meaner sort of people."

This list of grievances was quite conventional, as were the arguments by which Coke justified his attacks on particular economic abuses. Nevertheless, some of his contemporaries strongly disagreed with him about specific issues and about what was wrong with English economic organization. They generally concurred with his view that most monopolies were evil, but some disagreed with him about what constituted a monopoly and defended particular restraints on trade that he attacked. Some favored restricting imports in ways that he thought would damage English trade. Some were unconcerned about the growth of London's share of England's exports, while others were more insistent than he was about defending the interests of the outports. No one could countenance the overburdening of trade, but some upheld the legality and convenience of particular impositions. Some defended the Merchant Adventurers' privileges when he attacked them, while others wanted to prune that company's privileges in ways that he opposed. Moreover, some of his contemporaries defended what he called monopolistic restraints on trade as measures for governing trade, while others attacked as "monopolistic" measures that he thought were conducive to "good order" in trade. As a result, an understanding of Coke's position in these debates can emerge only from a study of *both* the general economic propositions that he advanced *and* the positions that he took on particular issues.

One may also attain further insight into his economic views by considering his ideas about the more basic causes of the economic abuses that he attacked. Stated in the most general form, his views about these issues were the following. First, certain individual subjects, informal groups, and corporations were ruthlessly promoting their own private ends at the public's expense. Second, people in positions of power and responsibility were either tolerating these abuses or positively promoting them. Third, certain basic principles of law and conveniency were being either ignored or deliberately flouted. Fourth, regulatory measures that allegedly promoted the public good were often being perverted so as to serve only the interests of a few private men, and the frequency with which this process was occurring raised questions about the value of certain types of economic regulation.

Coke's views about the "effects" of economic grievances also constitute an important part of his critique of English economic organization. He believed that specific abuses in trade, like individual grievances in law, posed particularly serious threats to the realm because of the complex interconnections between different parts of the commonwealth. Many of the same metaphors that he used when discussing the legal system also appear in his speeches on trade; and his use of them in the latter context indicates his fear that economic abuses, like legal ones, could spread and ultimately infect the entire commonwealth, or at least disrupt the workings of its parts. Moreover, he also believed that particular failures to observe certain general principles of economic organization could lead first to further violations of those principles and then to their complete abandonment. Nevertheless, a survey of both the remedies for economic abuses that he supported and the manner in which he promoted them shows that he did not regard these grievances as ultimate threats to the survival of the commonwealth and would not risk the success of entire parliamentary sessions by promoting remedies for them. This fact indicates, in turn, that he retained considerable faith in the ability of other institutions besides Parliament to deal with economic grievances, and that he did not believe that the court as a whole was deliberately following policies that seriously threatened the public good.

Coke's speeches on economic issues fall into three groups: analyses of the causes of the depression, detailed comments on the organization of the wool and cloth trades, and attacks on monopolies. He was convinced that members of Parliament could not find suitable remedies for the depression unless they could discover its causes; and as a result, the search for causes of this crisis is an important theme in his speeches of 1621 and 1624. He never developed a coherent explanation for the crisis and believed that it had many heterogeneous causes; but, like other members, he often attributed it to the decay of money, the unfavorable balance of trade, the overburdening of trade by impositions, and restraints on free trade. Implicit in this causal analysis were a critique of existing English economic institutions and several unformulated but still identifiable ideas about how the economy ought to be organized. These ideas can be identified and described after his views about the trade crisis have been outlined.

In two major speeches delivered in 1621, Coke followed the lead of the most informed economic analysts of his time in arguing that England's loss of coin was a principal cause of the depression. Although he never explained the precise connection between these two phenomena, his conviction that the commonwealth could not prosper without an adequate money supply did not result from any tendency to attach mystical significance to gold and silver but instead grew out of a practical understanding of foreign and domestic trade.[14] Merchants, privy councilors, members of Parliament, and pamphleteers like Mun, Misselden, and Malynes all maintained that the decay of money caused the decay of trade and disagreed with one another only about the reasons for England's lack of money.[15]

The Commons began to debate the decay of money early in 1621. On 6 February John Glanville "moved and proposed three things to the consideration of this honorable assembly . . . concerning the coin of England. 1, Whether there be a want of coin; 2, if so, what be the reasons thereof; 3, that a committee be chosen to think of some remedy." Glanville's motion typified the Commons's debates on both the decay of

---

14. Ibid., pp. 93–94, 198–99 and passim; and Charles Wilson, "Mercantilism." Both writers directly attack Heckscher's contention that the economic writers of this period put "a halo of significance around gold and silver not explained by functions consciously ascribed to them" (Heckscher, *Mercantilism*, 2:261). For other criticisms of Heckscher's views on mercantilism, see D. C. Coleman, ed., *Revisions in Mercantilism*, and the works cited at pp. 210–13.

15. Supple, *Commercial Crisis*, pp. 198–99.

money and the trade depression as a whole in that it reflected two strong convictions: that effective remedies for the current crisis could be found only after a careful analysis of its causes and that the depression was an aberration whose causes could be objectively determined. After establishing the existence of a want of coin, Glanville then listed some of the causes of this problem. Other members added to his list and the Commons ultimately referred the matter to a committee of the whole.[16] Almost three weeks later, on 26 February, they returned to this subject in a major debate opened by their leading analyst of economic problems, Sir Edwin Sandys. After he had explained the disastrous effects of the decay of money on all members of the commonwealth,[17] other members added to the list of causes of the decay of money begun by Glanville on the sixth.[18] By far the most loquacious participant in this debate was Coke, who showed himself to be quite well informed on the subject under discussion. He observed that the issue at hand was next in importance only to "the cause of religion" and noted that the king himself had specifically asked the House to consider it. He then emphasized the vital role that money played in the life of the commonwealth. It was the "measure of all things,"[19] he said, and it was one of the two things that enriched nations (the other being soldiers). Without it, a country could not live in peace or in war[20] and would become a nation of beggars; and if it were scarce, the price of all commodities would fall.[21] He produced statistics to show that much of the silver coined between 1558 and 1619 had been lost[22] and said that the Commons's first task was to discover why and how this loss had occurred, for otherwise they would find no cure for it. He had considered both its causes and the remedies for it, he said, but for the present would only note seven causes that had not been fully discussed. After first declaring that the Goldsmith's conversion of the king's coin into plate was one cause of the decay of money, he went on to express his support for "an act to make it treason" to melt the king's currency. He

16. *CD 1621*, 2:29–31 and n. 16; 4:19; 5:3–4, 439–40; *CJ*, 1:510–11; *P&D*, 1:16–17.

17. *CD 1621*. 2:137; 4:104–5; 5:490, 513–14: 6:10, 297 and n. 34. On this speech, see Heckscher, *Mercantilism*, 2:223.

18. *CD 1621*, 2:138; 4:105–6; 5:515; 6:10, 296; *CJ*, 1:527; *P&D*, 1:95.

19. For similar statements about money, see Malynes, *The Center of the Circle of Commerce*, p. 10.

20. On the tendency of writers in this period to see a close connection between a plentiful money supply and an ability to wage war, see Heckscher, *Mercantilism*, 2:46–47; and E. Lipson, *The Economic History of England*, 3:67–68.

21. For Misselden's most striking statement about the connection between economic well-being and an adequate money supply, see *Free Trade*, p. 28.

22. These statistics may have been taken from papers described in HMC, *Ninth Report*, pt. 2, p. 366. See *CD 1621*, 2:138 and n. 1.

then listed six other reasons for the weakened condition of English currency: "the consumption of gold and silver in vanities by gilding, painting, [and] silvering."; the undervaluation of silver;[23] exportation of silver by the East India Company;[24] England's generally unfavorable trade balance; increases in importation of French wines;[25] and the conversion of gold and silver into thread.[26] On the following day, Coke listed four further causes of the decay of money: the government's failure to enforce the statutes of employments;[27] the importation of Irish cattle;[28] the transportation of money into Scotland; and, finally, a "[w]ant of freedom of trade" that was due to the "overburdening of trade" with impositions.[29]

Three years later Coke advanced a somewhat similar explanation for the continuing economic crisis, but he now treated as its primary cause England's unfavorable trade balance, which was a factor that he had previously cited as merely a contributory cause of the decay of money.[30] As a preface to his motion for a Committee of Trade at the opening of the parliament of 1624, he advanced by far his most coherent analysis of the depression's causes. The "estate of the commonwealth" he said, "grows feeble and faint," and "the spirits and life of it are invaded by 3 especial wants": want of trade, want of money, and "want of labor and employment for the meaner people." These three wants, he suggested, were linked together in a single causal chain. Since trade was the "lifeblood of the state,"[31] its decay led to "the want of money," which was "the sinews of the body of a commonwealth."[32] The want of

23. On this issue, see Supple, *Commercial Crisis*, pp. 14, 31, 164–81, 190, 193, 198–99, 207; Heckscher, *Mercantilism*, 2:223; and Lipson, *History*, 3:75.

24. In 1609, the company had been granted a license to export foreign coin or imported bullion up to the amount of £30,000 in one voyage, and in 1618, this limit was raised to £100,000 (CD 1621, 7:356). On the views of those who claimed that such exports caused the decay of money, see Supple, *Commercial Crisis*, p. 185. In 1621, Thomas Mun wrote his *Discourse of Trade* to rebut this charge against the East India Company.

25. On earlier complaints about the French wine trade, see Lipson, *History*, 3:99.

26. For Coke's speech, see CD 1621, 2:138–39; 5:14, 515; 6:10, 296; CJ, 1:527.

27. On these acts, see Heckscher, *Mercantilism*, 2:141 and n. 22, 252–53; and Lipson, *History*, 1:460–62; 3:70–74. Mun approved of these statutes (see *Discourse of Trade*, p. 54); and in a Privy Council meeting in September 1615, Coke had called for their enforcement (see Spedding, *Bacon*, 12:194–206). For Coke's fullest statement about them, see *Institutes*, 2:741–43.

28. For Coke's views on a bill to bar cattle imports from Ireland, see pp. 96–97.

29. For Coke's speech, see CD 1621, 5:261, 524; 6:15–16, 298. On his other critical remarks about impositions, see pp. 99–100.

30. A change that seems somewhat similar also took place in Mun's views during this same period. See Supple, *Commercial Crisis*, pp. 211–14.

31. Blood was more commonly used as a metaphor for money. See Heckscher, *Mercantilism*, 2:217.

32. On this conventional image, see Heckscher, *Mercantilism*, 2:146–47; and Lipson, *History*, 3:67–68.

money, in turn, led to the want of employment for "the meaner people" and also exacerbated its initial cause, the want of trade, because it produced "a disvaluation of all . . . native commodities." He also noted that the want of labor for the meaner people was "attended with fearful consequences" since it led to disorder.

Coke then considered what he now saw as the "chief cause" of England's economic difficulties, which was the fact that "the importation of foreign commodities . . . did . . . far exceed the exportation of our own." To show how a favorable balance of trade would lead to economic health, he alluded, oddly enough, to the allegedly prosperous age of Edward III and produced statistics to show that in one year of his reign customs on exports exceeded those on imports by over £150,000.[33] He then argued that the unfavorable trade balance of the early 1620s was due to excessive importation, particularly of "trifles and unnecessary commodities," and that this excessive importation was the cause of "the decay of traffic, and consequently of the state and [was] the original of all our want." Coke apparently recognized, however, that the depression had other causes as well, for he urged the House to search out various obstructions and "offensive humours," like "impediment[s] to freedom of trade by patents," that were producing such a great "distemper in the body of the politic state." Once the Commons had discovered these causes, he said, they should apply what he called *"medicina removens"*; that is, they should remove those things that were causing sickness in the body of the realm. He went on to say, however, that *"medicina removens"* would not fully restore the commonwealth to health, and that the Commons would also have to apply *"medicina promovens"*: they would have to encourage trade by applying "some restorative and cordial medicines."[34]

In his speeches on the decay on money and on the unfavorable balance of trade, Coke was apparently arguing, *inter alia*, for restricting imports of certain commodities. Nevertheless, he never supported any bills to this effect and actually opposed the only such measures that the Commons debated in 1621. Some members favored restrictions on the importation of Spanish tobacco, Irish cattle, or foreign grain on the grounds that they would check the decay of money and improve the balance of trade. But such restrictions may have been designed simply to benefit certain interest groups whose members hoped to use the depression

33. On these figures, see Friis, *Alderman Cockayne's Project*, p. 11; Lipson, *History*, 3:90 and n. 5; and Stone, "Elizabethan Overseas Trade," pp. 32–33 and 32 n. 6. They are used in Misselden's *Circle of Commerce* (p. 119).

34. For Coke's speech, see Spring, 1624, ff. 13–14; Erle, 1624, f. 14v; Pym, 1624, f. 5; *CJ*, 1:672, 717.

as a pretext for enacting bills that would otherwise lack general support in Parliament. Because members could therefore support or oppose restrictions on particular imports for various reasons, Coke's views about such measures are difficult to interpret, but his opposition to them still seems noteworthy.[35] On 26 February 1621, Sir Edwin Sandys complained about the importation of tobacco in a debate on the decay of money;[36] and on the next day he succeeded in focusing the Commons's attention on this issue.[37] Needless to say, his position in the Virginia Company gave him a special interest in the tobacco trade, as was shown by the fact that he called for a proclamation or statute to ban not only the importation of Spanish tobacco, but also the growing of tobacco in England.[38] Although Coke often concurred with Sandys, he broke with him on this issue. He asserted that neither of Sandys's two proposals could be legally effected by proclamation—or at least not for any prolonged period—and argued that while Parliament could legally prohibit the planting of tobacco on the grounds that it was an "evil," it would be unreasonable to do so while simultaneously allowing the importation of tobacco from Virginia and the Somers Islands. He also maintained that any such prohibition would infringe on Englishmen's liberty to use their land as they wished, even though he conceded that Parliament could enact such a measure. Although he did not directly oppose a ban on the import of Spanish tobacco, he obviously did not support it either.[39]

Coke also failed to support another alleged remedy for the decay of money and England's unfavorable balance of trade. He had been one of the first to cite the importation of Irish cattle as a cause of the loss of coin,[40] but he later charged that a bill "against importing Irish cattle into England and transporting money into Ireland" struck "at the root of exportation," and he moved to have it committed.[41] His choice of words

---

35. On 6 February, when Coke had cited the conversion of gold and silver bullion into thread as causes of the decay of money (see p. 94, above), he had also complained that the gold and silver threat patent contained a provision that allowed the patentees to bar the importation of gold and silver thread. According to one report of his speech, he said that it was "*unfit*" that "any such thing should be prohibited without act of Parliament; because if we prohibit here, others will do [the same] beyond the seas" (*CJ*, 1:527; my italics). According to another version of his speech, he said, "It's *against law* to forbid the importation of any commodity without a[n act of?] Parliament" (*CD 1621*, 2:139; my italics).
36. *CD 1621*, 2:139.
37. Ibid., 4:113; 5:262–63, 524–25; 6:15–18, 298–99; *P&D*, 1:104–7.
38. *CD 1621*, 5:528. On Sandys's lobbying activities on behalf of the Virginia Company, see Prestwich, *Cranfield*, pp. 305–10; and Zaller, *1621*, pp. 101–2.
39. What appears in the text above is summary of the arguments that Coke made in three separate speeches: (1) *CD 1621*, 5:263, 528; 6:300; (2) *CD 1621*, 2:297; 5:74, 331; *P&D*, 1:263; *CJ*, 1:579; and (3) *CD 1621*, 3:8; 4:236; 5:76; *CJ*, 1:581.
40. See p. 94, above.
41. *CD 1621*, 2:357; *CJ*, 1:615.

probably reflects his general agreement with those who opposed the bill on the grounds that the Irish could not pay for English goods without the money that they received from England in return for their cattle.[42] Similar arguments are found in his speeches against a bill restricting the importation of foreign grain. This measure barred imports of wheat, rye, barley, beans, peas and oats, unless their prices were above certain fixed levels.[43] Its proponents argued that it was "for the maintenance of husbandry to have corn at a reasonable high price. For now farmers complain that they cannot pay their rents, so that farms are fallen twenty in the hundred." The bill's opponents replied, however, that Parliament "must not make a law for the farmer that we may make the poor to curse us," and that "at this time it's unreasonable when we shall set ourselves to praise God for the cheapness and plenty [of corn, that] we go about to bring a dearth upon ourselves." They also argued that "[t]o forbid the importation of corn is to forbid free trade" and that "to restrain the merchant from importing corn is the way to restrain the exporting and vent of our cloth, for much cloth is carried in[to] Danzig [and other parts] from whence few commodities are brought besides corn."[44] This second argument resembled the one used against the Irish cattle bill, and it seems to have convinced Coke. The corn bill, he said, was without precedent, or at least "not usual." Moreover, it would "overthrow navigation" for the reasons given by the bill's opponents; and it would also diminish the king's customs.[45] He therefore moved in a later debate that some other way might be "thought upon for easing the farmer without neglecting the merchant."[46]

While Coke proposed no specific method for stopping the decay of money and restoring a favorable trade balance, he suggested that another general cause of the depression could be easily eliminated if impositions that overburdened trade were simply abolished. In his second speech on the decay of money in 1621, he had argued that excessive impositions contributed to England's loss of treasure and that the overburdening of any commodity damaged "trade and traffic" in general and was "against law." If members of Parliament found any commodity to be overburdened,

---

42. *CD 1621*, 4:252.

43. See the abstract of the bill in Ibid., 2:97.

44. *CD 1621*, 2:178; *CJ*, 1:544–45. On the importance of grain imports, especially rye, to the trade of the Eastland Company, see Hinton, *Eastland Trade*, pp. 38–42; and Supple, *Commercial Crisis*, p. 7.

45. *CD 1621*, 2:379; 3:281 n. 26; 6:163; *P&D*, 1:88, *CJ*, 1:624. Malament claims that Coke opposed the bill because he wished to guarantee an adequate food supply at home ("Coke," p. 1330 n. 48). She does not note his other reasons for disapproving of the bill.

46. *CD 1621*, 3:323 n. 4; 4:381.

he had maintained, they should endeavor to "set a-foot a free trade and traffic," because "the life of trade" was "freedom" and trade was "the life of the commonwealth."[47] Several months later, the Commons returned to the twin issues of freedom of trade and overburdening of trade when Sir Dudley Digges proposed that the port towns farm out their customs on trade to merchants. He maintained that this proposal would increase the king's revenue and enrich the port towns, and he also argued that it would enlarge trade, which was currently suffering from being over-charged.[48] Coke strongly supported Digges's proposal and said that he should be "blessed" for having made it. After citing two statutes to support the dictum that "freedom of trade" was "the life of trade," he railed against the corruption of the current customs farmers. He also declared that Digges's proposal had come at a "fit" time, since the Great Farm of the Customs would run out in six months; and he therefore urged the Commons to reform the customs system while they still had the opportunity to do so.[49]

Nothing ever came of Digges's plan, but in 1624 Coke and other members mounted stronger and more wide-ranging attacks on overbur-dening of trade. They continued to regard it as a restraint on trade and also came to treat it as one of the principal causes of the depression.[50] In 1621, members of the Commons had attacked various individual burdens on trade, like royal impositions on cloth, the Merchant Adventurers' impositions on cloth, the pretermitted customs on cloth, and the imposi-tions levied by the corporate towns. Burdens like these were also occa-sionally cited as particular causes of the decay of money and/or the decay of trade.[51] But the lower house failed to mount a general assault on trade duties until 1624.[52] At the very beginning of this Parliament, the phrase "overburdening of trade" was used as a general heading under which at

47. Ibid., 5:261, 524; 6:298.
48. Ibid., 4:408.
49. Ibid., 2:422–23; 3:395; *P&D*, 2:154.
50. See Nicholas, 1624, f. 27v.
51. For references to debates on these various customs in 1621, see *CD 1621*, I, Index, s.v. "CUSTOMS ON CLOTH, complaints against," "CUSTOMS ON CLOTH, pretermitted, complaints against," and "CORPORATIONS, impositions by." On attacks against the imposi-tions of the Merchant Adventurers, see p. 107, below. On impositions generally, see Norman Scott Brien Gras, *The Early English Customs System*. On the pretermitted customs on cloth, see Friis, *Alderman Cockayne's Project*, pp. 48–50, 218–19, 382, 434–40. For some important comments on the Commons's failure to mount a strong attack on impositions in 1621, see Russell, "Parliamentary History in Perspective," pp. 22–23.
52. During the time between the meeting of the two parliaments, several different groups complained about several sorts of impositions. See Friis, *Alderman Cockayne's Project*, pp. 419, 422; Supple, *Commercial Crisis*, pp. 58–59, 60–61, 66; and Gould, "The Trade Depression." See also Misselden, *Free Trade*, pp. 50, 130–32; and Mun, *England's Treasure*, p. 30.

least six distinct trade duties could be subsumed;[53] and although the house considered each of them individually, members never ceased to regard them as particular instances of a more general grievance.

Coke did not actively discuss the economic impact of excessive duties on trade, but his failure to do so almost certainly reflects a calculated division of labor within the Commons rather than his lack of interest in this issue. While he attempted to show the illegality of various trade burdens, Sandys marshalled economic arguments against them; and it seems reasonable to suppose that Coke concurred with the position of his colleague. On 1 April Coke moved that the House give "some special consideration to those commodities which were over-burdened by impositions" and set a time for a report from the Committee of Trade on this issue.[54] Later that afternoon, Sandys strongly attacked impositions in the committee.[55] In his report to the House the next day, Sandys claimed that while English trade was subject to both "foreign" and "domestical" burdens, the latter were largely responsible for the former, because it was a "general rule" that "when any charge is laid here, it is done in other parts." He then attacked six different domestic burdens on trade: "the customs due by law"; "the subsidy of poundage and tunnage [sic] by act of parliament"; "impositions by royal prerogative"; "the exactions by officers"; the Merchants Adventurers' impositions; "the pretermitted customs"; and the "new" impositions on wine, sugar and grocery. He concluded by reporting the committee's opinion "that if these burthens continue it will bring a consumption upon the whole land and make people unable to support a war; for they do not concern the merchant alone but all the subjects."[56]

Coke gave no comparable speech on the general effects of the over-burdening of trade, but he lent indirect support to Sandys's views by attacking the legality of the pretermitted customs; the new impositions on wines; and, by implication, all impositions levied without parliamentary consent. Moreover, on at least one occasion, he declared that the continuance of such illegal taxes would overthrow not only all trade and commerce, but all property as well. On 6 April and 28 April he argued against the legality of the pretermitted customs;[57] and after the House had formally declared these taxes to be illegal on 3 May he was

---

53. See, for example, the speeches given on 26 February by Sherwill (Nicholas, 1624, ff. 5–5v; Erle, 1624, f. 15) and Sandys (Nicholas, 1624, f. 27).

54. *CJ*, 1:751; Pym, 1624, f. 44v.

55. *CJ*, 1:751; Erle, 1624, ff. 108v–109; Pym, 1624, f. 44v.

56. Pym, 1624, ff. 45v–46v; Erle, 1624, f. 112v; D'Ewes, 1624, f. 96v.

57. For the first of these arguments, see Nicholas, 1624, f. 115v. For the second, see *CJ*, 1:693, 778; D'Ewes, 1624, f. 109v.

ordered to join with Noy and other lawyers in drawing up "the reasons and arguments" that supported the House's position.[58] Although he said nothing about the economic impact of these duties, he presumably concurred with the Committee of Trade's opinion that the pretermitted customs led to four main "mischiefs": "(1) decay of clothing; (2) the abatement of the price of wool; (3) the hinderance of vent [of cloth]; (4) the loss of his majesty's revenue, being more diminished by decrease in number of cloths transported than advanced by this excess of charge."[59] On 9 April, Coke delivered another elaborate speech directly attacking the legality of the "new" impositions and implicitly questioning the validity of all impositions levied under the prerogative. He concluded by warning that if the king were allowed "by his prerogative to raise impositions," and if "this course of imposing" were continued, it would not only overthrow "all commerce and trade"; it would also "destroy all property," for then no man could say that "this or that" was "his." While he did no more than suggest that all such impositions were illegal, he insisted that the House explicitly deny the legality of the new impositions. He declared that just as "color upon color, or metal upon metal is false armory," so "imposition on imposition is worse policy and equity"; and in an obvious reference to Lord Treasurer Middlesex (who was soon to be brought to trial) Coke stated that whoever had advised the king to establish the new impositions was an offender against the commonwealth.[60]

An analysis of Coke's speeches on the general causes of the trade depression leads to four conclusions about his economic thought. First, it shows that he was acquainted with informed economic opinion of his era, that he regarded the English economy as an integrated mechanism, and that he perceived complex causal and functional relationships between different economic phenomena. Second, his remarks about England's excessive exports show that he did not believe that the pursuit of private gain by particular groups, like the East India Company, was necessarily compatible with the public good. Third, his causal analyses of the depression suggest that while he explained this crisis by referring to abstract phenomena like the decay of money, he was prone to blame England's economic plight on particular people and to regard it as the result of human error and immorality. He was apparently undecided,

58. CJ, 1:697, 698; Nicholas, 1624, f. 189v.
59. Pym, 1624, f. 62.
60. Erle, 1624, ff. 127–28; Nicholas, 1624, ff. 130v–31; D'Ewes, 1624, ff. 102–102v; Pym, 1624, f. 56v; Holles, 1624, ff. 126–126v. The attack on Cranfield had begun a few days earlier (see chap. 5), and in this speech, Coke gave indirect support to it by citing two potentially useful precedents: the case of Lyons and Latimer (see Institutes, 2:61); and the case of the duke of Suffolk.

however, about how much blame for the depression could be assigned to the court and obviously had no desire to mount a full-scale assault on royal economic policy or to have Parliament assume general responsibility for running the English economy. Finally, Coke's speeches on the general causes of the depression show that his notion of free trade was far from simple, but that he apparently felt no need to explain it fully to his fellow members. On the one hand, he attacked excessive impositions as restraints on "freedom of trade," and he may have objected on similar grounds to restrictions on particular imports. He also suggested that Englishmen had a general but not absolute right to use their lands as they wished. On the other hand, he clearly supported the enforcement of the statutes of employments and may have favored parliamentary restrictions on luxury imports. The fact that he took such positions suggests that his notion of free trade was a highly subjective one, but even though many of his contemporaries had different conceptions of free trade, Coke never attempted to explain the way in which he defined this crucial term.

Although Coke believed that the decay of money, the unfavorable trade balance, and the overburdening of trade were the principal causes of the depression and ought to be closely scrutinized by Parliament, he was also convinced that the current economic crisis was intimately related to problems in the wool and cloth trades. Like many writers of the early seventeenth century, he believed that the trade, like money, was "the lifeblood of the state,"[61] and that because nine-tenths of England's exports consisted of cloth,[62] this particular trade was "the axis of the commonwealth."[63] He realized that declines in the cloth trade led to widespread unemployment and social disorder,[64] but from this fact he deduced policies that were in keeping not with Elizabethan but with Jacobean economic thought. Whereas Burghley had maintained that "the diminution of clothing in this realm were profitable to the same,"[65] Coke

61. Spring, 1624, f. 13. On the importance that Coke's contemporaries commonly ascribed to trade in promoting economic welfare, see Supple, *Commercial Crisis*, p. 1; and Heckscher, *Mercantilism*, 2:277–81.

62. *CD 1621*, 3:318. For similar estimates by Coke's contemporaries, see *CD 1621*, 5:386; and a passage quoted in Supple, *Commercial Crisis*, p. 6. According to Supple, "perhaps as much as 90 percent and certainly over 75 percent of England's exports were of articles made of wool" (*Commercial Crisis*, p. 6).

63. The phrase is Misselden's (see *Circle of Commerce*, pp. 63–64; cf. *Free Trade*, p. 40). For comments on this prevalent attitude towards the cloth trade, see Supple, *Commercial Crisis*, p. 6.

64. See Supple, *Commercial Crisis*, pp. 6, 9–14, 19–20, 64.

65. *TED*, 2:45. For comments on this passage, see Supple, *Commercial Crisis*, pp. 6–7, 234–35. He argues that Burghley's attitude was expressed in the Cloth Acts of Edward VI and in the Statute of Artificers.

believed that the government should strive to maintain the cloth trade[66] and that it could do so by dealing with the problems that were generally cited by other diagnosticians of the decay of clothing such as "the poor quality of home textiles, the growth of manufacture abroad facilitated by the export of English wool and stimulated by the Cockayne project, the impositions on cloth at home and abroad, . . . the lack of home demand, . . . and the monopolistic character of the trading companies."[67] However much Coke may have praised the virtues of tillage,[68] he fully accepted the central role of wool and cloth in the English economy and therefore gave close attention in 1621 and 1624 to proposals designed to remedy abuses in these two trades.[69] In these two years, the Commons held lengthy debates on four bills of this nature: the bill for free buying and selling of wool, the bill to restore free trade to the Merchants of the Staple, the bill for free trade into all countries, and the bill for free trade in Welsh cloth.[70] In addition, the Commons also discussed various ongoing disputes between the Merchant Adventurers Company and several other groups that were involved in the wool and/or cloth trades. Coke actively participated in all of these debates; and the speeches that he made in them provide additional evidence about his views on economic organization in general and free trade in particular.

The complexity of Coke's views about the wool and cloth trades becomes apparent when one considers his role in the Commons's attacks on the Merchant Adventurers and on the Merchants of the Staple. While he disliked many of the restrictive privileges enjoyed by these two companies, he did not fully support measures aimed at opening the wool and cloth trades to anyone who wished to engage in them. The most hotly debated of these measures was the bill for the free buying and selling of wool.[71] This proposal would have repealed both the Staplers' patent

66. Malament, therefore, may overemphasize the similarities between Coke's economic views and Burghley's (see "Coke," pp. 1322, 1329 and n. 9).

67. Supple, *Commercial Crisis*, pp. 58–59.

68. See *Institutes*, 1:85b; and *Tyrringham's Case* (*Reports*, 4:36b). See also Malament, "Coke," pp. 1332–33 and 1333 n. 72.

69. It is unclear, however, whether Coke believed, as others did (see Supple, *Commercial Crisis*, pp. 236–37), that efforts should be made to expand England's cloth exports beyond their pre-depression level.

70. On proposals made for free trade in James I's first parliament, see Friis, *Alderman Cockayne's Project*, pp. 132–33, 149–56; Theodore K. Rabb, "Sir Edwin Sandys in the Parliament of 1604"; Robert Ashton, "The Parliamentary Agitation for Free Trade in the Opening Years of the Reign of James I"; Theodore K. Rabb, "Free Trade and the Gentry in the Parliament of 1604"; Robert Ashton, "Jacobean Free Trade Again"; Supple, *Commercial Crisis*, pp. 30–31, 237; and Notestein, *1604–1610*, pp. 106–25.

71. The editors of *CD 1621* found no draft of the bill, and its provisions must be reconstructed from the Commons's debates on it. For a brief discussion of the bill, see Bowden, *Wool Trade*, pp. 172–74.

(which gave them an effective monopoly over the internal wool trade) and a clothing statute of 1553, which placed restrictions on the types of people who could buy wool.[72] The bill would also have opened the cloth export trade to people who were not members of the Merchant Adventurers Company.[73] The bill's proponents advanced the following argument in its support. Since wool was the kingdom's chief commodity, its price should be kept as high as conveniently possible. This objective could be best attained by dispersing wool "into the hands of all sorts of manufacturers within this land," and by providing that "every one of his Majesty's subjects being able and willing; to be a merchant, may have free liberty to put his hand to so good a work."[74]

On the bill's first reading in 1621, Coke espoused positions similar to those of its principal supporters. England's trade policy, he argued, should be directed towards three main ends. It should "maintain the merchant," because "he vents our native commodities and brings us home . . . other wares for them"; it should "uphold the clothier," because he "keeps the poor on work"; and it should "keep up the wool at a reasonable price." To this last objective he attached particular importance. He told the House that at least one statute and one fourteenth-century case enunciated the common-law principle that wool prices should be kept high, and he produced statistics to show that a drop of twelve pence in the price of wool per tod could ultimately cost the commonwealth £100,000 per year.[75]

These remarks show that Coke basically supported the bill, but he also had several reservations about it. First, he probably opposed the radical step of throwing open the cloth export trade. Certainly he never supported such a measure in either 1621 or 1624, and his general remarks about the cloth trade show that he was afraid of changing it radically. The commonwealth, he told the House, was like a clock: if one wheel

72. On the Merchants of the Staple under Elizabeth and James I, see Bowden, *Wool Trade*, pp. 80, 115–17, 155–71; and on the new patent that they received in 1615, see pp. 166–71.

73. The bill was also designed to restore the Staplers' right to export cloth, but this part of it and the provision that would have thrown open the cloth trade seem to have been dropped from the bill. Each of these proposals was then incorporated into a separate bill. The first was presented in the bill to restore "the free trade of the Merchants of the Staple for the exportation of cloth and all other manufactures made of wool into parts beyond the seas" (*CD 1621*, 7:225). The second turned into the bill "for free trade into all countries" (*CD 1621*, 4:271). On these two bills, see p. 108.

74. Ibid., 7:574–75; cf. 2:75 n. 6.

75. The statute was 43 *Edw.* III, *c.* 1, and the case was 43 *Lib. Ass., pl.* 38. The case (which is summarized in Holdsworth, *History*, 4:376) had been cited in 1616 by serjeant Richardson to prove that the law's policy was "to maintain the price of wool" (*CD 1621*, 7:497). On Coke's later use of this precedent, see p. 105. For Coke's speech, see *CD 1621*, 2:76–77; 4:50; 5:10–11, 457; 6:77, 431; *CJ*, 1:521; *P&D*, 1:40.

were "out of order all goes wrong."[76] It was therefore exceedingly dangerous, he maintained, to alter "an established course in the vent of a staple commodity"; and as a warning against such alterations, he cited the example of the Cockayne Project and said that in spite of its laudable objectives, it had "so displaced and put the trade out of frame, that it was not yet thoroughly settled."[77] Besides having reservations about opening the cloth export trade, Coke also feared that the free wool bill, as it had been drafted, would allow complete freedom in the domestic wool trade, "take away the trade of clothing" established under the Statute of Artificers, and allow both engrossing and exportation of wool.[78] He probably thought that the trade of clothing had to be maintained so as to ensure the quality of English cloth, and he clearly believed that the exportation of wool had to be strictly limited.

In spite of these reservations, however, Coke supported the bill for free wool. The economic rationale for his support of it lay in the propositions that he had set forth on the bill's first reading and that he restated two days later: "When wools were dearest then was this kingdom richest; [and] scarcity of buyers causes cheapness." His adherence to these two principles led him to condemn two measures that the bill repealed, the clothing statute of 1553, which restricted the number of wool buyers, and the Staplers' patent, which he called "another great harm to our wools." He charged that the latter advanced "one man's private" at the commonwealth's expense and gave a monopoly over the right to buy wool to "the gentle Stapler, alias called a plain ingrosser."[79]

On the bill's final reading Coke also noted that the repeal of the Staplers' patent would benefit the wool converter, who would be allowed to receive his wool directly from the wool jobber;[80] but he spent most of his time developing his previous point about the importance of maintain-

76. This analogy was, of course, conventional and was used both by Malynes (*Maintenance of Free Trade*, p. 6) and by the author of the *Discourse of the Common Weal of this Realm of England*, p. 93. On the use of such analogies by writers on the commonwealth, see Ferguson, *The Articulate Citizen*, pp. 279, 293, 349, 368, 371 and passim; and Jones, *Tudor Commonwealth*, p. 196. Both writers suggest that an author's use of mechanical analogies, rather than organic ones, is an index of his more modern outlook. Coke, however, seems to have used the two types of analogy interchangeably.

77. Similar views about the project were expressed by Misselden (*Free Trade*, p. 41). The view that the project had contributed to the depression was expressed frequently, both in and out of Parliament (see *CD 1621*, 2:213, 290; 5:262; 6:60–61; and Supple, *Commercial Crisis*, p. 60 and n. 1). On Coke's initial support for the project, see Appendix B.

78. For comments on Coke's generally favorable view of the Statute of Artificers, see Malament, "Coke," pp. 1335–38 and p. 123, below. On his views concerning forestalling and engrossing, see Malament, "Coke," pp. 1333–34 and p. 111, below. On his opposition to the exportation of wool, see pp. 113–14, below.

79. For this speech, see *CD 1621*, 4:65; 5:468, 504; 6:171, 290.

80. On this issue, see Bowden, *Wool Trade*, pp. 171–72.

ing a high price for wool. "It is good," he said, "to keep our main commodities at a good rate, for that is according to the common law which [is] grounded upon such a rock of reason that it varies not as Act of Parliament." Coke was thus conferring a very special status on the proposition that wool prices should be kept high. He was not just presenting it to the House as a wise statement of economic policy; he was treating it as a main point, or maxim, of common law that had the same status as the principle that all land should be fee simple. By doing so, he was not only indicating that Parliament need not look outside the common law to find fundamental principles of economic policy, he was also expressing the opinion that Parliament should sooner tolerate particular "mischiefs" or declare a royal patent void than deviate from the principle that wool prices should be kept high. To prove that the policy of the common law with respect to wool prices was as he had stated it, he again summarized the case from the Book of Assizes that he had previously cited. In Edward III's reign, he said, "one [was] fined and ransomed for beating down the price of wool by reporting there would be wars, and had this judgement by the common law."[81] He then derived three main conclusions from the common-law principle that the price of wool should be kept high. First, since the statute of 1553 indirectly contravened this principle by limiting the number of wool buyers, it had to be "suspect," as was borne out by the fact that it provided for its own repeal by royal proclamation. Second, because the Staplers' patent also overthrew this same principle, it was certainly inconvenient if not actually illegal. Finally, since the bill for free buying and selling of wool upheld and restored a fundamental point of the common law, it should be speedily enacted.[82]

Coke's speeches on the free wool bill suggest that he opposed the Staplers more vehemently than the Merchant Adventurers and supported free trade in wool more fully than free trade in cloth. His other parliamentary speeches from the 1620s show, however, that he did not always favor the Merchant Adventurers Company and sometimes supported its critics and competitors. He criticized it for encroaching on the privileges of the Cinque Ports and argued that its impositions on cloth exports were illegal. Nevertheless, he never supported overthrowing all its privileges, and, unlike other members of the Commons, he never directly attacked it as a monopoly. His sharpest attacks on the company were made not in defense of every Englishman's right to export cloth, but in support of the privileges of the Cinque Ports, which was another legally constituted interest group that was involved in a bitter dispute with the Merchant

81. For this case, see fn. 75, above.
82. *CD 1621*, 2:293–94; 3:319–20; 4:378–79; 5:177; 6:170–71; *CJ*, 1:627–28.

Adventurers. When the company had received its new charter in 1617, it had also received the power to check interloping in the cloth export trade and soon began to use it to prosecute citizens of the Cinque Ports. In 1619 the ports complained to the Privy Council that the company was depriving them of their rightful privileges, but the council was reluctant to intervene in the dispute. A committee, on which Coke served, was ordered to investigate the dispute, but it took no action. The council later ordered the attorney and the solicitor to look into the matter, but they, too, did nothing. Finally, in 1621, the ports petitioned the Commons about their grievances.[83]

When the Commons debated the ports' petition in 1621, Sir Edwin Sandys (who sat for one of the ports) attacked the Merchant Adventurers and warned that the decay of the ports would seriously harm the commonwealth.[84] Coke then supported the ports even more vehemently than Sandys. They were "the gates of the realm," he said, and "if the gates be not well kept the kingdom cannot be in safety"; and it was for this reason, he claimed, that they had always been accorded great respect in law. He then charged that the company had illegally harassed citizens of the ports by imprisoning them, confiscating their goods, and examining them before commencing suits against them. He also suggested that this dispute raised the broader and more fundamental issue of London's increasing control over trade at the expense of the outports. "I love London well," he said. "I would have London . . . to subsist in all prosperity." But "other places as well as London must be provided for." For if the outports were to decay, then even London could not survive and the whole commonwealth would suffer. To emphasize this point, he then likened London to the head of the body of the commonwealth and claimed that if all humors were drawn to the head, "the body will calescere and apoplexia sequitur."[85] Two days later, Coke presented slightly different arguments on the ports' behalf. He stated that their claim to free trade was rea-

83. On the dispute between the Cinque Ports and the Merchant Adventurers, see Friis, *Alderman Cockayne's Project*, pp. 366–67, 369, 371, 373–75. On Coke's role in the council's investigations of the dispute, see Appendix B. For the Ports' petition to the parliament of 1621, see CD 1621, 7:593–96; 4:229.

84. Ibid., 3:245; 2:364; 5:162–63; 6:154; CJ, 1:520; P&D, 2:66. For brief notes on this speech, see Friis, *Alderman Cockayne's Project*, pp. 407–8; and Zaller, *1621*, p. 29. On Sandys's election to the parliament of 1621 as a burgess for Dover, see John K. Gruenfelder, "The Lord Wardens and Elections, 1604–1628," p. 14.

85. CD 1621, 3:246–47; 2:364; 4:338–39; 5:62–63; 6:155; CJ, 1:620; P&D, 2:67. On the question of whether the outports' share of England's export trade was really declining in this period, see F. J. Fisher, "London's Export Trade in the Early Seventeenth Century"; W. B. Stephens, "The Cloth Exports of the Provincial Ports, 1600–1640"; J. D. Gould, "Cloth Exports, 1600–1640"; and W. B. Stephens, "Further Observations on English Cloth Exports, 1600–1640."

sonable, was supported by law and precedent, and was necessitated by their obligation to maintain ships for the crown; and he implied that the company would need very strong arguments to defeat such a claim. Against the company's argument that its right to check interloping and its power to maintain government in trade should override whatever trading privileges the ports might possess, Coke made two counterarguments. First, he noted that the statute of 1521 provided that "for 10 marks any man might freely trade." Second, he argued that while the merchants of the ports had to be under "government," they did not have to be subject to the company's "government" or to the fines, extortions, and contributions which that "government" demanded.[86]

Coke also attacked the legality of the impositions on cloth exports that the Merchant Adventurers Company had been empowered to collect as a means of defraying the cost of buying back its charter in 1617.[87] The Commons cited these impositions in 1621 as a cause of the decay of money and trade[88] but did not attack them systematically until 1624, when they established that the overburdening of trade was one of the three main causes of the depression.[89] In early April, Sandys listed the company's impositions as one of the six principal burdens on trade,[90] and after his Committee of Trade had investigated them more thoroughly, he advised the House "to command, desire, or require" the company to "lay [them] down."[91] Some members "doubted" whether the Commons had the power to do this, and Sir George More therefore moved that they merely "advise" the company to discontinue the impositions.[92] Coke strongly opposed More's motion. He said that it was "unlawful for one subject to impose upon another" and moved that the House declare the company's impositions to be "against law." If the company persisted in levying them, he said, it would then do so at its peril. His motion carried, and the impositions were "declared unlawful and unjust and a grievance and to be taken away."[93]

Although Coke denounced the Merchant Adventurers' impositions and their harassment of the Cinque Ports, he was not one of those who wished to overthrow the company completely or to severely curtail its

86. *CD 1621*, 3:276; 2:375–77; 4:356; 5:378; *P&D*, 2:84–85. For a statement of Coke's about the legal status of the Cinque Ports, see *Institutes*, 4:222–24.

87. On these impositions, see Supple, *Commercial Crisis*, pp. 49, 60.

88. *CD 1621*, 2:215; 3:246; 4:150, 272; 5:351.

89. See pp. 98–99.

90. Pym, 1624, ff. 45v–46.

91. Holles, 1624, f. 129v; Pym, 1624, ff. 84v–85; D'Ewes, 1624, ff. 111–111v; Nicholas, 1624, ff. 184–86.

92. Pym, 1624, f. 85v.

93. Holles, 1624, f. 139v; Pym, 1624, f. 85v.

privileges. In 1621 the Commons debated two bills designed to limit the company's privileges: the bill to restore free trade to the Merchants of the Staple and the bill for free trade into all countries. Coke never supported the latter bill and expressed strong reservations about the former. Since the bill for free trade into all countries would have weakened and perhaps destroyed the exclusive privileges of all foreign trading companies, it naturally provoked great debate in the House.[94] The views of its strongest supporters were well expressed by Mr. Neale of Dartmouth, who declared that "[n]either law nor order ever did heretofore restrain the freedom of subjects in matter of trade," and that all restraints on trade had "grown from mere monopoly."[95] Coke is not recorded as having spoken in this debate, but his views on the bill restoring free trade to the Staplers suggest that he probably opposed the bill for free trade into all countries. The Staplers' bill was part of a unified program for the freeing of the cloth trade that included the bill for free trade into all countries and the bill for the free buying and selling of wool. Its supporters claimed that it would be "convenient and profitable for the common weal," because it would enhance wool prices and provide more work for the people.[96] Although these contentions resembled Coke's own arguments for the free wool bill, they did not induce him to support the Staplers' bill very forcefully. Sir Henry Poole claimed that the bill's passage would help to alleviate the depression. Neale charged that the "ingrossing" of the cloth trade "into a few hands" of the Merchant Adventurers was "very prejudicious" to the commonwealth. And Sir Robert Phelips said that it was "fit that this monopoly of the Merchant Adventurers be by this act regulated."[97] Coke, however, supported the bill much more cautiously. He warned the House not to do anything that might hinder the vent of cloth and again cited the failure of the Cockayne project as a warning against the institution of plausible schemes to improve trade. Moreover, in words that almost echoed the Merchant Adventurers' "reasons" against the bill, Coke told the Commons not to overthrow the "old course" of the cloth trade before making sure that the new course they instituted would remedy the defects of the old and would not introduce new defects besides.[98]

Neither the bill for free trade into all countries nor the Staplers' bill was introduced into the parliament of 1624, but this parliament attacked

94. For abstracts of the bill, see CD 1621, 4:271–72; 5:109, 267; 3:105. For a note on the bill, see Friis, *Alderman Cockayne's Project*, p. 402.
95. CD 1621, 3:106; 6:107.
96. Ibid., 7:225, 226. For arguments against the bill, see CD 1621, 7:231–38.
97. Ibid., 3:189; 2:352.
98. Ibid., 5:150; 3:190.

the Merchant Adventurers Company even more sharply than the previous one had and ultimately curtailed some of its exclusive privileges. Moreover, some of the company's critics in the Commons went on to condemn other trading companies and restrictive trading companies in general. How Coke viewed the "free trade" movement of 1624 is difficult to establish. Although he obviously favored parts of it, he was still very reluctant to support radical changes in the organization of the cloth trade, and he never directly attacked trading companies for being monopolistic.

Early in 1624, Sandys identified "the monopolizing . . . or restraining of trade" as one of the three main causes of the depression.[99] Neale claimed that "the patents procured for the bringing [of] trade into [a] few men's hands" were causes of the depression; and, as examples of such patents, he mentioned the Merchant Adventurers' charter, which restrained the "vent of cloth," and "that of the Eastland Company, by which means those in the west parts cannot have masts, pitch, and tar."[100] Two days later, when the Committee of Trade debated "the general causes of the decay of trade," Sir John Eliot moved "to consider first that which concerns monopolies." "[F]or it cannot there be," he said, "that the great business of trade can be discharged by a few, and usually those men's appetites that engross all trade into their hands exceed the strength of their stomachs to digest it well and that makes them surfeit and us suffer." Neale then stated flatly that "[t]he principal cause of the decay of trade is the imprisoning of it," and charged that "the principal cause of the decay of the price of wool is that there [are] no buyers and the Merchant Adventurers are the cause by their not buying of cloths and restraining of others from trading and transporting cloths."[101]

During the following months, several members proposed curtailing the Merchant Adventurers' privileges in various ways. Some called for the abolition of their rule against admitting nonmerchants and/or a reduction in their admission fees. Others wished to open the entire cloth export trade, or at least the trade in dyed and dressed cloth,[102] and it was also proposed that if the company failed to buy up all cloth at Blackwell Hall, others be permitted to buy there.[103] The Commons gave little attention to proposals concerning admission to the company, but in early

---

99. Nicholas, 1624, f. 27v.
100. Erle, 1624, ff. 14v–15; Pym, 1624, f. 5. On 10 March the Commons ordered that the patents of these two companies be brought into the House (Erle, 1624, f. 66v; Nicholas, 1624, f. 62; Pym, 1624, f. 23v).
101. Nicholas, 1624, ff. 26–27.
102. See D'Ewes, 1624, f. 93; Nicholas, 1624, ff. 127v–128.
103. This proposal was put forward as a proviso to the bill for the true making of woolen cloth. See p. 110, below.

May they held a long debate about whether "the trade of dyed and dressed cloths should be left or taken from the Merchant Adventurers." The company's supporters repeatedly stressed the need for "government" in the cloth trade and claimed that only the Merchant Adventurers could provide it. One of them argued that the company's valuable trading privileges on the continent would "all be lost if the trade be thrown open and no government [be kept] among merchants." Another warned that "if we labor too much to prune this company, we may destroy [it] and so bring a great mischief to the kingdom." The company's opponents, on the other hand, wished to open the trade in dyed and dressed cloths and to limit severely the company's power to regulate the affairs of its members.[104] In this debate, Coke seems to have held what was called the "middle" opinion.[105] He said only that he favored opening the trade in dyed and dressed cloths, and without mentioning any of the more radical proposals for curtailing the Merchant Adventurers' privileges, he moved that this proposal be put to the question.[106] On the issue of liberalizing the rules for buying cloth at Blackwell Hall, Coke again failed to side with the company's strongest opponents. In April, the bill for the true making of woolen cloth was reported from committee with a proviso that after Friday noon "any man" might "buy [cloth] freely at Blackwell Hall and carry it where he will."[107] Coke, who had been on the committee for the bill,[108] immediately moved that the proviso be withdrawn. He again warned of the dangers of innovation in the cloth trade by citing not only the usual example of the Cockayne project, but also the unsuccessful project of 1586–87 "for the free venting of cloth."[109]

In spite of his failure to join with the Commons's most extreme opponents of the Merchant Adventurers' restrictive privileges, Coke repeatedly presented himself in the Commons as a champion of free trade. On the first reading of a bill requiring Norwich clothiers to use only Norfolk wool, he attacked it for creating a "monopoly" and had it cast out of the House.[110] His most extreme diatribes against restraints on trade were made in the 1621 debates on the bill for free trade in Welsh

104. Nicholas, 1624, ff. 192v, 193v–194; Pym, 1624, f. 88v.
105. Pym, 1624, f. 89.
106. CJ, 1:689, 784.
107. Erle, 1624, f. 151v; Pym, 1624, ff. 73v–74.
108. CJ, 1:679, 730.
109. Holland, 1624, I, f. 40v; Pym, 1624, f. 73v; Erle, 1624, f. 151v. On the so-called free trade experiment of 1586 to which Coke was referring, see J. D. Gould, "The Crisis in the Export Trade, 1586–1587"; and George Unwin, "The Merchant Adventurers' Company in the Reign of Elizabeth," pp. 201–4. The proviso was ultimately withdrawn.
110. D'Ewes, 1624, f. 106v; CJ, 1:689, 773. On this bill, see Bowden, Wool Trade, pp. 64–65 and 65 n. 3. For the council's proceedings relating to the Norfolk wool trade, see APC, 1616–17, pp. 49, 252–53, 316; APC, 1621–23, pp. 295–96, 329, 445–46, 486–88.

cloth.[111] But an analysis of these debates shows that his support of free trade did not lead him to oppose all regulation of the wool and cloth trades and again raises the question of how he distinguished between unlawful restraints on trade and legitimate and necessary government of trade. As originally drafted, the Welsh cloth bill provided that "all merchants, native and foreign, were to be allowed to buy cloth anywhere in Wales" and to export it after paying customs to the crown.[112] Although the latter provision was quickly dropped, a compromise bill allowing freedom of export was eventually worked out, but it permitted free export "only after the cloth had been entirely finished at home."[113] Although the purpose of the bill was to end the quasi monopoly enjoyed by the Shrewsbury Drapers over the transportation of Welsh cloth to London,[114] it did not provide for complete freedom of trade. It prohibited the export of unfinished cloth and did nothing to check the French Company's effective monopoly on the export of Welsh cloth.[115] This last issue was never mentioned in the Commons, but it was of great concern to the drapers, who hoped that if they failed to block the bill entirely they might at least gain the right to export Welsh cloth.[116] Coke dominated the Commons's most important debate on this bill, but while he claimed that it would further freedom of trade, he never alluded either to the French Company's monopoly or the bill's prohibition on the export of unfinished Welsh cloth.

On the bill's third reading in 1621, the two burgesses for Shrewsbury tried to block it by raising four objections to it. They claimed that it would overthrow a statute specifying official dimensions for Welsh cloth, and allow forestalling and/or ingrossing. They also said that it would overthrow the charter of Shrewsbury and overturn the customs of the corporate towns by enabling Welsh clothiers to sell their cloth in any English town.[117] The main task of refuting these objections fell to Coke, who answered the last three of them point by point. He was "against forestallers," he said, for they were oppressors of the people and enemies

---

111. On this bill, see T. C. Mendenhall, *The Shrewsbury Drapers and the Welsh Wool Trade in the Sixteenth and Seventeenth Centuries*, pp. 162–77, 237–38; and on Coke's role in promoting it, p. 198.

112. Ibid., p. 171; cf. pp. 237–8; and *CD 1621*, 7:70–2.

113. Mendenhall, *Shrewsbury Drapers*, pp. 174–75. Later, the bill was further amended so as to provide that "anyone exporting unfinished cloth should forfeit its value" (*Shrewsbury Drapers*, p. 176).

114. See Mendenhall, *Shrewsbury Drapers*, pp. 169–70, 173.

115. On this point, see Mendenhall, *Shrewsbury Drapers*, p. 63.

116. Ibid., pp. 180–88 passim.

117. *CD 1621*, 3:66; 4:252; 6:94; *CJ*, 1:589. The statute that they cited was 34 *Hen.* VIII, *c.* 11. Mendenhall's account of this debate differs considerably from the one given here (see *Shrewsbury Drapers*, pp. 176–77).

of the commonwealth, but he denied that the bill legalized their activities.[118] He also presented two arguments to show that the bill would not contravene the custom of foreign bought and foreign sold. First, he pointed out that the Welsh clothiers would not actually violate this custom even if they were permitted to do so, because they would not find it profitable to retail their cloth in English town markets. Second, he noted that because the bill allowed the Welsh to sell cloth only to those who could "lawfully" buy it, it would not overthrow any borough customs; but he suggested that some borough customs were already illegal at common law.[119]

To the argument that the bill would overthrow the charter of Shrewsbury, Coke made a longer reply. If this town were to suffer from the bill, he maintained, it was only because it enjoyed monopolistic privileges. He declared that monopolies that restrained trades were "to be taken away" not only when they benefited individuals, but also when they benefited towns, for monopolies were "to be detested" and the "common good" was "to be preferred before any particular town." He also rejected the claim that monopolies of this sort could be justified by "reason of state" and said that such arguments were the most "desperate" ones that could be used "to put a man from the right way."[120] From this attack on private and corporate monopolies, Coke moved on to the general subject of free trade. After intoning the maxim that freedom of trade was the life of trade and trade was the life of England, he observed that "where the merchant may trade most freely and gain most, [there] will he trade most"; and then he warned that unless English merchants were given a chance of "reasonable gain," they would simply become usurers. To demonstrate the connection between free trade and prosperity, he then cited the example of the Dutch, who, he said, were now engrossing "all the trade of Christendom." Unlike the English, they had many staple towns and were not "troubled with impositions to burden trade nor monopolies to restrain it." England, he argued, should follow their example and would prosper more without impositions, monopolies, and contradictory regulatory statutes. He even went so far as to say that it would be better to have "no penal laws" at all than to have "so many contrary

---

118. For a reference to a brief note on Coke's attitude towards forestalling, see fn. 78, above. For a statement of his own on this subject, see *Institutes*, 3:195–97.

119. In *The Chamberlain of London's Case*, the court ruled, according to Coke, that customs of London "which are contrary or repugnant to the laws or statutes of the realm are void and of no effect" (*Reports*, 5:63–64).

120. Three days earlier, Coke had made a similar point in a debate on the salmon and lobster patent (see *CD 1621*, 5:89–90). On the use of arguments from "reason of state" in this period, see Berkowitz, "Reason of State."

to each other."[121] In conclusion, he maintained that both the ancient wisdom of Parliament and the ancient wisdom of the law supported his views, and he then asserted that in at least eight statutes, and indeed in "all acts of Parliament," "freedom of trade" was held to be "the life of trade."[122] Because the present bill gave freedom of trade, he concluded, it was " a good bill."[123]

In this speech, Coke had elevated to the status of a common-law maxim, or main point of common law, the principle that trade should be free. By doing so, he not only indicated that he attached the highest importance to the maintenance of this principle, he also provided a *legal* basis for arguing that a charter of incorporation that contravened this principle was void. In other words, he was treating as a principle of law what might otherwise have been considered as a mere statement of desirable economic policy. But while he thus attached great importance to the principle that trade should be free, his failure to attack the Welsh cloth bill for banning the export of unfinished cloth shows once again that he did not equate free trade with an absence of governmental regulation and that he somehow distinguished between restraints on trade and government of trade. The same conclusions emerge even more clearly from an examination of his views on the exportation of English wool. Like many of his contemporaries, both in and out of Parliament, Coke believed in the necessity of banning wool exports. He did so because he thought—quite correctly—that exported English wool would be used by England's competitors in the cloth trade, who could then make inroads into England's cloth markets abroad.[124] He had criticized the free wool bill for allowing the transportation of wool out of Ireland and Scotland and had also attacked the Staplers' patent for giving them "liberty to transport wools at such times as the council of state should allow them."[125] He also gave strong support in both 1621 and 1624 to a bill "to prohibit the transportation of wool, yarn made of wool, and fuller's earth into

121. He made a similar point in a conference with the Lords about the informers bill (see *CD 1621*, 3:39). Similar views about the penal laws regulating the clothing industry were held by Misselden (*Circle of Commerce*, p. 136) and by the trade commission of 1622 (see Lipson, *History*, 3:319).

122. The only citation recorded by the diarists is 27 *Edw.* III, *st.* 2, *cc.* 2–4. The other statutes that Coke apparently cited may have been the ones to which he referred in his *Third Institutes* (at p. 181) to prove that monopolies were "against the ancient and fundamental laws of the realm."

123. The bill was ultimately enacted as 21 *Jac.* I, *c.* 9 (*SR*, 4, pt. 2, pp. 1218–19). For Coke's speech, see *CD 1621*, 2:317–18; 3:66; 4:252; 5:93–94, 346; 6:94; *CJ*, 1:589.

124. For comments on this commonly held view, see Supple, *Commercial Crisis*, p. 60 and n. 1; and Lipson, *History*, 3:307–8. For expressions of it in the Parliament of 1621, see, for example, *CD 1621*, 2:214; 4:97; and 6:431.

125. *CD 1621*, 5:468.

foreign parts."[126] When the bill was debated in 1621, Sir Edwin Sandys attacked it because it made violation of its provisions a felony. Such a punishment, he declared, was "disproportionate and unjust."[127] Coke replied that "[if] the stealing of a sheep be felony, much more the robbing of a whole state by carrying out wool or fulling earth."[128] In 1624 he again defended the bill's severity after one member suggested that a proviso be added to it stating that "no man shall be questioned by this law but within a certain time." Coke replied that former laws of this sort had included no such provisos and that there was "now more need to punish exporters of wool than ever was," and he therefore wished to have no more provisos to the bill than were in former laws.[129]

An examination of Coke's parliamentary speeches on the causes of the trade depression and the organization of the wool and cloth trades leads to the following conclusions about his views on the economy. First, it shows that while he was deeply concerned about England's grievances in trade, he did not attach the highest priority to finding parliamentary remedies for them. Second, although his speeches on these issues clearly reveal his dissatisfaction with Jacobean economic policies, they show that he blamed England's economic problems not only on the court but also on privileged interest groups like the Merchant Adventurers, the Staplers, the East India Company, and the borough of Shrewsbury, as well as on various unspecified groups or individuals who ignored the public good by exporting wool or cloth of poor quality or who created demand for useless luxuries imported from abroad. Third, an analysis of these speeches also seems to clarify our understanding of what he meant by "freedom of trade." It shows that he regarded free trade not only as a

126. The exportation of wool was prohibited by 5&6 *Edw*. VI, *c*. 7, which would have been repealed by the bill for the free buying and selling of wool. On 13 March Mr. Berkeley noted that if this bill were to be enacted, then "wools" could be exported "without gainsaying" (*CD 1621*, 2:216). To meet this difficulty, a bill was introduced "to prohibit the transportation of wool . . . into foreign parts" (*CD 1621*, 5:337; 3:119). Violation of the act was to constitute felony, and accessories—like the masters of ships, searchers, and other officers—would come under the penalty of the act (*CD 1621*, 5:226). The bill stated that these commodities were "the riches of the kingdom," that "they can not beyond the seas make cloth without these natural blessings," and that "many poor are set on work" by the making of cloth (from the abstract of the bill in *CD 1621*, 5:114).

127. Sandys argued that "where a thing is malum per se the magistrate may extend the punishment to the measure of the offence; but when it is but malum prohibited it is not lawful to take away the life of a man." For his speech, see *CD 1621*, 4:276; 5:114–15; *CJ* 1:596; *P&D*, 1:354.

128. In his reply to Sandys, Coke discussed "the jurisdiction of the Parliament to make felonies." He said that things *malum in se* were felony by common law, but he denied that only things *malum in se* could be made felony. For his speech, see *CD 1621*, 5:115; 4:276.

129. Nicholas, 1624, ff. 178–178v. Coke expressed similar views about the exportation of wool and a few other commodities in *Institutes*, 3:95–97.

legal right of sorts, but also as a sound principle of economic policy that was, in some sense or other, part of the common law. It also demonstrates, however, that he regarded free trade and government of trade as complementary, and not antithetical, principles of economic policy. Nevertheless, though he believed that absolute economic freedom could be and should be restrained in the name of government of trade, he also recognized that certain groups, like the Merchant Adventurers, fallaciously claimed to be providing good order for trade when they were actually restraining it, promoting their own private interest, and undermining the public good. He must have realized, therefore, that there was no generally recognized way of distinguishing between government of trade and restraint of trade. But, oddly enough, he never urged Parliament to give statutory authority to the distinctions that he himself made. Furthermore, although he objected strongly to certain restraints that the crown had imposed on trade, his attacks of the early 1620s on royal economic policies and practices were much less forceful, embittered or combative than his attacks of the later 1620s on what he regarded as the court's attempts to curtail the liberties of English subjects. Finally, his speeches on the causes of the depression and on the wool and cloth trades clarify his ideas about the proper role of Parliament in remedying the economic grievances of the commonwealth. First, they suggest that he regarded Parliament as an appropriate and perhaps ideal forum for the discussion of economic grievances, but not as a body that should exercise total, or even extensive, control over English economic policy. These speeches also express his conviction that Parliament's traditional powers were adequate to the task that he thought this body should perform in dealing with economic affairs.

Coke's speeches on monopolies articulate ideas that are generally consistent with the ones discussed above, but these speeches also suggest that our picture of his economic thought should be slightly modified in three main ways.[130] First, Coke thought that he could not successfully

130. Coke's printed works contain three main passages on monopolies: (1) *Institutes*, 2:48; (2) *Institutes*, 3:181–87; and (3) *The Case of Monopolies* (also known as *Darcy v. Allen*) (*Reports*, 11:84–88; for other reports of the case, see *The English Reports*, 72:830–32; and 74:1131–41). The Statute of Monopolies (21 *Jac.* I, *c*. 3) has often been treated as a fairly direct expression of Coke's views on monopolies (see Wagner, "Coke," p. 35; Malament, "Coke," p. 1353; and Little, *Religion, Order, and Law*, pp. 215–17); but it will be shown below (see. p. 129) that this act differed markedly from Coke's original draft bill against monopolies. Also relevant to a discussion of Coke's ideas about monopolies are his reports of cases concerning the scope of the Statute of Artificers, or the legality of guild and municipal ordinances. See *The Taylors' of Ipswich Case* (*Reports*, 11:53–54); *The Chamberlain of London's Case* (*Reports*, 5, pt. 2: 63–64); *The Case of the City of London* (*Reports*, 8:241–58); and *Dr. Bonham's Case* (*Reports*, 8:226–40). See also *Tooley's Case*

remedy the grievance of monopolies without establishing Parliament's power to judge the validity of royal patents of monopoly and declare them void. While he was able to achieve these ends by appealing to precedents and to well-established arguments that had been used to justify voiding royal letters patent, his parliamentary campaign against monopolies depended upon somewhat novel interpretations of the law. Second, in attacking monopoly patents, Coke probably came closer to criticizing the court than he had in complaining about most other grievances in trade. Finally, his prominent role in drafting and promoting the Statute of Monopolies revealed his belief in the need for defining or clarifying certain legal principles that he thought were being violated. Nevertheless, his speeches on monopolies are not really inconsistent with his remarks on other economic issues. His sharpest attacks on monopolists were reserved not for prominent courtiers, but for lesser figures who were generally involved in the day-to-day administration of patents; and when he chose to attack a courtier, he had the good sense and tact to pick one, like Mompesson, who was vulnerable. Although he developed somewhat novel arguments to justify the Commons's quasi-judicial proceedings against patents, he faced no real opposition when he effected this slight expansion of the Commons's powers. He promoted the passage of a statute that defined the law governing monopolies, but he purposely refrained from making this act so precise as to leave little discretion to the common-law judges who would have to interpret it; and he did not protest strongly when his original bill was significantly weakened by both houses. Finally, although he treated monopolies as the principal economic grievance of the commonwealth, he avoided major conflicts over this issue by skirting truly controversial questions about whether regulated trading companies or borough corporations could be construed as monopolies in all cases.

Aside from his attacks on the Staplers and the Shrewsbury Drapers,

---

(*The English Reports*, 80:1055–60), which Coke decided but did not report himself, and *Davenant v. Hurdis* (*The English Reports*, 72:576), which Coke frequently cited when discussing monopolies. For modern discusions of Coke's views on monopolies, see Wagner, "Coke," esp. pp. 35–42; Wagner, "The Common Law and Free Enterprise"; Hill, *Intellectual Origins*, esp. pp. 233–35; Thorne, "Coke"; Malament, "Coke," esp. pp. 1338ff.; Little, *Religion, Order, and Law*, pp. 189–217; Knafla, *Law and Politics*, pp. 150–52; Russell, "Parliamentary History in Perspective," p. 15; and Foster, "Patents and Monopolies." Many other works discuss Elizabethan and/or Jacobean monopolies. Among them are William Hyde Price, *The English Patents of Monopoly*; Lipson, *History*, 3:352–83; Holdsworth, *History*, 4:343–54; E. Wyndham Hulme, "The History of the Patent System under the Prerogative and at Common Law"; D. Seaborne Davies, "Further Light on the Case of Monopolies"; and M. B. Donald, *Elizabethan Monopolies*. On complaints about monopolies in later Elizabethan parliaments, see Neale, *Elizabeth I and her Parliaments, 1584–1601*, pp. 352–56, 376–88. On attacks on monopolies in the parliaments of the 1620s, see, above all, Foster, "Patents and Monopolies."

Coke's parliamentary opposition to monopolies took three main forms during the early 1620s. First, as chairman of the Committee of Grievances in both 1621 and 1624, he was a leading figure in the quasi-judicial processes by which the lower house first judged numerous monopoly patents to be grievances in the creation and/or execution and then formally petitioned the king and his council to withdraw them. He also played an instrumental role in the parliamentary trials of two leading monopolists, Michell and Mompesson. He helped to persuade the Commons to punish Michell themselves before ultimately sending his case to the Lords, and he delivered a crucial speech in the conference at which the Commons presented formal charges against Mompesson to the Lords.[131] Finally, he expressed his opposition to monopolies by supporting a monopolies bill that he had drawn up himself. Although his original bill was seriously weakened by numerous provisos that were tacked onto it to placate its opponents, its passage in 1624 nevertheless marked the culmination of several generations of parliamentary complaints about monopolies.

Coke's attacks on monopolies were so numerous and blunt that his hostility towards monopolistic trading practices is not in doubt. He usually expressed this hostility by challenging the legality and/or conveniency of particular monopoly patents; but as his speech on the Welsh cloth bill shows, he regarded monopolies established by royal grants as only particular instances of a more general economic grievance, namely the restraint of free trade. He was not concerned solely with the legal origin of monopolies;[132] nor did his opposition to them simply reflect his distrust of the Stuart court.[133] Most of the monopolies that he attacked in 1621 and 1624 had originated in royal grants; but he also opposed statutory monopolies and the monopolistic privileges of corporate boroughs.[134] In 1621, he spoke against a bill concerning brick making in and around London because it would create a monopoly.[135] In 1624, he opposed the Norfolk wool bill for a similar reason; and in his exchange with the burgesses for Shrewsbury in 1621 he stated that corporate monopolies were detestable and should be abolished.[136] In both

---

131. See pp. 146–50.

132. As Heckscher suggests (see *Mercantilism*, 1:283–84).

133. As Malament implies (see "Coke," pp. 1347, 1350, 1351). Conrad Russell may also be slightly in error when he asserts that "to Coke . . . , a monopoly was first and foremost a method of law-enforcement by a private individual, rather than a restraint of trade" ("Parliamentary History in Perspective," p. 15).

134. Malament argues that Coke opposed royal, but not parliamentary, regulation of the economy ("Coke," pp. 1329, 1331, 1350). What she does not note, however, is that he opposed certain kinds of regulatory measures, regardless of their legal basis.

135. See *CD 1621*, 2:97; 4:66; *CJ*, 1:525.

136. See p. 112.

1621 and 1624 he opposed the inclusion of a proviso for corporate and statutory monopolies in the monopolies bill.[137] Finally, even if his opposition to monopolies reflected his medieval, moralistic attitude towards economic activity,[138] it was also related to his belief that they sometimes had demonstrably detrimental effects on certain sectors of the English economy. He believed, for example, that the Staplers' patent harmed the economy because it kept down the price of wool and that the removal of "impediments to freedom of trade by patents" would benefit the economy in substantive ways.[139]

Nevertheless, to say simply that Coke disapproved of monopolies is to say little about his economic ideas, unless one can also specify what he meant by this term. Things called "monopolies" were attacked throughout the sixteenth and seventeenth centuries by English and continental writers of widely disparate views.[140] And during Coke's own lifetime, the term "monopolist," like the terms "depopulator," "engrosser," or "usurer," had only a pejorative connotation. Moreover, one cannot illuminate Coke's views about economic regulation simply by saying that he favored free trade, when even a leading advocate of governmental economic regulation like Colbert believed that his policies actually promoted free trade.[141] In late Elizabethan and Jacobean England, men argued less about the conveniency or legality of monopolies than about the question of what sorts of economic activities and organization were truly monopolistic. The greatest disagreements about the proper application of the term "monopoly" probably arose in debates about the organization of foreign trading companies. When Thomas Milles attacked the Merchant Adventurers as a monopoly, the company's spokesman, John Wheeler, did not defend monopolies in general or the company's monopoly in particular. Instead, he argued that the company was not a true monopoly.[142] Disagreement also existed, however, about how the term was to be applied to domestic trading organizations. In the Commons's great monopoly debate of 1601, Bacon stated that "if her Majesty makes

137. See pp. 132–35.
138. Malament, "Coke," pp. 1346–47.
139. See pp. 95, 104–5.
140. Heckscher, *Mercantilism*, 1:270.
141. Ibid., 1:274–75; Charles Woolsey Cole, *Colbert and a Century of French Mercantilism*, 1:346. On support for free trade in mid-seventeenth-century France, see Cole, *Colbert*, 1:277.
142. Heckscher, *Mercantilism*, 1:386 and 372–92 generally. After Malynes had attacked the Merchant Adventurers' Company as a "monopoly" (*Maintenance of Free Trade*, pp. 60–73), Misselden complained that "some think that the reducing trade into order and government, is a kind of monopolizing and restraint of trade" (*Free Trade*, p. 54); and then, like Wheeler, he defined the term "monopoly" in such a way as to make it inapplicable to the company (see *Free Trade*, p. 55).

a patent, or a monopoly, to any of her servants, that we must go and cry out against: but if she grants it to a number of burgesses, or corporation, that must stand: and *that, forsooth, is no monopoly.*"[143] Others, like Coke, argued, however, that grants of exclusive privileges to boroughs and other corporate bodies did not necessarily differ from grants of monopoly privileges to private individuals. An understanding of Coke's use of the term "monopoly," therefore, is crucial to an understanding of his economic thought. His parliamentary speeches of the early 1620s provide no conclusive evidence about what sorts of activities he regarded as monopolistic, or about how he distinguished between monopolies and legitimate government of trade. But they nevertheless indicate his general hostility to restraints on free trade and his skepticism about most claims that such restraints actually promoted government or good order in trade and not a few private interests.[144]

Although Coke never clearly articulated the economic rationale for the parliamentary attacks on monopoly patents, he explained their legal basis in a crucial speech delivered in the Committee for Grievances on 19 February 1621. His first objective was to demonstrate that the Commons could question the legality of royal monopoly patents without challenging the king's prerogative. He conceded that some royal prerogatives, like the power to make war, were "indisputable." But he insisted that those that concerned "meum et tuum" were "bounded by law" and disputable; that royal patents of monopoly fell into this second category; and that such patents could therefore be questioned in courts, including the court

---

143. Heckscher, *Mercantilism*, 1:287–88.

144. Coke's writings do not clearly indicate what he meant by the term "monopoly." The fullest definition of it is found in his *Third Institutes*, where he wrote, "A monopoly is an institution, or allowance by the king by his grant, commission, or otherwise to any person or persons, bodies politique, or corporate, of or for the sole buying, selling, making, working, or using of any thing, whereby any person or persons, bodies politique, or corporate, are sought to be restrained of any freedom or liberty that they had before, or hindered in their lawful trade" (p. 181). It is not clear, however, that Coke always used the term "monopoly" in ways that are entirely consistent with this definition. On the one hand, as was shown above (p. 117), Coke did not believe that monopolies could be established only by royal grant, commission or allowance. But on the other hand, he was sometimes reluctant to characterize restrictive trading companies as "monopolies" and probably believed that some of them promoted government and order in trade. Nevertheless, in spite of the fact that he did not use the term "monopoly" with great precision or consistency, he was more generally opposed to monopolistic trading practices than Malament suggests (see fn. 133, above). Although he attached great importance to the maintenance of government in trade, he sometimes expressed great skepticism about claims that restrictive trading organizations promoted the public good. In his *Second Institutes*, he stated that "[n]ew corporations trading to foreign parts, and at home, which under the fair pretence of order and government, in conclusion tend to the hinderance of trade and traffic and in the end produce monopolies" (p. 540). For Malament's comment on this passage, see "Coke," p. 1354.

of Parliament.[145] He claimed that "mischievous" royal grants had been suppressed by courts and remedied by Parliament throughout English history; and to prove his point, he cited at least twenty-two cases from the last two-and-a-half centuries. Basic to Coke's argument was the unstated assumption that royal grants of monopolies were really grants of property rights and/or offices and not acts to regulate trade. If this assumption had been questioned and undermined, he would have had difficulty in sustaining his parliamentary campaign against monopoly patents. But as no one in the parliaments of 1621 or 1624 ever even attempted to raise this issue, Coke could attack monopoly patents with several arguments previously used to void royal letters patent of various sorts.

Having established Parliament's authority to judge royal monopoly patents and declare them void, Coke then explained that patents might be illegal " in the creation" and/or "in the execution." This distinction was important for him, because he believed that illegal patents of the latter sort could be "set afoot" again, whereas the others could not.[146] He never clearly formulated this distinction but seems to have used it roughly as follows. He regarded a patent as illegal in the execution either when it contained illegal provisions for its own enforcement, or when the patentee(s) committed illegal acts for which it did not provide. For example, the gold foliate patent was illegal in the execution, according to Coke, because the patentees had arrested some men and had seized the goods and tools of others.[147] On the other hand, he deemed a patent illegal in the creation when its provisions were inherently illegal. A patent would be illegal in the creation if the king granted away a right that he did not have or could not legally alienate, or if he was in any way "deceived in his grant," or if the consideration for which the grant was made were not carried out.[148] The distinction between illegality in the creation and illegality in the execution was not always clear-cut, however, for in arguing that a patent was illegal in the creation, Coke sometimes referred to facts that had become known only after the issuance of the patent. For example, a patentee's lack of competence to carry out the

145. On Coke's other remarks about such "indisputable" prerogatives of the king, see p. 173.
146. See Foster, "Patents and Monopolies."
147. CD 1621, 4:288; 3:130; 6:124.
148. For discussions of the circumstances under which royal letters patent might be declared void in law, see Arthur Legat's Case (Reports, 10:110–14); and The Case of Alton Woods (Reports, 1:26–53). Many other cases in Coke's Reports deal directly or indirectly with this issue.

express or implied purposes for which his patent had been granted,[149] or his actual failure to fulfill the express or implied purposes for which his patent had been granted[150] would, in Coke's view, make the patent illegal in the creation.[151]

Coke's speech of 19 February 1621 provided the main legal foundation for his later attacks on particular monopoly patents. These attacks all depended upon the assumption that Parliament could void monopoly patents in the same way that common-law courts could void other royal letters patent, and they all made use of the distinction between illegality in the creation and illegality in the execution. Of the several dozen patents that Coke discussed in the early 1620s, however, only seven directly raised questions about the legality or restraints on trade.[152] Six of them granted monopoly rights over the making and/or selling of particular commodities, and a seventh empowered a patentee to pardon offenses against a statute regulating economic activity. In addition, an eighth patent granting monopoly rights over the performance of a clerical office provided Coke with an occasion to discuss restraints on trade in general.

In the House's March 21st debate on this last monopoly, Sir Robert Flood's patent for the sole engrossing of wills, Coke gave one of his most forceful speeches in favor of free trade.[153] On 19 March 1621 he had argued in the Committee of Grievances that the patent was unlawful, because it restrained "the liberty of . . . subject[s] to go to whom they will for ingrossing or transcribing of wills,"[154] and on the twenty-first, when he informed the House of the Committee's opinion that the patent was illegal in the creation and execution, he developed this argument at considerable length. After suggesting that the patent concerned all subjects, because "[a]ll the sons of Adam must die," he said that it was in the commonwealth's interest to have last wills settled and that "[t]herefore[,] when men are dead their wills are to be proved." He then stated that

---

149. This was one of Coke's arguments against Lepton's patent. See *CD 1621*, 2:363; 4:336.

150. See his argument against the gold foliate patent, discussed on pp. 124–25. Coke was also prepared to argue against the legality of a particular patent if it granted a commission to a few patentees to perform a task that was too great for them to discharge themselves. See his argument against the patent for finding of arms (*CD 1621*, 2:264).

151. *CD 1621*, 4:79–81; 5:258; 6:249–51. On this speech, see Foster, "Patents and Monopolies," p. 64; and White, "Coke," pp. 317–19.

152. On some of these other patents, which granted rights to exercise governmental functions, see pp. 56–57, above.

153. On this patent, see *CD 1621*, 7:469.

154. Ibid., 5:53.

it was ever the liberty of the subject to engross [his will] himself if he would and bring it to be examined, and so to have the seal put to it. But now by this patent he may neither engross [it] himself nor go to whom he will [to have it engrossed]. He must come to Sir Robert Flood [who] must have his sole engrossing. . . . Here is liberty taken away, an heavy thing. If this be lawful, men may as well be confined to scriveners that none shall make bonds but such a scrivener, and to butchers that we shall buy flesh of none but such an one, which were a miserable servitude.

To show that Flood's patent illegally restrained "the liberty of the subject," he then cited the case of *Davenant v. Hurdis*. In the forty-first year of Elizabeth, he said, "There was a charter made to the Merchant Taylors [empowering them] to make constitutions, and they made a constitution that no man should put cloth to dress but one of the company. . . . But it was adjudged against law," because "they cannot restrain the liberty of the subject without common consent."[155] Coke concluded his speech by saying that projectors like Flood deserved to be hanged.[156]

Flood, who was a member of the House, denied that he was a projector and tried to justify his patent by explaining that the king had been informed of "the abuses and extortion" of proctors and had therefore granted the patent to reform the engrossing of wills.[157] Coke replied that the abusive practices of proctors did not establish the legality of Flood's patent and went on to make a highly significant point. If the existence of abuses in a trade were to constitute grounds for establishing a monopoly, he said, then trades like those of butchers and bakers (and presumably others as well) might be "put down" and "sole selling" established in their places. Moreover, he argued, the king's belief that Flood's patent would have beneficial effects did not constitute the ground for a conclusive argument for its legality, because the king had been misinformed about the law and had not known that patent was against Magna Charta and therefore illegal. "If a subject make a grant upon misinformation," Coke explained, "it's good. But if the king do, he may avoid it, for else he might do a wrong." The king, of course, could not do a wrong, for he was God's "[l]ieutenant" and "God can not do wrong." Because the king could not wrong, and because his grant to Flood would have done a wrong, the grant had to be held void.[158]

While arguing against the legality of Flood's patent, Coke had conceded that liberty of trade could be taken away by common consent.

155. For a report of this case, see *The English Reports*, 72:576. For comments on the case, see Wagner, "Common Law and Free Enterprise"; and Malament, "Coke," pp. 1341–42.

156. *CD 1621*, 2:250–51; 4:177–78; 5:58, 314–15; 6:79, 460–61.

157. Ibid., 2:252–53; 4:178–79; *CJ*, 1:566.

158. *CD 1621*, 5:59; 2:253.

Although the precise meaning that he ascribed to these two phrases is unclear, he obviously believed that common consent as expressed in an act of Parliament could take away free trade.[159] Although he once wrote that acts that restrained trade were usually short-lived,[160] his remarks on the apprentices patent show that he acknowledged the legality of statutory restraints on trade and approved of them in certain cases. This patent empowered four men "to grant pardons to offenders against the statute of apprentices,"[161] and when the Committee of Grievances debated it on 21 February 1621, Coke attacked it on the grounds that it defeated that statute's purposes. Those purposes were laudable, he said, because "[i]t breeds a corruption of manufactures" "[t]hat men should exercise that [trade] wherein they have no skill."[162] When Coke later reported that the committee had found the patent to be illegal in the creation and execution, he argued, in a similar vein, that "whereas by the statute of 5° Eliz[abeth], none can exercise a trade except he that have been an apprentice to the same for seven years, [the patentees] can give them licenses before they be of their crafts masters, to the great hurt of trades."[163]

In his speeches on the Apothecaries' charter in 1624, Coke took this argument one step further by arguing that Parliament could and should limit the access to occupations requiring skill, even if they were not trades within the Statute of Artificers. The Apothecaries had originally been members of the Grocers' Company, but in 1617 they had received a separate charter granting them the exclusive right to make and distribute medicines within seven miles of London.[164] When the Committee of Grievances debated the Grocers' complaint against this charter seven years later, Coke maintained that the charter was illegal in creation, because a company's members could not leave it and form another one without the first company's consent.[165] Nevertheless, he was highly sympathetic to the Apothecaries' argument that they should retain the monopoly granted them in 1617. When he reported the case to the House

159. See Wagner, "Coke," p. 31; and Malament, "Coke," pp. 1328–29, 1338–39.

160. *Institutes*, 2:37.

161. On this patent, see *CD 1621*, 7:327–29; Davies, *Apprenticeship*, pp. 31–36; and Price, *English Patents*, p. 167.

162. *CD 1621*, 4:92; 2:124–25; 6:266, 286.

163. Ibid., 2:250; 4:177–78; 5:58, 315; 6:79; *CJ*, 1:565; *P&D*, 1:206.

164. See *CD 1621*, 7:77–85; and C. R. S. Barrett, *The History of the Society of Apothecaries of London*, pp. xix–xxxix, 1–17. In 1618, the Grocers had petitioned the king to revoke the Apothecaries' exclusive right to make and distribute medicines (*CD 1621*, 7:326 and n. 2), and in 1621 they had supported a bill permitting all men exercising the trade of making and selling hot waters "[t]o distill, make and utter the same" (*CD 1621*, 7:80). On the dispute between these two companies, see George Unwin, *Industrial Organization in the Sixteenth and Seventeenth Centuries*, pp. 135–36.

165. Pym, 1624, f. 50.

the next day, he conceded that the charter was illegal for the reason that he had previously given in the committee, and that it was both "a hindrance of trade" and a "cause of the decay of trade"[166] because it gave the Apothecaries the "[s]ole trade of drugs and distillations." He further conceded that it took away "the greatest part of the Grocers' trade" and that merchants in general "had a great wrong" by it. Nevertheless, he reported the committee's opinion that "such physical composures or potions as are to be taken by sick persons should be composed and made by men of skill and experience," and that the Apothecaries should therefore prefer a private bill establishing their sole right to make and distribute such "composures" in London.

This speech indicates that Coke believed that Parliament had the power to limit the subject's freedom to practice whatever trade he wished and should sometimes use it. Moreover, although he attacked the legality of the gold foliate patent, he nevertheless stated that the king as well as Parliament could legally take away free trade in certain limited cases by granting a monopoly over the manufacture of a particular commodity to the discoverer of a new way of making it. This patent was, strictly speaking, a grant of incorporation to the Goldbeaters giving them exclusive rights to make foliate.[167] In February 1621, Coke had cited it as a cause of the decay of money[168] and later argued on 27 April and 2 May that it was also illegal in the creation for three reasons. His first argument against its legality was the same as the one that he had used against the Apothecaries' charter, but he then raised several new issues. The Goldbeaters' charter was void, he said, because they had "not performed their [express] covenant to bring in bullion enough of for the supply of the work . . ., and if the consideration fail the grant itself fails." Coke also argued that the charter was void because it did not meet the legal requirements for a monopoly patent. "A patent that restrains trade," he explained, "must have 3 incidents: 1, the commodity must be as good as before; 2, as good cheap; 3, it [the patent] must be [for] a new invention never used before." He then argued that the gold foliate monopoly was illegal, because it was not for "a new invention" and had neither of the other two necessary incidents of a valid monopoly. He also emphasized that the making of foliate was not a trade within the Statute of Artificers but an "ancient trade" that many had liberty to practice. The king, he said, could make a corporation of the Goldbeaters, after the Goldsmith's consent had been secured, but since the making of foliate was an ancient

---

166. *CJ*, 1:756; Nicholas, 1624, f. 114; Pym, 1624, f. 50v; Erle, 1624, f. 115.
167. *CD 1621*, 7:371.
168. See p. 94.

trade, this corporation could not then "seclude [other] men from their liberty" of making foliate. He probably thought, however, that if this manufacturing process had been either a new invention or a trade within the statute of 1563, then the king could have granted the Goldbeaters a monopoly over it for a specified number of years. He might also have argued that if this process required particular skill, Parliament could have granted the Goldbeaters a monopoly over it, even if it were neither a new invention of theirs *or* a trade within the 1563 statute.[169]

Coke's remarks on the apprentices' patent, the Apothecaries' charter and the foliate patent show that he recognized three main cases in which monopoly patents might be lawful. Nevertheless, his remarks on Sir Robert Mansell's glass patent show that he construed at least one of these cases very narrowly—the one for new inventions.[170] He began his attack on this monopoly by claiming that because the patentee had not actually invented a new method of glass making, his patent was void for two reasons. First, because it had been "grounded upon an undue consideration, that it was a new invention to make glass with sea coal," it was void for the reason that a grant would fail if the consideration for it failed. Second, because the king had granted the patent in the belief that Mansell had found a new way of making glass, whereas his claim to have done so was "expressio falsi and suppressio veri," the grant was void because the king had been deceived in his grant.

These arguments were not at all novel, but Coke then claimed that even if Mansell had invented a new way of making glass, his patent would still have been illegal. To support this position, he first repeated his claim that anyone holding a monopoly over the manufacture of any commodity had to make it "as well conditioned, [and] sized, and as good cheap" as his competitors, for otherwise his monopoly would be "hurtful to the commonwealth." He then stated that because Mansell's glass failed to meet these conditions, his patent was void in the creation. He further asserted that the patent was illegal because it contained certain illegal provisions. It barred all glass imports and gave Mansell the sole right to export his product. These privileges Coke regarded as superfluous for a patentee who could actually make as good a product at as low a price as other manufacturers, and there was, he said, "no law" for them. Coke also charged that the patent was void because it was granted for the

---

169. The text summarizes the arguments that Coke made in two speeches: (1) *CD 1621*, 5:105–6; and (2) 3:129–30; 2:336; 4:228; 5:362; 6:124; and *CJ*, 1:602–3.

170. On the glass patent, see *CD 1621*, 7:362–63. On Coke's involvement in the granting of this patent, see Appendix B.

period of twenty-one years, which he said was unlawful.[171] Finally, Coke attacked Mansell's patent on grounds that implied a very narrow view of the king's power to grant monopolies for new inventions. He suggested that even if a man invented a new way of making a particular commodity and could meet the specifications noted above he would not be automatically entitled to the "sole manufacturing" of it. Even if Mansell had discovered a new way of burning sea coal and pit coal for glass making, Coke claimed, he could legally have received a monopoly patent only for the "sole making of the furnace" in which the coal was burned. He could not have restrained those who had previously made glass with wood, sea coal, or pit coal from continuing to do so, because, Coke explained, monopoly privileges "are to be granted to new inventions, not to every device for improvement or amendment of manufacture formerly practiced." With respect to glass making, Mansell's alleged invention was "a new furnace but an old art" and was like "a new button upon an old coat."[172]

Like Mansell's glass patent, the salmon and lobster patent of Bassano and Vaudry was illegal in the creation, in Coke's view, because it contained several unlawful provisions and because the patentees had not actually made a new invention.[173] After stating that they had made no new discoveries about how or where to catch salmon or lobsters, Coke could then argue that their patent was void, because either the consideration for it had failed or the king had been deceived in granting it. He then argued, as he had in the case of Mansell's patent, that even if Bassano and his partner had made a new invention, their patent would still have been void, because it had been granted for an excessively long term, and because the prices of salmon and lobsters had actually increased under their administration. Coke also employed two other arguments against the patent's validity. First, it violated the provision of a statute of Edward III that "the sea shall be open for all manner of commodities." Second, whereas another statute had provided that no grant should "restrain [the marketing of food] but that all manner of victuals shall come to market,"[174] the patentees' marketing practices amounted to forestalling and diminished the food supply.[175]

171. On Coke's views about the time periods for which monopoly patents could be legally granted, see *Institutes*, 3:184.

172. The text above summarizes the arguments that Coke made in three different speeches: (1) *CD 1621*, 3:195; 5:153; (2) 3:257; (3) 3:272–73; 4:355; 5:170; 6:160–61; *P&D*, 2:80; *CJ*, 1:822.

173. On this patent, see *CD 1621*, 7:403–4.

174. The statute was 7 *Ric.* II, *c.* 11. In the committee, Coke had claimed that two statutes made it "lawful for all men to sell fish" (*CD 1621*, 5:90).

175. These arguments against the salmon and lobster patent were presented in two

In arguing against the legality of the lobster patent, Coke was thus relying partly on statutory provisions for free trade, but when he came to condemn the gold-and-silver thread monopoly he again supported certain kinds of trade restraints.[176] In his opinion, this patent was illegal in the creation because like other patents, it had been made "upon 3 false suggestions." Although the patentees had undertaken to sell a better product more cheaply than other producers and to make it from imported metal, they had done none of these things. Moreover, they had barred other men from practicing their "ancient trade" of wiredrawing. Thus far, Coke's argument resembled the one he had employed against the lobster patent, but it took a new turn when he claimed that the patent in question was also illegal in the creation because the patentees "were never brought up to the trade" of wiredrawing and "therefore both by common law and by statute law" could not "exercise and practice it," unless empowered to do so by statute.[190] The assumption underlying this argument was presumably that the making of gold and silver wire required special skill and/or was a trade within the Statute of Artificers.[177]

In his remarks in 1624 on the Newcastle Hostmen's monopoly over the buying of sea coal, Coke again upheld the legality of certain kinds of trade restraints and further asserted that such restraints could be established not only by statute and royal grant but by prescription as well.[178] When the Commons debated the Hostmen's monopoly on 9 April, he first said that it was "a common right of every man that all men may sell to whom they will" and that if a charter erected a new corporation "with a clause of restraint of good[s] foreign bought and foreign sold, it is void." He added, however, that "by prescription or Act of Parliament, such a restraint is good."[179]

Coke's campaign of the early 1620s against specific monopoly patents was obviously successful. Most of the patents condemned by the Commons were speedily withdrawn by the council. Nevertheless, Coke wished to carry his campaign even further. He wanted Parliament to use its ancient judicial powers to judge and punish a few notable monopolists so as to provide an example for future projectors, and, like previous par-

---

speeches: (1) *CD 1621*, 5:89–90; (2) 2:320; 4:255; 5:97–98, 349; 6:99; *P&D*, 1:317; *CJ*, 1:591.

176. On this patent, see *CD 1621*, 7:364. On Coke's brief remarks about it in 1621, see White, "Coke," p. 329 n. 119.

177. D'Ewes, 1624, f. 97v; Holles, 1624, f. 118.

178. On the sea-coal patents, see *CD 1621*, 7:429–32; and J. U. Nef, *The Rise of the British Coal Industry*, 2:21. The Hostmen's monopoly had been under continuous attack since the 1590s (see Nef, *Coal Industry*, 2:121–28), and attempts were made to abolish it in the parliament of 1621 (see *CD 1621*, 7:85, 97–99).

179. Nicholas, 1624, f. 132v; Pym, 1624, f. 57.

liamentary critics of monopolies, he also pressed for the passage of a monopolies bill that would constitute a remedy for this grievance in future times. His speeches on Parliament's proceedings against Sir Francis Michell and Sir Giles Mompesson reveal little about his views concerning free trade, but an analysis of his role in Parliament's proceedings on the monopolies bill helps to illuminate his views concerning economic regulation. The passage of this bill concluded almost fifty years of parliamentary agitation against monopolies. A complaint against this grievance had been heard in the Commons as early as 1571,[180] and in 1597–98 the House had petitioned the queen about it.[181] In 1601, a member had preferred a bill against monopolies, entitled "An act for the explanation of the common law in certain cases of letters patent,"[182] and in James I's first parliament, a monopolies bill was again under discussion in the Lower House.[183] In the spring of 1621, the Commons finally passed such a bill, and although the Lords rejected it the following fall it was ultimately enacted in 1624.[184] Although this statute declared and enacted that all monopolies and dispensations with penal laws were void, it also contained ten provisos stating that it did not extend to several classes of monopolies or to certain specific patents; and these provisos were held to allow Charles I to continue making grants of monopoly patents.[185] Although Coke drafted the bill introduced in the Commons in 1621,[186] he did not include any provisos in it and explicitly opposed their inclusion. As a result, the final Monopolies Act of 1624 provides no guide to his views about monopolies, which must be inferred from his original bill and from his remarks in the Commons's debates on it in 1621 and 1624.[187]

During the first month of the parliament of 1621, various members, including Coke, called for a bill against monopolies,[188] and on 12 March he finally brought in "An act concerning monopolies and dispensations

180. Neale, *Elizabeth I and her Parliaments, 1559–1581*, pp. 218–19.
181. Neale, *Elizabeth I and her Parliaments, 1584–1601*, pp. 352–56.
182. Ibid., p. 377; and Notestein, *1604–1610*, p. 515 n. 4.
183. Notestein, *1604–1610*, p. 51.
184. 21 *Jac.* I, *c.* 3 (*SR*, 4, pt. 2, pp. 1212–14).
185. See Gardiner, *History*, 8:71, 72; Price, *English Patents*, pp. 35–46; Cecil T. Carr, ed., *Select Charters of Trading Companies, A.D. 1530–1707*, pp. lxxiii–lxxx; and Holdsworth, *History*, 4:353 and n. 6.
186. One diarist later stated that two other members had drafted the bill. See fn. 199, below.
187. Several historians have mistakenly treated the Monopolies Act of 1624 as the direct expression of Coke's views about monopolies. See fn. 130.
188. Proposals for such a bill grew out of the Commons's investigations of individual monopoly patents in the Committee of Grievances; but the monopolies bills that had been brought into earlier parliaments were almost certainly known to some members. On 5 March Digges called for a bill very much like the one that Coke ultimately brought into the

with penal laws" that he had "penned" himself.[189] In its original form, this bill contained a preamble and four main enacting clauses, just as the final act did.[190] After referring in the preamble to James I's declaration against monopolies in his "Book of Bounty" of 1610, it "declared and enacted" that all grants of monopolies, grants in dispensation of penal laws and grants of power to pardon or compound for offenses against penal laws were "utterly void," and that they were to be tried "by the laws of this realm in the King's courts of record." It then "enacted" that all subjects, present and future, were now disabled from exercising rights conveyed by the types of grants listed above and that anyone exercising them would incur the penalties prescribed by Richard II's statute of *praemunire*. Finally, the bill "enacted" that any person grieved by the exercise of such rights could recover treble damages and double costs from the person exercising such rights.[191] Although the bill's preamble and enacting clauses resembled those of the final act, it differed significantly from the act in that it contained no provisos, and its legislative history thus consists largely of the process by which provisos were successively added to it.[192]

The debate following the second reading of Coke's bill revealed remarkable confusion and disagreement in the House about what sorts of monopolies the bill should declare void and about the meaning of the

---

House (see *CD 1621*, 2:67; 6:31; *P&D*, 1:122; Zaller, *1621*, p. 64), and his suggestion was "much applauded" (*CD 1621*, 5:272). Later that day, Sir John Walter made a similar suggestion and the House then appointed a committee to consider the drafting of a bill against monopolies (*CD 1621*, 5:25; *CJ*, 1:538). On 8 March Coke told the Lords at the conference on Mompesson's case that it was "necessary that some law be made for the time to come that no monopoly be granted, and [that] they that procure any such may incur some great punishment" (*CD 1621*, 2:194). On 12 March Sir Nathaniel Rich called for the enactment of a monopolies bill and suggested that it be drafted by Walter, Crew, and Noy (*CD 1621*, 6:53; *CJ*, 1:549).

189. *CD 1621*, 2:210; 5:290; 6:56.

190. A transcript of the original draft bill of 1621 is printed in *LD 1621*, at pp. 151–55. For comments on this transcript, see fn. 192. For abstracts of the bill, see *CD 1621*, 2:210; 4:147; 5:289–90.

191. *LD 1621*, pp. 151, 152, and nn. f, g, and h, 152–53.

192. In his transcript of the draft bill of 1621, S. R. Gardiner italicizes interlineations that he presumes to be "the alterations made in committee" (*LD 1621*, p. 151 n. a). In his transcript, parts of several provisos do not appear in italics and are thus made to appear to be parts of the original draft bill. These provisos, however, could simply have been added to the bill without any interlineation. This hypothesis is confirmed by three facts. First, the provisos were not written in the same hand as the enacting clauses, or on the same type or size of paper. Second, certain objections that were made to the bill on its second reading would have made little sense if the bill had already contained *any* of the provisos that appear in Gardiner's transcript as parts of the original bill. Finally, several diaries state explicitly that provisos were added to the bill during the early stages of its passage through the Commons.

word "monopoly."[193] William Hakewill said that although Coke's bill was "of the greatest consequence, for the good of the subject, of any in the House," he objected to it because it might "extend to new inventions" and to "some corporations, having the sole working" of certain commodities. He also complained that it did not seem to extend to monopolies for foreign trade.[194] Coke maintained, however that the bill ought not to be "over much clogged" with explanations and provisos, because it was "founded merely upon the King's own judgement" as expressed in the "Book of Bounty."[195] After commenting at length on the question of the royal dispensing power, he then turned to Hakewill's query about the meaning of the term "monopoly" and said that the bill used the word in the sense in which "the judges of the law" had previously used it. It was "derived from moinos et poleomos," he said, and signified the "sole buying and selling of anything," the "sole importation and exportation" of anything, and, presumably, the sole making or using of anything as well. To strengthen his contention that restraints on importation and exportation were monopolistic, he asserted that "merchandizing" was "the birth-right of the subject" and went on to note that as attorney general, he had successfully brought *Quo Warrantoes* against three patents for sole importation. He therefore indicated that Hakewill's last objection to the bill was groundless, because the bill already extended to import and export monopolies, which were in fact "especial" monopolies.[196] In conclusion, Coke admitted that the bill had been "drawn suddenly, by the commandment of the House" and might contain errors, and he therefore moved to commit it, after declaring that he would cease to support it if it were found to be "against the King's supreme prerogative."[197] Several members, however, were dissatisfied with his reply to Hakewill. Sir Thomas Wentworth wanted the bill to include a particular definition of the term "monopoly." Calvert proposed that it not extend to patents for new inventions, and Sir Thomas Roe wanted it to state "in

193. For the debate, see *CD 1621*, 2:218–19; 5:38, 296; 4:153; 6:61–62; *CJ*, 1:553–54; *P&D*, 1:55.

194. *CJ*, 1:553; *CD 1621*, 2:218; 4:153. It is barely possible that Hakewill could have made these objections even if the bill had already contained provisos for new inventions and/or corporations. He may have believed (correctly, in Coke's opinion) that the provisos did not validate the types of provisos that they mentioned but simply excepted them out of the penalty of the act. Bacon had apparently made this point about the monopolies bill of 1601 (see *TED*, 2:278), and Lord Mandevil was to raise a similar issue when discussing the provisos at a conference with the Commons in 1624 (see p. 133, below).

195. On the Book of Bounty (also referred to as "The King's Book"), see Price, *English Patents*, p. 28. For the text of it, see *CD 1621*, 7:491–96.

196. For the definition of the term that Coke later used when writing about the Monopolies Act of 1624, see fn. 144, above.

197. *CD 1621*, 2:219; 5:38, 295 n. 12, 296; 6:61; *CJ*, 1:553; *P&D*, 1:155.

express words" that patents for sole importation or exportation were monopolies.[198]

On 15 March, when a committee of the whole debated the bill, its critics expanded on an earlier objection of Hakewill's and claimed that "it extended too far" in three respects: "(1) [To] [t]he making void of divers charters of cities, (2) To the overthrow of companies, (3) To [the] taking away of that custom which was in most towns of foreign bought and foreign sold." No one at the committee could meet these objections, and they were referred to a subcommittee.[199] This subcommittee reported the bill back to the committee on 20 March with several alterations and four provisos. The first proviso stated that the bill did not extend to patents for new inventions previously made for twenty-one years or less and thus partially met the objections of Hakewill and Calvert. The second proviso met both Hakewill's second objection to the bill and the objections made in the committee on the fifteenth by providing that the bill "should not extend to any corporations of towns, cities, or companies." The third and fourth provisos excepted out of the bill's operation various existing monopolies over printing, saltpeter, alum, and iron ordnance.[200]

After a brief debate, in which further provisos were suggested, the bill was sent back to the subcommittee[201] which reported it back to the committee on 26 March with at least six alterations.[202] Both the preamble and the first clause now stated that monopolies were contrary to "the ancient and fundamental laws" of the realm,[203] and the third clause now disabled "bodies politic and corporate," as well as "single persons," from exercising monopoly privileges.[204] The second clause now said that monopolies should be tried "by the ordinary courts of common law," and

---

198. Calvert said that the king could establish a monopoly for a new invention, but not for "an old trade" (*CJ*, 1:554).

199. *CD 1621*, 4:160. Pym stated at this point in his diary that Noy and Crew had drafted the bill. They were two of the three men whom Rich had previously mentioned as suitable draftsmen of the bill (see fn. 188).

200. *P&D*, 1:199–200; *CD 1621*, 5:213; 4:173 and n. 1. None of these accounts indicates precisely what amendments had been made. Nicholas states that the bill had been changed so that it would not extend "to any patent made in 11 *Jac.* for any manufacture" (*P&D*, 1:199); but no such proviso is appended to the draft bill. The passage in Nicholas's diary must therefore refer to the proviso for new inventions, which contains the phrase "for the term of eleven years or under" (see White, "Coke," p. 738).

201. *P&D*, 1:200; *CD 1621*, 4:173–74; 5:312. Provisos for a license for the transportation of calveskins and for a license to export wine were proposed by solicitor Heath (*CD 1621*, 4:173; *P&D*, 1:200). Towerson, a member of the Merchant Adventurers' Company, complained that by limiting the royal dispensing power, the bill threatened his company's charter, which was "grounded and granted upon a non obstante" of 27 *Hen.* VIII, *c.* 13 (*CD 1621*, 4:173).

202. *CD 1621*, 4:197; 5:322; *CJ*, 1:575.

203. *LD 1621*, pp. 151, 151–52. On this amendment, see Zaller, *1621*, pp. 128–29.

204. *LD 1621*, p. 152 and n. h.

the amended proviso for new inventions excepted out of the bill only patents that "were not contrary to the law and unprofitable to the state by raising prices."[205] These four alterations were designed to strengthen the bill and partially compensate for the addition of the four provisos the previous week. Nevertheless, the subcommittee had further limited the bill's scope by adding two more provisos: one "for all monopolies erected by statute," and another for Lord Nottingham's license to sell wine.[206] Following the report from the subcommittee, the Commons definitely resolved to include provisos for iron ordnance and saltpeter and omit a proviso previously proposed for the exportation of white cloth.[207]

By the time of its third reading on 12 May, the bill apparently contained seven provisos. In addition to those for new inventions, printing, corporations, saltpeter, and iron ordnance, it included the two provisos reported on 26 March and a new one for "warrants to the judges to compound for any forfeiture."[208] In the debate following its third reading, Coke directly stated that he opposed all these provisos but would still support the bill's passage. He was probably willing to do so, not only because he thought that the bill could not pass without the provisos, but also because he believed that they validated no monopolies but simply excepted them out of the bill.[209] After another brief debate, the Commons passed the bill and sent it to the Upper House with a "special recommendation."[210] The following fall, however, the Lords rejected it[211] and the lower house was never able to draft a new bill agreeable to them.[212]

Nevertheless, the monopolies bill was quickly revived in 1624, like most other significant legislation considered in 1621. On 23 February Coke moved that it be read[213] and it received two quick readings on the twenty-fourth and the twenty-sixth. Its second reading precipitated a brief exchange between John Pym, who moved to commit it, and Glanville, who was continuing in his role as its principle spokesman. After Pym had noted that several members opposed certain features of the bill and hoped to "alter" it in committee, Glanville spoke in its defense. After reminding the House that it was "a law declaratory" whose purpose was not to state new rules concerning monopolies but merely to lay down new

205. CD 1621, 4:97. On these amendments, see Zaller, 1621, pp. 128–29.
206. CD 1621, 4:197; 5:322; LD 1621, p. 154.
207. CD 1621, 2:267; 4:197–98; 5:322; CJ, 1:575.
208. CD 1621, 4:333–34. Pym actually lists eight provisos, but he considers the two parts of the printing proviso separately.
209. CJ, 1:619; P&D, 2:62; CD 1621, 3:326.
210. CD 1621, 4:334; 3:326; 5:161, 373.
211. Ibid., 5:413.
212. See White, "Coke," p. 228, n. 107.
213. Holles, 1624, f. 81; Spring, 1624, f. 9; CJ, 1:716.

penalties and procedures, he conceded that it did not "fully meet with all inconveniences," particularly because it did not define the term "monopoly."[214] Coke was named to the committee for the bill, but on 13 March it was Glanville who reported the committee's twenty alterations in it to the House.[215] The Commons approved the committee's work, and after accepting a few further changes in the bill they had it engrossed.[216] They passed it on the seventeenth and sent it up to the Lords,[217] who considered it for several weeks[218] and then asked for a conference about it.[219] This conference was finally held on 17 April. Prior to it Glanville had acted as the bill's chief sponsor, but Coke now assumed the burden of answering the Lords' objections to it.

The conference fell into two main parts. First, Chief Justice Montagu propounded "five general scruples" about the bill, which Coke answered point by point. The king's attorney then presented a series of detailed objections to the bill to which Coke also responded. Montagu's first scruple was that the "savings" to the bill, of "special grants," as he called them, would be "of small effect." Because savings to a declarative law were of no force and because the present bill declared that all monopolies were against law, the judges, he said, would be "bound by the declaration" rather than by the savings. In reply, Coke first noted that the bill concluded with "provisoes" and not "savings" and then confirmed Montagu's interpretation of the bill's effect. "Our meaning," he said, "was not to confirm them that are mentioned [in the provisos] or any other monopoly, but to leave them as they were. And the proviso [will] help them [only] thus far, that they shall not be in danger of this law nor of a *praemunire*." Thus, they still might be found illegal at common law.

Montagu then explained the second part of his first scruple concerning the bill. "Though laws are to be penned in Parliament," he said,

yet they are to be expounded by judges. Therefore, he wished the declaration might be so drawn as to stand with the proviso[s]; as in the statute[s] against engrossing, forestalling, regrating, and bankrupt[s] it is carefully described what an ingrosser, forestaller, regrater, and bankrupt is, so it would be good [for] the bill to declare certainly what a monopoly is, for the etymology of the word may be larger than the true definition or civil description of the thing.

To this Coke responded that a "monopoly" was simply "a claim to use that solely which of right is common free to many" and that the bill

214. Spring, 1624, f. 33; Nicholas, 1624, f. 25; *CJ*, 1:674, 719.
215. *CJ*, 1:680, 731. Ten of these alterations are noted in Pym, 1624, f. 23.
216. *CJ*, 1:731; Erle, 1624, f. 63.
217. *CJ*, 1:685, 736; Erle, 1624, f. 82; Holles, 1624, f. 100; Spring, 1624, f. 113. Oddly enough, Coke declined to take the bill up to the Lords (see Holles, 1624, f. 100).
218. *LJ*, 3:261, 267.
219. Ibid., 3:286; *LD 1624–1626*, p. 50.

should include no such definition, because of the "rule" that "definitiones in lege sunt periculosissimae."

Montagu's second main scruple was that he was unsure as to what sort of action the bill would allow against a monopolist. Coke therefore explained that a plaintiff had a choice of suing either "generally at common law" or else "contra formam statuti" and then added that if the defendant's patent were covered by one of the bill's provisos, he would be "exempted from the penalty" of the act. With respect to the penalty prescribed for anyone who delayed a suit against a monopoly without a court order, Montagu had a third scruple and asked Coke the following question. If a judge should be delayed upon a royal message or a privy councillor's letter that supported a defendant in a monopoly case who was in the king's service, was it fit that the judge and councillor should incur a *praemunire*? Coke stated flatly that it was. Montagu then posed another question. If a suit brought under the present bill were to concern a "matter of state, wherein it will be fit to know the King's pleasure, which, if the King were absent, might require more time than ordinary proceedings would allow," how could the suit be delayed, in view of the fact that the bill gave only one "imparlance"? Coke then replied that while the bill gave only one imparlance, there could be an infinite number of continuances and that even if they were to reach issue there remained "dies datus [*sic*] which the judges may give as often as [they] please."

Montagu's fourth set of scruples concerned the proviso for new inventions, which he thought too restrictive in several respects. First, it extended only to existing patents and not to future ones. Second, it extended only to such new inventions as "should not be inconvenient," even though what was inconvenient for one time or place might not be so in other circumstances and in spite of the fact that a particular inconvenience might be accompanied by a greater good. Finally, he criticized the proviso for not extending to additions to, or improvements on, old inventions. Coke yielded to the first two of these objections and said that the proviso should be amended so as to extend to future patents for new inventions and to except out of the act all new inventions, present and future, that were not "*generally* inconvenient." He insisted, however, that the proviso should not extend to additions to old inventions. "A new invention," he said, "is that which brings to the Commonwealth [what] they had not before," whereas "[a]n addition to an old invention" was "but a new button" on "an old cloak."

Montagu's final scruple was that the bill abridged "his majesty's prerogative in making new corporations." Coke replied that if a royal charter of incorporation extended "only to government and choice of officers," the bill would not apply to it and thus could not possibly abridge the royal prerogative. He also said, however, that if a royal charter granted "any liberty of sole buying and selling" to a corporation, it would be "within the law." He could then have argued that if a court were to void such a charter, its action would not actually abridge the royal prerogative, because the case would concern only that "ordinary" prerogative that could be "disputed" in court.

In the second part of the conference, Coke responded to the king's attorney, who raised questions about the bill's provisos and about whether it would extend to certain specific patents.[220] After briefly debating Coke's report of this conference, the House appointed a committee to consider provisos for four monopolies: Vane's subpoena patent, Young and Pye's patent for sole writing under the Great Seal, Mansell's glass patent, and Chambers's patent for sheriffs.[221] On 1 May Coke reported that the committee had examined the first three of these patents and that "if the Lords shall add a proviso, to exempt them out of the act, and leave [them] as they be, the committee thinks it fit to consent, not in love to these patents, but to the passage of the bill." He also said that while the committee had "affirmed" none of the patents "to be good, nor condemned any of them to be ill," its opinion was that no one should be allowed to hold similar patents in the future, after the terms of the present ones had expired.[222]

A conference of both houses was then held at which the Lords tried to secure legal protection for numerous patents by either suggesting parliamentary confirmations of them or proposing specific provisos for them. At the same time, while the Commons were willing to make some concessions to the Lords for the sake of getting the bill enacted, they refused to accept more than a few further provisos, which would merely have excepted specific patents out of the bill without validating them. In the end, the two houses agreed to add provisos for several patents that had previously been debated, along with Baker's patent for making smalt.[223] Several weeks later, another proviso was added for Lord Dudley's iron ore patent,[224] and after a complex series of negotiations, the bill had finally passed both houses on 25 May[225] and received the king's assent four days later.[226]

---

220. For accounts of this conference, see Pym, 1624, ff. 71v–72; Erle, 1624, ff. 149–50; and *CJ*, 1:770–71.

221. *CJ*, 1:771; Erle, 1624, f. 150; Pym, 1624, f. 72v; Nicholas, 1624, f. 163v.

222. *CJ*, 1:696; Nicholas, 1624, f. 188v; Holland, 1624, II, f. 69v; Pym, 1624, f. 86.

223. *CJ*, 1:703.

224. *LJ*, 3:394; *LD 1624–1626*, p. 98.

225. *CJ*, 1:711, 794.

226. D'Ewes, 1624, f. 129.

The preceding discussion suggests several general conclusions about Coke's views concerning both the rights of English subjects to engage in various economic activities and the general principles that should govern English economic organization. It also illuminates his ideas about the relationship between the public good and the pursuit of private interest and about the conveniency and legality of various types of government of trade. First, he apparently believed that English subjects had certain rights to "free trade" that included the liberty to use their lands as they wished; to employ their labor as they chose; and to engage in agricultural, industrial, or commercial activities. Although he did not regard these rights as absolute and inalienable, he believed that they could be destroyed, qualified, or abridged only by due process of law. Moreover, by elevating this economic freedom to the status of a legal right under the common law, he took a very significant step. He implied that laws, grants, or customs that limited free trade or took it away were generally to be strictly construed and not extended by equity. Second, although he thought that every English subject had this right, at least potentially, he also believed in the existence of a stronger sort of economic right to free trade that could be established by legal process, custom, or long usage. Thus, he distinguished between the general right of every subject to engage in a particular trade and the right of particular subjects to continue in a trade that they had already been following. In addition to recognizing the subject's common-law right to free trade, he also accorded the status of maxims or main points of common law to certin principles of economic organization. The two such principles that he mentioned in the early 1620s were, first, that trade should be free and, second, that wool should be kept at a high price. By treating these policies as legal principles, maxims, or main points of law, Coke was implying that they were convenient for the commonwealth by definition and by law, and he could then argue that laws, grants, or customs that contravened these principles were inconvenient. Moreover, because he recognized the legal force of arguments from inconvenience, he could sometimes argue either that such laws, grants, or customs were legally void, or at least that they had to be strictly and narrowly construed by judges, including judges of the court of Parliament.

It is important to bear in mind, however, that by recognizing the subject's legal right to free trade and by positing the existence of a common-law principle that trade should be free, Coke was not implying that every subject's unbounded exercise of economic liberty necessarily promoted the public good, that rights to free trade could never be taken away, or that the principle that trade should be free could not be restricted in certain cases. His support for the subject's right to free trade and for the principle of free trade was qualified in several important ways. First, he did not believe that the pursuit of private interest by subjects who were apparently exercising their rights to free trade would necessarily benefit the commonwealth. In fact, he repeatedly stated in 1621 and 1624 that the pursuit of private gain was detrimental to the public good, at least in certain cases. Thus, his views on economic organization were such as to allow for the existence of a potential conflict between the right to free trade and the public good; but he could often avoid acknowledging the possibility that such conflicts could occur. If he thought that a particular use of economic freedom actually damaged the public good and ought to be checked, he would rarely state that free trade should be restrained in that particular case. Instead, he would generally call for a measure that would prohibit the ruthless pursuit of private gain in that case and would assert that such a measure would promote the public good. His ability to manipulate conventional rhetoric in this way was facilitated, moreover, by the fact that his support for free trade was qualified in another significant way. He sometimes used the phrase "free trade" to refer to trade that was not limited by unfair or unreasonable restraints. He was thus able to support limits on the subject's right to free trade and on the general principle that trade should be free, without having to admit that he was trying to abridge free trade. Another way in which he could simultaneously maintain that there was a common-law right to free trade and that certain economic activities could be legally banned was by emphasizing the importance of government or good order in trade. He did not posit the existence of a common-law maxim that trade should be under good government, but he certainly believed that government and good order in trade benefited the commonwealth, and he could therefore rationalize his support for limitations on free trade simply by calling them measures that promoted good government of trade.

It is clear, therefore, that Coke's support for freedom of trade, both as an individual right and as a principle of law and policy, was qualified in at least three ways: by his belief that the pursuit of private interest might be harmful to the commonwealth; by his tendency not to equate freedom of trade with absolute economic liberty; and by his claim that government of trade, like freedom of trade, promoted the public good. Nevertheless, the fact that his support for free trade was qualified in these three ways does not imply that he did not really believe in this principle of economic organization or that he was not prepared to defend it against those whom he believed were undermining it. He knew very well that the argumentative strategies that he himself used to justify certain effective restrictions on economic liberty were also being used by people who wished to retrain trade in ways that he opposed. As a result, he often expressed extreme scepticism about claims that apparent restraints on free trade promoted the public good, that they provided good order in trade, or that they were not really restraints on true freedom of trade. Moreover, during the early 1620s Coke was also becoming dubious about the efficacy of regulatory measures that supposedly promoted the public good by maintaining good order in trade. This was not because he opposed these measures on principle, but because he was highly suspicious of the processes by which these regulations were being enforced. He believed, for example, that informations on regulatory statutes often served only the private interests of informers and not the public good; that under the pretense of maintaining good order in trade, companies like the Merchant Adventurers were using their privileges and powers to harass their competitors; and that towns like Shrewsbury were also trying to justify their monopolies by arguing that they were not restraining trade but simply governing it. Finally, Coke's support for freedom of trade was not qualified as severely as might be supposed by his failure to equate the pursuit of private gain with the promotion of the public good. His parliamentary speeches and writings draw attention to conflicts between public and private interest, but he must have thought that public interest often coincided with the private interests of subjects pursuing private gain.

Coke's parliamentary speeches show, however, that he recognized many specific cases in which the promotion of government of trade was convenient for the commonwealth and should take precedence over the defense of freedom of trade. These cases fall into four main categories of which the first was by far the most important. First, Coke strongly believed in the conveniency of many measures for the good government of England's foreign trade. He thought that the commonwealth would benefit from bans on the export of bullion, wool, unfinished cloth, iron ordnance, and perhaps poorly made cloth as well. He also expressed qualified support for the restrictive privileges of the Merchant Adventurers, probably on the grounds that they were necessary for the maintenance of regular access to foreign markets for English cloth. Second, Coke may have recognized the convenience of restrictions on certain imports, particularly luxury goods; but even if such restrictions prevented short-run losses of bullion, he sometimes opposed them on the grounds that they would, in the long run, damage England's system of trade. Third, Coke believed that the commonwealth would benefit from certain restraints on the entry to particular trades and industries. He supported the restrictions laid down in the Statute of Artificers, but precisely how he construed its provisions is unclear. He also supported monopoly patents for new inventions, even though he believed that they should be carefully scrutinized both for their legality and conveniency. Finally Coke believed that in certain cases, which he failed to discuss extensively in Parliament, restraints on domestic trade might be beneficial to the realm; but he regarded many of them with suspicion and supported them much less strongly than restraints on foreign trade.

Coke thus recognized several cases in which government of trade (which in fact restrained freedom of trade) might be convenient for the commonwealth; but he nevertheless believed that such restraints could be legally valid only under certain circumstances. He recognized four possible legal bases for limitations on freedom of trade: statute, custom, prescription, and royal charter. But he did not think that *any* restraint established in one of these four ways was necessarily good in law. He of course recognized Parliament's power to take away freedom of trade by statute and believed that this power could sometimes be used to benefit the commonwealth. Moreover, he could think of no way of voiding certain parliamentary restraints on trade of which he disapproved. Nevertheless, he did not passively accede to all such expressions of legislative will. He was probably prepared to argue that statutes against freedom of trade, like penal statutes in general, should be interpreted strictly. He was also ready to declare void certain statutes that confirmed the powers of corporations to enforce their economic privileges; and by doing so he may have been able to undermine certain restrictive economic practices. Moreover, while he recognized the legality of customary restraints on trade, he insisted that they were illegal if they were unreasonable. The criteria that he used to determine their reasonableness are not clearly stated anywhere in his writings or speeches, but he was clearly prepared to void customary restraints of which he disapproved. He did not think that he could void unreasonable restraints established by prescription, but his parliamentary remarks on this question are too brief to provide any clear guide to his precise views on this subject.

Finally, although Coke recognized that royal charters could establish monopolies or restraints on trade, he developed many different ways of showing that they were sometimes void. First, he doubted the legality of those monopolies that were created under the royal dispensing power by royal grants to single subjects or corporations of the right to be exempt from the operation of a statute prohibiting certain kinds of economic activity. Second, he was sometimes prepared to argue against the legality of royal grants of monopoly privileges to borough corporations on the grounds that they took away the rights of those subjects who were not members of that corporation. Third, although he recognized the legality of royal charters granting monopoly rights over particular foreign trades, he could argue that they were void if the grantees failed to fulfill the purposes for which the grant had been made and could easily strike down enforcement provisions in such patents. Finally, Coke developed a whole battery of arguments that he could use to invalidate royal patents of monopoly for new inventions. He could argue against the legality of a patent of this sort if the patentee's invention did not constitute a distinctly new method of making a particular commodity, or if the patentee's product were not better and cheaper than the product of others who made it. He could do so, moreover, on three different grounds: that the patent did not have the three necessary "incidents" of monopolies for new inventions, that the king had been "deceived in his grant," or that the consideration for which the king had granted the patent had failed. Second, he could argue that such a patent was void if it had been granted for a period of more than seven years. The rationale underlying this argument was that subjects who were apprenticed to the patentee for the usual term of seven years in the first year of the patent's execution would otherwise be barred later from what was or had become their trade. Coke could also attack a monopoly patent if it secluded subjects from their ancient trade, or if it barred the practitioners of that trade from using a different method of making the same product as the patentee. Finally, Coke argued against the legality of monopolies granted to men who lacked the skill necessary to execute them and monopolies over activities that could not possibly be executed by the patentees themselves; and he would not necessarily accept as a justification for a monopoly the fact that the economic activity placed under monopolistic control was in a state of disorder.

Coke's parliamentary speeches of the early 1620s not only show that he accepted the legal force of numerous arguments against monopolistic, or restrictive, trading practices. They also indicate that he was dissatisfied with the organization of the English economy in this period and that a major source of this dissatisfaction was the existence of numerous restraints on freedom of trade. Although he recognized the need for good order in trade and supported certain measures regulating economic activity, he believed that arguments for restraining trade or putting it under government were often specious and merely served to cloak the promotion of private interests. He also thought that many potentially beneficial regulatory measures were being manipulated in such a way as to damage the public good. These convictions led him to attack various restraints on trade in the parliaments of the early 1620s and to promote the passage of an important law *in futurum* against monopolistic trading practices. Nevertheless, Coke's support for free trade in these years was muted for several different reasons. In the first place, he still believed in the value of particular regulatory measures, particularly when they concerned foreign trade, and was unwilling to support extreme proposals that would have overthrown the privileges of important trading organizations like the Merchant Adventurers or the Eastland Company. Second, although he knew about the corrupt methods by which regulatory statutes were often enforced, he nevertheless favored the continued enforcement of certain penal laws like the Statute of Artificers. Third, he obviously realized that attempts to abolish well-established monopolies would arouse considerable opposition within Parliament, that controversies over radical proposals for free trade would seriously disrupt Parliament's proceedings and prevent it from remedying other important grievances, and that he would have to accept certain compromises (as he did in the case of the Monopolies Act) in the interest of securing the enactment of any significant remedies for grievances in trade. Fourth, although he knew that there were institutionalized reinforcements for restraints on English trade, he tended to view these restraints as creations of particular corrupt individuals and to believe that attacks on particular abuses, rather than on general policies or well-established institutions, might constitute effective remedies at least for certain grievances in trade. Fifth, in spite of his opposition to many existing restraints on trade and his concern about the ongoing trade depression, he apparently did not regard economic abuses as immediate or potentially lethal threats to the commonwealth. Finally, his failure to press more strongly for the implementation of parliamentary remedies for economic abuses is probably attributable, in part, to his continuing faith in other governmental institutions besides Parliament. Although he believed that frequent, if not yearly, Parliaments were necessary because of the recurrent need for parliamentary remedies for certain types of grievances, he still believed that the Privy Council and the common-law courts were capable of taking actions that would promote the public good, even in the absence of clear, detailed legislative directions from Parliament. Moreover, while he may have distrusted certain influential courtiers like Buckingham, he did not believe in the early 1620s that the court was actively and deliberately subverting those fundamental legal and governmental principles on which the public good, in his opinion, depended. Nevertheless, if significant changes were to take place in his attitude toward the court and toward the grievances of the commonwealth, his parliamentary actions would be likely to change as well.

The Privileges and Powers
of Parliament

Coke's primary objective in the parliaments of 1621 and 1624 was to remedy specific grievances and not to expand parliamentary power, attack royal authority, or engage in constitutional controversies with the king or court. His efforts to remedy grievances by bill and petition, moreover, occasioned relatively little constitutional controversy. The substance of these remedies was sometimes heatedly debated, but only rarely did anyone dispute the Commons's or Parliament's power to implement them. Few questions were raised about Parliament's efforts to regulate court procedure, about the Commons's quasi-judicial proceedings against monopoly patents, or about the limits placed on the royal prerogative by the bills against monopolies and concealments. In fact, only two sorts of parliamentary actions were seen as constitutional novelties in 1621 and 1624 or provoked much debate: the Commons's petition of 1621 on war and foreign policy; and the parliamentary trials of 1621 and 1624. The Commons were obliged to construct highly complex arguments to demonstrate that Parliament as a whole and each of its constituent houses could act as courts in certain cases; and their efforts to judge and sentence Edward Floyd in 1621 involved them in a brief confrontation with both the king and the Lords. Much more intense parliamentary conflict arose in the fall of 1621, when the House offered James formal advice on foreign affairs in the hope of inducing him to take a firmer anti-Spanish and anti-Catholic position abroad. To justify this action, the Commons ultimately adopted a protestation of their privileges and the king responded by dissolving Parliament.

In spite of these clashes, however, one should not overestimate the importance of constitutional conflict in James I's last two parliaments or attribute it to the Commons's desire to expand their own powers at the expense of royal authority. In retrospect, Parliament's prosecutions of important crown servants like Bacon and Middlesex look like attacks on the crown that prefigured the more dramatic assertions of parliamentary power of the 1640s. During the early 1620s, however, the revival of parliamentary judicature was not thought to threaten the crown and was achieved with singularly little controversy. Only the Commons's ill-advised efforts to sentence Floyd provoked serious disagreements about Parliament's judicial powers, and even these disagreements were quickly resolved. The Commons's interest in expanding the scope of their privilege of free speech was less intense than one might suppose. They avoided possible clashes on this issue until the very end of the fall session in 1621 and only adopted the extreme statement of their privileges found in the Protestation after their various attempts to compromise with the king had failed. In 1624 they avoided reopening controversies over free speech that had led to Parliament's dissolution three years before; and although they formally expressed their views on war policy, they did so only after they had been explicitly invited to do so.

Nevertheless, while constitutional conflict did not dominate the parliaments of 1621 or 1624, those constitutional controversies that arose were not mere aberrations. They reflected tensions that would be more clearly manifested in the later 1620s. The Commons's debates on the Protestation and on Floyd's case indicate their increasing propensity to believe that minor concessions in controversies over their privileges and powers might undermine their ability to remedy grievances. They were coming to believe in four propositions whose implications were particularly conducive to parliamentary conflict and stalemate: that the survival of English subjects' liberties depended on Parliament's ability to remedy grievances effectively; that Parliament's ability to do this depended upon its ability to maintain its own privileges and powers; that all parliamentary privileges and powers had to be scrupulously maintained and actively defended if any of them were to survive; and that because these privileges and powers could be seen as "the inheritance" of English subjects, attacks on them threatened property rights and individual liberties. As members of Parliament became more prone to adopt these positions, their views on parliamentary issues became more rigid and monolithic and they gradually lost the freedom to maneuver without which parliamentary compromise and action were impossible. They were coming to see their interests as a circle, no part of which could be broken without damage to the whole. Such a situation had not yet developed in 1621 or 1624, but it was dimly foreshadowed in certain speeches from those years and would emerge more clearly in the parliaments of the later 1620s.

The most striking constitutional innovation of the early 1620s was Parliament's sudden assumption of broad judicial powers.[1] In James I's last two parliaments, the Commons and Lords used, or attempted to use,

---

1. On this development, see Tite, *Impeachment*; and Roberts, *Growth of Responsible Government*, chaps. 1–2.

these powers to try ten different men, including a lord chancellor, a lord treasurer, and several clients of the reigning royal favorite. The legitimacy of these proceedings was established by Coke and other lawyers who successfully argued that Parliament's right to act as a court in certain cases was supported by precedents from the later middle ages. The existence of medieval precedents for the judicial proceedings of James I's last two parliaments did not alter the fact that these proceedings marked a sharp break with the practices of Tudor parliaments. But despite the relative novelty of Parliament's judicial actions during the 1620s, its use of judicial powers in these years did not constitute radical political action. The Commons never attacked men whom the king really wished to defend and usually used procedures whose legitimacy could not be questioned by either the king or the Lords. Their judicial proceedings, moreover, were basically extensions of their more traditional attempts to remedy grievances and reflected their basically conservative propensity to find scapegoats for these grievances rather than seek their more fundamental, institutional causes. Only during the later 1620s did the Commons use Parliament's newly developed judicial power as a political weapon against the king's intimates or employ parliamentary trials as a means of focusing and dramatizing their attacks on court policies.

Coke played a very active part in the revival of parliamentary judicature during the early 1620s, but his speeches on Parliament's judicial proceedings during these years do not reveal him as a steadfast opponent of the court or as the proponent of a coherent theory of limited monarchy or parliamentary sovereignty. Although he saw practical value in Parliament's newfound judicial powers and helped establish their legitimacy, he had no plan to make Parliament supreme; and he showed relatively little interest in developing, articulating, or implementing a consistent theory of parliamentary judicature, or in working out a strict division of responsibility between the Commons and the Lords in parliamentary trials. Finally, he seemed so willing to cooperate and compromise with the king and the upper house that some of his fellow members actually attacked him for damaging the Commons's privileges. He was obviously eager to use Parliament's judicial powers against important figures like Bacon and Middlesex, as well as against less politically important men. But these two prominent courtiers had their enemies at court and were not royal favorites whom James wished actively to defend, and Middlesex had in fact alienated the king's most intimate counselor, the duke of Buckingham. Coke's attacks on these two men, moreover, reveal his inclination to blame major grievances on individual wrongdoers instead of explaining them by reference to more basic, structural features of

English government. And his attacks against Cranfield show how closely he was willing to work with the royal favorite.

The first person against whom the Commons proceeded in 1621 was Sir Francis Michell.[2] While Coke took part in these proceedings, he did little to clarify the legal issues that they raised. Since the Commons originally sentenced Michell themselves and only later forwarded charges against him to the upper house, his case raised difficult questions about the limits of their own jurisdiction and about the scope of their power to punish; but instead of fully answering these questions in accordance with a coherent theory of parliamentary judicature, Coke worked mainly to secure Michell's punishment so as to make an example of him to other monopolists who might challenge the legitimacy of the Commons's proceedings against monopoly patents. Although his attack on Michell was integrally connected with his more general attack on those monopoly patents that had been approved by prominent courtiers and granted by James I, it in no way reflected his "opposition" to the Stuart court or king. The king's supporters in the lower house supported Michell's punishment by the Commons.[3] The Lords chose to augment his sentence, and the king never indicated the slightest opposition to Parliament's proceedings against him.

Michell was an associate of Sir Giles Mompesson and was involved in the administration of both the alehouse patent and the gold and silver thread monopoly.[4] After examining him for several days about his role in enforcing the former patents[5] the Commons's Committee of Grievances received a petition from him on 23 February in which he denied having played any role in procuring the patent, noted that it had been approved by important royal advisors, and claimed that he had merely executed it to the best of his abilities.[6] At one point in his petition, he characterized certain objections to the patent as "ignorant" ones; but whether he was referring to the Commons's objections, as they later charged, or to those of the alehouse keepers, as he later insisted, is not entirely clear.[7] Later on the twenty-third, Coke reported to the House that the committee had condemned the alehouse patent "both for matter and manner" and went on to charge that Michell's petition was an affront to the honor of the

2. On Michell's case, see Tite, *Impeachment*, pp. 91–94; White, "Coke," pp. 86–89; and White, "Rev. Tite, *Impeachment*," pp. 1939–41.

3. See the speeches of Sir Thomas Edmondes and Sir George Calvert in *CD 1621*, 6:4–5.

4. Gardiner, *History*, 4:16; Tite, *Impeachment*, p. 91.

5. February 19: *CD 1621*, 7:501–2. February 20: 6:260–61; 5:483; 4:86; 6:284. February 21: 2:213; 6:263–64, 283–84; 4:91.

6. Ibid., 6:94; 2:127 n. 7; *P&D*, 1:82–83. For the petition, see *CD 1621*, 7:499–501.

7. See White, "Rev. Tite, *Impeachment*," pp. 1940–41.

House and therefore constituted contempt.[8] Sir Dudley Digges then stated that Michell deserved to be punished for this contempt, as well as for his "other faults";[9] and after the question had been proposed as to what punishment the Commons should impose on him,[10] Coke moved that he be removed from the Commission of the Peace and disabled from serving on it in the future and that he be imprisoned in the Tower until he had been put out of the Commission and made his submission to the House.[11]

Since Coke failed to specify the offenses for which these punishments were to be imposed on Michell, his proposal is difficult to interpret. But, as the conclusion of the Commons's debate showed, it raised several complex legal issues that he failed to discuss. In the first place, the Commons did not necessarily have the power to impose Coke's first proposed punishment on anyone, regardless of his offense. John Glanville later argued that they could not legally remove Michell from the commission, not because they lacked all jurisdiction over his offenses, but because the power to remove a man from the commission pertained to some other governmental body.[12] The Commons were apparently impressed by this argument, for instead of ordering Michell's removal from the commission, they voted only to declare him unworthy of serving on it both for the present and in the future.[13] Coke's proposals for punishing Michell also raised a second legal problem that he failed to discuss. Since the Commons had not clearly established their jurisdiction over any offenses besides ones committed against their privileges while Parliament was sitting, Coke's proposed punishments would have been difficult to justify if they had been construed as punishments not for Michell's contempt to the House, but for his other offenses.[14] Many members believed that they were sentencing Michell for offenses committed in enforcing the alehouse patent,[15] but Coke never indicated that they might lack the power to do this. Nor did he try to show that their jurisdiction actually extended further than was generally supposed.[16] His failure to discuss either the

8. CD 1621, 2:127–28.
9. Ibid., 4:94; 6:4; 5:485.
10. Ibid., 2:130.
11. CD 1621, 6:4; 2:130 and n. 14; P&D, 1:84.
12. CD 1621, 2:131.
13. Ibid., 2:132; 6:5; P&D, 1:85.
14. Under Elizabeth the Commons had established their right to punish their own members for offenses both when the House was sitting and when it was not (Elton, TC, pp. 260, 277–80), and their right to punish nonmembers for offenses committed against the House while the House was sitting (TC, pp. 261–62). In 1621, the Commons exercised this latter right on two occasions (see White, "Coke," p. 87 n. 9).
15. See, for example, CD 1621, 6:454.
16. On discussion of this point by other members, see Tite, Impeachment, pp. 91–92; and White, "Rev. Tite, Impeachment."

scope of the House's power to punish or the limits of its jurisdiction could be explained in one of three ways: he may not have considered these issues; he may have been reluctant to raise them directly because he had doubts about his ability to justify the punishments that he had proposed; or he may have hoped that the house would impose a sentence on Michell that he could later interpret either as a precedent for an extension of its jurisdiction or as a judgment consistent with a more restricted, traditional interpretation of its jurisdiction. Whatever the reasons for his proposal, it cannot be interpreted as part of a well planned, self-conscious campaign to develop and justify Parliament's powers of judicature.

It was only several days later, after questions had been raised about the legality of the Commons's sentence on Michell, that Coke attempted to rationalize their proceedings in the case. On 27 February, when they were debating Mompesson's case, it was argued that they had exceeded their jurisdiction in punishing Michell, because the offenses for which he had been sentenced had not been committed while Parliament was sitting.[17] In reply, Coke developed an entirely new justification for the Commons's sentence. He maintained that they had sentenced him not for his role in enforcing the alehouse patent (a point that he had not made clear on the twenty-third) but for justifying his role in enforcing a patent that the House had condemned as a grievance. Although the former offense or offenses had not been committed while Parliament was sitting, he claimed, the latter had been and constituted a contempt to the House.[18] Coke was thus attempting to do two things. First, he was directly denying, as he had not done on the twenty-third, that the Commons had sentenced Michell for his role in enforcing the alehouse patent. Second, he was constructing an entirely new interpretation of Michell's contempt. Whereas this contempt had been previously held to have consisted in Michell's derogatory comments about the Commons's objections to the alehouse patent, Coke now claimed that it consisted simply of his having attempted to justify his actions with respect to the condemned patent. Coke's reasons for developing this new interpretation of the case are not entirely clear; but his speech can be explained as follows. First, he was now prepared to state that the Commons had not sentenced Michell for his role in enforcing the alehouse patent because it had become clear that any such extension of their jurisdiction would encounter strong and perhaps conclusive objections. Second, his reinterpretation of Michell's contempt can be accounted for in one of two ways. Either he wished to enhance the status of the Commons's novel, quasi-judicial proceedings

17. CD 1621, 6:431.
18. Ibid., 4:11–12; 5:15 and n. 2, 523; 6:15, 356, 431–32.

against monopoly patents by construing any objection to them as a contempt, or else he realized that Michell had successfully raised doubts about whether he had actually characterized the Commons's objections to the alehouse patent as "ignorant" and that the Commons needed a new theory about what his contempt had consisted of.[19]

Coke's justification of the Commons's sentence on Michell provided no legal basis for their proceedings against Michell's associate, Sir Giles Mompesson. Like Michell, he was involved in the administration of monopoly patents that the Commons had condemned, but he had done nothing that could be construed as a contempt to their House. As a result, they were ultimately obliged to refer his case to the Lords for judgment.[20] During his trial, Coke cited numerous precedents to justify Parliament's proceedings against him, as well as the sentence on Michell and all future parliamentary judicial proceedings.[21] An examination of these speeches shows, however, that he had advanced no coherent theory of parliamentary judicature and that he revised his views on this subject whenever he found it convenient to do so. The most crucial issue on which he changed his position concerned the division of responsibility between Lords and Commons in cases judged by the former,[22] but he also seems to have altered his stance about the judicial powers that the Commons could exercise by themselves alone. In addition, he took no consistent position on the question of whether the Commons had the power to administer an oath.

The Commons's proceedings against Mompesson began with a series of examinations in the Committee of Grievances, in which Coke, as chairman, acted as Mompesson's principal interrogator.[23] By 27 February the committee had found that Mompesson had committed many offenses,[24] but it had no notion about how to proceed against him[25] until

19. See fn. 7.
20. On Mompesson's case, see Tite, *Impeachment*, pp. 92–110; Zaller, *1621*, pp. 56–60, 62–67, 77–78; *LD 1621–1628*, pp. xii–xv; Gardiner, *History*, 4:41–44, 54, 84; Tanner, *CD*, pp. 321–24; Kenyon, *SC*, pp. 93–94; Roberts, *Growth of Responsible Government*, pp. 23–25; White, "Coke," pp. 90–96; and White, "Rev. Tite, *Impeachment*," pp. 1941–44.
21. See Tite, *Impeachment*, pp. 44–47, 222.
22. On the differences between the analysis given here and the one given by Tite, see White, "Rev. Tite, *Impeachment*."
23. *CD 1621*, 6:251; 2:112–13; 5:481; 4:85. See also Zaller, *1621*, pp. 56–57.
24. For Coke's report of these offenses, see *CD 1621*, 2:145; 4:110–11; 5:260; 5:522–23; 6:14, 301, 378; *P&D*, 1:102–3; *CJ*, 1:530.
25. The Committee had left the question to the House (*CD 1621*, 2:145). After Phelips had moved that some be appointed to search the Tower for records to see "how far our power will extend to punish him," the House ordered that a committee "take consideration of [Mompesson's] offense" and that Noy and Hakewill search for records in the Tower and report back to the committee, which should in turn report back to the House on the next

Coke suddenly proposed on the twenty-eighth that the House refer his case to the Lords, who could then pass judgment on him.[26] In a complex, highly obscure speech delivered in committee, Coke explained and justified this course as follows. The Court of Parliament, he said, was and always had been both "a court of counsel" and "a court of pleas," but when it had been divided into two houses, "indivisible things," like the power of judicature, had "remained with the Lords." In many former cases, the Commons had heard complaints and examined grievances, and, after trying "matters of fact," they had "resorted to the Lords for judicature." The precise procedures that they had followed in going to the Lords, however, had varied. In some cases, the Commons had been made "plaintiffs" and the "delinquents" had answered their charges in the Lords. In other cases, the steward of the household had "made a complaint and the Commons were made a party" to the case in the Lords. In other cases, still, the Lords had had "the cognizance alone."[27] Whatever the procedure, Coke declared, no one who had been found guilty had been able to "bear out the storm of the common forces," and although "no judgement in this kind" had been rendered in Parliament since the time of Henry VI, many precedents existed for it from earlier reigns. He also noted that although one precedent from Henry IV's reign seemed to conflict with his position on Parliament's judicial power, it did not bind later parliaments since it was only an ordinance.[28]

Coke then reported to the Commons the committee's opinion that

---

day (*CD 1621*, 2:146). On the twenty-eighth, Noy and Hakewill reported to the committee that they could find no precedents in the Tower for punishment of Mompesson by the Commons alone (*CD 1621*, 2:146; 6:301–2).

26. On the twenty-seventh, a similar proposal had been made (*CD 1621*, 2:146; 5:260; *CJ*, 1:530) but seems to have gone unnoticed.

27. MS. 2 of Pym's diary (*CD 1621*, 4:115) reads, "And sometimes *the Commons* would have the cognizance alone" (my italics). However, MSS. 1 and 3 read, "And sometimes the Commons would have the cognizance alone" (see *CD 1621*, 4:115 and n. c.). Tite (*Impeachment*, pp. 44–45) follows the editors of *CD 1621* in preferring the MS. 2 reading. My own reading can be justified as follows. Because Coke had just said that after the division of Parliament into two Houses, "indivisible things remained with the Lords" (*CD 1621*, 4:115), and because he was apparently implying that the power to hear "pleas" was "an indivisible thing," it seems unlikely that he would have said a few moments later that the Commons could judge pleas alone. The readings of MSS. 1 and 3 lend some support to the view that he said no such thing, because they obviously require emendation and allow for the possibility that the subject of the verb of which "cognizance" is the direct object was originally "the Lords." This conjectural reading implies, however, that Coke changed his position on parliamentary judicature between the time of this speech and the time of his speech to the Lords on 8 March.

28. See *RP*, 3:427, no. 70. When the king later cited this precedent in Floyd's case to show that the Commons lacked the power to be parties in judicial cases, Coke dismissed it just as he did in this speech on Mompesson's case (see pp. 155–58). For other cases that Coke may have cited, see *CD 1621*, 4:116 and nn. 2–4. For the only report of Coke's speech, see *CD 1621*, 4:115–16.

"according to ancient precedents" they should refer Mompesson's case to the Lords.[29] This plan was quickly approved.[30] On 7 March, the Commons finished preparing the case for presentation to the upper house and on the following morning heard rehearsals of speeches by those who were to present the case to the Lords that afternoon.[31] The last of these speakers was Coke, whom the House had previously ordered to speak "for matter of precedents to justify our proceedings [,] for punishment [,] for the offences [,] and [for] the remedies to prevent the like in time to come [,] and so to conclude."[32] Cast in this role, he presented an elaborate justification of the Commons's proceedings in the case that differed from the one that he had given on 28 February.[33] He began by stating that "in Parliament the power of judicature and judicial proceedings is of four sorts: (1) Coram Domino Rege et Magnatibus, (2) Coram Magnatibus Tantum, (3) Coram Magnatibus et Communitate, (4) Coram Communitate Tantum." Although he cited numerous precedents for each of these four types of parliamentary judicature,[34] he spoke mainly about the second one (Coram Magnatibus Tantum) that was being employed in Mompesson's case. Proceedings before the Lords alone, he said, could take place in three sorts of cases. First, the Lords could judge alone in cases of "necessity," where otherwise "justice would fail[, as] upon a writ of error in a judgement in King's Bench."[35] Second, in other cases that he failed to characterize, the Lords had original jurisdiction. Third, the Lords could act as judges "at the prayer of the Commons," as they had done in at least five cases in the past and as they were about to do in Mompesson's case.[36]

Coke repeated these points at a conference with the Lords that afternoon[37] and ultimately incorporated many of them into his *Fourth*

29. CD 1621, 2:148; cf. 4:116; 5:264, 531; 6:10, 302.
30. Ibid., 2:149. The House also ordered the former committee for punishment to review all Mompesson's offenses (CD 1621, 2:149) and planned to have a select committee conduct further examinations into his case (CD 1621, 5:531; 6:19; CJ, 1:532).
31. Zaller, 1621, pp. 59–66.
32. CD 1621, 2:170–71; my interpolations. Hakewill observed on this occasion that Coke had been "a father of the law" (CD 1621, 2:170).
33. Tite minimizes the differences between the two speeches (see *Impeachment*, p. 45).
34. For the precedents, see Tite, *Impeachment*, pp. 44–47, 222.
35. Only the Lords could be judges in such cases, Coke said, for the king, being "pars gravata," could not serve as a judge.
36. For the discussion of punishment that concluded this speech, see White, "Coke," p. 93 n. 24.
37. CD 1621, 2:193–98; 6:43–45, 307–9. The afternoon version of the speech differed from the morning one in two respects. First, Coke omitted from the afternoon speech a precedent that was thought "to impugn the privilege" of the Commons (CD 1621, 4:137). Second, when Coke addressed the Lords, he apparently added a preoration on corruption (CD 1621, 2:127) that is discussed in chap. 3. On the rest of the proceedings against

Institutes.[38] But they reflected a view of parliamentary judicature that differed somewhat from the one that he had expressed on 28 February. In the first place, he now said that in certain cases a parliamentary judgment could be given not just by the Lords, but by the Lords and the king. Second, in his earlier speech he seems to have implied that judicial power was an "indivisible" thing that could not be exercised by both houses. But he now asserted that the Commons's power to judge was of the same nature as other sorts of parliamentary judicial power, which was a position that obviously fortified the Commons's earlier sentence on Michell and that provided a basis for their future proceedings against Floyd. Finally, Coke seems to have slightly altered his views about the Commons's role in cases judged by the Lords. On the twenty-eighth he had suggested that the lower house could initiate such trials in several different ways; but he was now apparently claiming that such trials could only be initiated at the "prayer" of the lower house.[39]

These changes in Coke's ideas were slight ones. But they still show the flexibility of his views about parliamentary judicature and his failure to develop a coherent theory to explain the procedures being employed in Mompesson's case. He obviously believed that the Lords were to judge Mompesson, but he had no fixed opinion about the Commons's role in the case. His failure to commit himself on this latter issue became apparent in a crucial debate on the case held on 16 March. This debate arose when the Lords suddenly requested that several members of the Commons who had knowledge of Mompesson's offenses testify under oath in the upper house. Like other members, Coke wished initially to deny this request on the grounds that it was somehow inconsistent with the legal theory underlying their previous proceedings in the case. As to what this legal theory was, however, Coke had no fixed opinion. Moreover, when he saw that a flat denial of the request would make it difficult, if not impossible, for Parliament to proceed successfully against Bacon, he quickly reversed himself and supported granting it.[40]

His first argument against acceding to the Lords' request ran as follows. Members of the Commons were judges who had "affirmative

Mompesson, see Tite, *Impeachment*, pp. 102–10; and Zaller, *1621*, pp. 66–67, 69, 72–4, 77–78.

38. See *Institutes*, 4:23–24 ("Of Judicature") and 21–23 ("Of Writs of Error in Parliament").

39. For reports of Coke's speech to the Lords, see *CD 1621*, 4:134–37; 5:32–33, 280–82; 6:38–39; *CJ*, 1:545–46; *P&D*, 1:133–4.

40. The sources for this debate are: *CD 1621*, 2:232–33; 4:162; 5:45–46, 302–13; 6:69; *CJ*, 1:557; *P&D*, 1:177. For discussions of the debate, see Zaller, *1621*, pp. 78–79; Tite, *Impeachment*, pp. 105–6; White, "Coke," pp. 94–96; and White, "Rev. Tite, *Impeachment*," pp. 1942–44.

and negative power and voice in making or rejecting of laws," and along with the Lords, they formed a single court. Just as judges of the Common Pleas or Star Chamber could not testify under oath in their own courts, even if they had knowledge of a particular case before those courts, so members of the Commons could not legally give sworn testimony before their fellow judges in the Lords.[41] This argument might have been difficult to sustain in the face of the counterargument that the Commons were not Mompesson's "judges" in the same sense as the Lords were and that their function in proceedings *coram magnatibus tartum* differed from that of the upper house. For this reason, perhaps, Coke quickly developed another rationale for refusing the Lords' request. The reason that members of the Commons were not "to be examined upon oath for [matters of] fact," he later claimed, was not only that they were judges but also that as representatives of the commonwealth, they were deemed to have "[n]otice of all things in the commonwealth," and their judgments for matters of fact, therefore, could never be questioned but had to be admitted.[42]

These two arguments of Coke's completely ruled out the possibility of the Commons's acceding to the Lords' request. But when the chancellor of the duchy of Lancaster noted that the Commons's proceedings against Bacon (which were rapidly progressing in the Committee for Courts) "did depend wholly" upon the testimony of two members of the House,[43] Coke saw the necessity of changing his views about whether the Commons could grant the Lords' present request in Mompesson's case. For any legal barrier that he erected against granting it would almost certainly prevent the Lords from getting the kind of evidence that they would require to convict Bacon. Coke's solution to this problem was inelegant but effective. After Sir Edwin Sandys had spoken persuasively for allowing the two members to testify against Mompesson in the Lords,[44] Coke recast his earlier arguments on this issue. He had previously stated that these members could not legally testify in the Lords about matters that had been previously resolved by the Commons. But he now claimed that they simply had a privilege against doing so. He could then argue that while they could not be compelled to testify, they could do so if they chose, because it was "a maxim in law" that "Qui libet potest renunciare iuri [sic] pro seipso."[45] The House then resolved that "upon request from the Lords any member of the House might offer himself to be examined

41. CD 1621, 2:233; 4:162; 5:45, 303; 6:69–70; CJ, 1:559.
42. CD 1621, 5:46–47; 6:70; CJ, 1:557; P&D, 1:177.
43. CD 1621, 4:162–63. See Zaller, 1621, p. 79.
44. CD 1621, 4:163. See Tite, *Impeachment*, p. 105; and Zaller, 1621, p. 79.
45. CD 1621, 2:235; 5:48, 303; 4:164; CJ, 1:558.

there and sworn." No further problems arose in the case, and on 26 March the Lords passed judgment against Mompesson.[46]

Although Coke's last speech in this case had helped to smooth the way for the Commons's proceedings against Bacon, his role in this latter case was relatively slight.[47] By attacking monopoly patents approved by Bacon,[48] as well as abuses in Chancery, Coke had helped to discredit the chancellor; and by justifying and explaining Parliament's judicial proceedings against Mompesson, he had laid the legal basis for Bacon's trial in the Lords. In the Commons's discussions of Bacon's case itself, however, Coke said very little.[49] He insisted that there were precedents to support their decision to refer his case to the Lords.[50] He easily persuaded them to ignore the king's proposal that a special, royally appointed parliamentary committee investigate the charges against Bacon.[51] And he answered questions raised in the House about the sufficiency of the evidence against the chancellor.[52] In the Commons's debates on Sir John Bennet's case, however, Coke resumed the position of leadership that he had held in their proceedings against Mompesson. He helped to support their case against Bennet by citing additional precedents for Parliament's power to punish corrupt judges and again demonstrated the flexibility of his views concerning the conduct of parliamentary trials. Bennet was a judge of the prerogative court of Canterbury and of several other tribunals, and he was also a member of the Commons in 1621.[53] In March he was accused in the Committee of Courts of taking numerous bribes.[54] After inquiring into some of these charges,[55] the Commons held several lengthy debates about whether to investigate all charges against him before sending his case to the Lords.[56] This question was difficult to

46. For the Commons's resolution, see *CD 1621*, 4:164. On the Lords' judgment on Mompesson, see Tite, *Impeachment*, p. 108.

47. On Bacon's case, see Marwil, *Bacon*, pp. 42–62; Tite, *Impeachment*, pp. 110–18; Zaller, *1621*, pp. 74–85; and White, "Coke," pp. 97–100.

48. On Bacon's role as a referee for patents, see Zaller, *1621*, pp. 57, 63–64.

49. His speeches are discussed in White, "Coke," at pp. 97–100.

50. *CJ*, 1:561; Zaller, *1621*, p. 80; Tite, *Impeachment*, p. 112.

51. *CD 1621*, 2:245; 4:170; 5:51, 309; *CJ*, 1:563. See Zaller, *1621*, pp. 82–83; Tite, *Impeachment*, p. 113.

52. *CD 1621*, 2:241–42; 4:168; *CJ*, 1:560. On the evidentiary question, see Tite, *Impeachment*, pp. 112–13; Zaller, *1621*, p. 81; and White, "Coke," pp. 98–99 and nn. 9–14.

53. On Bennet's case, see Tite, *Impeachment*, pp. 133–36; Zaller, *1621*, pp. 97–99; Gardiner, *History*, 4:108, 125, 350.

54. *CD 1621*, 2:279; 4:212.

55. See White, "Coke," pp. 101–3 and nn. 4–17.

56. See *CD 1621*, 3:28–32; 2:302–3; 4:238–39; 5:282–84, 339–41; *P&D*, 1:282–84; *CJ*, 1:583–84. See also *CD 1621*, 3:51–61; 2:310–15; 4:245–49; 5:90–93, 344–45; 6:467; *P&D*, 1:297–302; *CJ*, 1:587–88.

answer partly because Bennet was a member of the Commons and had not yet appeared to answer their charges against him. It was also problematical because it raised more questions about the division of roles between Commons and Lords in a parliamentary trial. Did the function of investigating an alleged delinquent belong solely to the Commons? Or could it be shared with the Lords? On 20 and 23 April, Coke argued that the lower house should in effect share its power of investigation with the Lords by having them inquire into most of the charges against Bennet. He recommended this course to the Commons, he said, because it would save them time and because the Lords' power to examine on oath, which the Commons lacked, would facilitate the investigation of those charges.[57]

Other members, however, opposed Coke's proposal for several different reasons. Some may have been reluctant to concede that the Commons lacked the power to give an oath, which was a concession that Coke himself later refused to make. Others claimed that the Commons still lacked sufficient evidence against Bennet to expel him and that their privileges would be maimed if they let the upper house investigate a sitting member of theirs.[58] The main arguments made against Coke's proposal, however, were that it would permit the Lords to usurp the Commons's investigative role in a parliamentary trial and that such a usurpation was either illegal or highly improper. Pym stated that parliamentary trials like Bennet's consisted of three parts, inquisition, judgment, and execution, and that the Commons should "reserve the power of inquisition solely" to themselves by investigating his offenses as thoroughly as possible "and so leave nothing but judicature to the Lords."[59] Serjeant Ashley, Digges, and Hakewill gave similar reasons for proceeding more slowly in the case than Coke had suggested,[60] but the Commons ultimately decided on the twenty-third to refer Bennet's case to the Lords.[61] On the next day, after Sackville had presented six charges against Bennet to the Lords,[62] Coke "knit up" the Commons's case with his lengthy speech on judicial corruption.[63] Bennet's trial began in the Upper House in late May but ceased with the June adjournment and was never resumed.[64]

57. For his speech of the twentieth, see CD 1621, 3:28; 2:302; 5:82–83, 339; for his motions of the twenty-third, see 3:352 n. 12; P&D, 1:297; CJ, 1:587.
58. See CD 1621, 3:31.
59. Ibid., 3:30.
60. Ibid., 3:53–55; 2:314; P&D, 1:299; CJ, 1:587.
61. They first found him "faulty" in the six cases charged to him and expelled him from the House. See CD 1621, 3:56; 4:248; 6:91.
62. Ibid., 3:75; 6:391–92.
63. Ibid., 3:75–77; 5:95–96; 6:392–93. On this speech, see pp. 54–55.
64. On the conclusion of the case, see Tite, Impeachment, pp. 135–36.

Although the Commons had assigned Coke the role of summing up the case against Bennet, his earlier proposals about how to proceed in the case had obviously displeased certain members who later claimed that he had "restrained the liberty of the [Lower] House by too often going to the Lords."[65] In the next case considered by the Commons, he again failed to take an intransigent position in support of their judicial powers; and although he made some blunt statements about their power to act as a court of record, he ultimately revealed his usual willingness to compromise with the Lords and king in the interests of saving time and preserving "good correspondency." This next case concerned Edward Floyd, a Catholic lawyer imprisoned in the Fleet, who had been overheard making derogatory remarks about the king's daughter Elizabeth and her husband, the Elector Palatine Frederick V.[66] His remarks were reported to a Commons committee investigating the Fleet, which reported them in turn to the house on 28 April.[67] Three days later, after denouncing Floyd as "a dangerous fellow" with a "popish heart," Coke urged the Commons "to punish all such offenders and so suppress such insolency as far as we can find it in any whomsoever" and moved for a special committee to examine the case that afternoon.[68] When this committee met several hours later, however, Coke mysteriously absented himself and was not even present when the full house upheld the committee's recommendation to pass a harsh sentence on Floyd.[69] On 2 May, the king stayed the execution of this sentence and informed the Commons that he "desired . . . satisfaction in the [two] doubts" that had induced him to take this action: "(1) whether this House be a court of record and has a power of judicature in such matters as do not concern our own privileges and members . . . ; (2) if there be such a power, whether it be fit to use it in inflicting punishment upon a denying party without proof upon oath." The king also brought to the Commons's attention a precedent from Henry IV's reign that seemed to show, according to Cranfield, that they had been "misled by those who affirmed the power of this House to judge alone."[70]

65. On Floyd's case, see ibid., pp. 122–33; Zaller, *1621*, pp. 104–14; and White, "Coke," pp. 107–17 and nn. 1–63.

66. Zaller, *1621*, p. 104.

67. *CD 1621*, 3:109; 4:298; 6:110; *CJ*, 1:596.

68. *CJ*, 1:600; *CD 1621*, 3:117.

69. For the Commons's May first debate, see *CD 1621*, 3:118–19, 121–27; 4:285–87, 296; 5:127–30, 258–60; 6:118–22, 397–98; *P&D*, 1:369–74; *CJ*, 1:600–602. For Coke's reference to his absence from these proceedings, see *CJ*, 1:604. For the Commons's sentence on Floyd, see *CD 1621*, 3:127–28; 4:287; 5:130, 361; 6:122, 398; 2:235; *P&D*, 1:374; *CJ*, 1:602.

70. *CD 1621*, 4:290–91; cf. 3:134–36; 2:337; 6:398; *P&D*, 2:5; *CJ*, 1:602. See also

This royal message obviously posed difficult problems for Coke. While he was not determined to support the Commons's sentence on Floyd in the face of such strong royal opposition, he would not accept the king's position about Parliament. James I was directly questioning not only the lower house's judgment on Floyd, but also its power to act as a court of record, its power to punish anyone other than its own members or those who offended against its privileges, and its power to punish any denying party without sworn testimony. Moreover, since the power to fine and imprison was thought by some to be reserved solely to courts of record, the message could be read as a challenge to the Commons's right to impose these punishments, even on its own members or those who offended against its privileges.[71] Finally, by citing the record of 1 Henry IV as an authoritative statement about Parliament's judicial powers, the king seemed to be making an even more serious challenge to the legality of Parliament's previous judicial acts. This record stated not only that the Commons were not parties to parliamentary judgments, but also that the power of judgment in Parliament was reserved to the Lords *and the king*. By citing it, therefore, the king seemed to be questioning the legality of all judgments by the Commons alone, all parliamentary proceedings to which the Commons had been a party, and all parliamentary judgments given by the Lords alone without the king. It could thus be read as a veiled legal challenge to all of the Commons's judgments (including those made against Michell or against the Commons's own members) and those given in parliamentary election cases, *and* to the judgments given by the Lords in the cases of Mompesson, Michell, and Bacon.

Because of its possible implications, the king's message obviously called for a response, but Coke had considerable difficulty in formulating a suitable one.[72] Initially, on 2 May, he tried to circumvent the problems that the message raised by insisting, on the one hand, that the Commons were a court of record while suggesting, on the other, that they lacked the power to give an oath and should refer Floyd's case to the Lords.[73] This

---

Zaller, *1621*, p. 106; Tite, *Impeachment*, p. 123–24. For the record and Coke's earlier remarks about it, see p. 149 and fn. 28.

71. For a detailed study of Coke's views about the nature of courts of record, see Samuel E. Thorne, "Courts of Record and Sir Edward Coke."

72. After hearing the king's message, most members of the Commons simply backed down. Hakewill said that he had been "a diligent searcher of precedents" for the Commons's power of judicature but had not found any. Sandys admitted that he had not spoken in the debate on punishing Floyd but said that his opinion then had been that the Commons should have informed the king of the charges and referred those charges to the Lords. Noy stated flatly that while the Lords had a power of judicature, the Commons did not (CD 1621, 3:137–38). Coke was obviously eager to refute Noy's contention.

73. Ibid., 3:138–39; 2:338–39; 4:292–93; 6:127–28, 399; 5:133, 363; CJ, 1:603–4. For a detailed discussion of the speech, see White, "Coke," pp. 111–13 and nn. 18–33.

solution, however, was not satisfactory. An admission that the Commons could not give an oath might justify referring Floyd's case to the upper house, but it could also be construed as an admission that the lower house was not a court of record. Moreover, because the Commons had already given a judgment against Floyd, they would either have to maintain it or annul it.[74] If they were to annul it, however, they would need some legal reason for doing so, and the only such reason presented thus far was that the lower house was not a court of record.

The House rejected Coke's suggestion and instead appointed a committee to draft an answer to the king's message.[75] On 3 May Coke reported this committee's recommendation that the Commons make the following points in response to the king: that in sentencing Floyd, they had not been trying to expand their power of judicature; that the precedent of 1 Henry IV did not bind them or impeach their authority to judge Floyd, because it was only an ordinance; and that they wished the king not to defer the execution of their judgment but rather to countenance that judgment with his authority and strengthen it.[76] The purpose of this proposed reply, which the Commons approved,[77] was to win James's support for their sentence on Floyd without conceding that the house was not a court of record. The Commons attempted to achieve this purpose by suggesting that their judgment in the present case did not differ from their previous judgments. Their efforts failed. In reply to their letter, the king stated that he could not support their judgment, because the case would then constitute a precedent for a new and "omnipotent" power of judicature vested in the Commons. Moreover, while he first made a promise to punish Floyd himself, he quickly retracted it and thus left the case at an awkward impasse.[78] James was determined to quash the Commons's judgment for the reasons given in his letter, while the Commons were intent on maintaining it because they feared that to abandon it would be to acquiesce in a serious diminution of their judicial authority. When the Commons reopened debate on the case on 5 May, most members tried to attack James's position head-on,[79] but Coke ingeniously construed the king's last message in a way that would allow the house both to avoid further clashes with James I and to preserve intact whatever judicial powers they might have. He claimed that this message

74. *CD 1621*, 4:137–43.
75. *CJ*, 1:604. See Zaller, *1621*, p. 107.
76. *CD 1621*, 5:137–38; 3:151–52; 4:195–96; 6:132; *CJ*, 1:606; and Zaller, *1621*, pp. 107–8.
77. *CJ*, 1:606; *CD 1621*, 3:154 n. 6; 4:196; 6:132. For Coke's speeches prior to this order, see White, "Coke," p. 114 and nn. 37–39.
78. Zaller, *1621*, 108–9.
79. Ibid., p. 109.

could be interpreted as a royal request to the Commons to suspend their judgment on Floyd. He then explained that although they could not properly grant such royal requests in cases between private parties, they could do so in the present case, because James I was in effect a party to their judgment against Floyd. Then, according to Coke, the House could refer the case to the king.[80]

While Coke was willing to accept a stay of judgment under such terms, he still refused to concede that the House was not a court of record. Although he had previously wished to send Floyd's case to the Lords, he now would not admit that the Commons had lacked the power to judge him, for such an admission might leave the impression that the invalidity of their judgment against him had been due to the fact that they were not a court of record. Therefore, when the Lords suggested in a conference on 5 May that the lower house was not a court of record,[81] Coke not only denied this proposition but also defended the Commons's judgment against Floyd more vigorously than ever before. To prove that the lower house was a court of record, he first said that every court of record had three "marks and effects": "(1) power to grant privilege and protections against actions for any sum, (2) power of imprisonment, [and] (3) power of fining." He then claimed that past cases proved that the Commons had all of these marks and effects. Next, he argued that if every court of record had the power to give an oath, the Commons must therefore possess this power, and he cited precedents showing that they had actually exercised it in the past.[82] Finally, to justify the Commons's judgment against Floyd, he presented the following argument.

A wrong offered to a member of the house or to the meanest servant of any member is examinable and punishable there. Now the king is the chief member and head of the house, and by presumption of law is always present there. And therefore a wrong to the king by the despite and dishonour to his daughter, who is pars patris, we conceived to belong to us to punish.[83]

The Lords found this last argument unconvincing and claimed that Coke's precedents showed only that the Commons had "jurisdiction" over their own members, and "would not justify such a power as [the Commons] had exercised by the judgement" against Floyd. Sandys then tried "to supply the defect of [Coke's] precedents by the access of reason," but the Lords still failed to recognize the legitimacy of the lower house's judgment

---

80. CD 1621, 3:168; 2:346; 5:141; 4:304; CJ, 1:608. On this argument, see White, "Coke," p. 116 and nn. 46–49.
81. On this conference, see Zaller, 1621, pp. 110–12.
82. On the precedents, see White, "Coke," p. 116 and nn. 53, 55.
83. CD 1621, 3:181–83; 4:312–13; 2:349–50; 5:145–46, 369.

on Floyd or to concede that the lower house was a court of record.[84]

At the end of the 5 May conference, therefore, the Commons's attempt to sentence Floyd seemed to have backfired. They had not only failed to have their sentence confirmed, they had also provoked the king and the Lords into questioning the legal basis of all judicial authority ever exercised or claimed by the lower house. Although Coke wished to salvage as much judicial authority as possible for the Commons, he still wished to avoid a major constitutional conflict, and he therefore adopted a new, conciliatory strategy that ultimately proved successful. Instead of defending the judgment against Floyd or trying to secure formal recognition of the Commons's claim to be a court of record, he worked to annul all previous parliamentary proceedings in Floyd's case, in order to prevent the Lords from formally declaring that the lower house was not a court of record. After a series of complex negotiations that stretched over several days,[85] he succeeded in getting both houses to agree that

A Protestation is to be entered in the House of Lords, by the consent of the House of Commons to the purpose: That the proceedings, lately passed in [the Commons] against *Edw. Floyd*, be not, at any time hereafter, drawn, or used, as a precedent, to the enlarging or diminishing of the lawful rights and privileges of either House; but that the rights and privileges of both Houses shall remain in the self-same state, and plight, as before.[86]

Two weeks later, with little further controversy, the Lords passed judgment on Floyd.[87] Although the compromise protestation clearly indicated the Commons's failure to expand their jurisdiction through their judgment on Floyd, it was not a total defeat for them because it also implied that that failure would not impeach their jurisdiction or undercut their previous claims to judicial power. Under its terms, the present Parliament and all future ones were to proceed as if the Commons's judgment against Floyd had never been given.[88]

When Parliament adjourned in June of 1621, its judicial procedures had been developed, justified, rationalized, and utilized to a point where they would not in themselves give rise to major controversy. The exact limits of the Commons's jurisdiction had not been determined. Nor had their precise role in trials held in the Lords been clearly defined. But after the seven parliamentary trials held between February and June of 1621, the fact of Parliament's judicial power could not easily be denied. As a

---

84. *CD 1621*, 4:313–14.
85. See White, "Coke," p. 117 n. 60.
86. *CJ*, 1:619.
87. Tite, *Impeachment*, pp. 129–30.
88. For slightly different interpretations of the settlement in Floyd's case, see Tite, *Impeachment*, pp. 129–31; and Zaller, *1621*, p. 114.

result, the two parliamentary cases on which Coke spoke in 1624 posed only a few legal problems for him to solve. In Middlesex's case, he had to show that apparently trivial offenses and dubious policies would justify Parliament in initiating judicial proceedings against one of the king's most exalted counselors.[89] In the case of Bishop Harsnett of Norwich, he had to demonstrate that Parliament could try men for ecclesiastical offenses.[90] In supporting the parliamentary trials of a prominent royal servant and an anti-puritan bishop, Coke was not attacking court policies or leading any "opposition party." Unlike religious leaders attacked in the parliaments of the later 1620s, Harsnett was not closely associated with the court or protected by the king; and an attack on him probably implied no blatant opposition to James I's religious policies. Parliament's proceedings against Cranfield, moreover, were instigated and actively promoted by the king's leading advisor, the duke of Buckingham, and Coke's active participation in them in fact signaled his rapprochement with the court after his long imprisonment in 1622.[91] Nevertheless, his speeches in these two cases still anticipate the trials of the later 1620s and even the early 1640s. By developing arguments to show that Parliament could put men on trial for religious offenses or for inconvenient policies, Coke laid part of the groundwork for Parliament's later proceedings against Montague, Manwaring, Buckingham, Strafford, and Laud.

Middlesex's enemies hoped to bring him down by having the Commons criticize his financial policies and his activities as master of the wards. His financial policies first came under attack on 2 April, when Sir Edwin Sandys reported the finding of the Committee of Trade that "the recent burdens imposed upon trade . . . had much to do" with the continued trade depression, and the committee was then ordered to investigate the referees for these novel burdens.[92] Middlesex's name was not mentioned at this time, but his support for the trade duties in question was well known.[93] A second line of attack against the treasurer was opened up three days later, when Sir Miles Fleetwood charged him with "innovations and gross corruptions" in administering the Court of Wards.

89. On Middlesex's case, see Tite, *Impeachment*, pp. 149–72; Ruigh, *1624*, pp. 303–44; Prestwich, *Cranfield*, pp. 423–68; Roberts, *Growth of Responsible Government*, pp. 36–38; Tawney, *Business and Politics*, pp. 231–74; and C. B. Anderson, "Ministerial Responsibility in the 1620s."

90. On Harsnett's case, see Tite, *Impeachment*, pp. 172–75. On his career, see Paul S. Seaver, *The Puritan Lectureships*, pp. 231, 242 ff., 323–24.

91. On Coke's relations with Buckingham in the parliament of 1624, see Ruigh, *1624*, pp. 70 and 88.

92. *CJ*, 1:752; Ruigh, *1624*, pp. 316–17; Prestwich, *Cranfield*, p. 441; Tawney, *Business and Politics*, pp. 239–40; Tite, *Impeachment*, pp. 150–51.

93. On Cranfield's general financial policies, see Prestwich, *Cranfield*; and Tawney, *Business and Politics*.

Middlesex had allegedly allowed his secretary to answer petitions himself and had taken "three or four great bribes."[94] As of 5 April, the Committee of Trade had made no specific accusations against Middlesex, and the only clear charges that had been made against him were Fleetwood's. Many members apparently believed that these charges were trivial and would not justify the Commons in prosecuting the treasurer,[95] but in a noteworthy speech given on the fifth, Coke tried to change their minds. After conceding that it was unjust to call great men to account for minor offenses, he insisted that bribery was "no small matter," because it concerned the "seminary of the kingdom" and because the "corruption of the fountains of justice" was a "hinderance" not only to the king but to the subjects. Moreover, he argued, a judge's acceptance of a bribe constituted perjury, because judges were sworn to do justice. Finally, he maintained that while Middlesex's innovations in the procedure of the Court of Wards might seem trivial to some members, they were in fact extremely dangerous. Any illegal proceedings in that court, he claimed, concerned "all the nobility and gentry, for all the sons of Adam must die and their sons come into the Court of Wards."[96]

One week later, after Phelips had summed up the charges against Middlesex,[97] Coke continued in his efforts to magnify their significance by telling the house that a medieval judge named Thorpe had once been hanged for having taken bribes "corrupte et felonice," but that the "reason of the judgement" against him was that "he had broken the King's oath which was committed to the Judges."[98] Coke then provided Parliament with a rationale for punishing Middlesex not only for taking bribes and breaking his oath as a judge, but for his financial policies as well. He suggested that Middlesex's offenses were graver than Thorpe's, because he had taken another oath imposing even greater obligations than the one broken by Thorpe. Not only was Middlesex a judge, by virtue of being master of the wards, but "as Lord Treasurer," he was "a judge of the King's revenue [and?] of the distribution thereof."[99] As treasurer, Middlesex had sworn "(1) To serve faithfully the King and his people. (2)

---

94. Ruigh, *1624*, p. 317; Holles, *1624*, ff. 118–19; Jervoise, *1624*, f. 111; Pym, *1624*, f. 48v; Erle, *1624*, f. 114v; Nicholas, *1624*, ff. 111–111v; *CJ*, 1:755.

95. On the attitude of some members towards the initial charges against Middlesex, see Ruigh, *1624*, pp. 326–27, 332.

96. *CJ*, 1:755; Holles, *1624*, f. 119. On Coke's later attempt on 15 April to inflate the importance of the charges against Middlesex, see Ruigh, *1624*, pp. 332–33.

97. Holles, *1624*, f. 130. On the proceedings of the preceding week, see Ruigh, *1624*, pp. 320–21.

98. Coke had cited this same case in Bennet's case (*CD 1621*, 3:17), and noted it in his *Third Institutes* (p. 145).

99. On Middlesex's appointment as treasurer in 1621, see Prestwich, *Cranfield*, pp. 328–29.

To do right to all[,] rich and poor. (3) To purchase the King's profit in all things with reason. (4) Justly . . . to counsel the King. (5) Truly to use and keep the King's secrets."[100] Because he had thus sworn an oath that imposed a greater obligation than mere abstention from wrong-doing, Parliament could legally punish him for his financial or governmental policies even if they did not constitute clear violations of existing law.[101] Even though the Lords ultimately rejected Coke's argument, it foreshadowed the ones used in the parliamentary trials of Buckingham.[102]

Three days later, on 15 April, Coke reported to the House that a select committee had drawn up a list of formal charges against Middlesex and had appointed Sir Edwin Sandys and himself to deliver these charges to the upper house. Coke was to present the charges of bribery and abuses in the Court of Wards, while all other charges were left to Sandys.[103] The House approved this proposal and later ordered the two men to go to Whitehall that afternoon "to deliver the business" to the Lords.[104] Coke opened the conference with an emphatic assertion of the Commons's power and duty to bring charges against the lord treasurer. "The assembly of Knights, Citizens, and Burgesses of the House of Commons," he declared, "do represent the whole body of the Commons"; and because they spoke for "great multitudes," they were therefore the "best inquisitors" of great offenses against the commonwealth. Acting in the role of inquisitors, he continued, the Commons had found evidence of "gross and sordid bribes" and of the "procuring of good orders [in the Wards] to be altered," offenses that constituted "oppression of the subject" and "deceit of the King." Then, after presenting the two charges assigned to him by the Commons, Coke concluded by emphasizing that

100. In his *Fourth Institutes*, Coke rendered this oath as follows: "1. That well and truly he shall serve the king and his people in the office of treasurer. 2. That he shall do right to all manner of people, poor and rich. 3. The king's treasure he shall truly keep and dispense. 4. He shall truly counsel the king. 5. The king's counsel he shall layn and keep. 6. That he shall neither know nor suffer the king's hurt, nor his disinheriting, nor that the rights of the Crown be decreased by any means, as far forth as he may let it. 7. And if he may not let it, he shall make knowledge thereof clearly and expressly to the king with his true advice and counsel. 8. And he shall do and purchase the king's profit in all that he may reasonably do" (p. 104).

101. Coke also cited an unprinted "statute" that provided punishments for great royal officials who took bribes (Pym, 1624, f. 60v). For the record, see *RP*, 3:626. For Coke's speech, see Pym, 1624, ff. 60v–61; Holles, 1624, ff. 130–130v; Erle, 1624, f. 134v; Nicholas, 1624, ff. 146–146v; D'Ewes, 1624, ff. 114–114v.

102. On Buckingham's trial in 1626, see Tite, *Impeachment*, pp. 178–217.

103. *CJ*, 1:767. Coke also delivered a long speech about innovations in the Court of Wards and bribes taken by Cranfield (see *CJ*, 1:767–68; Pym, 1624, ff. 65–65v; Erle, 1624, ff. 140–40v; Nicholas, 1624, ff. 152–53; Holles, 1624, ff. 132v–33; Spring, 1624, ff. 219–21; see also Prestwich, *Cranfield*, p. 445).

104. Holland, 1624, II, f. 30; Nicholas, 1624, f. 156.

Cranfield had "broken his 3 oaths of Treasurer, Privy Councillor, and Master of the Wards."[105] Sandys then presented his part of the Commons's charges,[106] and the Lords were left to their deliberations. After lengthy investigations and a long series of delays,[107] the Lords finally sentenced Middlesex on 13 May.[108]

During the later stages of these proceedings the Commons were also investigating charges against Samuel Harsnett, Bishop of Norwich. According to one letter writer, it was "a company of factious puritans" who had precipitated these investigations of the bishop by petitioning the Commons about Harsnett's repression of lecturers in his diocese.[109] The Committee of Grievances heard the petition in mid-April but could not proceed with it before deciding how far Parliament's jurisdiction extended in matters of religion and church government. One member went so far as to maintain that "this House may question every canon"; but another argued that the Commons could not themselves reform such matters because they were within the competence of the archbishop of Canterbury, but that they could complain to the king about them on behalf of the city of Norwich. Coke, who chaired this debate, did not directly contradict the first speaker, but he noted that no one had complained "against the constitution of the church" and that Harsnett was simply being attacked for failing to maintain preaching, as he was required to do by royal and archepiscopal orders. Nevertheless, while he did not assert Parliament's right to question every canon, he did claim that Parliament had "dealt in church government" at least from the time of King Alfred. The committee took no formal position on the issue of Parliament's jurisdiction over religious matters and simply resolved to "peruse" the petition against Harsnett.[110]

The matter was little discussed for several weeks, but on 3 May, Coke made a point of proving that the Commons could legally inquire into complaints about the maintenance of preaching. First, he claimed that "[e]ven in the midnight of popery" parliaments had frequently heard complaints "against the clergy for neglecting their callings." He then went on to note cases from the reigns of Edward III, Richard II, and

---

105. Erle, 1624, ff. 142–43v; *LJ*, 3:307.

106. Erle, 1624, ff. 143–43v.

107. Ruigh, 1624, pp. 332–43; Prestwich, *Cranfield*, pp. 445–68; Tawney, *Business and Politics*, pp. 245–63; Tite, *Impeachment*, pp. 158–67.

108. Prestwich, *Cranfield*, p. 445 and n. 1; Tite, *Impeachment*, pp. 167–68. On the Commons's dissatisfaction with this sentence, see Tite, *Impeachment*, pp. 168–70.

109. Locke to Carleton, 1 May, 1624. S. P. Dom. 14/165:21; quoted in notes to Yale transcript to Nicholas, 1624.

110. For Coke's speech and the committee's resolution, see Holland, 1624, II, ff. 36–37.

Henry IV in which "complaint in parliament was made that [the] people wanted instruction." Second, to prove that Harsnett's alleged offenses were violations of both canons and statutes and were therefore fit matters for Parliament, he cited the forty-fifth canon of 1604, which provided that "[b]eneficed preachers [are] to preach every Sabbath day; [and] so every preaching minister." He also noted that a statute of 1559 provided for the punishment of those who disturbed a minister's sermon. Finally, to prove that the king had ultimate responsibility for the maintenance of preaching, he declared that "the ancient law of England" was that the king should provide for "sufficient ministers" and that "if the ordinary fail of his duty, then is the King to take order." Parliament, Coke reasoned, was obviously obliged to help the king carry out this duty.[111]

On 7 May, Coke reported Harsnett's case to the House, and after summarizing the bishop's alleged offenses, he showed by citing numerous precedents that the House had "cognizance" over them.[112] He reported in the following day that the charges had been reduced to six main heads,[113] and he was then ordered to request a conference with the Lords about the matter, at which he was "to vouch precedents for maintenance of [the Commons's] proceedings in this case."[114] After a series of delays, Coke finally presented the charges against Harsnett to the upper house on 19 May,[115] and the archbishop of Canterbury replied that the Lords would "take care of" the case and "do in it according to justice."[116] Instead of judging the case, however, the upper house simply referred it to an ecclesiastical tribunal that did nothing about it.[117] Although the Commons were thus thwarted in their efforts to have the bishop punished and to establish Parliament's judicial power over ecclesiastical offenses,

---

111. Erle, 1624, ff. 167v–68v; cf. Holland, 1624, II, f. 72 v. For the possible sources of Coke's statements, see *RP*, 2:271, no. 23; and 3:321, no. 43.

112. Erle, 1624, ff. 174v–75; Holles, 1624, ff. 139v–40; D'Ewes, 1624, ff. 113–13v; Pym, 1624, ff. 89–89v; Holland, 1624, II, ff. 79v–80v; *CJ*, 1:699, 784. For the precedents, see White, "Coke," p. 127 and nn. 21–26.

113. According to Pym (Pym, 1624a, ff. 32v–33), these charges were "1, the inhibiting of preachers; 2, allowing of images carved and painted of Christ, his saints and of the holy ghost, and the setting up of crucifixes on the high altar; 3, new order for praying to the east, excommunicating and vexing men for breach of those orders; 4, a recognition enjoined to one for being present at catechism, prayers and singing of psalms in his minister's house; 5, divers extortions; 6, not registering institutions" (Pym, 1624a, ff. 32v–33). For other versions, see Erle, 1624, ff. 175v–76; Nicholas, 1624, ff. 197–97v; Holland, 1624, II, f. 83v. See also Tite, *Impeachment*, p. 173.

114. Pym, 1624, f. 33; cf. Erle, 1624, f. 176; *CJ*, 1:701, 786.

115. *LJ*, 3:388. For Coke's report of the conference, see Nicholas, 1624, ff. 207v–8; *CJ*, 1:705, 709.

116. Nicholas, 1624, f. 208.

117. Tite, *Impeachment*, p. 147.

Coke accepted these defeats without protest.[118] He had actively helped to promote the revival of Parliament's long-unused judicial powers and had done so without provoking controversies that would jeopardize the success of his other more mundane efforts to remedy grievances through parliamentary action.

Major controversies could not always be avoided, however, when Parliament debated the other major constitutional issue of the early 1620s, namely the scope and legal basis of the Commons's privilege of free speech. Although members of the lower house had acquired a privilege of free speech during the preceding century, two major questions about it were still unresolved in the early 1620s: What was its legal basis, royal allowance, statute, prescription, or inherent right? and What were the limits on the subjects that the Commons could legally discuss without fear of prosecution?[119] These two questions were of immediate political importance in 1621, because many members wished to criticize the king's foreign policy while the king wished to prevent them from doing so. By 1624 the king or court had come to adopt foreign policies more to the Commons's liking and was even willing to allow Parliament some role in debating foreign policy. But the two basic questions about the Commons's privilege of free speech had still not been clearly answered and still troubled some members.

In 1621 the king maintained that the Commons held their privilege of free speech by royal grant or allowance and could not discuss "matters of state" in general, or foreign policy and war in particular. Against this royalist position on free speech, certain members of the Commons periodically argued that they held this privilege by right and could at least sometimes discuss matters of state. Although they never claimed that members could say whatever they wished with impunity, they insisted that those who misspoke themselves were subject only to punishment imposed by the House itself. This view of free speech was formally expressed in the Protestation of 8 December 1621, which described the privilege as "the ancient and undoubted birthright and inheritance of the subjects of England" and declared that members had "liberty and freedom" to debate all matters mentioned in the parliamentary writ of summons.

The adoption of the Protestation marked the culmination of almost

---

118. Phelips, however, did protest. See Tite, *Impeachment*, pp. 174–75 and n. 62.

119. On the Commons's privilege of free speech during the Tudor-Stuart period, see Elton, *TC*, pp. 253–57, 263–67; and Kenyon, *SC*, pp. 24–32. On Coke's speeches in 1621 and 1624 concerning the Commons's privilege to grant protections from arrest to their servants, see White, "Coke," pp. 55–59 and nn. 1–26.

a month of intense debate in the Commons about the king's foreign policy and about their right to discuss it; and it led James to dissolve Parliament and thus frustrate months of parliamentary work on the remedy of specific grievances. This open clash over free speech, however, was not characteristic of the Commons's proceedings on this issue in either 1621 or 1624. Conflict over free speech had almost broken out early in 1621 but had been skillfully suppressed; and it was again avoided in May, when certain members wished to debate Irish grievances against the king's wishes. Although the fall session ended with a clear-cut confrontation between the king and the Commons over this same issue, both sides adopted intransigent positions only after weeks of debate and tactical skirmishing and after several attempts at compromise had failed. Moreover, in 1624 the Commons's support for the court's new foreign policy and the crown's efforts to cultivate that support diminished parliamentary concern about abstract constitutional questions and made most members of Parliament work to avoid clashes over them. The Commons clearly preferred actual influence over foreign policy to mere formal recognition of their abstract right to discuss it.

Coke played a highly prominent role in the Commons's debates on free speech in both 1621 and 1624. While he significantly influenced the form and content of the Protestation and repeated its claims about free speech in his *Fourth Institutes*,[120] he generally took more compromising and flexible positions on this issue and usually showed little interest either in formulating a coherent view of free speech or in pressing for its acceptance. Early in 1621 he worked to avoid a clash over free speech and several months later failed to insist strongly on the Commons's right to discuss Irish affairs. In late November and early December he conceded that the Commons had no right to meddle in matters of state and attempted to justify their petition on foreign policy in ways that would not contradict the king's position on free speech. Although he ultimately took a strong stand on this issue in the last weeks of the parliament and soon suffered imprisonment for doing so, he vigorously attacked those who attempted to raise the same issue in 1624.

A study of his remarks on free speech during the early 1620s shows that he did not consistently espouse any single position on this issue, that he was more interested in using Parliament to achieve certain limited goals than in establishing the Commons's abstract right to free speech, and that he hoped to avert constitutional clashes on this as well as on other issues. His speeches of later November and early December also show that he was sometimes prepared to adopt more dogmatic stands on

120. *Institutes*, 4:819.

the question of free speech, even if they led to a dissolution of Parliament and the termination of his efforts to remedy grievances of the commonwealth. His sudden intransigence on this issue can be accounted for in the following way. He saw James I's attacks on the Commons's claims to free speech as a serious threat to their immediate efforts not only to influence foreign policy, but also to transact any controversial parliamentary business at all. This threat appeared particularly serious to him for three main reasons. First, because it was directed against the Commons's efforts to promote what they conceived of as true religion, it had a distinctly sinister cast and raised questions about the motivation lying behind it. Second, it seemed to threaten the Commons's parliamentary proceedings at a time when Coke was increasingly prone to regard parliamentary action as essential to the common weal. Finally, this threat to what was increasingly seen as a legal right of English subjects could be construed as an indirect threat to all vested legal rights, for if the king could deny English men the inheritance that they had in Parliament's liberties, he could deny any other right at all. Coke's decision in late 1621 to take a strong stand on the issue of free speech was therefore an index of his concern not only about this particular issue, but also about the condition of the commonwealth as a whole. It reflected his belief that only Parliament could remedy certain grievances of the commonwealth and his increasingly strong conviction that certain basic rights had to be defended against royal attack if any rights were to be preserved. Although these anxieties of his were quickly alleviated, they did not disappear. They were expressed even more clearly in his parliamentary speeches of the later 1620s.

At the beginning of the parliament of 1621, one of Coke's principal concerns was to avoid any serious clash over free speech. The Commons began to debate this matter on the first working day of the session and continued to discuss it for over a week.[121] Debate on this issue initially arose because certain members feared that the king would prevent the lower house from freely debating his policies on the current religious and political crisis on the continent. These fears seemed to have some basis in reality. Six weeks before the opening of Parliament James I had issued a proclamation against "lavish speech of matters of state," and it seemed reasonable to suppose that among those against whom he had directed it were members of the Commons who opposed his conciliatory stance towards Spain.[122] On 3 February 1621, moreover, Lord Chancellor Bacon

---

121. On this debate, see Zaller, *1621*, pp. 37–41; and Harold Hulme, "The Winning of Freedom of Speech by the House of Commons," pp. 836–39.

122. This proclamation was drafted by Bacon. See Bacon, *Works*, 14:165–67; and Zaller, *1621*, p. 28.

had replied to the speaker's petition for free speech by warning the Commons "[n]ot to turn liberty of speech into license."[123] In response to these apparent threats to the Commons's privilege of free speech, Sir Edward Giles moved on 5 February that the Commons supplement their traditional petition for free speech with another petition to the king for free speech, for the right to act on their own to punish "those that spake extravagantly," and for immunity from prosecution after the end of the session for words spoken in Parliament.[124]

Although Giles's motion was generally supported by those who had interpreted the Commons's privilege of free speech broadly and who wished to express themselves on controversial issues, Coke spoke against it on three separate occasions, probably because he wished to avoid unnecessary controversy at the very outset of what was hoped would be a productive parliamentary session. To prevent contestation from arising over this issue, he had to show that Giles's motion was unwise, and he was willing to attack the motion by espousing views of free speech that were mutually inconsistent and that he later abandoned or substantially revised. His use of such varied arguments against Giles's motion reveals his concern about maintaining good correspondency in Parliament and his willingness to sacrifice legal consistency and coherence in his legal arguments in order to promote parliamentary action.[125]

On 5 February Coke first opposed Giles's proposed petition on the grounds that it was directed against only an illusory threat to the Commons's privileges. Although he later denied that these privileges had merely a statutory basis, he now adopted this position, because he could then argue that since no proclamation could be in force against a statute, the king's recent proclamation against lavish speech posed no threat to the Commons's privileges. He also advanced another argument against

123. CD 1621, 4:10; cf. Zaller, 1621, p. 37. The king also warned the Commons not to abuse their privilege of free speech on 30 January (CD 1621, 2:12; 6:372; 4:10), and 3 February (2:15).

124. CD, 1621, 2:17; cf. 4:11; 6:375; Zaller, 1621, p. 37. Giles's motion, which also provided for actions to be taken against recusants (CD 1621, 2:17), was seconded by Phelips, who said that the Commons could not "well proceed either to the King's supply or our own grievances" (CD 1621, 2:17–18; cf. 4:11–12; 5:533; 6:437; CJ, 1:508–10). For the first debate on this motion, see CD 1621, 2:17–24; 4:11–16; 5:433–34; 6:289, 437.

125. Prestwich claims that in the debates on Giles's motion, Coke was "speaking as a moderate and indeed as a supporter of the Crown" and "saved" the situation for the court (Cranfield, pp. 291–92); and Zaller takes a similar position (1621, p. 40 and n. 16). Both writers ignore the possibility that those who were not supporters of the crown could easily have had a strategic or tactical interest in avoiding a clash on free speech. Zaller, moreover, misinterprets Coke's position, partly because he attributes to him a speech that he characterizes as "conservative" but that was actually made by Mr. John Coke (see 1621, p. 40 and n. 16; and CD 1621, 2:56–57). The same error is also made by Mosse (Struggle for Sovereignty, p. 114 and n. 16). See fn. 128.

the petition on the morning of the fifth. He maintained that a petition to the king for free speech would only raise questions about the legal basis of this privilege and might bar the Commons from later claiming that they held it by statute. The presentation of such a petition to the king, he suggested, would constitute an admission by the Commons that they did not hold their privilege of free speech by statute, for if this privilege had a statutory basis it would require no royal confirmation. He went on to say that if this privilege were even slightly undermined, the house would be losing one of "the greatest things that belonged to it." Meddling with these liberties was dangerous, he said, because they were "like a circle which if any part be broken the whole is broken." Although this same analogy could have been used to justify a strong defense of the Commons's privileges, he now employed it in order to warn the Commons against disturbing the status quo.[126]

On the afternoon of the fifth, Coke advanced a third argument against the proposed petition. He now asserted that the House held its privileges not by statute, but by right, and that the proposed petition might therefore damage them in one of two ways. After noting that the petition would have to be either of right or of grace, he said that both sorts of procedures held dangers. A petition of grace for free speech would be "in derogation" of the House's claim to hold its privileges by right, for the king could later claim that the House could not enjoy them until or unless he had granted a petition for them. On the other hand, in a petition of right, the Commons would be "bound to an exact enumeration" of their privileges and would run the risk of losing any privilege that they failed to enumerate.[127] Four days later, Coke advanced a similar argument against petitioning the king for their privileges. Such a course, he claimed, could do no good and might do harm. If the Commons were to complain about past imprisonments of members for words spoken in Parliament, the king might then support such actions by citing precedents that they might not be able to answer fully. Moreover, he argued, if the king were to refuse to confirm their privileges, then the Commons might lose them because they would have acknowledged that they did not hold them by right. Finally, if the king were to confirm their privileges, he would only do so, Coke thought, on the condition that they would proceed dutifully, in which case they would be no better off than before. Petitioning the king, therefore, would at best accomplish nothing and would

---

126. *CD 1621*, 2:22–23; 4:15–16; 5:435; *CJ*, 1:510. In this speech, Coke also discussed supply, grievances, and recusancy. For the precedents that Coke cited, see White, "Coke," p. 47 and n. 8.

127. The only direct report of Coke's speech is in *CD 1621*, 2:25. *CD 1621*, 4:17 and 5:438, mix his remarks in with those of other speakers.

only indicate the Commons's anxiety about their privileges and their distrust of the king, which were sentiments that Coke thought unworthy of the House. He therefore moved to let Giles's motion "sleep."[128] This motion failed, but three days later he got his wish. On 15 February James I informed the House that he granted their "liberty and freedom of speech in as ample manner as ever any of his predecessors ever did,"[129] and the Commons responded by ending their debate on Giles's motion and on "all other propositions concerning liberty of speech."[130]

Coke's arguments against Giles's motion could have been used to show that the Commons should devote all their time and energy to identifying and then defending their privileges. But he obviously thought at the outset of the parliament of 1621 that such action was unnecessary and would accomplish nothing. In 1628 he would support the Commons's effective decision to put aside more substantive parliamentary business in the interest of settling a few crucial constitutional questions. But in February of 1621 he thought that Parliament could use its time in other, more productive ways. Several months later he adopted the same posture when the Commons briefly discussed their right to treat Irish affairs. On 26 April a privy councillor for Ireland complained that "corruptions" there were "wonderfully overgrown" and moved that the House "take some course to give the king notice hereof."[131] Sir John Davies conceded that the House should be "sensible" of Ireland's wants and sufferings and that Parliament could make a "representation" to the king about Irish affairs. But he noted that the English Parliament could not reform Irish abuses by statute, because that power belonged to the Irish Parliament.[132] Although Davies acknowledged the Commons's right to discuss Irish affairs, he obviously hoped that they would not exercise it. Initially, Coke refused to drop the matter. Although conceding that the Commons should deal with it "warily," he insisted that Parliament had not only the right to discuss Irish grievances, but that it had actual "jurisdiction" over them. After citing precedents for this position, he may have anticipated one of his later, more extreme statements about the Commons's privilege of free speech. He claimed that "the great dependence of the safety of [England] upon the peace of Ireland" would justify

---

128. *CD 1621*, 2:57–58; 4:39–40; 5:448–49; *CJ*, 1:517. Mr. John Coke also spoke in this debate (*CD 1621*, 2:56–57), but his remarks are not to be confused with those of Sir Edward. See fn. 125.

129. *CD 1621*, 2:84.

130. Ibid., 4:55.

131. Ibid., 4:249; cf. 3:89–90; 2:323; 5:101, 350; 6:100–101; *CJ*, 1:593; *P&D*, 1:327. On the ensuing debate, see Zaller, *1621*, pp. 118–19; Willson, *Privy Councillors*, p. 252.

132. *CD 1621*, 3:91; 5:101.

the Commons in discussing Irish grievances, because the parliamentary writ of summons stated that members of Parliament were called to discuss matters concerning "the defense of the realm." In December of 1621 he would use this same argument to establish the Commons's right to debate "matters of state," but in the April debate on Ireland he did not press his argument from the writ of summons to such an extreme conclusion. He initially suggested that the Commons cast their complaints about Ireland "in the form of a law" and hold further debates on Irish grievances.[133] But when the king asked the House to drop this subject on 30 April,[134] Coke was not among those who protested against this interference in the Commons's proceedings or who insisted strongly on their right to continue their debates on Ireland.[135]

Only in the fall of 1621 did Coke finally take a militant position on free speech, and even then he took several weeks to reach it. The debates that led to the Commons's adoption of the Protestation began on 21 November, when the king's ambassador, Sir John Digby, told both houses that England had to prepare for a war in the Palatinate for which Parliament would have to provide funds.[136] When the Commons discussed this speech on the twenty-sixth and twenty-seventh, many members supported a direct sea war against Spain over the limited engagement in the Palatinate that Digby had outlined and further argued that James I should break off his ongoing negotiations for the Spanish match.[137] Instead of directly communicating these views about foreign policy to the king, however, the House initially chose to express them obliquely through a petition against domestic recusants. They hoped in this way to alert James to the intimate connection between the Catholic threat at home and the Spanish threat abroad and thereby induce him to make war against Spain directly and to abandon all thoughts of a Spanish alliance.[138] On the twenty-seventh Coke helped to promote this strategy by harping on the threats to the realm posed by domestic and foreign popery,[139] and

---

133. Ibid., 3:91; 2:323–24; 4:259–60; 5:101, 350; 6:101; *CJ*, 1:593; *P&D*, 1:327–28.

134. *CD 1621*, 5:118–19, 355–56; 4:278–80; 6:112–13, 396. James I admitted directly, however, that the Commons could "treat of the affairs of Ireland" (*CD 1621*, 5:118).

135. The only two whose protests were recorded were Edward Alford (see *CD 1621*, 3:163; and Zaller, *1621*, p. 118) and Sir Edward Cecil (see *CD 1621*, 3:143).

136. Zaller, *1621*, p. 145.

137. On the debates held on these two days, see Zaller, *1621*, pp. 146–48.

138. The main proponent of this strategy was John Pym, whose speeches of 27 and 28 November are discussed by Zaller (*1621*, pp. 147–51).

139. *CD 1621*, 3:465–68; 2:445–57; 4:444–45; 5:218–19, 406; 6:201–2, 323–24; *CJ*, 1:648; *P&D*, 2:222–23. For a detailed reconstruction of this speech, see White, "Coke," pp. 60–61 and nn. 6–10.

he was later placed on a committee to draft the recusant petition.[140]

On the twenty-seventh no clash over the Commons's right to debate foreign policy seemed imminent. Although many members wanted a full-scale war against Spain, they seemed content to express their views indirectly in the recusant petition. On 29 November, however, Sir George Goring urged the house to declare its views more openly by petitioning the king for a war with Spain and by promising to support him in it.[141] The Commons apparently took Goring's proposal as a signal from the king and ordered that it be incorporated into the recusant petition, which would then directly express the views hinted at in its original draft version. The subcommittee's new draft stated that the Commons did not mean to "press upon" the king's "undoubted and regal prerogative" to conduct foreign policy, but it nevertheless urged him to make war against Spain, to direct this war against Spain generally and not merely against Spanish forces in the Palatinate, and to abandon the Spanish match and marry Prince Charles to "one of our own religion."[142]

When Coke reported this draft to the House on 3 December, the king had already seen it and instructed his servants in the House to oppose it.[143] Sackville charged that its clauses concerning "war, matches and alliances" encroached on the "King's prerogative," while Weston declared that "for parliament to advise the King of war was presumptuous," because no precedents existed "of the best time" for the Commons's treating such a "point of sovereignty."[144] In response, over a dozen speakers, including Coke, defended the legality and propriety of the petition.[145] The most striking thing about Coke's speech is that it contained two distinct and even contradictory defenses of the petition. It indicated his readiness to challenge the king's views about the Commons's privilege of free speech, but it also left room for the king to yield to the Commons's petition without making concessions to the House on the

140. CD 1621, 2:459.
141. Goring was acting on Buckingham's instructions. See Zaller, 1621, p. 153; and Russell, "Foreign Policy Debate," p. 290.
142. Tanner, CD, pp. 277–78. Russell convincingly argues that because the Commons thought that they were following instructions from the king when they began to debate foreign policy, their early debates on this subject and their decision to petition the king about war and foreign affairs do not reveal their desire to expand their powers or to engage in a constitutional conflict with the king ("Foreign Policy Debate," pp. 290, 309). He nevertheless concedes quite rightly that "the debates beginning from the receipt of the king's first letter on 5 December, do deserve a place in the study of constitutional conflict" ("Foreign Policy Debate," p. 309).
143. CD 1621, 2:487; 6:220. Coke had wished to report the draft petition on 1 December (CD 1621, 6:220), but several courtiers had succeeded in stalling for time (Zaller, 1621, p. 154 and n. 54).
144. CD 1621, 2:488–89; 5:229; 6:220; cf. Zaller, 1621, p. 154.
145. See Zaller, 1621, pp. 154–56.

more general question of free speech. Coke's first argument in justification of the Commons's petition raised no serious questions about the scope of their privilege of free speech because it neither asserted their right to debate foreign policy and war nor denied the king's exclusive power to direct them. He conceded that such matters were all "arcana imperii," that they fell under the "indisputable" and "inseperable prerogatives of the crown and king," and that they were "not to be meddled with" by others. Nevertheless, he justified the Commons's petition on two grounds. First, because it was merely a petition of grace, and not a petition of right or a bill, it could have "no hurt in it," for the king could "give it life if he please and quash it at his pleasure."[146] Second, the Commons had had "good warrant" for the petition, because it expressed views that had originated with the king himself.[147] The king's servant, Digby, had told the Commons to prepare for war with Spaniards in the Palatinate and they had merely started from Digby's remarks and then moved "a concreto ad abstractum—from warring with Spaniards to war with Spain."

Having provided the king with a way of gracefully acceding to the Commons's petition, Coke then indicated that he could also defend it much more forcefully when he asserted that the Commons could lawfully "treat of the state of the . . . kingdom and of the remedies for it." In supporting this assertion not only by precedent but also by the words of the parliamentary writ of summons, he succeeded in showing that Parliament's right to treat of war and foreign policy was inherent in its very nature.[148] According to writ, Coke said, the king had called Parliament "pro magnis arduis et urgentibus negotiis nos[,] statum et defensionem regni nostri et statum et defensionem ecclesiae concernentibus."[149] These words showed, he said, that Parliament could lawfully treat the matters contained in their petition, because these matters were urgent and concerned the king, the state, and the defense of the realm and church.[150]

146. Similar arguments had been made by Wentworth, Recorder Finch, Brooke and Crew (*CD 1621*, 2:490–94).

147. Similar arguments had been made by Moore, Brooke, and Crew (*CD 1621*, 2:493–94).

148. For the precedents cited, see White, "Coke," p. 64 and nn. 43–47. Precedents for the petition had been cited by Wentworth, Perrott, Phelips, Brooke, and Crew. In addition, Wentworth, Moore, Phelips, Brooke and Crew had argued that the Commons were carrying out a legitimate parliamentary function in preferring the petition (see *CD 1621*, 2:490–95). Brooke and Crew, therefore, had anticipated three of Coke's main arguments for the petition. But Coke was apparently the only member to use the parliamentary writ of summons to support the petition.

149. On Coke's use of the writ of summons, see Russell, "Foreign Policy Debate," p. 290 and n. 3. Russell shows that Coke quoted the writ correctly.

150. Coke said that the Commons should take the writ as their guide, because it "set down why the parliament is called" (*CD 1621*, 6:223; 2:497). In his opening speech to this Parliament, on 30 January 1620, James I had cited this passage from the writ, but he had

After other speakers had replied to Sackville and Weston, the Commons approved the petition with only minor amendments;[151] but in a letter delivered to the Commons on the morning of 4 December, James I rejected even their more conciliatory arguments in support of it and directly forbad them to treat of war or foreign affairs. After complaining that some members had presumed "to argue and debate publicly of . . . matters far above their reach and capacity, tending to our high dishonor and breach of the royal prerogative," he commanded the Speaker to inform them "that none therein shall presume henceforth to meddle with anything concerning our government or deep matters of State, and namely not to deal with our dearest son's match with the daughter of Spain, nor to touch the honor of that King or any other [of?] our friends and confederates." He also stated that if the Commons had "already touched on any of these points which we have forbidden in any petition of theirs which is to be sent unto us[,] except they reform it before it come to our hands we will not deign the hearing nor answering of it."[152]

When the Commons discussed this message the next morning,[153] Coke defended their petition against the king's attacks; but he still did so without insisting on their absolute right to debate war and foreign policy. He did not dispute James's contention that their petition treated matters above their "reach and capacity." Nor did he directly question the king's right to forbid them to discuss certain subjects. Instead, he first restated the milder defense of the petition that he had made on 3 December and then claimed that the king would not have attacked the Commons's petition if he had been truly informed about their proceedings, because they had not encroached on his prerogative but had left it intact. Finally, he expressed his anxiety about the king's command to the Commons to "talk of no matters of government," for he did not know how far this prohibition might be "stretched." He therefore moved that the Commons draft a "declaration" containing "a narrative" of their proceedings and a "justification of them by precedents."[154] Subsequent speakers supported this motion, and a subcommittee was then appointed to draft this so-called declaration.[155]

Coke's precise role in drafting this document is unclear, but it contained certain points that he had made on 3 and 4 December. It attributed

---

gone on to say that the Commons were not to treat of war or peace unless they were commanded to do so (CD 1621, 2:4; 4:2–3). For reports of Coke's speech of 5 December, see CD 1621, 2:295–97; 5:231; 6:222–23; P&D, 2:273–74; CJ, 1:657.

151. CJ, 1:657. For the amendments, see CD 1621, 2:498; and Zaller, 1621, p. 156.
152. Tanner, CD, pp. 279–80; cf. Zaller, 1621, p. 156.
153. In a committee of the whole (CD 1621, 6:225).
154. CD 1621, 6:225; 2:502–03; 5:232–33; P&D, 2:284; cf. Zaller, 1621, p. 158.
155. CD 1621, 2:506.

the king's misunderstandings of the Commons's recent actions to the "partial and uncertain reports" of them that he had received, and it expressed concern about the meaning and scope of his order that they cease discussing "matters of government." It also stated that their petition did not encroach on the royal prerogative, because it was a petition of grace and because the king himself had induced them to discuss the matters that it treated. The most significant feature of the declaration, however, was that it did not contain the most extreme arguments for the legality of the petition that Coke had made on 3 December. Although it stated that the Commons's privileges were theirs by right and not by royal allowance, it did not assert their right to debate all matters mentioned in the parliamentary writ of summons.[156] The substance of the declaration indicates, therefore, that in early December the Commons had not yet adopted a militant position with respect to the scope of their privilege of free speech.

While awaiting the king's answer to the declaration, which they sent to him on 7 December,[157] the Commons abandoned work on legislation[158] and they ignored a royal order of 12 December to resume business,[159] because, as Coke put it, they were "under a cloud and not free."[160] On the fourteenth, James's answer to the declaration finally arrived. In it, he continued to denounce the petition of December third for encroaching on his prerogative and meddling with things far above the Commons's reach. He also stated that he could not "allow of the [declaration's] style," because it described the Commons's privileges as their "ancient and undoubted right and inheritance" instead of stating that they were "derived from the grace and permission" of the king's ancestors and himself. Nevertheless, James assured the Commons that as long as they contained themselves "within the limits" of their "duty," he would be "as careful to maintain and preserve" their "lawful liberties and privileges" as any of his predecessors.[161]

When the Commons debated this new message on the fifteenth, Coke strongly supported a proposal made by Phelips and others that they respond to it with a protestation of their liberties. Ordinarily, he said, he would not dispute with the king over words, but "when the King says he

156. Tanner, *CD*, pp. 280–83.

157. Zaller, *1621*, pp. 161–62. For Coke's speech in this debate, see White, "Coke," p. 69 n. 76.

158. For the Commons's debate on whether to proceed with regular business, see Zaller, *1621*, pp. 159, 162–64; and White, "Coke," p. 69 and nn. 77–81. Coke favored abandonment of all regular business.

159. *CD 1621*, 2:513–14; Zaller, *1621*, p. 164.

160. *CD 1621*, 6:234.

161. Tanner, *CD*, pp. 283–87; Zaller, *1621*, pp. 165–67.

cannot allow our liberties of right," he said, "this strikes at the root," because the Commons's liberties were "the nurse and life of all laws." Coke then claimed that his own inheritance was threatened by the king's denial of the Commons's right to their liberties and that he would there- fore have to "[f]ly to Magna Charta" in order to defend both the Com- mons's liberties and his own inheritance.[162] This speech signaled Coke's belated decision to engage in direct contestation with the king over the issue of free speech. He now construed the king's statements as not just a denial of the Commons's right to debate foreign policy and war, but as an arbitrary and unlawful seizure of the subject's property and as a direct assault on the subject's most fundamental liberties. He was thus reinter- preting the political and legal situation in which he found himself. He was treating a somewhat dubiously established privilege of the Commons as a property right or "inheritance" of every English subject, and he was representing the House of Commons as not merely a part of the English central government, but as the principal guardian of the subject's liberties. He was thus able to portray the king's statement that the Commons's privileges were not theirs by right as an attack on the fundamental liberties and property rights of English subjects.[163]

The Commons ended their debate of 15 December by ordering an- other committee of the whole to meet two days later to discuss a new "declaration of [their] privileges and liberties."[164] On the seventeenth this plan was disrupted by the arrival of yet another royal letter. The king now claimed that in his last message to the Commons,

we never meant to deny them any lawful privileges that ever that House enjoyed ... in our predecessors' time and we expected our said answer should have sufficiently cleared them; neither in justice whatever they have any undoubted right unto, nor in grace whatever our predecessors or we have permitted unto them. And therefore we made that distinction of the most part, for whatsoever privileges or liberties they enjoy by any law or statute shall be ever inviolably

162. For an analysis of Coke's views as to what sort of committee should draft the Protestation, see White, "Coke," pp. 71–72 and nn. 103–11. It is there argued that when Coke said that the Commons served "for thousands of ten thousands [sic]," he was not making a "political" appeal, as Margaret Judson suggested (The Crisis of the Constitution, pp. 286–87). His argument was simply this: to entrust the task of defending the Commons's privileges to a *select* committee, as had been proposed, would be inappropiate if not illegal, because members of a select committee would be acting as proxies for other members. But, according to Coke, members of the Commons could not appoint proxies because they represented others—in fact, thousands of others.

163. For Coke's speech, see CD 1621, 2:256–57; 5:239–40, 417; 6:240; P&D, 2:337; CJ, 1:665.

164. CD 1621, 2:528.

preserved by us and we hope our posterity will imitate our footsteps therein. And whatsoever privileges they enjoy by long custom and uncontrolled and lawful precedents we will likewise be as careful to preserve them and transmit the care thereof to our posterity.

James then expressed the hope that the Commons would proceed "cheerfully . . . in their business, rejecting the curious wrangling of lawyers upon words and syllables."[165]

Despite the conciliatory tone of this message, the Commons were not satisfied with it or willing to return to business. Although Coke claimed that the message contained "an allowance of our privileges, which indeed [are] ours by law, by custom, by precedent, and by act of Parliament," he also stated that the terms of this allowance were too general and that neither king nor Commons was sufficiently well acquainted with the Commons's privileges to bring his or their debates on this subject to a satisfactory conclusion. He therefore moved that "all precedents of the House should be collected and presented to the King." Once this had been done, he predicted, the king would "allow" the Commons their privileges and "so remove many rubs."[166] He abandoned this proposal, however, when others suggested that the Commons draft a "protestation" of their liberties modeled on the Apology of 1604.[167] He then tried to influence the content of this Protestation by urging that it refer to particular privileges of the Commons that the king had denied, and that it assert that the House held these privileges by right and not by royal allowance. He also wanted the document to inform the king that if he would not allow the Commons their privileges, they would keep silent and do no business.[168] When the House reconvened on the eighteenth to continue their discussion of the Protestation, they received a warning from James that he would dissolve Parliament if they did not "seriously apply themselves" to regular parliamentary business.[169] After approving a noncommittal reply to this message,[170] the Commons quickly approved Coke's motion to draft a Protestation of the particular privileges that the king had denied.[171] They then resolved to divide this text into six parts

165. Ibid., 2:529–30.

166. For this speech of Coke's, see *CD 1621*, 2:530; 6:241, 332; *P&D*, 2:341.

167. Ashley, Hakewill, Strode, and Pym all favored a protestation (*CD 1621*, 2:533; 6:243). On the Apology of 1604, see Notestein, *1604–1610*, pp. 124–40; G. R. Elton, "A High Road to Civil War," and Hexter, "Power Struggle, Parliament, and Liberty," pp. 32–38.

168. *CD 1621*, 2:534; 6:243, 336; 5:241; cf. Zaller, *1621*, p. 174.

169. *CD 1621*, 2:535; for the full message, see 2:534–36 and 6:425. For comments on it, see Zaller, *1621*, pp. 175–76.

170. *CD 1621*, 6:340.

171. Ibid., 2:537; 6:245 and n. 1, 340. On some procedural problems that arose at this point, see White, "Coke," p. 75 n. 144.

and appointed a subcommittee to draft it.[172] Later in the day, the Protestation was brought into the house and was debated, passed, and entered into the Commons's journal.[173]

This Protestation bore the mark of Coke's influence. As he had twice suggested, it was cast as an assertion of those of the Commons's privileges that the king had challenged; and its treatment of these privileges conformed closely to his recommendations. In dealing with the issue of free speech, he had advised the Commons to "insist but upon universals, not upon particulars to[o] particularly."[174] He had also suggested that instead of explicitly asserting their right to debate "[p]eace and war and marriage," they should simply state "[t]hat in Parliament we may treat[,] and have freedom of speech concerning[, the King], the state [and defense] of the realm, and [of] the Church of England." He had also urged that the Protestation state that the house could treat of and have freedom of speech concerning the making of laws and the redress of grievances and mischiefs "[t]hat happen or are in the kingdom." In its final form, the Protestation's clauses concerning free speech used language very similar to Coke's. It stated "that the arduous and urgent affairs concerning the King, state and defense of the realm, and of the Church of England, and the maintenance and making of laws, and redress of grievances which daily happen within this realm, are proper subjects and matters of counsel and debate in Parliament."[175] Another clause in the Protestation may also have originated in one of Coke's suggestions. The Committee of the Whole had originally resolved that it should contain five heads, but on his motion, a sixth head was added that he said should run roughly as follows: "What soever the King shall hear to be done in the House, the King shall give no ear or belief to it till the whole House inform [him of] it; for no body ought to inform anything but what shall be informed by the whole House."[176] The sixth head of the Protestation stated that "if any of the said members be complained of and questioned for anything done or said in Parliament, the same is to be showed to the King by the advice and assent of all the Commons assembled in Parliament before the King give credence to any private information."[177] Coke's acceptance of the positions set forth in this document is further demonstrated by the

172. Originally, the Protestation was to have had five "heads" (CD 1621, 6:342; Zaller, 1621, p. 177), but a sixth was added on Coke's motion (P&D, 2:358). See fn. 176.

173. See Zaller, 1621, p. 177.

174. CD 1621, 5:244; 6:342; 2:541; P&D, 2:358. Coke had said that the Protestation as a whole should deal with particular privileges, but that each particular section should be cast in general terms.

175. Kenyon, SC, p. 47.

176. CD 1621, 6:342–43; P&D, 2:358. See fn. 172.

177. Kenyon, SC, pp. 47–48.

fact that he closely followed its wording in the sections on parliamentary privilege in his *Fourth Institutes*.[178]

By the end of the parliament of 1621, therefore, Coke had adopted an extreme position on the issue of the Commons's privileges, even though he knew that by doing so he would probably undermine his own efforts to implement parliamentary remedies for grievances. Nevertheless, his support for the Protestation did not mark an irreversible turning point in his parliamentary career. Although he obviously knew of James's emphatic rejection of the Protestation[179] and was himself imprisoned for several months while royal agents confiscated his papers,[180] he showed no inclination in 1624 to engage in further contestation with the king, to use Parliament as a forum for the debate of constitutional issues, or to attack the Stuart court. Instead, he made even greater efforts than he had in 1621 to avoid conflicts within Parliament. His success in attaining these objectives is shown by his later reference to this parliament as "foelix," in contrast with its relatively unhappy predecessor.[181]

Coke signaled his desire to avoid any clash over free speech at the very outset of the new parliament when he opposed an attempt to reopen the controversies that had led to Parliament's dissolution two years earlier. On 27 February Sir John Eliot alluded to previous parliamentary conflicts over free speech and moved that the Commons send a petition to the king containing a comprehensive statement of their privileges and liberties.[182] Coke had to concede that Eliot's motion raised important issues, but he opposed it because it might cause an immediate rift with the king. After declaring that the privilege of free speech was the "quintessence" of Parliament's proceedings[183] and urging the Commons to preserve their liberties, he also warned them to "take heed of contestation" with the king. Ignoring the House's experience in 1621, he also argued that Eliot's proposed petition was unnecessary, "for there was no fear that [the king] would deny [their privileges] since he had given . . . his word for them in

---

178. *Institutes*, 4:8–9.
179. On the king's response, see Zaller, *1621*, pp. 185–87.
180. Ibid., pp. 184–85 and n. 183. See also p. 9 and fn. 33.
181. *Institutes*, 3:2.
182. On this motion and the Commons's subsequent debate on it, see Ruigh, *1624*, pp. 171–4; and Hulme, *Eliot*, pp. 47–8. Hulme claims that those who opposed Eliot's proposals were "opportunists" who were "no longer interested in obtaining the privileges of freedom of speech in theory when they had it in practice" by virtue of the king's opening speech to Parliament (p. 48). According to John Pym, many members were "afraid this motion would have put the House into some such heat as to disturb the greater business," that is, the breaking off of the Spanish treaties (Pym, *1624*, ff. 8v–9).
183. Coke said that the four sorts of parliamentary proceedings—bills, judicature, petitions of grace, and petitions of right—were the four "essences" of Parliament (Holles, *1624*, f. 84).

his speech at the beginning of the Parliament." He instead recommended that the Commons prefer "a petition that his Majesty will not after the passing of laws, dissolve the Parliament but that he would show cause for it." Coke may have hoped that such a petition might dissuade the king from dissolving Parliament as James had done in 1622, on the bare pretext that the Commons had overstepped the limits of their privilege of free speech.[184] But he advanced even this modest proposal very cautiously. He insisted that he was proposing merely a petition of grace. He also advised the Commons to "learn of Solomon in the ending of differences" and not bring up old grievances, as Eliot had done, because such "repetitions," he said, "do aggravate more than the former discourtesies." Instead, they should cite precedents for their liberties. In conclusion, he again pleaded that there be no contestation with the king and urged the Commons to "consider the state of Christendom, and the desire of our enemies to break off our meetings without success."[185] He then moved that they refer all questions concerning their privileges to a small committee "of the ancientest Parliament men" and that this committee not "give ear to disturbers."[186] After a brief debate, the House appointed a committee headed by Coke "to deal in all the liberties and privileges of the House [and] to provide the best remedy for time to come." The effect of this order was to put Eliot's proposal to sleep. Coke's committee never reported back to the House.[187]

During the remainder of the parliament of 1624, Coke's position with respect to the Commons's privileges was characterized by vacillation and inconsistency, but he always succeeded in avoiding a clash over this issue. On the twenty-seventh he had opposed Eliot's attempt to raise explicitly the issue of the Commons's privileges, but two days later he adopted a somewhat different stance. On 1 March he urged the Commons not only to debate foreign affairs, but to assert directly their right to do so. When the Committee of the Whole was considering a proposal to break off England's treaties with Spain,[188] Coke made a point of declaring that the Commons were to give formal "advice" on this foreign policy issue and not merely express their "opinion," and that they had an absolute right to give advice on this matter. "In advice," he said, "there must be a demonstration of the grounds whereupon we ground our advice," and he therefore claimed that it was "necessary that some select commit-

184. See Zaller, 1621, pp. 185–87.
185. For Coke's speech, see CJ, 1:719–20; Nicholas, 1624, ff. 29–29v; D'Ewes, 1624, ff. 61v–62; Holles, 1624, f. 84; Pym, 1624, ff. 8v–9; Holland, 1624, ff. 5–5v; Erle, 1624, ff. 31v–32.
186. Holland, 1624, I, f. 5v.
187. See Ruigh, 1624, p. 174.
188. On this debate, see ibid., pp. 177–85.

tee be appointed to collect the reasons which every one delivers[, and] to draw them to some heads that we may be able to show the reasons from whence our opinions shall receive life." The House should follow such a formal procedure, Coke said, because they were "justly moved to the care and consideration of these things." There were precedents for their proceedings on matters of foreign policy and war, and these proceedings were in keeping with the purposes for which they had been called to Parliament. Because "parliament precedents are fittest for parliaments, and held there in most esteem," he said, he would "acquaint the House with some passages of the parliament concerning the articles of treaty and contract made in Parliament between King Philip and Queen Mary." After summarizing seven parts of the statute 1 Mary, *st.* 2, *c.* 1,[189] he argued, just as he had on 3 December 1621, that "the *natural sense* of the words in the Parliament writ" demonstrated Parliament's right to give formal advice on the breaking off of the treaties. After quoting the relevant passage from the writ, which he had thrice cited in 1621 and which was quoted in the Protestation, he glossed it as follows. "[T]he advice is ex [*sic*] arduis," which are "difficult things"; "the speed of it [is] implied in urgentibus"; "it concerns the King in the word nos and his children"; "et statum regni, how the land itself may subsist"; "et defensionem [,] how to keep off the enemy."[190]

Coke was thus arguing that the Commons could discuss the Spanish treaties not because they had been asked to do so, but because they had the right to debate such matters.[191] Four days later, however, he showed himself to be more concerned with "expediting a declaration of war" than with defending the Commons's privilege of initiating proposals for supply. On 4 March subcommittees of both houses drafted a statement of the reasons for breaking off the Spanish treaties. Later, in the upper house, one of the members of the Lords' subcommittee moved that those who were to deliver this statement to the king have the power to add that "if this breaks off the treaty . . . his Majesty need not doubt but we will be ready with our persons and our estates to be assistant." The motion passed the Lords, and the additional words were written on a separate piece of paper that was delivered to the chairman of the Commons's subcommittee, Sir Edwin Sandys.[192] When Sandys brought "the paper," as it was called, into the House of Commons on 5 March, Edward Alford

189. See *SR*, 4, pt. 1, pp. 200–201.

190. Coke also glossed the words "ecclesiae Anglicanae." They showed, he said, that even under Henry V, when these words had come into the writ, Parliament was "interested in the care and reformation of abuses" in the Church (Spring, 1624, f. 57).

191. For Coke's speech, see Spring, 1624, ff. 56–57; Erle, 1624, ff. 39–39v; Jervoise, 1624, f. 27; Holles, 1624, f. 88.

192. Ruigh, 1624, pp. 192–94.

"dissented" from receiving it, "saying [that proposals for] supply of money should properly proceed from this House, not from the Lords."[193] Coke agreed that the Lords had proceeded improperly in sending the paper. "If any subsidy or aid come," he said, "it ought to be from the Lower House," because such taxes came from "the body of the realm," which the Commons represented. Nevertheless, he denied that any great offense had been committed and urged the Commons not to protest to the Lords about the paper. Instead, he simply moved that "a mannerly message may be sent to the Lords that in due time in a parliamentary way we may give answer" to the paper.[194]

This incident suggests that Coke was so anxious to preserve the "good correspondency" between the Commons, the Lords, and the king, that on this occasion he was "willing to risk privileges which [he] had jealously guarded in preceding Parliaments."[195] Two days later, however, he seemed to reverse his posture with respect to the Commons's privileges. When the Commons debated the subsidy on 11 March, he moved that they pass a resolution "on the necessity and justice of war." This proposal was more extreme in its constitutional implications than any he had advanced in 1621,[196] and eight days later he made a similar suggestion. On 19 March, in another debate on the subsidy, Sir John Savile moved that the Commons not only supply the king but also specify "the thing to be done and the necessity of it."[197] Savile was suggesting that the Commons explicitly state that supply was being given for a war with Spain, and that they give explicit reasons for the adoption of such a policy. Supporters of Savile's motion cited various cases in which the Commons had granted supply for a particular war, but it was Coke who argued most forcefully for Savile's proposal. He said that "if the King will make a war and require no aid he may do it where he will, but if he demand aid he must be advised" by Parliament, and he then cited five precedents to support this statement.[198] Once again Coke quickly retreated from his extreme position on the Commons's power to advise the king on matters of military and diplomatic policy. When Savile's proposal was attacked and ultimately watered down on the following day, Coke failed to protest.[199] He was still proceeding on the assumption that he could work with Buckingham and the court; that parliamentary "contestation" was

193. Holles, 1624, f. 92.
194. Ibid., f. 92v; Holland, 1624, I, f. 33; Nicholas, 1624, f. 52.
195. Ruigh, 1624, p. 195.
196. Spring, 1624, f. 105; cf. Ruigh, 1624, p. 206.
197. Ruigh, 1624, p. 222; for a discussion of the full debate, see pp. 217–27.
198. Holles, 1624, f. 106v; Erle, 1624, f. 97; Spring, 1624, f. 137; cf. Ruigh, 1624, p. 221. For the precedents, see White, "Coke," p. 84 and n. 67.
199. Ruigh, 1624, pp. 221–22.

to be avoided; and that there was no necessity for him to adopt strong, consistent positions about Parliament's privileges and powers or about the liberties of the subject. In little more than a year his attitude would change when he realized that Buckingham could not be trusted to pursue sound religious, foreign, or military policies and that the duke would obstruct many parliamentary attempts to remedy the grievances of the commonwealth.

Part Two

The Later 1620s

Six

Coke in the Parliament of 1625

In spite of its brevity and the relative simplicity of its proceedings, the parliament of 1625 marked a significant turning point in Coke's career and in the history of early Stuart parliaments.[1] It was the scene of more continuous contestation than the parliaments of 1621 or 1624, and it saw a significant breakdown of good correspondency between the court and the leaders of the Commons. It was also marked by a significant change in Coke's attitude towards the grievances of the commonwealth and towards Parliament's role in remedying them. Although Charles I's servants continually called on the lower house to display its love for the king and trust him, members like Coke frequently expressed deep suspicions and strong reservations about his foreign and military policies and opposed granting him the financial support that he requested and allegedly needed. In addition to complaining about the toleration of recusants, they expressed skepticism about the court's devotion to true religion by persisting in attacking an Arminian clergyman, Dr. Richard Montague, even after the king had made him his chaplain. The main theme of the Commons's debates in this year, moreover, was that the king was being guided by "evil counsel," and as the parliament progressed, some members became bolder and bolder about suggesting that the source of this evil counsel was the duke of Buckingham. These complaints against Buckingham constitute their first all-out attack on a highly favored royal servant, and they were all the more significant because they were integrally related to a new mode of discussing and accounting for the grievances of the commonwealth. In the early 1620s, the Commons had focused their attention on specific abuses that they could blame on individual scapegoats rather than on the court; and they had supported only limited parliamentary reforms in the state, because they did not conceive of Parliament as having a general responsibility to reform the whole realm. In 1625, however, these attitudes were in the process of changing. Although leaders of the Commons had not yet constructed either a coherent critique of court policy or a general plan to reform it

1. On the main sources for the history of this parliament, see Johnson, "Parliamentary Diaries." For secondary accounts of it, see Gardiner, *History*, 5, chapters 52 (pp. 337–74) and 54 (pp. 397–435); Hulme, *Eliot*, pp. 72–93; J. N. Ball, "Sir John Eliot at the Oxford Parliament, 1625"; and Conrad Russell, *The Crisis of Parliaments*, pp. 300–302.

(and would not do so until the Long Parliament), they were increasingly prone to note close logical, causal, or organic connections between their various grievances, to attribute them to the action or inaction of courtiers, and to subordinate their complaints about individual abuses to their sweeping criticisms of the court in general and the duke in particular.

A striking feature of the Commons's debates in 1625 was the way in which their leaders shifted their discussions from one type of grievance to another. An interesting example of this process was later noted by Sir John Eliot, who wrote that

> where ever that mention does break of the fears or dangers of religion, and the increase of popery, their [the Commons's] affections are much stirred, and what ever is obnoxious in the state, it is then reckoned as an incident to that: for so it followed upon the agitation of that motion [for a recusant petition], first the danger of religion was observed in some general notes of prejudice; then by induction it was proved in the enumeration of particulars; to that was urged the infelicities of the kingdom since that disease came in. this had an aggravation by a syneresis and comparison with the days of Q[ueen] El[izabeth]. to that was added the new grievances and oppression, wholly inferred and raised since the connivance with the papists: the monopolies that had been, the impositions that then were, all were reduced to this.[2]

Eliot's only purpose in this passage was to demonstrate the Commons's "apprehension" about popery and their "affection" in religious matters,[3] but the same associative processes that he described could be seen in other Commons's debates in 1625. Questions about royal policy towards domestic Catholics would lead to further questions about the purposes of the king's foreign policies, which would lead in turn to objections against the king's requests for supply. Comments on the subsidy would turn into criticisms of the court's general financial policies and complaints about the country's inability to pay. Debaters could then attack any and all abuses that allegedly prevented the king's subjects from supplying him, criticize the court for its failure to remove them, or complain about the "evil counsel" that was at the root of all these problems. Complaints about evil counsel could then serve to raise further questions about the religious policies of the court, and the whole cycle of complaints could then begin once more. As the Commons became more conscious of the interconnections between different grievances and developed a political explanation for the abuses that troubled the realm, their debates became less compartmentalized. They are therefore less susceptible to a topical analysis and must instead be treated chronologically.

Superficially at least, what precipitated the Commons's attacks on

2. Eliot, *Negotium*, 1:69.
3. Ibid., 1:69–70.

the court and duke in 1625 was their cynicism and suspicion about the king's continental designs. But foreign-policy issues were so closely identified with religious ones that questions about the former inevitably raised questions about the latter. The support for royal foreign policy that the Commons had expressed in 1624 quickly evaporated the following year[4] as they gradually realized that Charles and Buckingham were not pursuing the policies that the Commons had formally supported the year before. Instead of preparing for a direct war against Spain, that was to be carried on mostly at sea, the king and the duke were working mainly to recover the Palatinate. Their efforts to reach this goal, moreover, were proceeding with singularly little success. Although Charles I had recently married a daughter of Louis XIII, he had not gotten French support against Spain or even induced the French king to make peace with the Huguenots at La Rochelle. He had also failed to secure effective support from his Scandinavian or Dutch allies, or to prepare his own army or fleet for real military action. Besides being ineffectual, the king's foreign policy, like that of his father, raised doubts in some minds about his commitment to the Protestant cause. He had gone against the Commons's advice of 1621 by marrying a Catholic princess and had made extensive concessions to domestic Catholics. He had also done little to support England's coreligionists in France. In addition, his diplomatic ventures were open to attack simply because of their expense. By the time Parliament met in June of 1625, he had exhausted the huge parliamentary subsidy granted to his father the year before and had incurred obligations far larger than any subsidy that Parliament was ready to grant. Finally, Charles I and Buckingham further alienated parliamentary members by failing to explain their policies in a timely or politic way. Although they never clearly stated the king's financial needs, they repeatedly and obtusely insisted that Parliament's actions in 1624 obligated its present members to give the king whatever sum he asked for.[5]

On 18 June, when Parliament opened at Westminster in the midst of an outbreak of plague, Charles informed members of both houses that "ye have heretofor engaged my father in a war . . . for the Palatinate, so that by succession, I am not only involved therein, but can challenge a particular promise of your loves and affections to that purpose in the last Parliament, when I labored all I could to bring my father to assent thereto."[6] Charles went on to say that it would be "a dishonor" to

4. For a clear and detailed analysis of the fragile consensus that was maintained on foreign policy in 1624, see Ruigh, *1624*.

5. See Gardiner, *History*, 5:337–74, 397–435 passim; and Russell, *Crisis of Parliaments*, pp. 300–302.

6. Add. MS. 48091, f. lv; cf. *CD 1625*, p. 1; Eliot, *Negotium*, 1:44; *LJ*, 3:436.

himself and to both houses if the present Parliament were not to "perfect" their previous engagement "by yielding such supply as the greatness of the work and the variety of provision did require."[7] Parliament's alleged "engagement" to support the king's war policy was also mentioned by Lord Keeper Williams[8] and was a recurrent motif in major speeches by courtiers during the remainder of this parliament. As early as 30 June, however, the very existence of this engagement was challenged in the lower house, where serious complaints were made both about the king's foreign policy and about the general state of the commonwealth, and the Commons then granted the king a much smaller supply than he requested. They also indicated their lack of confidence in the court by granting the king tonnage and poundage for only a year and not for life and by investigating the writings of Montague, whom James I had supported and who was soon to receive favor from the new king.

Obviously displeased with this parliament, Charles I adjourned it on 11 July, but in the hope of getting a further grant of supply he called it back into session at Oxford on 1 August. He and two courtiers explained his policies and financial needs to both houses on 4 August, and on the fifth another courtier moved that the Commons grant the king further supply. Instead of approving this motion, however, the leaders of the House launched a comprehensive attack on the court and its policies and all but named Buckingham as the source of all evil counsel in the state. Three days later, the duke tried to defend himself in an address to both houses and to justify the king's requests for funds, but on 10 and 11 August the Commons continued to oppose all supply motions and criticized the Duke even more sharply than before. On the eleventh, moreover, they discussed various scandals in the admiralty, probably with the intention of initiating judicial proceedings against the duke modeled on their actions in Middlesex's case the year before. Their attacks on the duke and their refusal to approve another subsidy impelled the king to dissolve Parliament. Immediately prior to the dissolution, on the twelfth, the Commons adopted a protestation, declaring their readiness "in convenient time and in a parliamentary way freely and dutifully to do our utmost endeavor to discover and reform the abuses and grievances of the realm and state, and in the like sort to afford all necessary supply to his Majesty upon his present and all other his just occasions and designs."[9] Just after the Commons had given formal expression to their opinion that the commonwealth was in need of general reforms that only Parliament could implement, Charles I dissolved his first parliament.

7. CD 1625, p. 2.
8. Ibid.; cf. Eliot, Negotium, 1:45; LJ, 3:436.
9. Cobbett, PH, 2, col. 27.

This Parliament marked as clear a turning point in Coke's career as it did in the history of early Stuart parliaments as a whole. While he was less active in it than in the two previous parliaments,[10] he cooperated closely with other parliamentary leaders like Phelips and gave several general speeches on the grievances of the commonwealth that signaled a significant change in his political outlook. Like other members of the Commons, he ceased to complain about isolated abuses or promote piece-meal legislative reform and instead made more general attacks on the crown's foreign, military, and financial policies and strongly criticized Buckingham. Instead of moderating his criticisms of the court in the interest of implementing limited remedies for grievances through par-liamentary compromise, he strongly implied that the commonwealth's grievances were so deeply rooted and intricately interconnected that they could be effectively remedied only through systematic, comprehensive parliamentary action.

Although Coke's political outlook was obviously changing, the na-ture of the shift in his viewpoint is difficult to characterize. At first, his parliamentary priorities merely seem to have shifted so as to lead him to devote less attention to individual grievances than to the court's foreign and religious policies and to the malign influence of Buckingham. How-ever, an examination of his parliamentary speeches of 1625 shows that far from abandoning his earlier concerns, he had found a new way of articulating them. Certain abuses that he had previously characterized as grievances in their own right he now treated as causes of the king's financial plight, or as reasons for the Commons's refusal to satisfy royal financial requests. He also came close to describing them as effects of the duke's evil counsel, because he now blamed Buckingham for not only court corruption but also for the court's failure to repress corruption throughout the realm and its obstruction of the Commons's efforts to undertake this task themselves. This change in Coke's political outlook rendered his critique of English society less simplistic insofar as it now proceeded from a heightened awareness of the structural interconnections between different social institutions; but it was also becoming less sophis-ticated in that it reflected a belief that the grievances of the commonwealth were primarily political, or even personal, in origin. Coke's political progress through the 1620s therefore involved a paradox. The processes that led him into more and more clear-cut opposition to the ruling politi-cal regime may also have led him further and further away from promot-ing the institutional and impersonal reforms that would have benefited

10. On the prominent position held by Phelips in this parliament, see Gardiner, *History*, 5:432–33.

those for whom he spoke in Parliament. Thus, one might argue that the development of his political outlook reflected his increasing propensity to espouse a simpleminded form of political "realism" and to lose sight of his original objectives. But one might also maintain that his increasing preoccupation with broad political and constitutional issues arose out of an accurate assessment of the English political situation, according to which the resolution of such issues had to precede the implementation of changes in the legal system or in economic organization. In other words, the elimination of corruption and the promotion of free trade, legal certainty, and quietness of possession had to await some sort of constitutional and political transformation.

Charles I's requests for supply and religious problems at home were the only two issues that significantly engaged Coke's attention in the parliament of 1625, and he discussed only the first of them at any length. Nevertheless, his fixation on the supply question did not narrow the scope of his criticisms of the condition of English society, because he was able to organize his comments on numerous grievances around this one issue. Although he and other leaders of the Commons decided not to debate specific abuses or promote individual legislative reforms, they were not abandoning these issues. They realized that most of them could be at least mentioned in supply debates since their existence provided several reasons for opposing large subsidies. They could argue that the existence of these grievances diminished the commonwealth's ability to give, that the grant of a large supply should be accompanied in a later parliament by the redress of major grievances, and that the country should not be asked to give money to compensate the king for the improvidence of his courtiers. Moreover, supply debates provided a useful pretext for attacking Buckingham, because he could be blamed for the king's financial plight, and because his position of power could be cited by itself as a reason for refusing the king a large subsidy. Coke was thus in a position to justify his decision in this year to abandon his earlier efforts to remedy grievances by bill and petition. Early in the Westminster session, he made a conscious decision not to focus attention on individual abuses by successfully opposing the appointment of a committee for grievances—a committee that had served as his main forum for attacking miscellaneous abuses in 1621 and 1624. Moreover, while he expressed dissatisfaction with Charles I's answers to the petition submitted to James I in 1624, he did not strongly press the new king for more satisfactory responses; and he barely alluded to the many severe economic problems that had so greatly concerned him in the two previous parliaments.

Coke's failure to promote legislation in 1625 is even more striking than his failure to support the drafting of a petition of grievances and a petition for trade. In both 1621 and 1624 he had delivered dozens of speeches and committee reports on proposed legislation and had labored to secure the passage of dozens of significant bills, but in 1625 the promotion of bills hardly concerned him at all. The records of this parliament mention only a handful of speeches that he made on proposed legislative measures. On 25 June he commended the bill "to prevent lapse in the case of qualifications"[11] and the bill for secret offices,[12] but he failed to secure the passage of either. On 4 August he reported to the House both the habeas corpus bill and the bill "for the quiet of ecclesiastical persons,"[13] but these two measures also went unenacted. His lack of interest in passing bills is further evidenced by this parliament's failure to pass more than four public bills besides the subsidies and the act providing that the king's assent to bills on 12 July would not determine the session. The act for the duchy of Cornwall, the act concerning licenses for alienations, and the Sunday act were all bills that he had supported in the early 1620s, but he had never attached much importance to any of them.[14] The fourth bill enacted in 1625 was "for the restraint of tippling."[15]

The main problem confronting Coke and other leaders of the Commons at the outset of the parliament of 1625 was to devise some general strategy for the session. They would need some plan of action if they were to succeed in attacking the duke of Buckingham, in criticizing royal foreign policy, and in blocking their king's plan to secure a large grant of supply. It is difficult to tell how closely Coke worked in 1625 with members like Phelips or Sir Francis Seymour or with opponents of Buckingham at court, but it seems likely that these members, at least, had formed a common strategy by late June and were working closely with one another by the time of the Oxford meeting in August. Their strategy seems to have been, roughly, the following. The Commons would spend little or no time investigating or debating individual grievances and would consider only a few minor, uncontroversial bills. Instead, they would devote their energies to debating two main issues: religion and supply. In discussing the first of these topics, they would call, as usual, for the enforcement of antirecusant legislation and would continue the attack, begun in 1624, against Dr. Richard Montague. Although they could not have known that Charles I would try to protect this ecclesiastic by making him his chaplain, they probably realized that by debating religious grievances

11. *CD 1625*, p. 16.
12. Ibid., p. 17. On this bill, see pp. 64–65.
13. *CJ*, 1:180.
14. 1 *Car.* I, cc. 1–3 (*SR*, 5:1–3).
15. 1 *Car.* I, c. 4 (*SR*, 5:3).

they could not only express their sincere concerns about them, but also discredit certain court policies and further their objectives with respect to the second major issue that they planned to discuss which was, namely, supply. Coke and his colleagues in the Commons obviously knew that the king would ask Parliament for a large subsidy, and although they were not prepared to deny him any funds, they were unwilling to vote him as much money as he needed and wanted, particularly if they could get nothing in return. They were also planning to use the Commons's deliberations on the king's request for money as a pretext for debating a host of other issues that might otherwise have been discussed in debates on grievances. First, they would raise serious questions about the foreign and military policies that the court had pursued since the prorogation of the parliament of 1624 and about the king's and Buckingham's plans for a war. They would be in a particularly good position to do this if the king were to request that Parliament pay off his past debts and fulfill its alleged promise of 1624 to support a war. Second, they would use the debates on supply as occasions for raising questions about other royal revenues, notably impositions and tonnage and poundage. Third, Coke in particular would take the opportunity afforded by the supply debates to attack royal financial policy in general and would argue that the king would not need a large subsidy if he were to reduce expenditures and devise sound policies to augment regular revenues. He would also argue that the king was violating a basic norm of English financial policy by asking Parliament for money to cover his ordinary charges. Finally, Coke and his allies would continually suggest that the king was receiving evil counsel and would ultimately charge that the duke of Buckingham was the source of this malevolent advice. This plan presumably reflected their belief or hope that they could persuade the new king to abandon the old favorite and appoint counsellors who were more to their liking.

Coke and the other leaders in the Commons had probably agreed on this plan by the end of June, but their failure to have developed it before Parliament opened was made clear in the Commons's debates of 21 and 22 June, both of which revealed their disagreements with one another about how the session should proceed. On the twenty-first a burgess of Ripon, Mr. Mallory, moved that the House petition the king to adjourn Parliament till Michaelmas "in respect of the plague."[16] Sir William Strode tried to divert attention from this motion by making another one, but Mallory's motion was seconded and strongly supported by Phelips. He argued that instead of supplying the king, the Commons ought rather to

16. CJ, 1:800. On this motion, see Eliot, *Negotium*, 1:61–63; Gardiner, *History*, 5:34–41; CD *1625*, pp. v–vi.

"supply the commonwealth," but that since they lacked the time to do this, they should simply adjourn. Although Wentworth supported adjournment, Solicitor Heath strongly opposed it on the grounds that it would weaken the king's reputation, and he persuaded the House not to put Mallory's motion to the question.[17] Coke's apparent failure to support Phelips's position is surprising in view of their close collaboration in many debates later held in this parliament. It seems likely, therefore, that if Coke had supported Phelips's plan to adjourn, he would have said so openly and forcefully on the twenty-first.

Coke's failure to have agreed on a strategy with other prominent members was also revealed in the debate of 22 June. After Sir Thomas Hoby moved that the Commons follow their customary procedure of appointing a committee of grievances,[18] a courtier opposed the motion, arguing that "the first Parliament of the King should have a temperate proceeding and prosperous success" and that the Commons should therefore conduct themselves "with sweetness, with duty, [and] with confidence in and towards his majesty."[19] Coke took the same position, but for different reasons. He maintained that the House should not appoint a committee for grievances, because members were in danger from the plague, and because no new grievances had arisen under the new king. He also argued that the Commons should not investigate new grievances when they had not yet gotten an answer to their petition of grievances of 1624; and he therefore moved that they petition the king for an answer to the earlier petition.[20] This motion was uncontroversial and Solicitor Heath later informed them that the king would comply with their request.[21] Because Coke's subsequent speeches show his readiness to attack new grievances, it seems likely that he opposed Hoby's motion simply because he had formulated the general strategy, noted above, of attacking grievances in the Commons's debate on supply. Nevertheless, he wished to uphold the principle that redress of grievances should accompany parliamentary grants of supply, and he therefore wanted the Commons to petition the king about the grievances of 1624.

As yet, however, Coke had not said what else the Commons should do; and when this question arose it again became clear that the leaders of the House had not yet agreed on any overall strategy. Sir Francis Seymour believed that the House should both petition the king against recusants and grant him supply as well, and he therefore moved for a committee "to

17. *CD 1625*, pp. 7–8 and 8 n. c.
18. Ibid., p. 9; *CJ*, 1:800; Eliot, *Negotium*, 1:63.
19. *CD 1625*, pp. 9–11.
20. Ibid., pp. 11–12; *CJ*, 1:800.
21. *CJ*, 1:800.

consider of religion and . . . supply." Wentworth opposed any deviation from "the ancient form of Parliaments," even though he had supported adjournment the day before; but although he favored the appointment of a Committee for Grievances, he wished to allow it discretion "to entertain nothing unfitting." Phelips apparently disliked all the motions previously made. He did not support Wentworth's position and directly opposed Seymour's motion on the grounds that it was "not yet timely for a Committee for Religion and Supply." Instead, realizing that a strategy for the session had to be worked out, he moved that the Commons appoint a committee of the whole to debate and resolve "a fitting course to be holden" in their consultations and resolutions. Nevertheless, he briefly indicated what course they should follow when he attacked a previous speaker who had opposed Hoby's and Seymour's motions on the grounds that "[t]he King's supply [was] now 'hoc unum necessarium.'"[22] Phelips now developed at greater length the views that he had expressed the day before and insisted that the House must deal not only with the needs of the king, but also with the needs of the kingdom and with the matter of religion. He then anticipated some of the points that would be made in subsequent supply debates by urging the House to investigate the new impositions and the act of tonnage and poundage, to scrutinize "the account of the last subsidies," and to determine "how the revenue of the Crown might be supplied" so that it could support "public charges."[23] Coke grasped the strategic significance of these suggestions; and although he opposed "meddling" with impositions generally (at least for the moment) he wanted the Commons to look into the act of tonnage and poundage and to establish "a settled book of rates." Nevertheless, instead of supporting Phelips's earlier motion, he made a new one of his own that closely resembled Seymour's, except that it stated explicitly that the Commons should deal with tonnage and poundage.[24] The House approved Phelips's motion and not Coke's and ordered a committee of the whole to meet the following morning "to consider of all the aforesaid propositions and of whatsoever else shall be offered."[25] On the twenty-third this committee quickly resolved to establish a committee for religion and supply, which resolved in turn to deal first with religion.[26]

   As of 21 and 22 June, the leaders of the House had obviously not formulated their strategy for the session, but they had still raised several major issues that they meant to discuss further. Phelips, who was already

22. Ibid.
23. CD 1625, p. 12.
24. CJ, 1:800–801; cf. CD 1625, p. 13.
25. CJ, 1:801.
26. CD 1625, p. 16.

emerging as the dominant figure in the Commons, had urged the House to investigate the accounts of the subsidies granted in 1624, the inadequacies of royal financial management, impositions, and tonnage and poundage. Coke, too, had indicated that he would not entirely ignore grievances and wished to discuss the book of rates. By the time the Committee of the Whole had moved on to debate supply, Phelips and Coke had obviously joined forces and secured the cooperation of such influential figures as Seymour, Wentworth, and Sandys. On 30 June, after "the business of religion" had been settled, Seymour suddenly brought up the matter of supply. In what was obviously a prearranged maneuver to catch the courtiers by surprise, he moved that the Commons vote the king one subsidy and one fifteenth.[27] Because most of the courtiers were absent, it was left to Rudyard to speak for the court by stating that "the sum propounded" was "too little both in respect of [the king's] wants and of his reputation." It would not cover "his great charges in domestical occasions," he said, "[like] the funeral [of James I], entertainment of ambassadors, [and the] coronation." Nor would it meet the king's needs for the navy, for Mansfeld's army at Breda, and for subsidies to the Low Countries and Denmark.[28] Rudyard was unable, however, to specify the sum that would meet the king's needs, and his failure to do so was quickly exploited by Phelips, who presented himself as a moderate by moving for two subsidies and no fifteenths. Obviously, this sum was also inadequate to meet the king's needs, but Phelips argued that "[d]ivers circumstances in this gift will express the affections of the subjects more than the value." He then began to implement the strategy that he and the other leaders had probably worked out during the preceding week. After noting that the Commons were proceeding unusually quickly with the king's supply and that his proposed subsidy was unusually large, he launched a strong attack on court policy. First, he maintained that the Commons's willingness "to lay aside the right of the subject" and grant the king supply was the greatest possible "argument" for their "love" of the king, in view of the fact that "never [had a] king found a state so out of order." The privileges of the kingdom and of the Commons had been "so broken," he declared and "such burdens [had been] laid upon the people, that no time can come into comparison with this." Phelips then directly rebutted the king's claim that the previous parliament's "engagement" to his father obliged members of the present one to vote him a large supply. "There is no engagement," Phelips asserted. The previous parliament had made certain "promises" and "declarations," but only

27. Ibid., p. 30. On the debate that followed, see Eliot, *Negotium*, 1:75–78; Gardiner, *History*, 5:344–48.
28. *CD 1625*, p. 30.

"in respect of a war" against a particular enemy, and as yet the Commons had been apprised of "no war nor of any enemy." He also maintained that the Commons's readiness to vote any funds to the king was particularly remarkable, because they had received no accounting of royal funds and no satisfactory account could ever be given of the money and men that had already "been expended without any success of honor or profit." "It was not wont to be so," he claimed, "when God and we held together; witness that glorious Q[ueen], who with less supplies defended herself, consumed Spain, assisted the Low Countries, [and] preserved Ireland." Finally, he urged the Commons to be "suitors to the King to take these things into his consideration, and to proceed in his government by a grave and wise counsel."[29]

After Sandys and Wentworth had also supported a grant of two subsidies,[30] Coke delivered a speech that he had probably worked out in advance and in consultation with Phelips. On 22 June Phelips had suggested that royal funds were being mismanaged, and Coke now made a similar point, which he was to develop even further when Parliament met again at Oxford. He reminded the House that while a king might require "relief" from his subjects for "extraordinary" expenses, his regular revenues should support his "[o]rdinary charges." Coke was implying that the Commons should not be asked to pay for the mismanagement of the king's ordinary revenue. To make his point even clearer, he contrasted recent English monarchs with one from the past, just as Phelips had done. He claimed that Edward III had waged war for fourteen years without any help from his subjects and that he had been able to do so "because he had good officers." Clearly, the officers of the present king were not as good as their predecessors, and the commonwealth was being asked to pay for their incompetence. He then observed that "[a]ncient Parliaments did so limit their gifts, that they [would] meet again," and he was obviously suggesting that the Commons should revive this practice so that future parliaments could remedy the commonwealth's grievances. He also noted that in 1589 Sir Walter Mildmay had actually opposed a large parliamentary subsidy, even "though he were a great officer." The contrast between Mildmay and his successors was obvious and did not have to be stated. In conclusion, Coke anticipated the argument that the Commons were voting the king a paltry sum by noting that tonnage and poundage and the subsidies of the clergy yielded substantial sums and were "all by gift of Parliament."[31] At this point in the debate some of the courtiers appeared, but "though divers were provided to have spoken and meant

29. Ibid., pp. 31–32.
30. Ibid., p. 32.
31. Ibid.

to have urged for a larger proportion, yet not knowing how the debate had passed, and seeing no likelihood of prevailing, they held their peace." The Commons then voted to grant the king only two subsidies.[32]

The strategy employed by Phelips, Coke, and Seymour had clearly worked. By alluding to various grievances and noting past military and diplomatic failures, they had provided a justification for granting Charles I a smaller supply than he wanted. They had also laid the groundwork for further attacks on the court while maintaining the pretense of debating nothing but the king's supply. Five days later Coke struck another blow against the court by first noting the inadequacy of some of the king's answers to the Commons's petition of grievances of 1624 and then moving to petition him for better ones.[33] To make matters worse for the king and the duke, the Commons soon followed up Coke's and Phelips's earlier suggestion that they raise questions about the bill for tonnage and poundage. After its second reading on 5 July, Sir Walter Erle first observed that "the consideration upon which this grant was first made" was that the narrow seas be better guarded and then argued that the recent capture of English ships on English shores showed that this was not being done. Moreover, he moved that Parliament make this grant for only one year, and not for life, so as to provide an opportunity for examining the royalist claim that the tonnage and poundage bill authorized the collection of the pretermitted customs.[34] After Phelips had moved that an examination of the pretermitted customs not preclude investigations into the legality of other impositions, Coke objected to the bill because its wording suggested that the Lords were initiating the grant of tonnage and poundage, and he provided a precedent for his objection by noting that when the Lords had moved for a subsidy in 9 Henry IV, the Commons had protested vehemently.[35] An earlier suggestion of Coke's was then revived by Mr. Bateman, who moved that the Commons survey the book of rates.[36] Solicitor Heath was willing to accept a proviso to the bill saving the Commons's rights with respect to the pretermitted customs and other impositions, but he opposed granting tonnage and poundage for only a year, because it had been granted for life to every monarch since Henry VI, and because any limitation on Charles I's right to collect it "might be distasteful to the King, who would be as inclinable to do

---

32. Ibid., p. 33.
33. Ibid., p. 41; *CJ*, 1:802.
34. *CD 1625*, p. 43; *CJ*, 1:803.
35. *CD 1625*, pp. 43–44; *CJ*, 1:803. Coke may have been objecting to words like those found in the Tonnage and Poundage Act of 1604 (1 *Jac.* I, *c.*33): that the Commons made the grant "by the advice and consent of the Lords . . . and by the authority of the same" (*SR*, IV pt. 2, 1063).
36. *CJ*, 1:803.

matters of grace to us as any of his ancestors."[37] According to Eliot, "this argument was much forced for the persuasion of the house . . . ; but it prevailed not against those other considerations that were being raised, upon which it was concluded for a limitation and restraint."[38] The bill passed the Commons in this form and was read once in the Lords, but it was never enacted.[39]

While the Commons were thus frustrating the king's hopes for a large parliamentary grant of supply, they were also about to embarrass the court by investigating Dr. Montague.[40] His case had first arisen in 1624, when two ministers named Yates and Ward had complained to the Commons that Montague's recently published treatise, A New Gag for an Old Goose, questioned several established articles of faith and promoted a rapprochement with papists. The House had referred the complaint to Archbishop Abbot, who began to investigate it but could not report on it before the dissolution of James I's last parliament. In 1625 the Commons quickly reopened the case by voting on 1 July to send a deputation to the archbishop to find out what he had done about the matter.[41] Abbot explained in a letter to the House that after securing James I's permission he had summoned Montague, told him that his book had caused a "disturbance" in the church and in Parliament, and then advised him to review his book and reform it if necessary. Abbot also informed the House that in May of 1625 he had "expostulated" with Montague for not consulting him about the publication of a second work called Appello Caesarem.[42] A committee, which the Commons ordered to examine Montague's two books, debated the case for several days and then interrogated Montague, who stated that the late king had supported his views and had given him permission to publish his second book.[43]

On 7 July the Commons heard the recorder summarize the committee's main conclusions.[44] First, the committee's opinion was that A New Gag contained "tenets . . . contrary to the Articles of Religion established by Act of Parliament," but it recommended that the Commons await "a more seasonable time to desire a conference with the Lords that course may be taken to repair the breaches of the Church and to prevent the like

37. CD 1625, p. 44.
38. Eliot, Negotium, 1:94.
39. See Gardiner, History, 5:364–65; Russell, Crisis of Parliaments, pp. 300–301.
40. On this case, see Tite, Impeachment, pp. 207–11; and Gardiner, History, 5:351–64, 399–403.
41. CD 1625, p. 33.
42. Ibid., pp. 34–35.
43. Ibid., pp. 33, 36, 42, 46–47.
44. CJ, 1:805; CD 1625, pp. 47–51.

boldness of private men hereafter."[45] As for the second book, *Appello Caesarem*, the committee found the manner of its publication to be "dispiteful and contemptuous" to Abbot and "derogatory to the dignity of this House."[46] The committee also found that the book contained "divers factious and seditious passages [that were]: 1. to the dishonor of the King that is dead. 2. Apparently tending to the disturbance of the Church and State. 3. Offensive to the House as being against the jurisdiction and liberty of Parliament."[47] After first showing how James I had been dishonored by a book that he had praised and approved for publication and then indicating how *Appello Caesarem* threatened to disturb both church and state,[48] the recorder explained the committee's opinion that the book offended the House in two ways. First, although Montague had known that Parliament had received a complaint against his first book and had referred it to the archbishop, he had "presumed to print his second book in defense of the first before the same was examined and approved." Second, because Montague's book contained "divers reviling and scornful speeches" against Yates and Ward, whom he knew to have complained to Parliament about his first book, and because Parliament was still investigating their complaint, the publication of *Appello Caesarem* was an offense against the Commons's privileges, because "every man that makes any complaint to the Parliament is to be protected by privilege of Parliament, both in his person and his fame, during the prosecution of his complaint." It was then moved for the committee that the Commons send thanks to Abbot; that they inform the Lords about Montague's books; and that "for his offense to the House he should for the present stand committed to the Serjeant, but his further punishment respited till the complaint with the Lords were adjudged."[49] The first of these motions "endured no debate,"[50] and although the second and third were attacked on the grounds that notice ought not to be taken of offenses against former parliaments, "the vanity of that argument was discovered by the clear light of reason and authority."[51] The second motion was also opposed by those who supported Montague's views and maintained that the charges against him were doctrinal in nature and therefore fell outside the "cognizance" of the House. Coke, however, rebutted these arguments "by difference and distinction of the fact, in that the points insisted on were but civil, for the honor of the K[ing], the privilege of Parliament, the

45. *CD 1625*, p. 47.
46. Ibid., p. 48.
47. Ibid., pp. 48–50.
48. Ibid., p. 51.
49. Ibid.
50. Ibid.
51. Eliot, *Negotium*, 1:93; cf. *CD 1625*, pp. 51–52.

peace and quiet of the state, the virtue and tranquility of the church, which it was said, by *Fleta*[,] were appropriate to the secular courts and magistrates."[52] The third motion was also opposed not only by the chancellor of the duchy but also by Sandys. They asserted that it was no offense for Montague to have justified himself in a cause that had not been judged and that an offense to the complainants Yates and Ward was not an offense to the House.[53] Coke insisted, however, that by "traducing" Yates and Ward for petitioning the Commons, Montague had committed a contempt against the lower house.[54]

The House ultimately approved the committee's three motions and also resolved that Montague had, "super tota materia committed a great contempt against [the] House," that his punishment should be respited until the next meeting of Parliament, and that he should be committed to the serjeant in the meantime. Montague then appeared and knelt at the bar while the Speaker pronounced judgment against him, and Coke was then placed on a small committee "to set down, in writing, the particulars against" him.[55]

Two days later, Charles I finally interfered with the Commons's proceedings against Montague, but ultimately succeeded only in alienating them further. On 9 July Solicitor Heath reported to them on a brief conversation he had had with the king about Montague. The king had told him that he had heard about the Commons's proceedings against Montague and that as Montague was his chaplain in ordinary, he had taken the cause into his own consideration. Heath had replied that Montague had never claimed to be a royal servant and that his position at court "was hardly known but to very few in the House." The king had expressed his conviction that had the Commons known of it, they would have proceeded differently in the case. He had also expressed his wish that the Commons set Montague at liberty and promised to give them satisfaction in the matter. Heath had then explained to Charles that Montague's commitment had been for his contempt to the House, and after he had satisfied the king's wish by giving him the "particulars" of the case, Charles had "smiled without any further reply."[56]

When Parliament met again at Oxford three weeks later, the Commons were prepared to pursue their proceedings against Montague. But before doing so, they took up another issue that raised further doubts about the court's religious policies and sympathies. When they reas-

52. CD 1625, p. 52.
53. CJ, 1:805; CD 1625, p. 52.
54. CD 1625, p. 53; CJ, 1:805.
55. CJ, 1:806.
56. CD 1625, p. 62; CJ, 1:807.

sembled on 1 August, they heard a complaint about a pardon recently granted to "divers recusants"[57] and later learned that it had been issued the day after the king's answer to the Commons's petition for religion.[58] Heath tried to minimize the significance of the pardon's date by noting that it had had its "inception" much earlier, but Coke claimed that it had been issued irregularly and went so far as to move that the House refer the matter to the Lords. Phelips supported this proposal while elaborating on it, and the Commons ordered a committee to consider the pardon that afternoon.[59] The Commons did not pursue this matter much further,[60] but it obviously raised questions about the king's religious views, and such questions in turn reinforced their desire to pursue both Montague's case and their more general inquiry into court policies.

The Commons's resumption of debate of Montague's case at the beginning of the Oxford meeting demonstrated their unwillingness to be put off by the royal message delivered by Heath on 9 July. On 2 August, after the serjeant had reported that Montague was sick and could not attend the House,[61] Coke indicated the importance that he attached to this case by warning the House about "the danger that grows by divisions in matters of religion." After citing Tacitus's statement that "the old Britons" were conquered because of their "want of united counsels" in war, he said that the modern Britons might suffer a similar fate because of their religious divisions. Such divisions would grow, he said, if "every private man" were allowed to put out "books of divinity," and he found fault with "the course now used for every particular man to put out books of all sorts." He said that Montague's book was "as dangerous a book as [he] ever saw," and he wished that no man might "put out any book of divinity, not allowed by the Convocation." Heath then reminded the Commons that Montague was a royal servant and moved that they refer the case to the king, who, he said, would assuredly permit them to proceed in it.[62] Alford replied that royal servants were not exempt from parliamentary inquiry and warned the House against "dismissing causes upon [royal] messages." Wentworth reminded the Commons of their recent proceedings against two more powerful royal servants, Bacon and Middlesex, and moved that they request a conference with the Lords about Montague.[63]

57. *CJ*, 1:805; cf. *CD 1625*, p. 68. On this issue, see Gardiner, *History*, 5:397–99.
58. *CD 1625*, p. 68.
59. *CJ*, 1:809; cf. *CD 1625*, p. 69.
60. See *CJ*, 1:812, 813, 815; *CD 1625*, pp. 90, 92, 118–19.
61. *CJ*, 1:809.
62. Ibid.; *CD 1625*, p. 69.
63. *CJ*, 1:809; *CD 1625*, p. 70.

After a brief speech by Eliot,[64] Coke requested and received permission to speak again. His most obvious reason for doing so was to clarify the jurisdictional issues that Montague's case raised; but by insisting at the end of his speech that Parliament could proceed against even the highest royal servants, he may also have been preparing for the Commons's later attacks on Buckingham. He first noted that at present the Commons were only "meddling" with Montague for his contempt to the House and had the power to do so. Montague had offended against the Commons's privileges by attacking Yates and Ward, and because these privileges were "the heart strings of the commonwealth," it was vital that the Commons punish all offenses against them. He further explained that the Commons would not themselves "meddle" with judging Montague's "tenets," for although they were "the general inquisitors" of the commonwealth, they had no power to judge on points of doctrine. Nevertheless, they could still "inform" the Lords about Montague's books and "transfer" his case to the upper house. The Lords' power to judge such a case, he continued, was clearly "warranted" by the words of the parliamentary writ of summons, which stated that Parliament was called "pro defensione ecclesiae Anglicanae," and was also justified by the fact that bishops sat in the upper house. Then, anticipating the argument that Charles I should have some role in the case, he pointed out that after both houses had "done their duties," the matter would "come to the King at last." Finally, Coke took up the question of whether Parliament could proceed against royal servants. He presumably conceded that the king could always pardon any servant of his whom Parliament had condemned. He nevertheless observed that a previous parliament had beseeched Henry III "not to pardon those who were condemned in Parliament," and he may have suggested that the present parliament follow a similar course, if Montague were to be condemned by the Lords. After noting that John of Gaunt and Lord Latimer had been "questioned" in Parliament "for giving the King ill counsel," he emphasized that "[n]o man, not [even] John of Gaunt, is to be excepted" out of Parliament's jurisdiction. If Coke had ended his speech here, his reference to Gaunt could be interpreted simply as an attempt to show that if Parliament could question such a great man, it could certainly proceed against a minor royal servant like Montague. His concluding words suggest, however, that his allusion to the most powerful courtier of the later fourteenth century had a deeper purpose. Coke ended his speech by stating, "Many men (and I myself) will speak in Parliament that which they dare not speak otherwise." This remark drew attention to the fact that Coke had not simply cited a precedent for

64. *CJ*, 1:809.

Parliament's proceedings against Montague, but that he had been hinting that the Commons might proceed against Buckingham, whose political role could easily be likened to Gaunt's.[65]

In fact, whereas the Commons deferred further proceedings against Montague until the next parliament, their attack on Buckingham would soon begin in their debates on supply. Three days before the adjournment of 11 July, Sir John Coke had unsuccessfully pressed the Commons to express their willingness to relieve the king "in some farther proportion,"[66] and when Parliament met again at Oxford the king and his servants renewed their efforts to get a larger parliamentary supply. On 4 August both houses heard addresses from Charles, Lord Conway, and Sir John Coke about the crown's foreign policies and financial needs. The king again recalled "their joint and mutual ingagements" to undertake a war and stressed "the impossibility he had to go through with so many great affairs as were now in hand without further help." Conway stated that "[t]he honor and safety of [the] nation and religion" depended upon the success of the king's policies, which depended in turn on "the help" of his subjects. He also stated that the fleet could not leave London unless thirty or forty thousand pounds were voted. Sir John Coke indicated that the king's other military ventures would require far more money and that his "coffers" were already empty.[67]

These speeches still left the Commons in doubt as to how much money the king needed and what sort of policy he was pursuing or wished to pursue.[68] When they debated the supply question on the fifth, Seymour, Phelips, and Coke opposed granting any subsidy and directly attacked royal policies and the duke of Buckingham.[69] Seymour claimed that previous parliamentary grants had not helped the queen of Bohemia. He then noted, as Phelips had done on 21 June, that no one had yet named the enemy whom England would fight, and he also observed that previous parliamentary taxes had "consumed" the people. He then anticipated the impending attack on the duke by declaring how "unhappy" kings were who relied on counsellors more skillful at flattery and begging than at giving counsel. He concluded, however, by stating that the Commons would vote the king "a seasonable and bountiful supply" if he would "deal freely" with them and give them "time to do somewhat for the Country."[70]

65. For the speech, see *CD 1625*, p. 71; and *CJ*, 1:809–10.
66. *CD 1625*, p. 59.
67. Ibid., pp. 73–77.
68. Gardiner, *History*, 5:406.
69. On this debate, see Gardiner, *History*, 5:406ff.
70. *CD 1625*, p. 78.

Sir Humphrey May tried to counter these remarks by lauding the king's diplomatic achievements and by noting that if the Commons failed to vote the king money, Parliament would be blamed for any foreign failures that the king might suffer.[71] Phelips responded, however, by attacking the foreign policy of Charles and his father and then went on to consider "the present state of the kingdom." After complaining about the levying of impositions and noting the Commons's forebearance in ignoring this issue in both 1621 and 1624, he then declared, "In governm[en]t there hath wanted good advise. Counsels and powers have been monopolized. There have been more assaults upon the liberties of the people, more pressures within [these last] seven or eight year[s] than in divers ages." Having concluded this veiled attack on Buckingham, who had been in power for some seven or eight years, Phelips reminded his listeners of previous parliaments that had sat at Oxford; and while criticizing their "disordered proceedings" he praised them for investigating "the disorders of the time" and persuading the king to reform his government. He also observed that "[w]hen Kings are persuaded to do what they should not, subjects have been often transported to do what they ought [not]." After urging the Commons to "look into the estate and government [of the realm], and, finding that which is amiss, make this Parliament the reformer of the Commonwealth," he then tried to further this reformation by moving for a select committee "to frame a petition to his Majesty upon such heads as may be for his honor."[72]

Sir Richard Weston tried to answer Phelips by stressing the "necessity" of Parliament's supplying the king[73] and then moved for two subsidies and two fifteenths, because a lesser amount would not "serve for the present occasion."[74] Instead of getting a second to his motion, he heard a mammoth oration by Coke, who answered the courtiers' arguments for supply and developed several points previously made by Seymour and Phelips. This speech began with a historical introduction. Coke recalled that when that "valliant and wise King," Edward III, was "in the height of his glory," the Commons had petitioned him to command the clergy to pray for three things: for his majesty's estate; for the peace and good government of the kingdom; and for the continuance and increase of good will and love between the king and his subjects. Even though this petition was not accompanied by any grant of subsidies, he said, the love between the king and his people continued. Although he then expressed the fear that "some evil star hath ruled that hath brought

71. Ibid., pp. 78–80.
72. Ibid., pp. 80–82.
73. Ibid., pp. 82–84.
74. CJ, 1:810.

us hither," he nevertheless urged the Commons to fear no "evil" and put their trust in God, because they surely had "a gracious and religious King." He then told another story for the House's instruction. Under that "stout and valiant King," Henry IV, the Commons perceived that things were going awry and petitioned the king, who then "rectified" the problems in the state. The lesson to be drawn from these two stories was clear. Things in the English commonwealth were now going "awry," resulting in an unusually great need for the Commons to petition for those things petitioned for in Edward III's reign. The preservation of the king's "state" [estate?], peace and good government, and love between king and subject were vital to the commonwealth and could not be secured simply by voting supply.

Coke then propounded the question of whether the Commons should further supply the king, but he indicated that this question was inextricably bound up with another one: How could the king subsist without charging his people? He was again suggesting that a subsidy would not remedy the grievances of the commonwealth and that discussion of supply had to treat more fundamental issues. Turning to the first question, he immediately stated that the House should vote no further supplies. Then, after warning that it was unlawful for anyone to report members' speeches to the king, he justified his position on supply by stating that "subsidies can do no good for the present" and that the king could have "credit" without the Commons's help. He then answered the two arguments that had been previously advanced for granting supply: that the Commons had to honor their "engagement" to the king by voting him money, and that supply should be given because of "the greatness of the [King's?] necessity." To the first argument, he replied that the Commons had no obligation to supply the king, because he had not named the enemy against whom he would fight. He also maintained that they had power to engage their constituents only by act of Parliament, and that even if they had entered into an engagement with the king in 1624, they had fulfilled it by supplying James I in 1624 and by voting Charles I two subsidies and tonnage and poundage the month before at Westminster. He then rebutted Weston's argument from necessity by criticizing the way in which royal finances were being managed. He first observed that according to Bracton there were three kinds of necessity: feigned necessity, unavoidable necessity, and necessity arising from improvidence. He acquitted the king of feigning necessity. He conceded that inevitable necessity broke all "laws and orders," but did not believe that the king was in "such a pinch" that his necessity was inevitable or invincible. He then asserted that the king's necessity grew up by want of providence and should therefore not be supplied by the House.

Coke then specified the sort of improvidence that he had in mind and, in doing so, moved closer and closer to attacking Buckingham. "Offices," he declared,

ought to be held and used by men of experience and understanding, of good years, discretion and judgement to execute such offices, or else they were void in law; and so be our books and law cases . . . . And a kingdom can never be well governed where unskillful and unfitting men are placed in great offices and hold the great offices of the Kingdom; for if they are unexperienced and unskillful themselves, they cannot execute them nor make choice of fit men under them, by reason of want of experience and judgement. Neither are young and unskillful persons to be trusted with such great offices; besides multiplicity of offices to be held by one man, it is a great prejudice to the merit of honor and his Majesty's well-deserving subjects; and by this means, that which is wont to be thought fit to advance divers as their rewards for their good service, or as a token of his Majesty's favor and grace, and bestowed only upon men of great desert both of King and Kingdom, is now held and ingrossed by one man only; which is neither safe for his Majesty, nor profitable for the Kingdom; and whereas the King might anciently have rewarded servants whom he found most fit for it, and another, and by such means keep his revenue to himself, it is now come to pass that, by ingrossing of offices, his Majesty's Exchequer stands charged with many pensions for the reward, at least alleged; naye, his ancient crown land granted away to gratify men in this kind.

In the preceding passage, Coke had attacked the duke of Buckingham; but he now suggested that the duke's corruption and incompetence were related to the mismanagement of England's military forces. "The office of Lord Admiral," he stated,

is the greatest office of trust about the King for the benefit of the Kingdom, it being an island consisting of trade, and, therefore, requireth a man of great experience and judgement, which he cannot attain unto in a few years, and such a one as shall have spent his time in the understanding of it. And . . . for his part, were he to go to sea, he had rather go with a man that had been once on the seas, and able to guide and manage a ship or fleets, than with him that had been times at the haven.

Then, looking back into earlier English history, he declared that the "wisdom of ancient time was to put great men into places of great title; but men of parts into such places as require experience." He observed that although Beomond had held the office of lord steward to himself and his heirs, no lord admiral had ever held his office in this way. And to show how taxing a position lord admiral was, he noted that under Edward III, the office had been divided in two.

The pretext for this attack on the duke was that it showed that the kingdom's necessity grew from improvidence, and that subjects should therefore not be called upon to remedy it. Coke now alleged another set of reasons for not supplying the king: "the affliction of the time, the cessation of trade, London shut up with the plague, the commons decayed." Once again he employed historical examples to fortify his position. He cited the Peasants' Revolt of 1381 and a rebellion in Henry VII's reign as "woeful examples" of what could happen from "pressing the people above their abilities." And once again, he turned his argument against giving supply into an attack on the duke, this time by telling a story about the reign of Henry VIII. In the fourteenth year of that king's reign, he said, "one eighth of every man's estate in land, money or plate, was granted to the King, but the [earl of Northumberland] was slain [by "the people"] in the North in collecting of it." When the king received complaints about the matter, he disclaimed responsibility for it, "laying it on the Council. They put it off upon the judges, and they upon the Cardinal," "and there it rested." The point of this story was too clear to be missed. A great monopolist of state offices had caused turmoil in the state by foolishly ordering the collection of a heavy tax.

Having shown why the Commons should refuse the king's request for supply, Coke then turned to the second question that he had posed at the beginning of his speech: "how the King might subsist without charging his subjects." By introducing this subject into the supply debate, Coke was accomplishing two things. First, he was again implying that the Commons were now being asked to grant subsidies to cover the king's ordinary expenses. Second, he was noting the need for general financial reforms that Parliament should help to implement. He conceded that it had become increasingly difficult for the king to subsist on his ordinary revenues, because James I's policy of neutrality had caused wars to increase and had neither helped England's friends nor harmed her enemies. He therefore stated that as matters now stood, it would be "a good project for a Parliament, and a worthy action" to insure that the king could "subsist of his own estate," because the king's estate was "now in a consumption, and the ship hath a great leak, which may be stopped yet; but if it be not stopped in time, it will all come to naught."

Before showing how that leak might be stopped, Coke insisted that Parliament should not grant subsidies to make up for what was lost by the leak in the ship of state, because "ordinary" expenses were to be discharged by "ordinary" revenues. He then told the House that he would divide the remainder of his speech into three parts. First, he would show "the causes of the King's wants." Then, he would propound "the remedies both removent and promovent" for those wants. Finally, he would "answer some objections and . . . show the ground of parliamentary proceedings." He began the first part of this disquisition by flatly asserting that the deficiencies of the king's estate arose "not for want of income, but through the ill ordering of it, which groweth either by wasting, or sur charging it," and then listed at least nine causes of the king's wants. First, he mentioned "fraud in officers," and to illustrate the problem he cited the example of the customs officers. Second, he noted that the treaty of the Spanish match had cost the king money, although he failed to say precisely how. Third, he alluded to the "erecting of new offices and new fees," and the establishment of new fees for old offices; and as an example of the former, he cited the Councils of the North and of the Marches, which he claimed "put the King to a great charge." Fourth, he noted "[a]buses in the King's household by increasing of tables and misemploying that which comes from the subject" and stated that this abuse could not be remedied by giving authority to men like Cranfield or Sir Simon Harvey, who had leapt "from the shop to the greencloth." As a fifth cause, he mentioned "[e]xcess of annuities, which upon all occasions former parliaments have used to retrench." "All the Kings since the Conquest," he declared, had not been "so much charged in this kind as the King now is, and by using to be bought and sold they [the annuities] are made perpetual." Sixth, he referred to "[t]he unnecessary charge of portage-money for bringing in revenue; and as a seventh cause of the king's wants, he cited "[o]vermuch bounty in the grant of fee farms and privy seals for money" and observed that the king's servants "should be rewarded with offices and honors; not with the inheritance of the Crown." Eighth, he declared that "[i]n the time of want and dearth, (as it now is) costly apparell diet, and lady vanity is to be abandoned." Finally, he mentioned the monopolization of offices as another cause of the king's financial plight.

These causes of the king's wants, he said, could be eliminated by *medicina removens*; that is, the abuses that he had mentioned could simply be checked. He also stressed the necessity of administering *medicina promovens*, so that the king's revenues could be increased. The three main remedies that he now proposed were the following. First, he called for "the improving of [the king's] waste grounds." He pointed out that the king's thirty-one forests and innumerable parks now stood him "in great charge" but would be a source of profit to him if they were peopled; and he then observed rhapsodically, "[w]hat greater honor can there be to a king, than by building of churches and increasing of his people, without doing wrong to others, to grow rich." Coke also claimed that the king's revenue could be increased through the employment of good officers, particularly in Ireland, which had once yielded the crown £30,000 a year but was now a great charge to the king. Third, he claimed that "[u]pon all the King's leases the rents may be raised at least a third part" while also claiming that "there is no farmer that had any lease made unto him by King James, but will give half a year's rent to have the same confirmed by King Charles." Coke then observed that "if the King would take these courses, he did hope, as old as he was, to live to see King Charles to be styled Charles the Great." He also made the significant claim that "[a]ll objections to these courses will be taken away if these things be done in Parliament" and added that nothing useful could be done out of Parliament, "because no man will speak so freely."[75]

This speech of 5 August was one of the most powerful and sweeping condemnations of court policy made in this parliament, and it illustrates the changes that were taking place in Coke's political outlook. None of his later speeches in 1625 were of comparable importance, but on 10 August he made a brief but even blunter attack on the royal favorite. Buckingham had defended his actions and policies before a meeting of both houses on the eighth,[76] and on the tenth Charles I informed the Commons that if they immediately voted him a supply, he would call them back that winter and not dismiss them until they had discussed proposals for reforming the commonwealth.[77] Although certain members supported the king's proposal,[78] Phelips strongly opposed it,[79] as did many other speakers, including Coke.[80] Coke ultimately argued against voting the king a supply on the grounds that it was against precedent for the Commons to give a second subsidy, particularly in a case in which their grievances had received no redress. But after again referring to "the leak in the King's estate," he devoted most of his "long discourse" to a discussion of "the qualities of a counsellor, and of the danger to great men if they misled the king, or affect to counsel alone against the counsels of other men." Although only fragments of this speech are recorded, they show that Coke may have referred to five great men who had been the objects of parliamentary attack: Hubert de Burgh, Chief Justice Segrave,

---

75. For Coke's speech, see *CJ*, 1:810–11; *CD 1625*, pp. 84–87; *CD 1625*, pp. 130–33; Eliot, *Negotium*, 2:39–44. Coke concluded by citing numerous precedents to show the past acceptance of the principle that only ordinary revenues should be used to meet ordinary expenses; and he then moved for a general committee to set down the heads of the various grievances that he and other speakers had been discussing. Heath tried to answer Coke's arguments and those of Phelips as well. Without directly rebutting Coke's contention that the king's necessities arose through improvidence, he insisted that the whole realm had to help their sovereign, for his necessity was theirs. Then turning to Coke's charge that "places were possessed by men that want experience," the solicitor "professed his obligation to the great man intended [i.e., Buckingham]," but he then said that even if Coke's charges were true, they should be examined "but not so as to retard the public." If Buckingham deserved blame, Heath said, "let the burden light upon himself, not upon the commonwealth" (*CD 1625*, pp. 87–88).

76. *CD 1625*, pp. 93, 94–105; Gardiner, *History*, 5:418–20.

77. *CD 1625*, pp. 106–7; *CJ*, 1:813.

78. *CD 1625*, pp. 107–9; *CJ*, 1:813–14.

79. *CD 1625*, pp. 109–10; *CJ*, 1:814.

80. For Coke's speech, see *CD 1625*, p. 115; and *CJ*, 1:814.

John of Gaunt, Lord Latimer, and the duke of Suffolk. Although he seems not to have named the duke in his speech, he voiced his approval of the policy observed between the Conquest and Edward III's time of not making dukes. He also stated that the Commons had evidence of "evil council" having been given to the king in at least two cases. In his opinion, the calling of the Oxford meeting of Parliament and the failure to provide for the fleet's support were both the result of evil counsel given to Charles I. These remarks signaled Coke's belated decision to use Parliament as a forum for direct attacks on a favored royal advisor and as a center of political opposition to the court.

Seven

Coke in the Parliament of 1628

Coke's concluding speeches in the parliament of 1625 suggest that he would have strongly supported Parliament's judicial proceedings against Buckingham in 1626 if the king had not prevented him from sitting in the Commons by appointing him sheriff of Buckinghamshire.[1] Although the lower house never upheld his claim that he could still sit there,[2] he must have followed its proceedings with interest.[3] This parliament witnessed even more contestation between king and Commons than the previous one and was marked by one of the harshest parliamentary attacks ever made on a favored royal minister.[4] Moreover, the policies of Charles I and Buckingham had become even more vulnerable to criticism than they had been in 1625. The duke's naval expedition to Cadiz had been a total failure. England was now on the brink of war with France, and the king's financial position was more desperate than ever before. Although Charles I had excluded the duke's most outspoken critics from the Commons, the court still came under attack in the lower house where Sir John Eliot assumed the position of leadership previously occupied by older members of parliament like Coke, Phelips, and Sandys.[5] Early in the session Eliot insisted that the Commons inquire into the government's

---

1. On Coke's exclusion from the parliament of 1626, see Hirst, *The Representative of the People?*, p. 77 and n. 28; Russell, *Crisis of Parliaments*, p. 303; Holdsworth, *History*, 5:448–49; Gardiner, *History*, 6:33. See also chap. 1, p. 10 and n. 38.

2. On 10 February, the king informed the Commons that even though Coke had been made sheriff of Buckinghamshire, he had been returned to Parliament as a knight of the shire for Norfolk "contrary to the tenor of the writ [of election]." The king then expressed the hope that the Commons would "do him that right, as to send out a new writ." The matter was then referred to the Committee of Privileges (*CJ*, 1:817). On 27 February, Sir John Finch reported the case from the committee; but the committee had reached no opinion about it and neither did the House (*CJ*, 1:825). The case does not seem to have been resolved prior to the dissolution of Parliament on 15 June (*CJ*, 1:871).

3. In the first week of this Parliament, Sir John Eliot seemed to be continuing with the strategies and plans developed by Coke and others in 1625, when he moved for a special committee to consider "the king's estate," the accounts of the subsidy granted in 1624, and "misgovernment, misemployment of the king's revenues, miscounselling, &c." (*CJ*, 1:817).

4. On the main sources for the history of this parliament, see Johnson, "Parliamentary Diaries." For secondary works dealing with it, see Gardiner, *History*, 6:59–121; J. S. Flemion, "The Dissolution of the Parliament of 1626"; Vernon F. Snow, "The Arundel Case, 1626"; J. N. Ball, "The Impeachment of the Duke of Buckingham in the Parliament of 1626"; Tite, *Impeachment*, pp. 178–211; and the works cited below in fn. 5.

5. On Eliot's role in the parliament of 1626, see Hulme, *Eliot*, pp. 94–151; Harold H.

foreign and military policies, and the information that they unearthed led them to initiate formal judicial proceedings against Buckingham. They did not halt these proceedings even when it became clear that the king had initiated the policies for which they were attacking the duke. Charles I responded to these attacks on his favorite minister by ordering the Commons to abandon all business except their proceedings on the subsidy. Instead of voting the king supply, however, the Commons continued their attack on Buckingham, and in order to avert the duke's conviction Charles I had to dissolve Parliament. The Commons's final action was to draft a lengthy remonstrance, which they never formally adopted but which attacked the duke with unprecedented vehemence. In this text they noted the importance of searching "into the causes of those mischiefs, which this your kingdom suffers, and divers of the grievances that overburden your subjects" and then informed the king of their conclusion "that the most pressive [sic] and comprehensive mischief that we suffered, was fundamentally settled in the vast power and enormous actions of the said duke."[6] In addition to cataloging the duke's misdeeds, the Commons stated that God's religion "was directly undermined by the practice of that party" that he supported. Once the king had removed the duke from power, they said, they would not only grant money to the crown but also apply themselves to "the perfecting of divers other great things, such as no one parliament in one age can parallel, tending to the stability, wealth, strength, and honor of this kingdom; and the support of your friends and allies abroad."[7]

When Parliament again assembled in 1628, the Commons initially chose not to undertake the reforms adumbrated in the Remonstrance of 1626, because their attention was engaged by new issues that had arisen during the intervening two years.[8] First, England's foreign policy was in even more disarray than ever. In a dazzling display of diplomatic ineptitude, Buckingham had somehow brought England into wars with both Spain and France, and he had further revealed his military and naval incompetence in an expedition to the Isle of Rhé that was even more disastrously unsuccessful than his earlier expedition to Cadiz.[9] Second,

Hulme, "The Leadership of Sir John Eliot in the Parliament of 1626"; and Ball, "The Parliamentary Career of Sir John Eliot, 1624–1629."

6. Cobbett, *PH*, cols. 201–2.

7. Ibid., cols. 206–7.

8. The only lengthy, narrative account of the parliament of 1628 is Gardiner's (*History*, 7:230–338). It is based on only a small body of sources and is deficient in many respects, but it has not yet been superceded. On the sources for this parliament, see Johnson, "Parliamentary Diaries"; and *CD 1628*, 1:1–48.

9. For brief notes on English foreign policy during this period, see J. P. Cooper, "The Fall of the Stuart Monarchy," pp. 553–55; and E. A. Beller, "The Thirty Years War," pp. 319, 325.

the raising of troops for ultimate dispatch abroad and the return of troops from the 1627 expedition to the Isle of Rhé created further "grievances of the commonwealth." The soldiers were often billeted on an unwilling populace, and the commissions for martial law that were given jurisdiction over these troops sometimes exceeded their delegated powers by judging civilians. In addition, troops were sometimes used to menace the political opponents of court policy.[10] Third, the king's need to pay for these military operations and his failure to obtain financial relief from the parliament of 1626 gave rise to further grievances. He revived the Tudor practice of levying "forced loans" assessed on property holdings and of forcing "collectors and taxpayers [to] swear to the accuracy of their valuation."[11] In the meantime, two clergymen named Sibthorpe and Manwaring printed sermons, in spite of Abbot's protests, upholding the legality of the forced loan.[12]

These three issues were significant enough; but it was the refusal of numerous landholders and merchants to pay the loan that gave rise to the complex issue that would dominate Parliament's debates in 1628. This issue was commitment by the king without cause shown. Not all the refusers were imprisoned, but a significant number were and many of them were men of substance. Faced with imprisonment, many "recusants of the loan," as they were called, payed their tax; but others, like Eliot, preferred to remain in prison as a symbolic protest against a tax that they thought to be illegal.[13] In 1627 five men tried to test the loan's legality by applying for writs of habeas corpus. The writs were granted and the chief justice of the King's Bench, Lawrence Hyde, consented to a trial. After the judges had stated that according to the returns of the writs, the five men had been committed by the king's special command, the first of the five knights, named Darnel, refused to plead. The other four chose to continue with the case and retained as legal counsel Selden, Noy, Calthorp, and Bramston. These lawyers argued that any person committed by the king or council without cause shown was bailable, while Attorney General Heath maintained that such a person should be kept in prison until the king was ready to bring him to trial.[14]

---

10. See Lindsay Boynton, "Billeting"; Boynton, "Martial Law and the Petition of Right"; and Berkowitz, "Reason of State," p. 189.

11. See Russell, *Crisis of Parliaments*, p. 305; and Perez Zagorin, *The Court and the Country*, pp. 109–10.

12. On the support for the forced loan expressed by Sibthrope and Manwaring, see Berkowitz, "Reason of State," pp. 182–83. On Manwaring's impeachment in 1628, see Tite, *Impeachment*, pp. 211–17; and H. F. Snapp, "The Impeachment of Roger Manwaring."

13. See Russell, *Crisis of Parliaments*, pp. 305–16.

14. For the case, known as *Darnel's Case* or the *Five Knights' Case*, see Howell, *ST*, 3,

    As Selden later explained to the Lords on 7 April 1628, the judges in this sort of case were in a position to make three different awards. First, "when the prisoner comes thus to the bar, if he desire to be bailed, and that the court upon the view of the return think him in law to be bailable, then he is always first taken from the keeper of the prison that brings him and committed to the marshal of the King's Bench, and afterwards bailed; and the entry perpetually is committitur marescallo, et postea traditur in ballium, for the court never bails any man until he first become their own prisoner, and be in custodia marescalli of that court." The second possible award that the judges could make was explained by Selden in this way: "If upon the return of the habeas corpus it appear to the court that the prisoner ought not to be bailed nor discharged from the prison whence he is brought, then he is remanded or sent back again there to continue until, by course of law, he may be delivered; and the entry in such a case is remittitur quousque secundum legem deliberatus fuerit, or remittitur quousque etc." Finally, the judges could proceed in a third way: "If the judges doubt only whether in law they ought to take him from the prison whence he came, or give a day to the sheriff to amend his return, as often they do, then they remand him [the prisoner] only during the time of their debate or until the sheriff hath amended his return; and the entry upon that is remittitur only, or remittitur prisonae predictae, without any more."[15] After having heard the arguments on both sides of the case, Chief Justice Hyde said to the four knights, "We cannot deliver you, but you must be remanded." These words were taken as a final judgment by Selden and other participants in the case, who assumed that a return of "remittitur quousque" would be entered. Most members of Parliament interpreted the judgment in the same way, and it was only later that they discovered their error.[16]

    When Parliament assembled in March, the Commons's agenda for the session almost drafted itself. Prominent members and obscure ones as well all assumed that three pressing issues had to be dealt with: the nature and scope of the subject's remedies for imprisonment without cause shown and for other forms of allegedly illegal detention; the forced loan and other forms of nonparliamentary taxation; and the various grievances related to the king's troops, such as billeting, unlawful commissions for martial law, and the abusive acts of the deputy lieutenants. Leaders of the Commons attached the highest priority to the resolution of these issues, but they also hoped that after resolving them, they could move on to

---

cols. 1–59. For comments on it, see Relf, *Petition of Right*, especially pp. 1–12; Berkowitz, "Reason of State," pp. 183–88; and Berkowitz, *Selden*, chap. 9.

15. CD 1628, 2:343–44; cf. Relf, *Petition of Right*, pp. 3–4.
16. Relf, *Petition of Right*, pp. 1–10. See also pp. 231–32, 235–36.

attack the duke of Buckingham, if necessary, and to implement the various reforms that had been mentioned in recent parliaments.[17] This decision to subordinate substantive institutional reform to the redress of certain specific constitutional grievances is so well known that it is usually taken for granted and thought to require no special explanation. But it probably proceeded from a particular political outlook whose characteristics must be examined and studied against the background of at least the previous decade of parliamentary activity. In order to understand the Commons's decision to focus all their attention on the three issues noted above, one must try to determine how these issues may have been perceived by leading members of the Commons like Coke. For although Coke did not determine the House's course of action in this parliament and obviously did not speak for all of its members, it was he, perhaps more than almost any other member, who publicly expressed the views that were supported, if not shared, by a majority of members. And although his actual beliefs cannot necessarily be reconstructed in full from his parliamentary speeches, it is neverteleess necessary to speculate about how he perceived the grievances that dominated the lower house's attention in the parliament of 1628. In the first place, Coke almost certainly regarded the forced loan, imprisonments of respectable merchants and landholders by the king's command, and the powers exercised by the king's loathsome army as immediate threats to the material interests of those for whom he spoke. Nevertheless, it seems probable that he was much more concerned about the secondary, tertiary, and more remote "effects" of these grievances. He saw commissions for martial law and imprisonment for matters of state as instruments that the court could use to stifle opposition to its policies; and he regarded the forced loan as an institution that could destroy Parliament, because it could procure money for the king whenever he wanted it. The destruction of Parliament, moreover, probably seemed like a particularly ominous threat to him, not only because he clearly enjoyed the power that their membership in it brought him,[18] but also because his recent experience had led him to believe, rightly or wrongly, that only Parliament, together with the king, could effectively remedy the grievances of the commonwealth.

Coke's views about the causes of the three main grievances that were debated in 1628 may also have led him to attach special significance to these grave abuses. He apparently regarded arbitrary arrest, arbitrary

---

17. See pp. 205–12, 214.

18. Conrad Russell argues that Parliament was not really a very powerful institution in this period (see "Parliamentary History in Perspective," pp. 3–18) and thereby suggests that a seat in Parliament conferred no great authority. Nevertheless, Coke at least had good grounds for thinking that he could exercise some power as a member of the Commons.

taxation, and unbounded military power with particular apprehension, because he thought that these grievances reflected a kind of malevolence at court that could obviously express itself in other ways in the future. Coke's anxieties about the court probably assumed particularly grand proportions in 1628 for two reasons. First, because he usually equated his political enemies with his religious opponents and assumed that a few powerful enemies of true religion could easily corrupt God's church, his anxieties were naturally aroused by any evidence that he might find of evil at court. Second, his heightened awareness of the possibility that particular grievances could eventually harm the whole commonwealth may have made him particularly fearful of the potential effects that the court's malevolent actions might have on the realm. His recent experience had made him acutely conscious of the various processes by which a single abuse could conceivably damage the whole commonwealth. His tendency to conceive of policies in legalistic terms also served to make him particularly sensitive to the legal doctrines espoused by the king's more ardent supporters.[19] It made him fear not only the actual consequences of particular royal actions, but also the possible consequences of a royal action that implied the overthrow of a valued legal principle. Moreover, his increasing propensity to conjure up the most fearful hypothetical cases was intensified by his belief that the enemies of God at court might be capable of any evil action imaginable.

The grievances debated in 1628 also seemed worthy of the most extended discussion, because they almost constituted archetypes of the grievances that parliaments had been attacking for decades. The forced loan could thus be construed as the latest and most blatant of a whole series of attacks on the propriety of the subject in his goods. The abuses committed under the martial law commissions were extreme examples of the exercise of arbitrary judicial power. Commitment without cause shown by the king's special command could almost be seen as a metaphor for any legal restraint on the liberty of the subject in his person. Because of the metaphorical power of these three issues, the Commons's debates on them frequently took on universalistic and apocalyptic overtones. The Commons could present themselves as defenders of all human rights against arbitrary power, if not as true believers struggling with the Antichrist. Their assumption of such roles, moreover, was not undercut by the vocal presence of those who might offer different interpretations of human rights or express other social ideals. No one in the Commons argued that freedom and liberty might be differently defined, or questioned

19. For a recent discussion of the royalist legal theories developed to justify the forced loan and imprisonment "for matters of state," see Berkowitz, "Reason of State."

whether the defense of existing property rights and certain liberties of the subject was the noblest action that a member of the commonwealth could take. Within the group of men who spoke out in the parliament of 1628, the only people to question the views of Coke and his colleagues were the proponents of an absolutist state.

When Coke returned to the Commons in 1628 after an absence of almost two-and-a-half years, his political outlook underwent further changes that carried him even further from his views of the early 1620s about the grievances of the commonwealth, their causes, and the appropriate remedies for them. In 1625 his ideas about these matters had become more clearly focused than they had been in 1621 or 1624 as he either abandoned earlier plans to remedy specific abuses through parliamentary action or else subordinated this objective to his new goal of attacking both Buckingham and the financial and foreign policies of the court. In 1625 Coke had also simplified his explanation of the grievances of the commonwealth and his ideas about how they could be remedied. Instead of blaming them on corrupt individuals or certain minor structural deficiencies in the English state, he had identified the duke as their principal cause and stated that they could be remedied only through a cooperative attempt by the king and Parliament to purge the court of novelties introduced or exacerbated by the favorite.

In 1628, Coke's political outlook, like that of other parliamentary leaders, continued to undergo a process of simplification as he became even more prone to blame the commonwealth's grievances on the duke. But he also began to express a novel kind of distrust of the court and crown. Instead of simply attacking Buckingham and proposing administrative reforms, he decided to devote his energies primarily to developing constitutional safeguards against arbitrary arrest and taxation. This decision suggests that his distrust of unchecked royal power arose not simply from his personal suspicions about Buckingham but also from his growing antagonism to the court and to certain royalist legal theories. Another novel feature of his parliamentary behavior in 1628 was his relatively new insistence, first, on securing formal, legal recognition of certain basic legal norms that he thought were being continually and knowingly violated by crown officers, if not by the king himself, and, second, on clarifying and even expanding the so-called liberties of the subject. Prior to 1628 he had only undertaken actions of this sort when dealing with such limited issues as monopoly law and parliamentary privilege. In 1628, however, he spent most of his time over a period of two-and-a-half months working out and defending a position on the king's power to imprison without showing cause—a position, moreover, that differed totally from the one that he had taken on this issue as late as 1621. Although he sometimes attributed the sudden change in his views on this issue to his acquisition of new, technical understanding of the law, perhaps his most convincing explanation of it was that he had become fearful of royal power and distrustful of the court and could now imagine the highest state officers acting in ways that had been inconceivable to him only a few years before.[20]

That a major shift had occurred in Coke's political outlook is also shown by his willingness to abandon, for the time being, his efforts to deal with those economic and legal abuses that had held so much of his attention during the early 1620s. Although it was a group of leaders in the Commons and not Coke alone who shaped the House's agenda in 1628 (and in previous Parliaments), Coke's active collaboration in the process of shaping this agenda and insuring that it was implemented indicates that a significant change had taken place in his political priorities. For though he obviously could not have dictated the House's agenda and though he might even have quietly acquiesced in parliamentary strategies and tactics that he actually opposed, he almost certainly would not have acted as an active, articulate, and dogmatic spokesman for a position with which he was out of sympathy; and if he had been intent on resurrecting the major issues debated in earlier parliaments, he almost certainly would have made some attempt to do so. In 1628, however, he barely mentioned the economic grievances that he had discussed at such length in 1621 and 1624. In those years, he had had much to say about company organization, particularly in the wool and cloth trades, but in Charles I's third parliament he made only brief speeches on the affairs of the Greenland Company[21] and the Turkey Merchants,[22] and only spoke once about the cloth trade in introducing a bill concerning the making of new draperies at Norwich.[23] He had also complained, in the early 1620s, about the ill effects of various impositions on England's trade balance, but by 1628 he limited himself to a few complaints about the impositions on malt[24] and wines.[25] Where he had argued against the legality of numerous monopolies in 1621 and 1624, including several not created by royal grant, and had promoted a bill to ban them, in 1628 he merely attacked five of them: the saltpeter monopoly,[26] the royal exchange patent,[27] Peck's

20. See Hexter, "Power Struggle, Parliament, and Liberty," p. 45.
21. See: (1) CD 1628, 3:610, 612, 619; (2) 2:612, 616, 619; and (3) 4:468.
22. See: (1) CD 1628, 3:450, 453; and (2) 3:595, 601.
23. Ibid., 2:41, 42, 47.
24. See CD 1628, 4:376, 381.
25. See: (1) CD 1628, 2:127, 136, 139; and (2) 2:211, 216.
26. See CD 1628, 3:71, 78, 82, 88. On this monopoly, see CD 1628, 3:71 n. 11.
27. See CD 1628, 4:425–26, 429, 434, 436.

patent for brokers,[28] Gorges' fishing monopoly,[29] and Monson's patent for drafting royal letters for the Council of the North.[30] His only other speeches on economic issues were delivered in minor debates on regulations for weights and measures,[31] and a project for the Medway River.[32]

Coke's interest in legal reform underwent a similar decline in 1628. Aside from economic regulatory measures and bills closely related to the Petition of Right, the legislative proposals to which he spoke dealt with either the interests of private parties, religion and morals, or minor and heterogeneous legal issues. Although he spoke on at least seven private bills, he did not attach high priority to their passage.[33] Although he believed in Parliament's duty to promote true religion through legislation, he was not overly concerned about the fate of the Sunday bill, the bill to promote preaching, the bill for the better maintenance of the ministry, the bill to prevent children from being popishly bred abroad, the bill concerning apparel, or the bill concerning adultery and fornication.[34] Four bills to which he spoke in 1628 concerned legal reform, but neither individually nor collectively were they comparable to the measures that he had promoted during the early 1620s. The new bill for continuance and repeal was conceived on a much smaller scale than the act of 1624 and the bills concerning forfeitures and subscription were of little consequence whatsoever.[35] Although he strongly favored the bill limiting the power of the Council of the Marches, he did not actively promote it in 1628 and failed to secure its enactment.[36] He also failed to use the Committee for Courts of Justice as a forum for attacking specific courts or court officers. The only issue to arise in this committee that concerned him at all was the dispute over Bowdler's case; and because this intricate case of an intestate bastard raised important issues concerning the king's prerogative, Coke's interest in it reflects concerns very similar to those expressed in his major speeches on the liberties of the subject and royal power.[37]

28. Ibid., 3:324, 326, 327. On this patent, see *CD 1628*, 3:324 n. 3.
29. Ibid., 3:512, 514.
30. See: (1) *CD 1628*, 4:22, 23–24, 26, 28; and (2) 4:26, 32.
31. Ibid., 2:550.
32. Ibid., 3:375.
33. These bills concerned: Sutton's Hospital; the earl of Devonshire; two men who wanted to be naturalized; Lord Arundel; Carew Ralegh; and two men called Herbert and Lownes.
34. The Sunday bill, the bill of alehouse keepers, and the bill concerning children being sent overseas to be popishly bred were enacted as 3 *Car.* I, cc. 2, 3, and 4 respectively (see *SR*, 5:25–26).
35. The subscription bill did not become law. The new bill for continuance and repeal was enacted as 3 *Car.* I, c. 5 (*SR*, 5:27–30).
36. For his two speeches on the bill concerning the Council of the Marches, see: (1) *CD 1628*, 3:452; and (2) 3:466, 473, 479.
37. For his speeches on this case, see: (1) *CD 1628*, 4:362, 367, 368; (2) 4:363–64,

Despite the obvious shifts that had taken place in Coke's interests by 1628, however, he had still not completely abandoned his concerns of the early 1620s. In 1621 and 1624 he had frequently expressed worry about uncertainty in law; threats to the subject's quiet enjoyment of his rights; the absence of proper incentives for subjects to improve their economic position; actual invasions of the subject's rights and liberties; and the absence of effective remedies for the various injuries, abuses, and mischiefs that subjects suffered. In 1628 these issues still concerned him, but he now alluded to them not in debates on specific legal and economic abuses, but in more abstract, constitutional discussions about the arbitrary and illegal exercise of royal power. The threats to the subject's liberties that concerned him had obviously changed somewhat during the course of the 1620s; but it is also important to recognize that his ideas about the origins of these threats had changed as well. He still took a highly moralistic view of the grievances of the commonwealth and blamed them on the actions of malevolent individuals. But he now believed that those evil individuals were ensconced in the royal court, where their capacity to do evil was greatly enhanced. This change in his ideas about the origin of evil in the state significantly affected his views about Parliament's constitutional role and its specific function in remedying the grievance in the commonwealth. He came to believe that Parliament had both the power and the duty to deal with matters that he had previously thought were better dealt with by other organs of the central government. He also suggested that one of Parliament's primary responsibilities was to articulate, and give legal force to, certain basic constitutional norms that he had previously regarded as requiring no explicit formulation. Finally, his newly developed view of the grievances of the commonwealth and the appropriate remedies for them led him to oppose the kind of parliamentary compromises, or "accommodations," that he had repeatedly favored during the early 1620s.[38]

These changes in Coke's political outlook become apparent only through an examination of his role in the Commons's proceedings leading to the enrollment of the Petition of Right. These proceedings were so complex as to defy simple narrative treatment, but they can be broken down into five main stages.[39] The first stage consisted mainly of debates

---

367, 368; (3) 4:451–52, 460–61, 463. This complex case is discussed in Maija Jansson Cole and Charles M. Gray, "Bowdler's Case."

38. On Coke's general opposition to "accommodation" in this parliament, see Berkowitz, "Reason of State," especially p. 207.

39. For a recent summary account of the proceedings that culminated in the King's Second Answer to the Petition of Right, see Berkowitz, "Reason of State," pp. 190–210. A

in the Committee of the Whole on imprisonment without cause, as well as on the forced loan, confinement, foreign employment, martial law, and billeting. Discussion of the first two of these topics concluded in early April when the Commons adopted four resolutions concerning commitment without cause, habeas corpus, bail, and nonparliamentary taxation. Shortly thereafter, on 4 April, Charles I stated that he would "give way unto" any reasonable parliamentary proceedings that they might employ to secure their "rights and liberties" with respect to these issues. During the second stage of the proceedings, which ran from 7 April to 17 April, the Commons attempted to obtain the Lords' support for their four resolutions. In the meantime, they worked toward formulating further resolutions on confinement, foreign employment, martial law, and billeting and concluded their proceedings on one of these issues, for the time being, when they presented a petition on billeting to the king on 13 April. During the third stage, running from 18 April to 8 May, the Commons debated and rejected five propositions drafted by the upper house as an alternative to their original four resolutions, whose substance they then incorporated into a bill for the subject's liberties. By continuing to proceed on this bill they indicated their unwillingness to rely upon the king's promise of 26 April to maintain their liberties. And when Charles I revealed on 1 and 2 May that he had abandoned his position of 4 April and would probably veto any bill that did more than confirm medieval statutes concerning the subject's liberties, the Commons decided to proceed by a petition of right that would include their four resolutions and several other clauses on martial law and billeting.

Once the Commons had passed the petition on 8 May and sent it up to the Lords, their proceedings entered a fourth stage, which lasted until 26 May. During this period the Lords made several largely unsuccessful attempts to weaken the petition by what was known as "accommodation," that is, compromise. On 12 May they proposed several "Altera-

---

much fuller account of these proceedings constitutes the tenth chapter of Berkowitz's forthcoming study on Selden (*Selden*, chap. 10). Other accounts of these proceedings are to be found in Relf, *Petition of Right*, especially pp. 1–58; and in the sections of Gardiner's *History* cited above in fn. 8. The editors of *CD 1628* have meticulously reconstructed the Commons's proceedings on the petition in the "Orders of Business" that precede each set of daily entries from the diaries for this parliament. Their work will enable historians to construct a definitive account of these proceedings. Earlier writings dealing with the Petition of Right are far too numerous to note fully here, but among the most important of them are: E. R. Adair, "The Petition of Right"; Harold Hulme, "Opinion in the House of Commons on the Proposed Petition of Right"; Foster, "Petitions and the Petition of Right"; Fleming, "The Struggle for the Petition of Right"; Ball, "The Petition of Right"; Elizabeth Read Foster, "Printing the Petition of Right"; Lois G. Schwoerer, "*No Standing Armies,*" pp. 15–32, and the articles of Boynton cited above in fn. 8. See also the writings noted in fn. 40.

tions" for it and also suggested on the fourteenth that it be revised so as to accord with a recent royal letter to them concerning prerogative arrest. On the seventeenth they further proposed that the petition end with a saving, or "addition," for the king's power to imprison for matters of state. By 23 May, the Commons had rejected these three attempts at accommodation, although they had made a few concessions to the upper house, and on the next day they also voted down the Lords' proposal for a joint protestation that would somehow make the petition more palatable to the king. Finally, on 26 May, after the Lords had made a declaration of their own concerning the royal prerogative, the petition was passed by both houses with only minor amendments.

During the fifth and final stage of the Commons's proceedings, their three main concerns were to decide on a method of presenting it to the king, to secure a satisfactory royal answer to it, and to insure that it would be of record, so that judicial notice would have to be taken of it. They quickly decided to have it presented to the king and answered in full parliament. It was accordingly presented to him on 28 May, and on 2 June Charles I answered it. This first royal answer clearly dissatisfied members of both houses; and after the Commons had begun an attack on Buckingham that would culminate in a remonstrance against him, the king gave way on 7 June and gave a second answer again in the presence of both houses. Having received what they regarded as a satisfactory answer to the Petition of Right, the Commons then undertook to secure its enrollment; and several days prior to Parliament's adjournment on 26 June this task was completed.

Many members of the lower house played important roles in promoting the petition. Phelips, Eliot, Digges, and Wentworth helped to develop the parliamentary strategies and tactics that this enterprise required; and the task of formulating and justifying the legal declarations contained in the petition fell largely to Selden, Coke, and Edward Littleton, with frequent assistance from other lawyers like Glanville, Noy, and Hakewill.[40] Coke cannot be regarded as the petition's principal proponent, because its adoption resulted from collective action, and, in fact, he did not even carry the main burden of drafting its individual clauses or arguing for its acceptance. He was still deeply venerated in both houses of Parliament, but because he now suffered, at the age of seventy-six, from occasional memory lapses and betrayed sporadic tendencies towards irrelevant flights of oratory, the Commons understandably relied less heavily on him for technical legal advice than on younger (and more

40. On Eliots's role in this Parliament, see Hulme. *Eliot*, pp. 184–265 and Ball, "Eliot, 1624–1629." Selden's role is treated in great detail in Berkowitz, *Selden*, chap. 10.

learned) lawyer-antiquarians like John Selden, who enjoyed the additional advantage of having served as Hampden's counsel in the Five Knights' Case. Moreover, Coke's previous statements about prerogative arrest, made as both a judge and a member of the Commons in 1621, may have made him something of an embarrassment to the Commons in 1628, particularly because the king's solicitor and attorney made a point of citing those earlier statements in their arguments against the Commons's (and Coke's) position in 1628.[41]

In spite of these disabilities, however, Coke still played an active role in every stage of the Commons's proceedings on the petition. At the very outset of the parliament, he proposed to remedy some of the grievances connected with imprisonment without cause shown by a bill that he drafted "against long and unjust detaining in prison," and also proposed that the Commons insert into the preamble of the subsidy bill a declaration against the legality of the forced loan. The Commons adopted neither of these proposals, but Coke still participated actively in the committee's debates on grievances and strongly supported the Four Resolutions of 4 April. He also made significant contributions to the second stage of the Commons's proceedings by presenting arguments from "reason" to support their resolutions at a conference with the Lords on 7 April and by debating Attorney General Heath and Serjeant Ashley in later conferences held on 16 and 17 April. During the third stage of the Commons's proceedings, he joined with Selden in opposing the Lords' Five Propositions and helped to devise answers to the king's various messages concerning their proceedings. He was also involved in drafting and promoting their bill for the subject's liberties; and when the king indicated his opposition to any such bill, Coke convinced his fellow members to proceed by petition of right. He continued to oppose any compromise with respect to the subject's liberties in the fourth stage of the Commons's proceedings by attacking the Lords' "alterations" and proposed "addition," by refusing to modify his positions in response to the king's letter of 12 May and by attacking the Lords' plan for a joint protestation. He also took part in the final stage of the Commons's proceedings by advising the House on how to present the petition to the king; and after expressing dissatisfaction with Charles I's first answer to it, he made a calculated and successful effort to extract a better answer from the king by joining in the Commons's direct attacks on Buckingham. Once the king had satisfactorily answered the petition, Coke joined in the Commons's deliberations on how judicial notice might be secured for it.

41. This hypothesis was suggested to me by Professor Berkowitz in a private communication.

Throughout all five stages of the Commons's procedings, Coke almost always worked closely with other members of the House, but his role in these proceedings was still unique. Although younger lawyers like Selden and Littleton were eminently capable of showing that statutes, records, and judicial decisions supported the Commons's positions on prerogative arrest, arbitrary taxation, and martial law, Coke was peculiarly skillful and eloquent when it came to giving "reasons" for the House's positions on these subjects. In performing this important task, he could not only call on his vast knowledge of precedent and earlier English history and his four decades of personal experience in English government; he was also able to exploit his singular capacity for formulating abstruse legal arguments in simple terms, and his highly developed skill at quoting or inventing aphorisms, maxims, figures, etymologies, and parables. By using these skills, he was apparently able to convince his listeners that his views were completely consistent with not only the common law, but also natural reason and traditional wisdom. His ability to use these skills was somewhat undercut, to be sure, by his audience's knowledge that he had completely reversed his position on prerogative arrest during the last seven years. Nevertheless, although his initial attempts to obscure or explain this reversal were fumbling, inept, and unconvincing, he ultimately accounted for it in a way that probably aroused the sympathy and approval of many members of both houses. While flatly admitting that he had changed his mind on prerogative arrest, he said that the crown's recent actions, coupled with his own personal misfortunes, had raised doubts in his mind and conscience about the validity of his earlier position. These doubts had obliged him to reconsider the whole question, he explained, and when he had done so, he discovered that he had been in error. This explanation might not have won him credit in a law court, but in the highly politicized atmosphere of Parliament it may well have convinced members to whom immediate political issues appeared more important than abstract legal argumentation.

Coke was apparently involved in planning for the parliament of 1628, even before it officially opened on 17 March. On the thirteenth he supposedly met with various leaders of the Commons at Sir Robert Cotton's house to devise a common strategy for the upcoming session. Although they all apparently decided not to risk a quick dissolution by immediately attacking Buckingham and to deal initially with more impersonal grievances, they did not reach agreement on the parliamentary tactics to be employed during the first week of parliament.[42] Their failure

---

42. On this meeting, see Forster, *Eliot*, 2:114–15; Gardiner, *History*, 6:230–31;

to do so was revealed on 21 and 22 March, when Coke proposed remedies for arbitrary imprisonment and taxation that he had obviously devised independently and that received no support from other leaders of the House. The first of these remedies was a bill "against long and unjust detaining in prison" that he brought into the House on 21 March and introduced with a brief speech. After observing that "liberty" was the most "precious" thing that a man could have "in this life," he then turned to the subject of restraint of liberty and said that "imprisonment" was "always a heavy punishment" and was even heavier if it were unjust. Because the law gave a remedy "if a horse or a sheep be taken," he declared, "[i]f a man be in prison, God forbid but the law should give remedy." He then told his listeners that, as they knew "right well," the law gave several remedies in such a case and that this fact showed that it was "against the law of the land" for a man to "lie in prison forever and never be called to answer." "For seeing a man has surety for himself," he stated, "God forbid the law should hold him in prison." After noting that "[t]he law is curious in this, touching the liberty or freedom of a subject," he then said that "[t]o give strength to the law," and "[t]o prevent" men from suffering perpetual imprisonment, he had drawn a bill which was then read.[43]

According to its preamble, "the laws of the realm" provided that "no person in prison, or committed to prison, for any offense done, or supposed to be done, ought to be [long] detained, but justice in convenient time is to be executed." The bill then enacted, first, that "no person now in prison, or restrained of liberty, or which shall [be], by any commandment or other warrant, . . . for any contempt done or supposed to be done, shall, after the end of this session, be kept in prison . . . , but in due time may [be] called to trial while the matter is in memory and the witnesses living." It further enacted that if there were "no proceeding for attainder" against a prisoner "within two months" after his imprisonment, he should be bailed, "until [he] be attained or delivered," if he could find "sufficient sureties" or bail, and that "for want of such delivery," he should be "acquitted and pardoned, and clearly discharged and delivered of and from all imprisonment." The bill then enacted that "if any person so committed shall not within three months be attainted, discharged, or come to his trial, he shall be bailed," and that "for want of such bail [he], shall be delivered and pardoned." Finally, it enacted that if any person

---

Hulme, *Eliot*, pp. 184–85; and Berkowitz, *Selden*, chap. 10, pp. 6–7 and n. 17. The memorandum that Forster cited as evidence for the holding of this meeting has never been found by later scholars.

43. *CD 1628*, 2:45, 47, 48–49, 50, 51. See also Hulme, *Eliot*, p. 187; Berkowitz, "Reason of State," p. 191; and Berkowitz, *Selden*, chap. 10, pp. 9–10 and nn. 29–32.

"that shall be so bailed shall not be convicted within three months after bail," he shall "be set at liberty." The bill then concluded with a proviso stating that any person "so imprisoned may take any other course for his delivery."[44]

The Commons's debate on the following day, 22 March, showed that Coke's bill was not supported by those with whom he had met at Cotton's house nine days before and that only a single member of the House was prepared to speak in favor of it.[45] Sir Benjamin Rudyard said that the bill was "very fit" and "necessary for the preservation of the liberty of the subject,"[46] but Phelips indicated his opposition to it when he advised the House "not to make a law to give us new liberties" and instead to pass a declaratory act on imprisonment with penalties for those who violated it.[47] This same debate also revealed that Coke differed with his colleagues about how the House should proceed with grievances. Wentworth wanted a grand committee to determine how the subject might be made secure in the "propriety" of his goods and the liberty of his person, while Eliot and Phelips favored similarly wide-ranging investigations on grievances. While none of these leaders flatly opposed a grant of supply, they clearly indicated that it should be conditional on remedies being found for various grievances of the subject.[48]

Coke, however, did not wish to "fly at all grievances" at once. Instead, he wanted to deal separately with the forced loan by declaring it illegal in the preamble of the subsidy bill, and he had drafted a bill to this purpose. His failure to secure advance support for this proposal became apparent, however, when he asked to have his bill read. No one supported his proposal and his request was denied.[49] Nevertheless, his other remarks about the loan and the subsidy showed his general agreement with other parliamentary leaders. Two of Charles I's supporters in the House had previously urged the Commons to ignore trivial domestic grievances and grant a large subsidy that would enable the king to defend the realm against France and Spain. Coke, however, declared himself "absolutely," "yet cautiously" for supplying the king and said that he did not fear England's "foreign enemies" but only prayed that God would grant them "peace at home." "The state," he said, "was inclining to a consumption" and Parliament's main business should be to "propound remedies" for this "disease." He then indicated that while he would not hunt after

44. For abstracts of the bill, see CD 1628, 2:45, 47, 49–50.
45. On this debate, see CD 1628, 2:55–71. See also Berkowitz, "Reason of State," pp. 191–92; Berkowitz, Selden, chap. 10, pp. 10–14; and Hulme, Eliot, pp. 187–89.
46. CD 1628, 2:58, 60.
47. Ibid., 2:63.
48. Ibid., 2:55–71 passim.
49. Ibid., 2:74.

grievances, he believed that any grant of supply would have to be conditional upon a satisfactory resolution at least of the loans issue. "Let us not flatter ourselves," he said, "[w]ho will give subsidies if the King may impose what he will, and if after a parliament the King may enhance what he pleases? I know the King will not do it. I know he is a religious King free from personal vices, but he deals with other men's hands and sees with other men's eyes. Will any give any subsidy that he may be taxed after parliament what *they* please?" He then attempted to "prove out of records of Parliament in 11 kings' time that it is not lawful [for the king] to compel any man to give [a] loan"; and among the records that he cited was one proving that "[y]ou shall not cut a part of my substance without my will," and another showing that "[l]oans against the will of the subject are against reason and the franchises of the land."[50]

Three days after the rejection of his proposed remedies for arbitrary imprisonment and the forced loan, Coke joined with other leaders of the House in a common effort to frame defensible resolutions concerning the subject's liberty in his person and propriety in his goods. He also concurred in the House's decision to have grievances and supply go "hand in hand."[51] Between 25 March and 3 April he spoke frequently in the Committee of the Whole's debates on the forced loan; confinement; foreign employment; and, above all, commitment without cause shown. In his speech of 22 March, he had presented a general argument against the legality of forced loans, and when the committee took up this subject on 26 March, he argued more pointedly against the legality of the commissions for the loan issued by Charles I in 1626. He maintained that even though these commissions had been deemed "necessary," they had not been issued "according to law." "No commission," he insisted, "can be granted but it must be warranted by the laws." It could not be "new" but had to be "such as are in the register . . . in Chancery." He then argued that because the commissions of 1626 did not meet these requirements, they were "all against law."[52] He therefore supported the committee's resolution, later adopted by the House, "that the ancient and undoubted right of every free man is that he hath a full and absolute property in his goods and estate, and that no tax, tallage, loan, benevolence, or other like charge ought to be commanded or levied by the King, or any of his minister [*sic*], without common assent by act of parliament."[53]

50. For his speech, see *CD 1628*, 2:64–65, 69–70, 74.
51. Ibid., 2:129.
52. Ibid., 2:124, 130, 134–35, 138, 140, 142.
53. Ibid., 2:276. This was the last of the four resolutions adopted by the House on 3 April. For the other three, see p. 236 and n. 77.

During this same two-week period, Coke also delivered several speeches on the subject of "confinement" or house arrest, which was a form of punishment that had been frequently imposed of late and that he himself had suffered in 1622. When the committee first debated confinement on 26 March, Coke argued that although it was "a new-growing evil" and "a new kind of punishment," it was still "against Magna Carta," because it was a "kind of imprisonment." He then contrasted the present age with the glorious reign of Elizabeth by stating that "[t]his Queen of ever blessed memory would not confine any, though a delinquent." In her time, it had been resolved that "no free man should be confined to any place whatsoever," and she had not even confined recusants, until a law had been made allowing her to do so. While he did not directly state that the present monarch was less gracious in this regard, he said that it was "much against the liberty of the subject that a Norfolk man should be confined to Cumberland," and that "to be removed from Buckingham to Norfolk, from Westminster to Westchester, what a misery this is!" He then stated that although confinement was a kind of imprisonment, it still ought to be "taken into consideration by itself," and he therefore moved that the committee resolve "that it is the ancient and undoubted right of the subjects of England not to be confined to a particular place but by act of Parliament."[54] Instead of approving this motion, the committee voted to defer "the resolution of this point . . . until the other points of the liberty of the subject should be ended";[55] but it returned to the subject of confinement on 3 April and ultimately adopted a resolution similar to the one that Coke had proposed a week before: "[T]hat no free man ought to be confined by any command of the King or Privy Council or any other, unless it be by act of parliament, or by other due cause [sic—for course] or warrant of law."[56]

Although Coke had little to say about foreign employment, the committee's debate on this subject on 3 April gave him a chance to offer its members a bit of legal wisdom. He first told them (in Latin) what a miserable servitude it was when the law was vague and unknown and then declared (again in Latin) that whosoever receded from law should suffer vagueness and uncertainty in all things. He also said that the royal prerogative was "like a river, which men cannot live without, but if it swell," he warned, "it will overflow, and perhaps run out of the course." He nevertheless believed that the matter of foreign employment was a

---

54. CD 1628, 2:122–23, 129, 133–34, 137, 140, 141–42.
55. Ibid., 2:142; cf. 123, 134, 137, 140.
56. Ibid., 2:281. For brief speech made by Coke prior to the adoption of this order, see CD 1628, 2:279, 286, 292.

matter "of more weight than difficulty" and moved for "a select committee to draw a bill for this business."[57]

Aside from these few remarks on arbitrary taxation, confinement,
and foreign employment, Coke's major speeches during the first phase of
the Commons's proceedings all dealt with imprisonment without cause.
He first discussed this issue on 25 March, in the committee's first major
debate on what Selden then characterized as "the greatest [question] that
ever was in this place or elsewhere."[58] Early in the debate, Phelips, Eliot,
and Selden all criticized the King's Bench decision in the Five Knights'
Case and suggested that the crown's legal advisors come into the House
to explain it. Solicitor Shelton said that he could not satisfy them in this
regard and wished to consult with the king's attorney before either of
them would "undertake to answer" the Commons's questions about the
case.[59] After observing that Shelton would have "much" to answer, Coke
said that "time" should be given him, because the matter was "very
weighty." Then, after protesting that he was "ever as ready to maintain
the King's prerogative as any man," he indirectly attacked arguments
from "reason of state" used by Heath before the King's Bench by saying
that he would not hear or speak of foreign laws in debates on this issue
and would "only speak of the laws of England." Then, to insure that
Shelton would have something to answer, he said, he would make a few
remarks. Assuming his most oracular pose, he told the committee that he
himself would say nothing, but "the records" themselves would speak
through him. The legal question at issue, he said, was "[w]hether" the
commitment of a man "by the Council [merely] upon signification to
them [that] it is the King's pleasure shall stand or no." His own answer to
this question was a flat no, because, he said, "[n]o free man ought to be
committed but the cause must be showed in particular [or in general?],"
and because "[i]t is against reason to send a man to prison and not show
the cause." Then, after expressing his hope that the king would be "truly
informed of the laws, which I dare say he will defend with his sword as
well as his predecessors," he concluded by saying, "I have now given a
preparative to Mr. Attorney, according to the old course of physic, which
is before you purge a man to give him a preparative." He doubted "not
that we shall deal with him well enough," he said, because he had "much
more in store" in the way of precedents and arguments.[60]

Two days later, however, the solicitor revealed that he and the attorney had had something in store for Coke. On 27 March Shelton stunned

57. Ibid., 2:281, 288, 293.
58. Ibid., 2:99.
59. Ibid., 2:109; cf. 100, 107, 113.
60. Ibid., 2:100–102, 107–8, 109–10, 113–14.

the committee by telling them not only that the judges had not given a final decision in the Five Knights' Case, but also that Coke had upheld the legality of commitments without cause in a King's Bench case decided in 1615.[61] Coke failed to explain this ruling satisfactorily when he spoke again on the twenty-ninth, but he made a start at doing so and also began to develop the arguments from "reason" that he would later use in the great conference of 7 April. He began on the twenty-ninth by declaring that the committee was now debating "[t]he greatest question in the world" and then praised his fellow lawyers like Selden for having spoken to it "pithily and learnedly, and . . . with all reverence due to his Majesty and the Council." While he also commended Shelton "for his temper," he complained that the solicitor "would not answer what was said" against him but merely slighted and scorned it "as nothing to the purpose." Coke then announced that such rhetorical tricks would be useless, for he would now leave the supporters of commitment without cause "as naked as Aesop's crow."

Because his opponents' position had so little authority to support it, he claimed, they were obliged to "beat upon reason," but he would now answer their reasons with even better ones. He proceeded to set forth four arguments against commitment without cause shown. The first two of them were designed to show that Shelton's interpretation of the law would lead to absurd, unreasonable, or unjust results, because of "the universality of the persons" whom the king could allegedly commit without cause, and because of "the indefiniteness of the time" during which such persons might be imprisoned. According to his third argument, Shelton's position implied that a man imprisoned without cause would have no remedy, but this would be absurd, because the law gave remedies for many lesser evils. Finally, Coke argued that the power to commit without showing cause could not be part of the prerogative for the following reason. "Nothing that is against the good of the King and his people" could be part of the prerogative. Statutes that bound the king to imprison only by due process and thus barred him from imprisoning without showing cause were made for the common good of the king and the people. The power to imprison without showing cause was therefore against the good of the king and his people and could therefore be no part of the prerogative. Having delivered these four reasons against prerogative arrest, Coke then responded to the argument that the king would suffer inconvenience if denied this power by pointing out that the king

<hr/>

61. Ibid., 2:152, 155–56, 159–60, 162, 165. See also Berkowitz, *Selden*, chap. 10, pp. 25–26; and Relf, *Petition of Right*, pp. 4–5.

could always give a general cause for imprisoning a subject. "Make the cause for suspicion of treason," he said, "who is there that suspects it not? Does not all Cheapside know it, as one is carried to the Tower?" And if the cause were to be contempt, he asked, "why is there not some certainty set down?"

Finally, Coke had to confront the objection that "[w]hen you were Chief Justice you did otherwise than now you speak" and cited Stanford's *Pleas of the Crown* in support of prerogative arrest. "I confess freely," Coke replied, that "when I read Stanford only[,] perhaps I was of his opinion, but when I saw such a company of authorities against it, God forbid that I should follow my guide [Stanford] when my guide goes wrong." After reviewing those other authorities and showing that "[t]here is no authority or opinion in law but Stanford for this imprisonment," he asked, rhetorically, whether "but one judge only in Queen Mary's time" should "overrule" the Commons's otherwise well-supported position on commitment without cause.[62]

This response at first seemed adequate, but Shelton then told the committee that when Coke was chief justice of the King's Bench

some [men] were committed by word of the King and Lords of the Council, and this came in question in 13 *Jac.* and continued divers terms. There was then recourse to those arguments. I have a report here of that time which doth witness it, part whereof I will read:

It was resolved by Croke, Coke, Doddridge and Houghton that the return was good and that the cause need not be disclosed being *per mandatum concilii* as *arcana regni.*[63]

This quotation obviously flustered Coke, and his efforts to respond to it were utterly unconvincing. He first tried to discredit the report from which the solicitor had read by saying that it was "under age" (being not yet twenty-one years old) and had obviously been written "by some young student that did mistake" the court's true ruling. He then made the peculiar claim that a case from the "ill time" of the powder treason was not a good precedent, because the judges may have had reason to "remand" conspirators like Fawkes back to prison, as their names were disguised in the warrants. Finally, he resorted to his earlier defense of attributing his opinion in the case to his reliance on Stanford, whose views he had since abandoned. Precisely when he had abandoned Stanford's opinion he did not say. This was a fortunate omission, because

62. For Coke's speech, see *CD 1628,* 2:190–92, 195–97, 200–202, 204–6, 207, 208–9.

63. Ibid., 2:192–93.

Heath would later show that Coke had supported prerogative arrest as late as 1621.[64]

By 31 March, when the committee returned to the subject of imprisonment, Coke had had time to collect his thoughts and was ready to explain his earlier rulings more convincingly. He must also have been pleased when Phelips first praised him as a "monarcha juris" and then said that "though it were the pleasure of the state to remove him from the King's Bench here, yet he hopes he shall have a place in the King's Bench in heaven."[65] Undoubtedly buoyed up by this saccharine platitude, Coke tried to engage the committee's sympathies even further by declaring that he "expected blows" for having attacked the forced loan and then said that he would "say somewhat" "[c]oncerning that which I did when I was a judge," even though he insisted that whatever decisions he had rendered "must not rule against acts of Parliament." After suggesting that he was rather hazy about the details of the cases in question, he resolutely stated that the would "never palliate with this House." He then made a further play for the committee's sympathies by stating, "I think there is no judge that hath a good heart toward God and hands toward men but would be glad to have someone to second his opinion." And when he was a judge, he confessed, he had found such support in Stanford. He had once held, with that author, "that a man committed by the King without showing cause could not be bailed" and had argued for this position "at the Council Table." Later, however, "when I perceived some members of this House were taken in the face of this House and sent to prison, and when I was not far from that place myself, I went to my book, and would not be quiet till I had satisfied myself. Stanford was my guide and my guide deceived me; therefore I swerved from it. I have now better guides. Acts of Parliament, and . . . other precedents, these are now my guides." Directed by these new guides, he was now "satisfied that such commitments [without cause shown] are against the liberty of the subject." "And now," he said, "the wit of man cannot deceive me, as I have showed you heretofore in what I have said and cited, and now I desire to be freed by the House" "from the imputation laid upon me."[66] Eliot then expressed what were presumably the committee's public sentiments when he said that he could not "think of flattery to commend" Coke "in his presence," that he need to say nothing in his defense, and that "we may here thank him now, whom posterity will hereafter commend."[67]

64. Ibid., 2:193, 197, 202, 206, 208.
65. Ibid., 2:224.
66. Ibid., 2:213, 218–19, 221, 224.
67. Ibid., 2:213, 221–22.

Having finally succeeded in responding to Shelton's remarks about his earlier opinions, Coke then had his chance to retaliate against the attorney and solicitor by making insinuating comments about the mysterious entry, or entries, for the judges' ruling in the Five Knights' Case. When the committee had discussed this case on the twenty-seventh, the solicitor had suggested that the Commons were "prematurely debating a matter that had not yet been finally resolved."[68] According to Shelton, the judges in the case had, in fact, reached no "determinate resolution" on the question of whether the king could commit subjects who refused to pay the forced loan; their resolution had concerned only the return of the prisoners' writs of habeas corpus, according to which these prisoners had been commited "per mandatum [or preceptum] domini regis." Moreover, Shelton claimed, the court's judgment in the case of "remittitur quouosque, etc." did not "authorize" the imprisonment of the five men; it simply gave the judges further time "to advise" of this broader question, as distinguished from the question of the returns, before trial.[69] On 28 March, however, Selden expressed his doubts about the accuracy of the solicitor's statements about the judges' ruling in the case. He said that when he had searched the roll for the word quouosque on the twenty-seventh, he had found "only a remittitur." He therefore moved for a subcommittee to make a further investigation of the rolls and was supported by both Phelips and Coke.[70] On 31 March Selden reported that this subcommittee had "caused the records of the judgement of the late habeas corpus to be brought before them and there in the record found only a remittitur." Selden went on to say that Shelton had then shown the subcommittee "a copy of the judgement" in the case, which had not been entered in the roll but which Shelton believed to be in the form of the entry in the roll.[71] After this entry had been read to the committee,[72] Phelips declared that it determined the question against the Commons "for ever and ever," because it in effect upheld the king's power to commit the recusants of the loan.[73] Although Shelton now claimed that this judgment was a clerk's rough draft and that no one had ever intended that it be entered in the roll,[74] Coke expressed great skepticism about the solicitor's remarks about the judgment in the case.[75] He thought that this so-called draft was actually "the intended judgement" and that it "would

---

68. Berkowitz, *Selden*, chap. 10, p. 25.
69. *CD 1628*, 2:152, 155–56, 159, 162, 165.
70. Ibid., 2:176, cf. 173–74, 180, 183.
71. Ibid., 2:211–12, 217–18, 219–20, 222; cf. Berkowitz, *Selden*, chap. 10, p. 29.
72. *CD 1628*, 2:212 and n. 3.
73. Ibid., 2:212, 218, 220, 224.
74. Ibid., 2:212, 218, 223.
75. See Berkowitz, *Selden*, chap. 10, p. 30.

have been entered had not the Parliament sat," since Parliament always brought "judges and all other men into good order." It was "ridiculous" to think that "an ordinary clerk" had drawn it, he said, for if he had done so "he would have done it by a precedent, and no precedent warrants it, and therefore some other did it." Coke then stated his opinion that Attorney General Heath had himself drafted it, and that when or if it were entered, it would reflect the judges' final judgment that persons committed without cause shown were not bailable.[76]

On the following day, 1 April, the Commons's Committee of the Whole completed its debates on the liberty of the subject in his person and unanimously adopted three resolutions on this issue:

That no free man ought to be committed, or detained in prison, or otherwise restrained by the command of the King, or the Privy Council, or any other, unless some cause of the commitment, detainer, or restraint be expressed, for which by law, he ought to be committed, detained or restrained.

That the writ of habeas corpus may not be denied but ought to be granted to every man that is committed, or detained in prison, or otherwise restrained, though it be by the command of the King, the Privy Council, or any other, he praying the same.

That if a free man be committed, or detained in prison, or otherwise restrained by the command of the King, the Privy Council, or any other, no cause of such committment, detainer, or restraint being expressed for which by law he ought to be committed, detained, or restrained, and the same be returned upon an habeas corpus granted for the said party, that then he ought to be delivered or bailed.[77]

When the House adopted these three resolutions on 3 April, along with the fourth resolution on nonparliamentary taxation, the first stage of the Commons's proceedings on the Petition of Right was over.[78] The second stage began that same day as they appointed a committee to decide how they should proceed with their Four Resolutions. On the fourth, Coke reported the committee's unanimous recommendation that the House request a conference with the Lords concerning "certain ancient and fundamental liberties" "of the subject," at which four of its members should speak. Selden, Littleton, and Coke, after an introduction by Digges, would "make known to their Lordships the full state of the cause."[79] As soon as the Commons had accepted this recommendation, Secretary Coke informed them that the king

76. For references to reports of this speech, see fn. 66.

77. CD 1628, 2:276. The texts quoted above are taken from entries in the Commons Journals under 3 April, which is the date on which the resolutions were approved by the House. For the approval of these resolutions by the Committee of the Whole on 1 April, see CD 1628, 2:231–41.

78. For the fourth resolution, see p. 229 and n. 53.

79. CD 1628, 2:296, 302, 313.

graciously taketh notice of that which is in agitation amongst us touching the freedom of our persons, and propriety in our goods. And, that this particular care (which he no way disliketh) may not retard our resolution for the general good, he willeth us cheerfully to procede in both, and to express our willingness to supply his great occasions upon assurance that we shall enjoy our rights and liberties with as much freedom and security in his time as in any age heretofore under the best of our kings. And whether you shall think fit to secure yourselves herein by way of bill or otherwise (so as it be provided for with due respect of his honor and the public good, whereof he doubteth not but you will be careful), he promiseth and assureth you that he will give way unto it. And the more confidence you shall show in his grace and goodness the more you shall prevail to attain your own desires.[80]

In response to this encouraging message, the Commons quickly gave the subsidy bill a second reading and after committing it to the Committee of the Whole, they overrode the efforts of some parliamentary leaders to make them proceed more slowly by deciding to grant the king a very large subsidy.[81]

The conference with the Lords was arranged for the afternoon of 7 April, and on the morning before, the Commons clarified the roles to be played by the four speakers appointed on the fourth. After Digges's introduction, they resolved, "Mr. Littleton is to justify the declaration of this House by acts of Parliament, [and] Mr. Selden is to insist on the remedy when the law is violated, and shall cite the precedents and answer the objections against them, and shall also show there was a draft of a judgement intended to be entered [for the Five Knights' Case]." Coke's assignment was slightly more complex. He was "to show that those acts[, precedents] and records are but affirmations of the ancient[, common] law." He was also to present "the reasons" for the Commons's resolutions on imprisonment and "to answer" general objections and the particular argument that "the showing of [the] cause of imprisonment" was "against reason of state." He was then "to leave" the matter "to the Lords" and "to desire their Lordships [that] they would use all expedition to join with us in our resolutions."[82]

That afternoon, after Digges had given his introduction, and Littleton and Selden had discussed, respectively, the statutes and precedents,[83] Coke concluded the conference with a lengthy oration consisting of four main parts. First, he briefly summarized Littleton's and Selden's speeches,

80. Ibid., 2:297; cf. 302, 313.
81. The Committee of the Whole voted to grant the king five subsidies (CD 1628, 2:303). For an outline of the committee's 4 April debate on supply, together with full references to the speeches made in it, see CD 1628, 2:294–95. For Coke's speeches in this debate, see CD 1628, 2:301–2, 308, 312, 316, 319.
82. CD 1628, 2:327. See also CD 1628, 2:324, 330, 331, 332.
83. See Ibid., 2:332–56; Cobbett, PH, 2, cols. 260–66; Howell, ST, 3, cols. 83–126.

and, after expounding a crucial and difficult passage from the statute of Westminster I, he commented briefly on the state of the cause and the nature of the authorities previously cited. In the second and main part of his speech, he presented "the reason of all those laws and precedents" that his two colleagues had previously discussed. Third, after citing four additional authorities for the Commons's resolutions, he answered two objections that might be made against their proceedings. He then concluded his speech by recapitulating all of the Commons's main arguments.

He began by noting that the Lords had just heard Littleton and Selden present seven statutes and thirty-one precedents "with great understanding," and, that having "perused" them himself and understood them all "thoroughly," he knew that "there was not one of them against the [Commons's] resolution[s]." He also said that twelve of Selden's cases were "all in point" and utterly conclusive, and that they constituted "a whole jury of precedents" and admitted "no answer." He then observed that "the very theme and subject" of the conference promised success, "which was 'Corpus cum causa,' the freedom of an Englishman not to be imprisoned without cause shown; which it is my part to show, and the reason and the cause why it should be so." After clearing some "doubts made of the Statute of Westminster [I]" and commenting on the general character of Littleton's and Selden's arguments, he then explained that his own part in the conference was "short, but sweet." It was to show "the reason of all those laws and precedents," he said, and then added that such arguments from "reason" "must needs be welcome to all men; for all men are not capable of the understanding of the law, but every man is capable of reason." Coke then announced that he would offer the Lords six "reasons . . . in affirmance of the ancient laws and precedents made for the liberty of the subject, against imprisonment without cause expressed, and [would] show them in order and method to confirm the same." These six arguments, in outline form, were:

1. A re ipsa
2. A minori ad majus
3. From the remedies provided
4. From the extent and universality
5. From the infiniteness of the time
6. A fine
    (i) Ab honesto
    (ii) Ab utili
    (iii) A tuto
        (a) of loss
        (b) of destroying the endeavors of men

Coke's first argument was drawn from the very nature of imprisonment and fell into three main parts. He first asserted that "no man can be imprisoned upon will and pleasure of any, but he that is a bondman and villein, for that imprisonment and bondage are 'propria quarto modo' to villeins. Now, 'propria quarto modo,' and the species, are convertible; whosoever is a bondman, may be imprisoned upon will and pleasure, and whosoever may be imprisoned upon will and pleasure is a bondman." He then maintained that "if a free man of England might be imprisoned at the will and pleasure of the King or his commandment, then were they in worse case than bondmen or villeins; for the lord of a villein cannot command another to imprison his villein without cause." Finally, he stated, "A free man imprisoned without cause, is so far from being a bondman, that he is not so much as a man, but is indeed a dead man, and so no man: [because] imprisonment is accounted in law a civil death." What Coke had done here was to argue that the existence of a power vested in the king to commit subjects without cause was logically incompatible with the free status of those subjects and even with their very existence. Implicit in this argument was the basic assumption that the king could not legally possess any powers incompatible with the free status of his subjects and that free status logically entailed freedom from arbitrary imprisonment.

In his second argument, "a minori ad majus," Coke started from Bracton's statement that "the smallest corporal punishment is greater than any pecuniary punishment whatsoever," and a resolution of "all the judges of England" that "the King himself cannot impose a fine upon any man, but it must be done judicially by his judges." He could then argue that because the king could not legally impose the lesser punishment of fining on the subject, except by legal process, he could not legally impose the greater punishment of imprisonment on the subject, except by legal process. This argument also depended upon certain unstated assumptions: that the king could not personally impose punishments but had to do so through his judges; that imprisonment without cause was an extralegal, if not illegal, process of a sort that judges could not employ; that it would be absurd for such principles governing imposition of punishment to apply to a small punishment and not to to large ones; and, finally, that the law could not admit of such absurdities. This last assumption also underlay Coke's third argument, which was "taken from the number and diversity of the remedies the laws give against imprisonment." Five such remedies had once existed at common law, he said, and although two of them were now "antiquated," three were still available to the imprisoned subject. Then, proceeding on the assumption that absurdities were not tolerated by the common law, Coke argued that "the law would never have given so many remedies [for imprisonment], if the freemen of England might have been imprisoned at free will and pleasure."

The assumptions underlying Coke's fourth "general reason" were somewhat more complex and included not only the one concerning absurdity but several others as well. This reason was "drawn" "from the extent and universality of the pretended power to imprison." This power, Coke warned, "should extend not only to the commons of this realm, and their posterities, but to the nobles of the land, and their progenies, to the bishops and clergy of the realm, and their successors. . . . Nay, it reacheth to all persons, of what condition, or sex, or age soever; to all judges and officers, whose attendance is necessary . . . without exception." Coke then stated that "an imprisonment of such an extent, without reason, is against reason" and was therefore against law. It is important to note that Coke was using this argument from natural reason not by itself, but to confirm the interpretation of the law that Littleton and Selden had arrived at through the use of the artificial reason of the law. Nevertheless, as Heath was later to note, the argument depended upon several questionable assumptions that Coke failed to state: first, that whatever trust the law accorded to the king did not extend to the power to imprison; and, second, that the law concerning the king's power to imprison had to be construed so as to provide for contingencies that were somewhat more improbable than those generally considered in the discussion of most legal questions.

Coke's fifth general reason resembled his fourth one and was "drawn from the indefiniteness of the time" for which a subject, according to the crown, could be imprisoned without cause. Since "the pretended power" was "limited to no time," Coke argued, "it may be perpetual during life." This argument in itself showed that imprisonment without cause was "against reason," in Coke's opinion. But he still went on to observe that the "pretended power" was unreasonable for another reason. It was clearly "an unreasonable thing," he said, "that a man had a remedy for his horse or cattle, if detained, and none for his body thus indefinitely imprisoned; for a prison without a prefixed time is a kind of hell." Coke had thus presented yet another reductio ad absurdum, which depended for its validity upon the unstated argument that a subject imprisoned without cause could have no remedy.

Coke's last argument, a fine, was by far the most complex and important of his "reasons" for the Commons's resolutions on imprisonment. The first part of it was drawn "ab honesto," or "a damno et dedecore." "It would be no honor to a king," he asserted, "to be a king of bondmen or slaves"; nor would it be honorable for a kingdom to be a kingdom of slaves. Yet, as Coke's first and fourth reasons together showed, such results could legally ensue were the king to have the "pretended power" of imprisoning without showing cause, and, he asserted, these

results would be "both dedecus et damnum, both to the King and kingdom, that in former times hath been so renowned." He then presented as
a reason "ab utili" the argument that he had previously advanced on 29
March to show that the pretended power was against the profit of the
king and people and called it "a binding reason" that "the wit of man
could not answer." Next, he proceeded to the reason "a tuto." The
power to commit without cause, he said, was "dangerous to the King [in]
two respects." First, if any subject were so committed and were to escape,
he said, "albeit the truth be it were for treason or felony, yet the escape is
neither felony nor treason." Second, in what was his last and perhaps his
most telling point of all, he asserted that "such commitments will destroy
the endeavors of all men. Who will endeavor to employ himself in any
profession, either of war, merchandize, or of any liberal knowledge, if he
be but a tenant at will of his liberty? For no tenant at will will support or
improve anything, because he hath no certain estate; Ergo, to make
tenants at will of their liberties destroys all industry and endeavors whatsoever."

Thus, after indicating that he regarded the grievance of imprisonment without cause as the ultimate form of "uncertainty in law," Coke
moved on to the third main part of his speech by adding further au-
horities to Selden's list of precedents. The last of his book-cases came
from the fourth year of Elizabeth's reign, which he called a time "blessed
and renowned for justice and religion," and it held, he told the Lords,
that "the common law hath so admeasured the King's prerogative, as he
cannot prejudice any man in his inheritance." And "the greatest inheritance a man hath," he continued, "is the liberty of his person, for all
others are necessary to it." He then considered an objection "in point of
state" by asking, "May not the Privy Council commit, without cause
showed, in no matter of state where secrecy is required? Would not this
be an hinderance to his Majesty's service [were he denied this power]?"
To these questions, Coke replied, "It can be no prejudice to the King by
reason of matter of state, for the cause must be of higher or lower nature.
If it be for suspicion of treason, misprision of treason, or felony, it may
be by general words couched; if it be for any other thing of smaller
nature, as contempt, and the like, the particular cause must be showed,
and no . . . uncertain cause [is] to be admitted." Then, anticipating another possible objection, this time to "the course held by the . . . Commons," Coke asked, "If the law be so clear as you make it, why needs the
declaration and remonstrance in Parliament?" To this, Coke replied that
"[t]he subject has in this case sued for remedy in King's Bench by habeas
corpus, and found none; therefore it is necessary to be cleared in Parliament."

In conclusion, Coke told the Lords that they had just been "advised by the most faithful of counsellors that can be; dead men, these cannot be daunted by fear, nor misled by affection, reward, or hope of preferment, and therefore your lordships might safely believe them." After reminding them once more of the many statutes and judicial precedents that supported the Commons's position, as well as the "manifest and apparent reasons" that he had just set forth himself, he said:

[T]hey of the House of Commons have, upon great study and serious consideration, made a great manifestation unanimously, nullo contradicente, concerning this great liberty of the subject, and have vindicated and recovered the body of this fundamental liberty, both of their lordships and themselves, from shadows, which sometimes of the day are long, sometimes short, and sometimes long again; and therefore we must not be guided by shadows.

After alluding yet again to the records that the Commons had shown the Lords, he finally ended by telling them that because they were "involved in the same danger" as the Commons, the Commons "had desired a conference to the end their lordships might make the like declaration as they had done; [for] 'commune periculum requirit commune auxilium'; and thereupon take such further course as may secure their lordships and them, and all their posterity, in enjoying of their ancient, undoubted and fundamental liberties."[84]

Five days after the conference of 7 April, the Lords listened to Attorney General Heath present the crown's position on commitment without cause,[85] and on 14 and 15 April they heard the judges speak on the same subject.[86] While the Commons were waiting to respond to these attacks on their resolutions, they continued their debates in the committee on billeting and martial law and responded to the king's complaints about their delays with the subsidy bill. The issue of billeting was quickly settled on 8 and 9 April. When the committee debated it on the eighth, Coke naturally condemned it as a grievance and cited numerous precedents demonstrating its illegality. Before moving that a subcommittee draft a petition to the king about it, Coke attacked the king's soldiers for invading the home of the subject, which he called his "tutissimum refugium." He also hinted that the practice of billeting these "vermin" on the subject would not only "disable and dishearten the country," but might also hinder "these unanimous subsidies," if it were not quickly

84. For Coke's speech, see CD 1628, 2:356–58; Cobbett, PH, 2, cols. 266–72; Howell ST, 3, cols. 126–31; LJ, 3:728.

85. LD 1621–1628, pp. 87–95; Howell, ST, 3, cols. 133–48.

86. LD 1621–1628, pp. 100–102, 104–8; Howell, ST, 3, cols. 161–62; LJ, 3:738–40; Cobbett, PH, 2, cols. 287–92.

abolished.[87] The committee then resolved that billeting was against law,[88] and on the following afternoon the House approved a petition against this grievance and ordered that it be sent to the king.[89]

The committee then moved on to the subject of martial law on the afternoon of 11 April, but Coke obviously thought it time to make some further progress on the king's financial needs so as to convince him that the Commons were actually keeping their promise to proceed "hand in hand" with grievances and supply. On the morning of the eleventh he had suddenly called "to mind the bill of tonnage and poundage" in order to forestall the complaint that "there is nothing done in it because . . . the House has no mind to it." Such a "misconception," he had said, might "beget a monster" by destroying good correspondency between the Commons and king. He had therefore explained that "[t]he retardation" in the House's proceedings on the bill was simply due to the committee's failure to agree upon the rates at which this tax should be collected.[90] That afternoon he again tried to make some show of progress with the king's supply by moving that the committee set a time for the payment of the subsidy. As a preface to this motion, he expressed the hope that the present parliament would be called "benedictum," just as the one of 1624 had been termed "foelix"; and to remind the Commons how much they had to gain from Charles I, he observed that they now had "many petitions with the King and they are petitions of right." He then declared, "I stand now to move you in a business which may much advantage our own proceedings, and may as much ingratiate us with his Majesty; and it is to take into your consideration the time for the payment of the 5 subsidies granted to his Majesty."[91] This sudden motion was opposed, however, by several prominent members,[92] but the committee finally resolved that the subsidies should be paid within a year "in a parliamentary wise." Then, to placate those who wished to proceed more slowly with supply, the committee also resolved not to entertain further debate on supply before having resolved upon "all the heads . . . concerning the liberty of the subject . . . agreed upon."[93] Coke's motion had probably been intended to further the Commons's proceedings against grievances by promoting good correspondency with the king, but lest any

87. For Coke's two speeches in the 8 April debate, see: (1) *CD 1628*, 2:362–63, 367, 368, 370; and (2) 2:369.
88. Ibid., 2:364.
89. Ibid., 2:375–76.
90. Ibid., 2:415. For references to the dates on which this bill was debated, see the "Order of Business" for Wednesday, 2 April in ibid., 2:242.
91. Ibid., 2:413, 417, 421.
92. Sir John Eliot and Sir Walter Erle. See *CD 1628*, 2:416.
93. Ibid., 2:419.

members misinterpret his motives in making it, he professed "before God and this House" that it "came merely from myself, not from the court, nor any desire of any man living to me."[94]

How effective this protestation was is unclear, but a royal message brought to the Commons the next morning showed that Coke had correctly predicted the Commons's need to make some progress on supply. Charles complained about the "unexpected stop" in their work on "his business" and bid them "take heed that [they] force not him to make an unpleasing end of that which was so well begun." After Secretary Coke had urged them "not to undervalue or overstrain this message,"[95] Sir Edward warned them to be careful about what they said about it, but he nevertheless claimed that it might "prove gracious." After meticulously analyzing it, he moved that they "go [on] with grievances" but also "make an humble remonstrance [to the king] that there has not been any stop" in their work on supply, "and . . . make it appear that what is behind is but the work of a few days."[96] The House decided to proceed in this way,[97] and on the fourteenth the Speaker made a circumspect response to the king's message of 12 April[98] while also presenting him with the Commons's recently adopted petition against billeting.[99] Charles I was apparently placated by the Commons's reply to his message and they were then left free to continue the task of supporting their resolutions on imprisonment before the Lords.[100]

On 12 April, in a speech made in the Lords, Heath had responded to the Commons's arguments of 7 April partly by criticizing Littleton's discussion of the statutes and Coke's arguments from reason, but he had spent most of his time attacking Selden's interpretation of the precedents.[101] The Commons received no official report of his speech, but because they heard "whisperings" that it had been well received, Eliot wished to arrange a further conference at which they could reargue their own case.[102] Selden, Littleton, and Coke, however, were all confident that their own arguments would prevail, and the motion was defeated.[103] On 14 April, Justice Whitelocke told the Lords that the judges of the King's Bench had given "no judgement at all" in the Five Knights' Case and had "only remitted the party [sic] to prison . . . until the court might

94. Ibid.
95. Ibid., 2:430.
96. Ibid., 2:431–32, 435, 438, 439, 440.
97. Ibid., 2:429, 433, 436–37.
98. Cobbett, PH, 2, cols. 281–83; CD 1628 2:449–51, 455–56, 456–57.
99. Cobbett, PH, 2, cols. 283–86; CD 1628, 2:451–52.
100. CD 1628, 2:452–53, 455–56.
101. For a reference to reports of this speech, see fn. 85.
102. CD 1628, 2:437, 433.
103. Ibid.

be better advised."[104] After the other judges had informed the Lords on the fifteenth that Magna Charta and the other six statutes still stood "in force,"[105] the upper house requested another conference at which the Commons might directly respond to the crown's position on imprisonment without cause.[106]

This conference opened on the sixteenth with the lord keeper's report of the judges' opinions.[107] Heath then rose, and after stating that Magna Charta and the six statutes were in force and bound the king, he said that the legal question at issue turned on "the interpretation and application" of the twenty-ninth chapter of Magna Charta. This chapter, he explained, used "general" words. "[I]t did not restrain the King from imprisoning a subject," he said, except by saying that he could only do so "per legale judicium parium suorum, vel per legem terrae"; "and how far lex terrae extends, is, and ever was the question." After briefly discussing some precedents bearing on this question, he paused to let the Commons's representatives answer.[108] Coke responded by scoring some cheap but possibly effective points off the attorney. It was "a good symptom" for the Commons, he said, that Heath had been late in coming before the upper house, because his delay showed that he was "loath" to answer the Commons.[109] He also declared magnanimously that his house would "take no hold of threads" by protesting that Heath's speech was a breach on order and would "allow him a voice here, where he ought not to speak." He further noted that while he and his colleagues had come "with ears, not with tongues" and could speak to no "new matter," they were "glad of" the judges' resolutions touching Magna Charta and the other six statutes and were "confident [that] never a judge in England" would oppose the Commons's resolutions on imprisonment. After these brief rhetorical exercises, he complained that the attorney had used mere rhetorical artifice to mask his inability to respond to the statutes previously cited by the Commons, and he therefore asked that these acts be read. Coventry replied that they were well known and had been already read to the Lords; but Coke insisted that it was wrong to slight them and "so pressed on that [they] might be read and opened."[110] After the statutes in question had been discussed (and read) by Littleton and again by

104. Howell, *ST*, 3, cols. 161–62.
105. Ibid., cols. 162–64; *LD 1621–1628*, pp. 104–8.
106. *LJ*, 3:741.
107. *CD 1628*, 2:499–500.
108. Ibid., 2:490–92.
109. Ibid., 3:5.
110. Cobbett, *PH*, 2, cols. 294–95; *CD 1628*, 2:500.

Heath,[111] the conference of the sixteenth ended with a long exchange between Selden and the attorney about the precedents.[112]

On the morning of the seventeenth, before the continuation of the conference, Coke faced another embarrassing reminder of his earlier views on imprisonment without cause. When Heath had addressed the Lords on 12 April, he had specifically noted Coke's previous defenses of the crown's present position on imprisonment not only as a judge, but even as a member of the Commons in 1621.[113] The Commons's opponents in the upper house wished to exploit this revelation and waited for the most opportune time to use it. That moment came on the morning of the seventeenth, just before the continuation of the conference at which Coke and Heath were sure to confront one another. In a message sent to the Commons that morning, the Lords asked that the clerk of the lower house bring "a journal book of 18 Jac." "to be used at this conference, as occasion shall serve." To explain this unusual request, the message further stated that when the Commons had been considering a bill explaining Magna Charta in 1621, "[s]omething" relevant to the issues to be debated that afternoon had been "then delivered by a learned member" of their house.[114] The "learned member" in question was, of course, Coke, who had criticized the Magna Charta bill of 1621 because it did not allow for commitment without cause.[115] After a Mr. Spencer had opposed granting this request,[116] Coke warned that it would be "dangerous" for the House "to allow this." Since "the clerk with his pen may mistake in setting down words . . . or leave out somewhat," it was "very unfit" that his book "should stand for evidence." It would also be "very disadvantageous," he claimed, "that any notes of debate of matters here should be binding to this House." After making these feeble attempts to divert attention from the real issue, he finally admitted that in the debate on the Magna Charta bill in 1621, he "himself or some other" might have advised the House "not to proceed with" it. He insisted, however, that "a man may speak that which he will upon good reason alter," and that "[w]e speak our consciences as it is for the present."[117] After Glanville had spoken in Coke's support, the Commons put off answering the Lords' message,[118] but, according to Nicholas, they resolved "by a tacit

111. Cobbett, *PH*, 2:295; *CD 1628*, 2:500–501.

112. Cobbett, *PH*, 2, cols. 294–304; *CD 1628*, 2:492–99, 501–503.

113. See *LD 1621–1628*, pp. 87–95; Howell, *ST*, 3, cols. 133–48. See also Berkowitz, *Selden*, chap. 10, p. 48.

114. *CD 1628*, 2:512, 513, 516, 519, 520.

115. See ibid., 2:509 nn. 6–7, citing *CJ*, 1:609–10 and *CD 1621*, 3:172.

116. *CD 1628*, 2:516, 519.

117. Ibid., 2:512, 516, 519, 520–21.

118. Ibid., 2:512, 516.

consent" not to send up the clerk's book or a copy of the bill to the upper house.[119]

Although Coke was thus spared embarrassment at the conference that afternoon, his recent views on imprisonment were still attacked vigorously by Heath, with the aid of Ashley. After Heath had concluded his discussion of the precedents and had noted the three occasions on which Coke had previously supported the crown's present position, the attorney summarized Coke's "reasons" against imprisonment without cause and asked the Lords to weigh them against other reasons that he would now present. His own reasons would show, he said "why personal liberty, in such sort as is desired by the resolutions of the Commons, cannot possibly be allowed of in that latitude therein set down." Heath's strategy, like Coke's, was to argue *a posse ad esse*[120] or by reductio ad absurdum and show that if the Commons's position were pursued to its logical conclusions, it would lead to absurd, unreasonable, and/or dangerous results. He therefore maintained that the following conclusion "*necessarily*" followed from the Commons's position on the king's power to imprison: "That in no case whatsoever, may any man be committed or restrained for anything, never so much concerning the state; but that forthwith the keeper of the prison must be acquainted with the cause so fully, as that he may truly and without variation, inform the court thereof, when it shall be required; and that cause must hold the strictest examination and trial of law." If this conclusion were to be admitted, Heath argued, then the Lords would see "what infinite peril it might bring, not only to the persons of private men (which are not to be neglected), but to the whole state; the very fabric and frame of government under which we live." Heath then attacked the heart of Coke's main arguments from reason by showing that their validity depended upon the assumption that the king might not only do wrong, but do infinite wrong. According to Heath, Coke had in effect argued "that if the King, or council may commit without showing cause, it would be infinitely full of mischief; for as the King may commit one, so he may commit any, or many; as he may commit for a just cause, so he may commit without a cause; as he may commit for a time, so he may commit to a perpetual imprisonment." To these arguments, based upon hypothetical cases, Heath answered "that it cannot be imagined of the King, that he will at any time, or in any case, do injustice to his subjects. It is a maxim of our law that the King can do no wrong."

After presenting two examples to show that "in some cases of importance . . . one may and must be imprisoned, and yet the cause of it not

119. Ibid., 2:521.
120. For an example of the use of this apt phrase, see *LD 1621–1628*, p. 131.

be presently rendered," he reminded the Lords that the Commons's resolutions would not allow for them, because their "general tenet admits of
no exception," and then he added that "[i]nfinite other examples might
be given." He then attempted to show that there were other cases in
which the state was not obliged to act in accordance with strict law. He
said that "the state" frequently "interposed" itself to "order" matters
like trade or the organization of companies and private corporations on
which "the common law," he said, "can give no rule." He also claimed
that conciliar orders concerning dearth and famine were "entirely fit and
yet governed by no law." After noting that the imprisonment of papist
plotters under Elizabeth had been done "by the acts of the state only," he
asked if it would have been fit "to have delivered, or bailed these [men]
upon a habeas corpus." "[T]he true answer for these, and the like cases,"
he said, was "that it was not contrary to the laws: for as God had trusted
the King with governing the whole; so had he therefore trusted him with
ordering of the parts: and there are many cases, of infinite importance to
the subject, and of undoubted trust, reposed in the King; wherein, not-
withstanding, it was never questioned by a subject of the King, why he
did thus or thus." One could argue, he conceded, that the king might
abuse powers with which he was trusted, like the powers to coin money,
make war, or "conclude peace or leagues," and that he might thereby
injure his people. Such arguments had indeed been used by Coke; but
Heath's answer to them was simply that the king would not do such
things "to the hurt of his people." He was not saying, he insisted "that a
King hath liberty to do what he lists." "No, God forbid: he is set over his
people for their good; and if he do transgress and do unjustly, there is a
greater than he, the King of Kings; respondet superiori. And as Bracton
. . . said, 'Satis ei sufficit ad poenam, quod dominum expectat ultorem.'"
In conclusion, Heath stated that while the Commons had behaved "like
true Englishmen" in maintaining their liberties by all good and fit means
at their disposal, they had also behaved like true Englishmen by advancing
a proposition about those liberties that was "so unlimited, and so large,
that it cannot possibly stand" and that was "incompatible with that form
of government, which is monarchy, under which we happily live."[121]

The attorney was then followed by Serjeant Ashley, who advanced
an even blunter argument from "reason of state" than Heath. His first
main point was that the phrase "lex terrae" in the twenty-ninth chapter
of Magna Charta did not stand only for "that part of the municipal law
of this realm, which we call common law; for there are divers other
jurisdictions exercised in this kingdom, which are to be reckoned in the

121. Cobbett, *PH*, 2, cols. 311–15. For other versions of Heath's speech, see *CD
1628*, 2:524–25, 527–28, 529–30, 534–35.

law of the land." Among them, he said, were not only ecclesiastical law, admiralty law, martial law, the law of nations, the law merchant, and natural law, but also "the law of the state." "[W]hen the necessity of the state requires it," he contended, the king and council "do, and may proceed according to natural equity . . . : because in cases, where the law of the land [sic] provides not, there the proceeding may be by the law of natural equity: and infinite are the occurrents of state unto which the common law extends not; and if those proceedings of state should not also be accounted the law of the land, then . . . the King should not be able to do justice in all cases within his own dominions." After noting that every state had secrets "not communicable to every vulgar understanding," Ashley concluded, "that for offenses against the state, in cases of state government, the King or his council has lawful power to punish by imprisonment, without showing particular cause; where it may tend to the disclosing of the secrets of state government."[122]

After Littleton had responded to Heath and Ashley,[123] Coke did likewise. He first said that "it was a wonder for him to hear [that] the liberty of the subject should be thought incompatible with the regality of the King," and, after responding to an argument of Heath's about commitments by the king's special command, he then considered those cases in which it was fitting, according to Heath, for subjects to be committed without cause shown. Whereas the attorney had said that such causes were "infinite" in number, Coke thought that they were exceedingly rare and therefore called it "[a] strange proviso, that a thing happening once in 100 years should overthrow and mar so many statutes in continued use." Coke then took up an argument that he said "came close to him." According to Coke, the attorney had asserted that because the king was trusted in "greater things" than imprisonment, such as wars, money, pardons, naturalization, and the like, he must have a trust in the lesser matter of imprisonment. Coke denied the validity of this argument, because, he said, "the liberty of the person is more than all these; it is maximum omnium humanorum bonorum, the very sovereign of human blessings." Coke also rebutted Heath's argument on this point by showing that the king's prerogative to coin money and issue pardons could be, and had been, limited by statute.

After craving the Lords' pardon for being "a little more earnest than seems fitting" and explaining that the issue in question concerned him "near," Coke concluded with a string of miscellaneous but interesting points. He hinted that Heath was not speaking his own mind and conscience by saying that "if they two were alone," they would agree "in all

122. Cobbett, *PH*, 2, cols. 315–19; *CD 1628*, 2:528–29, 530–31, 535–36.
123. Cobbett, *PH*, 2, cols. 319; *CD 1628*, 2:528–29, 530–31, 535–36.

things." After observing that Littleton's *Tenures* never mentioned a freeman's being a tenant at will for his liberty, he amplified on his earlier argument from universality by conjuring up a striking image. If "this new doctrine" were accepted, he warned, "the judges themselves, when they should sit on the Bench, must be walking towards the Tower." He then concluded, by protesting that "he intended no prejudice at all to the King for matters of state; for the honorable must be maintained in honor or this commonwealth could not subsist; but the question was, Whether they ought not to express the cause?"[124]

After Noy, Glanville, and Selden had responded to Heath's arguments,[125] Coke reminded the Lords, first, that they were considering "the greatest cause in hand, that ever came into the Hall of Westminster, or, indeed, into any Parliament"; and second, that because their "noble ancestors," whose "places" they held, "were parties to Magna Charta," they themselves were "commanded . . . to thunder out . . . anathemas against all infringers" of the charter. He then called on them again.

Put together, my noble lords, in one balance 7 acts of parliament, records, precedents, reasons, all that we have spoken, and that of 18 Edward III, whereto I found no answer; and, in God's name, put into the other balance what Mr. Attorney hath said, his wit, learning, and great endowments of nature; and, if he be weightier, let him have it; if not, then conclude with us. You are involved in the same danger with us; and therefore we desire you, in the name of the commons of England, represented in us, that we might have cause to give God and the King thanks for your justice, in complying with us.[126]

After Heath had summed up his arguments,[127] Coke had brief but acrimonious exchanges not only with the attorney, but also with the duke. When he attempted to respond to Heath's conclusion, the attorney challenged his right to do so on the grounds that the "privilege of speaking the last word belonged to the king. Coke replied that that privilege held "good in a court of Westminster Hall, but that there was no such privilege . . . in the court of Parliament." A few moments later, Heath moved "for an accommodation" on the issue that had been so long debated and called on the Lords "to find out a middle way" between the two extreme positions that they had heard argued for. Coke seized on this remark in the hope that the Lords would construe it as an admission of weakness by the king's attorney. Unlike Heath, he called for "[n]o accommodation" and "no dividing of the child"; and to distinguish his position even more clearly from Heath's, he observed that "[t]he true mother will not divide

124. Cobbett, *PH*, 2, cols. 323–25; *CD 1628*, 2:537.
125. Cobbett, *PH*, 2, cols. 325–29; *CD 1628*, 2:525–27, 529, 538.
126. Cobbett, *PH*, 2, cols. 327–28; cf. *CD 1628*, 2:534, 538.
127. Cobbett, *PH*, 2, cols. 327–28; cf. *CD 1628*, 2:534, 538.

the child." The point of this last remark was not lost on Buckingham, who rebuked Coke sharply for using words that implicitly likened Coke's master, the king, "to a whore." On this embittered note, the two-day conference ended.[128]

The conclusion of the conference of 16 and 17 April marked the end of the second main stage of the Commons's proceedings on the Petition of Right. The third stage got underway on the eighteenth as the Committee of the Whole resumed its debates on martial law, which were to go on intermittently until 8 May.[129] Although Selden dominated discussion of this issue, Coke also spoke to it several times and expressed complete agreement with the views of his younger colleague. On 11 April he had stated that the question at issue was "when martial law be used, and when not," and that since it was obvious that "when the Chancery is open, this [martial] law sleeps," "the time is only in question."[130] Four days later, on 15 April, he had again helped to clarify matters by stressing that "[t]he question is not of the King's power to grant commissions of oyer et terminer," for it was indisputable that he had such power. The real questions concerned three "disputable" issues: the "form" of such commissions, the "manner" in which they were "to be executed," and the time during which they were to be executed. Thus, the Commons were not questioning "the King's power" in this regard but simply trying to "regulate it."[131]

On 18 April Coke developed these views at greater length in response to a speech by the civil lawyer, Sir Henry Marten, who had defended the legality of the recent commissions of martial law.[132] According to Coke, Marten had maintained that "martial law is to be used in convenient time." But "Who shall judge of that?" Coke asked. After praying that God would keep him and his fellow subjects "to the discretion of our common law" and never let them live "under the law of conveniency or discretion," he said that Marten's statement of the law would "bring all to an absolute power." Marten had also stated, according to Coke, that "the laws common and martial may stand together." But, Coke asked, "[s]hall the soldier and the justice sit on one bench?" "One place," he insisted, "cannot serve for martial and common law together: the trum-

128. For this exchange, see *CD 1628*, 2:514, 529, 538.
129. For outlines of the Commons's debates on martial law between 18 April and 8 May, together with references to speeches made in these debates, see *CD 1628*, 2:539, 562–63; 3:21, 68–69, 299, 322.
130. Ibid., 2:412, 416, 420, 423.
131. Ibid., 2:466, 469, 473, 475, 476.
132. For Marten's speech, see *CD 1628*, 2:542–43, 548–49, 552–53, 556–57, 558–59, 560–61.

pets will deafe[n] the crier." "The question" of when martial law should be in force, he said, "must be determined by the law of England [that is, the common law], and the martial law is bounded by it. If you bring me other laws it is not to the purpose. The common "law is the great and principal law."

After this introduction, Coke divided his argument on martial law into five parts. The first question, he said, was "[w]hen the time of peace is and the reason of it." The answer was "when the courts of Westminster be open," because "then you [may] have a commission of oyer and terminer; [and] you may [therefore] proceed according to the course of the common law." And "when the [common] law can determine [a cause], he added, "the Constable and Marshall are not to do anything." The second question was "[h]ow it shall be tried" "[w]hether the land were in war"; and the answer was that it was to be "tried by the King's record and not by jury." The third question was "[w]hether martial law may be [executed] in time of peace"; and the answer was clearly no. The fourth question was "[w]hether the King may enlarge the power of the deputy lieutenants by commission." The answer to it was also negative, because "[t]he King cannot add anything to the jurisdiction of any court," and because "no commission can [be] give[n] power to exercise a power that is not in the original power of such a court." The fifth and final question was whether the present commissions for martial law were legally valid. Coke argued that they were not, not only because they had been issued in peace time and had expanded the scope of the deputy lieutenants' power, but because they could be, and had been, used "against others than soldiers." Marten had defended the commissions on the grounds that they were used "only for actual soldiers," but Coke countered this argument by saying that "the commission goes to all soldiers and all that shall join with them. And who shall judge of this, who are soldiers and who they are that join with them? There are now 60 articles to which that commission hath reference: 40 of them are written in blood. How shall the soldier know how to obey them? They are not under the great seal."[133]

Coke delivered several more speeches on martial law during the next few weeks,[134] but the main subject that engaged his attention in this period was the Lords' reaction to the Commons's resolutions and arguments on imprisonment. After debating these resolutions on 21 and 22 April, the Lords told the Commons at a conference on the twenty-third that they agreed "in general . . . to the just liberties of the subject," as the Commons had stated them, and (or but) that they also desired that "the just prerogative of the King" might be preserved "for the benefit of the

133. Ibid., 2:545–46, 549–50, 554–55, 558, 559–60, 561.
134. See: (1) CD 1628, 2:567; (2) 2:569, 573, 575; (3) 3:307, 315.

whole kingdom." They then expressed their hope that they could maintain both of these legal interests and thus bring "this great business to a happy issue."[135] These statements naturally led the Commons to believe, rightly, that the upper house would support some kind of compromise. At another conference held on 25 April, the Lords presented them with a set of compromise proposals, known as the Five Propositions, which were meant to replace the Commons's Four Resolutions.[136]

The Commons' first debate on these proposals, held on the twenty-sixth, showed that certain members found them acceptable, but Coke and Selden were unwilling to accept any accommodation.[137] Coke bluntly stated that he "would receive none" of the Lords' Five Propositions in place of the House's previous resolutions. Their own resolutions, he said, "are plain and open and clear" and "do conclude something; these do not." He first laid it "as a foundation" that the Commons should not "recede" from their own resolutions, which he believed to be "good and wholesome" "according to his knowledge" and "conscience." He then turned to the Lords' propositions and attacked them one by one. The first proposition was, "That his majesty would be pleased graciously to declare, that the good old law called Magna Carta, and the six statutes, conceived to be declarations or explanations of that law, do still stand in force to all intents and purposes." Coke said that these words, while "good," were too general to "conclude" anything about the cases in which Magna Charta and the other statutes were in force and did not say whether these acts barred commitment without cause shown. He also objected to the word "conceived," because he wanted it "positively" stated that the six statutes explained the charter, and he then complained that the Lords had omitted a seventh statute cited by the Commons. Finally, he objected to the Lords' use of the word "graciously," because "[w]hen a thing is done graciously, it is not of right." "I pray you mistake me not," he said, "I love the word 'grace' very well." "[B]ut will you have Magna Carta as a grace?" "[I]t is an act of right, not of grace, that we stand upon."

Coke then turned to the second proposition, which stated, "That his majesty would be pleased graciously to declare that, according to Magna Charta, and the statutes aforenamed, as also according to the most ancient customs and laws of this land, every free subject of this realm hath a fun-

135. For Coke's report of this conference, see *CD 1628*, 3:45, 46–47, 48–49, 51–52, 54, 55 (*bis*).

136. Cobbett, *PH*, 2, col. 329. For the text of the Lords' Propositions (which are quoted on pp. 253–55, below), see *LJ*, 3:769–70; *CD 1628*, 3:74–75, 81, 87. For a note on the text see *CD 1628*, 3:74 n. 34.

137. For an outline of the debate, together with references to the speeches made in it, see *CD 1628*, 3:92–93.

damental propriety in his goods, and a fundamental liberty of his person." This proposition "determines nothing," he said, because it omitted the Commons's direct exposition of Magna Charta stating that "lex terrae is the common law." The proposition could therefore be construed as supporting the king's power to commit without showing cause by those who believed that Magna Charta allowed of that power. Coke then attacked the third proposition, "That his majesty would be pleased graciously to declare that it is his royal pleasure to ratify and confirm unto all and every his loyal and faithful subjects, all their several, ancient, just liberties, privileges and rights, in as ample and beneficial manner, to all intents and purposes, as their ancestors did enjoy the same under the best of his majesty's most noble progenitors." After again objecting to the word "graciously" for the same reason as before, Coke claimed that since this proposition did not specify the subject's "just liberties," it would not prevent "the King's learned counsel" from arguing that these liberties were not taken away by the king's power to imprison without showing cause. The fourth proposition also failed to satisfy Coke. It stated "that his majesty would be further pleased, graciously, to declare, for the good contentment of his loyal subjects, and for the securing [of] them from future fears, that, in all cases, within the cognizance of the common law concerning the liberty of the subject, his majesty would proceed according to the common law of this land, and according to the laws established in this kindgom, and in no other manner or wise." After objecting yet again to the word "graciously" and complaining about the omission of any reference to "the statutes or customs of the realm," Coke expressed his fear that the Lords' vague reference to "the laws established in this kingdom" could be taken to refer to "the law martial"; and indeed he was "sure" that it was meant to be so construed. He did not "like" "to have the common law matched with other laws," he said, and was afraid that this proposition would be construed as meaning that at least in some cases "the common law must yield to the martial law."

It was the fifth and last proposition, however, against which Coke protested most violently. It stated:

And as touching his majesty's royal prerogative intrinsical to his sovereignty, and intrusted him withal from God, "ad communem totius populi salutem, et non ad destructionem," that his majesty would resolve not to use or divert the same, to the prejudice of any of his loyal people in the property of their goods, or liberty of their persons; and in case, for the security of his majesty's royal person, the common safety of his people, or the peaceable government of his kingdom, his majesty shall find just cause, for reason of state, to imprison or restrain any man's person, his majesty would graciously declare, that, within convenient time, he shall and will express the cause of the commitment or restraint, either general or special; and upon a cause so expressed, will leave him immediately to be tried according to the common justice of the kingdom.

Of all the Lords' propositions, Coke said, it was this one that most moved him "to keep to" the Commons's own resolutions. First, he objected to the characterization of the king's prerogative as "intrinsical." "It is a word we find not much in the law," he said; and, in fact, "it was no word of the law," for it meant "inward, not according to the outward ordinary law." To call the prerogative "intrinsical," therefore, was to say that it was "not bounded by any law, or by any law qualified." If the Commons were to concede that the king had an "intrinsical" prerogative, he warned, then all their laws would be "out." He also disliked the statement that this "intrinsical" prerogative was "entrusted by God" to the king, because it might imply that acts done under the prerogative were "done by the Law of God." Because this would imply in turn that no "human" law could "take away" such acts, he argued, the use of this phrase would allow the king to commit without showing cause in the face of any human law against such commitment. Moreover, if the king could imprison "for reason of state," as the fifth proposition indicated, then the Commons would be back where they had started. To this, Coke said, "we cannot yield."

He also complained that while the fifth proposition might bind the king to state a cause of commitment "within the convenient time," it did not say "[w]ho must be judge of this 'convenient time'?" The king had had this power "before Magna Carta," he said, "but now [it was] otherwise settled." Moreover, if the king were bound merely by general words to state a general cause of imprisonment, he could then declare that the imprisonment was "'per mandatum domini regis', or 'for matter of state'." If this were allowed, Coke said, "we are gone, and we are in a worse case than ever. . . . We shall leave Magna Carta and the other [seven] statutes and make them fruitless, and do what our ancestors would never do. We shall say [that] 'for matter of state' and [within] 'a convenient time' a man may be committed without cause." After declaring that he would "never yield to alter Magna Carta," he said that if the Commons meant "to declare Magna Carta," they must not "yield to any accommodation of it," and that since "all statutes against Magna Carta are deemed void," the Commons might not alter the charter. He then warned the House, "We are now about to declare and we shall now introduce and make a new law, and no king in Christendom claims that law, and it binds the subject where he was never bound." After further warning the House of the "infinite inconveniences" that would arise if "any pillars or maxims of the common law" or if "any of the old statutes or Magna Carta" were "shaken," he then said, "We have declared what the law is for the liberty of [the] subject, and shall we now weaken the law?" "[S]hall we go back and consent to these commitments [without cause]?" "The end of our conference with the Lords was that their Lordships would declare with us." "Consider the trust we reposed in the Lords." "We showed them our evidence. We desire[d] them to declare the like, but to be against us we begged it not." "If they shall out of their doubtfulness use any hesitation," or "if the worst of all should happen, that they should oppose us herein," then "we go on by ourselves" and "rely upon the gracious and benign disposition of our noble King," for "I doubt not our gracious sovereign will comply with us."[138]

After other members had spoken to the Five Propositions,[139] Coke successfully moved to defer further debate on them until Monday, 28 April.[140] When the Commons reassembled on that morning, however, they were called up to the Lords to hear a royal message read by the lord keeper. Charles I informed both houses

> that he holds the statute of Magna Carta, and the said other six statutes insisted upon for the subject's liberty, to be all in force, and assures you that he will maintain all his subjects in the just freedom of their persons, and safety of their estates, and that he would govern according to the laws and statutes of this realm, and that you shall find as much security in his Majesty's royal word and promise as in the strength of any law you can make, so that hereafter ye shall never have cause to complain.[141]

When the Commons returned to their own house, Secretary Coke unsuccessfully moved that because the king "had now showed himself the best of Kings, they would acknowledge his goodness, and apply themselves" to the subsidy.[142] Instead, after some debate they appointed a committee to draft a bill "wherein should be contained the substance of Magna Carta and the rest of those laws concerning the liberty of the subject in their persons and goods, and to make use of the resolutions of this House."[143]

On 29 April, Coke reported that the committee had drafted "an act for the better securing of every free man touching the propriety of his goods and liberty of his person." "[T]he first work of its members," he said, had been "to agree of capita" or heads, and they had decided upon three: "1, the liberty of the person, 2, the propriety of the goods, [and] 3, the matter of billeting soldiers." They had then considered what statutes the bill should mention and decided on a list including the twenty-ninth

138. For Coke's speech, see CD 1628, 3:94–96, 100, 104–5, 109–10, 114–15, 116–17.

139. See CD 1628, 3:99–116. In the course of this debate, Coke had a brief exchange with Sir Francis Nethersole (see CD 1628, 3:101, 106, 110) and made a few other brief remarks (see 3:112).

140. CD 1628, 3:108.

141. Ibid., 3:125.

142. Ibid., 3:126–27, 132–33, 136–38, 140–41.

143. Ibid., 3:139; cf. 123, 130, 134, 141, 142, 143.

chapter of Magna Charta and eight or nine other acts. Third, they had agreed not to look "backward" or lay any "imputations" in the bill. Finally, Coke explained that after making "the best preamble that ever was" by beginning with Magna Charta, they then set down in the bill "the resolutions of this House."[144]

The committee's debate on the bill of 29 April revealed a significant split among the leaders of the Commons. Whereas Wentworth wanted the bill not to deny directly the king's power to commit without showing cause, Coke, Selden, and Eliot all refused to compromise on this issue.[145] Coke expressed his views on the bill by answering several basic questions that previous speakers had raised about it. First, did it correctly state the law in providing that a cause had to be expressed on commitment? Second, should the Commons's earlier resolution on this point, even if legally correct, be "inserted into the body of the bill"? As one of the bill's principal spokesmen, and perhaps one of its main draftsmen as well, Coke naturally answered both questions affirmatively and then defended these answers at length. After protesting that his tongue should cleave to the roof of his mouth if he were to "touch on" the royal prerogative and repeating some of his earlier "reasons" against imprisonment without cause shown, he then proposed to use two methods, authority and experience, to demonstrate that "[t]here must be a cause shown upon the commitment." Once having cited several authorities for this position, he quickly turned to his argument from experience; and it soon appeared that it was of his own experience that he would speak. To show how "fearful" it was to be committed without cause being shown, he told the House how he had been committed to the Tower, and had all his books taken and his study searched. "Every man was upon me," he said, "nay more, after I was committed men did inquire where I rode circuit, what I did do there, only to find me in fault." This plainly showed, he said, how a cause of commitment might easily be found out "after the commitment" itself. "All men's mouths are open against the party," he said, "and our friends afraid as well to come to us."

Coke then responded to an objection that he had previously cleared in the Lords. Some said that because the statutes recited in the present bill's preamble "concluded" the question of imprisonment and had been declared to be in force by the judges and by the king, no provision for this question was needed in the body of the bill. To this argument Coke said that in his own opinion the statutes concluded "these questions in sub-

---

144. Ibid., 3:149, 152, 155, 161, 163, 164–65, 167. For the bill, see *CD 1628*, 3:149, 152, 161.

145. For outlines of the debates on this bill, which continued on 30 April and 1 May, see *CD 1628*, 3:144–45, 168–69, 183.

stance," but they did so only implicitly and not conclusively. As matters now stood, therefore, "Mr. Attorney with a whiff or a distinction may blow away all." He also reminded his listeners that "it is not now without occasions, that we insist upon this. Were there ever such violations [of the subject's rights] offered? Were there ever such commissions and oaths?"

After thus hinting at the intimate connection between the grievance of imprisonment and all the other grievances of the commonwealth, Coke then responded to those who opposed including the imprisonment resolution in the bill because it would "tie the King that never was tied." Coke simply pointed out that Magna Charta tied the king and that some of the other statutes explaining the charter named the king and the council. He then turned to the objection that the Commons should say nothing about imprisonment in their bill, because no final judgment had been given in the Five Knights' Case. Coke conceded that the judges had not yet ruled that "they could not be bailed who were . . . committed" without cause shown; but he emphasized that they had not "disclaimed" such an opinion or indicated that they would not so rule once Parliament was no longer sitting. Finally, to cap his speech, Coke reminded his listeners that those who opposed the inclusion of the resolution on imprisonment in the body of the bill were out of order, because they were speaking against a previous order of the House.[146]

On 30 April and 1 May, the committee continued to debate the bill for the subject's liberties without further comment from Coke.[147] This debate was suddenly interrupted on the first by Sir John Coke, who said that the king had commanded him "to desire this house clearly to let him know, Whether they will rest upon his Royal Word and Promise, made at several times, and especially by my lord-keeper's speech made in his own presence; which, if they do, he doth assure you, that it shall be really and royally performed."[148] After Sir John had explicated this message,[149] Sir Edward observed that "[n]ow is the axe laid to the root of the tree" and successfully moved to defer debate on the message until the following day.[150]

On 2 May, after many other members had spoken in the committee on the king's message,[151] Coke finally rose to say that he had never been "in so great a strait in all his life." After stating that the committee's first task was "[t]o consider . . . what the King's desire" was, Coke then interpreted Charles's latest message in the following way. After stating

146. For Coke's speech see *CD 1628*, 3:150–51, 153–54, 159, 162, 164, 166, 168.
147. See fn. 145.
148. Cobbett, *PH*, 2, col. 342; cf. *CD 1628*, 3:189, 191, 195, 198.
149. *CD 1628*, 2:189, 195–96, 198, 201, 203–4, 205.
150. Ibid., 3:189, 191.
151. For an outline of this debate, see *CD 1628*, 3:206–7.

that "the royal word" mentioned in the most recent message had "reference unto" earlier royal messages to the Commons, Coke ignored the king's special reference to Coventry's speech of 28 April and suggested that Charles had been referring, *inter alia*, to his promise of 4 April to "give way" to any attempt by the Commons to secure themselves in their liberties. This construction of the king's most recent message allowed the Commons to proceed with their bill without appearing to act in direct opposition to the king's will. It also upset the strategy that probably lay behind the king's message. By referring "especially" to the lord keeper's speech of 28 April, Charles I may have meant to suggest that the Commons should simply rely on his promise of the twenty-eighth and that he would not be receptive to their bill for the subject's liberties. Nevertheless, he had expressed his wishes in a way that caused relatively little overt offense. Coke's response to the royal message forced the king either to allow the Commons to proceed with their bill or else to command them explicitly to abandon it. No matter which alternative the king chose, Coke would have gained a small tactical advantage. He would clearly gain if the king allowed the Commons to proceed with the bill. And if the king directly forbad them to proceed on it, he would be put in the position of infringing on their liberties and of directly repudiating a public promise that he had made to them only a month before.

Having thus outmaneuvered the king, Coke could then say that Charles would see "how we are singly tied to his royal word," by which Coke meant the royal word of 4 April and not 28 April. After calling on the Commons to "deal clearly" with their "sovereign," he said that "the sense of the House is not to rest on a naked confirmation of the statutes, but, because they have been questioned by the King's learned counsel and some great Lords, let us make . . . a clear exposition [of them] that shall not trench [on] his honor." He then said that he would not have this bill "come from us, but from the King, and not in these terms that 'he ought not,' but in these terms, 'we will,' etc. 'that neither ourselves nor successors' shall do such and such things." He insisted that an oral promise could not satisfy him, since "it is the King's honor [that] he cannot speak but by record." Coke also said that his "heart" went with a bill. If the king were to assent to a bill expounding Magna Charta and the six [or seven?] statutes, he predicted, then "Henry 3 shall be no more famous for Magna Carta than King Charles shall make himself to posterity in this happy explanation [of the Charter]." Finally, Coke moved that the Commons do two things. First, they should thank the king "for his gracious care," because he was "the foundation" of their proceedings on the subject's liberties. Second, they should "humbly . . . beseech him graciously" to "declare" that a law might be made to explain that which lay hidden in the words of Magna Charta and the other statutes.[152] In the end, however, the Commons adopted a somewhat different motion framed by Wentworth that a subcommittee should draft a reply to the king's message, while the committee itself proceeded with the bill for the subject's liberties.[153]

Before the Commons had drafted a reply to the king, however, they received yet another royal message that promised them their liberties but also warned them not to encroach on the king's sovereignty. Charles I commanded that in proceeding with their bill, they stay "within the bounds and laws of our forefathers, without straining them or enlarging them by new explanations or additions in any sort; which he tells us, *he will not give way unto.*"[154] This message directly threatened the Commons's proceedings on their bill, but it nevertheless served the interests of those, like Coke and Selden, who opposed "accommodation" on the bill's substance, and it cut the ground out from under those like Wentworth who favored compromise, for it clearly served to raise doubts in the minds of those who were inclined to repose great trust in the king.[155] When the committee considered the message on 3 May, Coke made three short speeches, all of which served to transform a debate on the royal prerogative into a debate on the privileges of the House of Commons.[156] Meanwhile, the subcommittee previously appointed to draft a reply to the message of 1 May had drafted a declaration that responded to the message of 2 May. This declaration was presented to the king by the Speaker of the House on 5 May.[157] After thanking the king for his "royal word and promise," the Speaker reminded Charles of his promise of 4 April and stated that without encroaching on the prerogative or enlarging the laws, the Commons's bill would merely make "some necessary explanation of that which is truly comprehended within the just sense and meaning of laws, with some moderate provision for execution and performance." Replying for the king, the lord keeper expressed some displeasure with the Commons's proceedings but nevertheless consented to the drafting of a bill confirming Magna Charta and the other six statutes, "but so as it may be without additions, paraphrases, or explanations."[158]

When the committee resumed debate on 6 May, its members quickly

---

152. For Coke's speech, see *CD 1628*, 3:211–12, 216, 221, 223–24, 228, 230. It is possible that Coke willfully misinterpreted the king's message.

153. *CD 1628*, 3:212, 216.

154. Cobbett, *PH*, 2, col. 345; cf. *CD 1628*, 3:212.

155. See Berkowitz, *Selden*, chap. 10, p. 78.

156. See: (1) *CD 1628*, 3:234, 237, 244; (2) 3:235, 238, 241–42, 243, 245, 247, 248; (3) 3:236, 239, 243, 247.

157. Ibid., 3:252.

158. Cobbett, *PH*, 2, cols. 346–48; cf. *CD 1628*, 3:253–54.

indicated their unwillingness to rely simply on the king's oral promise or to proceed with the only kind of bill that the king would apparently accept—a "bare bill" simply confirming Magna Charta and the other six statutes. They saw the futility, however, of proceeding with a bill like the one they had been debating, because the king would obviously veto it. They were also unenthusiastic about Alford's proposal to insert something into the preamble of the subsidy and were clearly not encouraged by Secretary Coke's statement that his master would probably grant a petition against the forced loan.[159] Sir Edward then proposed that the Commons abandon their bill and instead proceed by petition of right. In order to gain support for this proposal, however, he had to show that it would indicate no distrust of the king on the part of the Commons. He conceded that "[f]or any not to rely on the King it is not fit trust. In him is all the confidence we have under God. He is God's lieutenant. Trust him we must." Still, Coke asked, "Was it ever known that general words were sufficient satisfaction to particular grievances? Was a verbal declaration of the King verbum regium?" Assuming the answers to these questions to be negative, he then indicated that the procedure he had proposed was a well-established "parliamentary way."

When the grievances be, the Parliament is to redress grievances and mischiefs that happen. Imprisonments are our grievances, billeting of soldiers, unnecessary loans, [martial law]. Did ever Parliament rely on messages? [No.] They ever put up petitions of their grievances, and the King ever answered them. The King's answer is very gracious, but what is the law of the realm? That is the question. I put no diffidence [?] in his Majesty. [But] [t]he King must speak by a record, and in particulars, and not in general.

Then Coke finally came to his own motion. "Let us have a conference," he said, "and join in a petition of right to the King" "for particular answer[s] to [all] our grievances." Anticipating a possible objection to this proposal, he then explained why the so-called answers in the king's previous messages were unsatisfactory and would still be unsatisfactory even if they were inserted in to the preamble to the subsidy bill. After dividing the king's earlier oral promises to the House into five parts, he explained that because they were contained in mere messages to the House, they were "not yet verbum regium." They were not yet of record; and if the Commons were to accept them on trust, he warned, then "[a]ll succeeding Kings will say, 'You must trust me as well as [you] did my predecessors.'" As for putting the promises contained in these messages into the subsidy, it was simply an unheard-of procedure, even if it were to result in the promises being of record. Since there were de-

159. For an outline of this debate, see *CD 1628*, 3:266–67.

ficiencies in all other procedures that the Commons might use to secure their liberties, he argued, "[l]et us put up our petitions; not that I distrust the King, but because we cannot take his trust but in a parliamentary way," "because we are parliamentary men."[160]

Coke's proposal was generally supported by those who followed him in debate. Glanville, Littleton, Pym, Wentworth, Eliot, and Digges all endorsed it and differed with one another only about whether the petition should incorporate the Commons's earlier Four Resolutions. Coryton, however, wanted to press on with the bill for the subject's liberties; and Hakewill raised the crucial question about Coke's proposal when he declared that a petition of right would not "amount to a law."[161] Whether Hakewill was right and whether Coke really disagreed with him are questions to which definitive answers cannot be given. The Petition of Right has sometimes been regarded as some sort of statute,[162] as a declaratory act,[163] or at least as a parliamentary instrument that was worthy of judicial notice and that bound not only the king but all subjects.[164] Those who view the petition in one of these ways are thus in a position to argue that by proceeding with it, the Commons were not backing off from their earlier positions on the subject's liberties but were merely adopting a different and more tactically efficacious method of securing judicial notice of their interpretation of the laws concerning the subject's liberties.[165] On the other hand, other writers have claimed that the petition was not a public or a private act (even though it bore some resemblance to the latter[166]) and that the statements of law contained in it were "not binding on the judges."[167] The proponents of this view can thus maintain that the Commons's decision to proceed by petition of right instead of by bill constituted a weakening of their position on the subject's liberties. But these same historians also maintain that the petition was superior to a mere confirmation of Magna Charta and the six statutes, because it "placed on record the King's acceptance of the statement that according to these laws certain definite grievances were illegal."[168] And they can therefore regard the adoption of the petition as a victory for moderates whose position in the constitutional crisis lay midway between that of

160. Ibid., 3:271–72, 277, 282–83, 286, 289, 293, 296.
161. For an outline of the debate on Coke's proposal, see CD 1628, 3:267.
162. This was Hallam's view, as quoted in Adair, "Petition of Right," p. 99.
163. This view is noted by Foster, who does not endorse it ("Petitions and the Petition of Right," p. 22).
164. See Berkowitz, "Reason of State," pp. 201–2.
165. Ibid., p. 203.
166. Relf, Petition of Right, p. 54.
167. Ibid., p. 57; cf. Adair, "Petition of Right," p. 102.
168. Adair, "Petition of Right," p. 102.

the king, on the one hand, and that of the members like Coke on the other.[169]

Unfortunately, it seems impossible to establish conclusively which of these interpretations of the petition is correct. The Petition of Right of 1628 was a unique parliamentary act.[170] It was interpreted differently by different people. And there are probably no absolute criteria by which its true nature can be determined. There is also no absolute test by which Coke's true opinion about the petition can be established. While he made several clear statements about its legal force, he always commented upon it as an interested party or advocate who hoped to persuade others to construe the petition in a way that was most favorable to his own interpretation of the law. In the debate of 6 May and in subsequent speeches, Coke usually took a position diametrically opposed to Hakewill's. That is, he maintained that the petition *would* "amount to a law," so long as it were to receive a satisfactory royal answer and be enrolled. How fully he believed in this position, however, is unclear. What is clear is that he thought that the only way in which he could achieve his objectives was to have the Commons and Lords join in a petition of right and to have it enrolled along with a satisfactory royal answer to it. This was his only hope, because Charles I had made clear that he would veto any bill for the subject's liberties that did more than declare that Magna Charta and the six statutes were in force. In supporting a petition of right rather than some type of bill, however, Coke was not making any sort of real compromise. He was not altering his position on the substantive legal issues that he had been debating for the past several months. He was simply proposing a procedure that he hoped would effectively secure legal recognition for his views about the subject's liberties. Instead of incorporating those views into a bill that the king could simply veto, he proposed to present them in a form that the king might be less likely to reject.

Once the Commons had reached a general consensus that they should abandon their bill and proceed by petition of right, Coke moved that the Commons "join with the Lords" in the petition and then have it "exemplified under the great seal," and that it "specify the several grievances previously mentioned."[171] The committee then ordered that the subcommittee appointed to draft the petition "should take into consideration

169. See Thompson, "The Origins of the Parliamentary Middle Group." See also Relf, *Petition of Right*, p. iii; Judson, *Crisis of the Constitution*, esp. pp. 258–59; and Hulme, *Eliot*, p. 227.

170. See Adair, "Petition of Right," p. 103. Foster has shown that "[b]y 1628, the parliamentary petition of right had acquired a specific meaning" ("Petitions and the Petition of Right," p. 43). But her investigations have not led to definitive conclusions about the precise juridical status of the Petition of Right of 1628.

171. *CD 1628*, 3:278.

the name of these grievances in the petition: loans, commissions, instructions, imprisonment, confinement, with all the illegal raisings of money, billeting of soldiers, etc."[172]

On the afternoon of 7 May, one last substantive question was resolved when first the committee and then the House resolved that the recent commissions for martial law were "against law."[173] This resolution was then incorporated into the petition, which was then presented to the Lords at a conference the next afternoon.[174] At this conference, Coke prefaced the reading of the petition with a brief speech. After first expressing his hope that "this meeting will prove a great blessing to us," he said that the Commons had commanded him "to express the singular care and affection that they have of concurrence with your Lordships in these urgent affairs and proceedings in this Parliament, both for the good of the commonwealth and principally for his Majesty." Moreover, if the Commons had "a hundred tongues," he said, they could not "express that desire which we have of that concurrence with your Lordships," since "it is evident that necessity there is, both in respect of ourselves and our posterities, to have good success of this business." Since the Commons had previously acquainted the Lords "with the reasons and grounds" of their position on the subject's liberties and had later conferred with them about the Five Propositions, "it behooves me," he said, "to give your Lordships some reasons why you have not heard from us before now." He then explained that while the Commons were considering "this weighty business," they had received several royal messages, which they had closely examined. Then, after considering "in what way we might go for our most secure way (nay yours)," they had decided "to go in a parliamentary course," because they believed that "old ways are the safest and surest ways." Finally the Commons had "drawn up a Petition of Right, according to ancient precedents, and left space for the Lords to join therein with them."[175] The petition was then read to the Lords.[176]

With the presentation of the petition to the Lords, the third stage of the Commons's proceedings ended, and the fourth stage began, during which the Lords would try unsuccessfully to alter the petition. When members of the upper house first debated it on 9 and 10 May, they seemed to approve of its substance. But they still expressed concern lest it

172. Ibid., 3:278; cf. 273, 284, 287, 291, 294, 296–97.
173. See CD 1628, 3:302–18, 326–31. For clear outlines of the procedures followed by the House in working out its final resolution on martial law, see CD 1628, 3:299, 322.
174. Ibid., 3:332.
175. Cobbett, PH, 2, cols. 350–51; CD 1628, 3:338; cf. 3:336, 344, 346.
176. See fn. 64, above.

be distasteful to the king; and they therefore wished to "sweeten" it by making several alterations in its wording.[177] In their debates of 9 and 10 May, however, the Lords had not directly touched on the central issue dealt with in the petition—"the commitment by the King and the Council without expressing the cause."[178] And before they had had an opportunity to debate this matter on the morning of 12 May or to reach any accord about it with the Commons, they received a royal message informing them of the king's reservations about the clause in the petition concerning imprisonment. Charles I wrote that even though he had tried to "satisfy all moderate minds, and free them from all just fears and jealousies" on this matter, he found it "still insisted upon" that "in no case whatsoever (though they should never so nearly concern matters of state or government) we, or our Privy Council, have power to commit any man without the cause shown." The acceptance of this proposition, he continued, "would soon dissolve the foundation and frame of our monarchy"; and "without overthrow of our sovereignty," he said, "we cannot suffer this power to be impeached." Nevertheless, "to clear" his "conscience and just intentions," he now made a declaration that closely resembled the previously rejected fifth proposition of the Lords. He was now pleased to "publish" that neither he nor his council would imprison any subject "for not lending money unto us, nor for any other cause which in our conscience does not concern the state, the public good, and the safety of us and our people." Nor would he "be drawn to pretend any cause which in our judgment is not, or is not expressed." He also promised that "in all cases of this nature which shall hereafter happen," he would on petition from the party or request by the judges "readily and really express the true cause of their commitment or restraint so soon as with conveniency and safety the same is fit to be disclosed and expressed." He further promised that "in all causes criminal of ordinary jurisdiction," the judges would deliver or bail the prisoner "according to the known and ordinary rules of the laws of this land, and according to the statutes of Magna Carta and those other statutes insisted upon, which we do take knowledge stand in full force, and which we intend not to abrogate or weaken against the true intention thereof."[179]

This royal message was read to the Commons at a conference held later in the morning of 12 May, at which the Lords also proposed that eight "alterations" be made in the petition;[180] and soon afterwards, the Lords also proposed that the petition's clause on imprisonment be brought

177. *LD 1621–1628*, pp. 148–49 and p. 149 n. 1.
178. *CD 1628*, 3:372; cf. *LD 1621–1628*, p. 150 and n. 1.
179. *CD 1628*, 3:372–73.
180. Ibid., 3:372. For the text of these alterations, see *CD 1628*, 3:382.

within "the compass" of the king's letter.[181] The Commons, however, refused to give any consideration to this second proposal and also showed little inclination to accept the alterations proposed by the Lords. When the Commons debated the Lords' alterations on 13 May,[182] Coke strongly opposed them all, except for one minor change in wording that Selden was also ready to accept,[183] and the House seemed ready to reject them all, aside from the one approved by the two lawyers. At a conference held on the fourteenth, the Commons informed the upper house of this decision and also stated that they would not "meddle with the [king's] letter," because, they said, "it is no parliamentary way."[184] The Lords, however, still favored some kind of compromise, and at a conference on the seventeenth, they proposed that this "addition" be made to the petition: "We humbly present this petition to your majesty, not only with a care of preserving our own liberties, but with due regard to leave entire that sovereign power, wherewith your majesty is trusted, for the protection, safety, and happiness of your people." Nevertheless, they also indicated that this proposal was "offered to be considered of, for an accommodation only," and that it should not "conclude their Lordships of their opinion, nor exclude the Petition of Right presented to them by the Commons."[185]

On the morning of 20 May, the Commons had agreed to one more change in the petition,[186] but they had still not decided whether to accept the upper house's "addition." That afternoon, Coke strongly urged them to reject it once and for all. After noting that its alleged purpose was simply to make the petition "more sweet and passable," he told them that it was actually "magnum in parvo"—"a little thing of great weight, and of such weight that it will destroy all our petition of right." "It trenches to all parts of it," he said. "It flies at loans, and at the oath, and at imprisonment, and billeting of soldiers" "and martial law." It "turns all about again." "[I]t lets loose and frees all at once; this is the extent of it."

He then subjected the addition to the same sort of analysis that he had employed in attacking the Lords' Five Propositions. He maintained

181. LD 1621–1628, p. 152.
182. For an outline of the debate, see CD 1628, 3:384–85. The "alterations" had been read to the House on the twelfth, but debate on them had been deferred (CD 1628, 3:374).
183. See: (1) CD 1628, 3:391, 395, 398; (2) 3:391; (3) 3:399; (4) 3:396.
184. Ibid., 3:427.
185. Cobbett, PH, 2, col. 355; cf. CD 1628, 3:452.
186. This change was not one of the "alterations" originally proposed by the Lords. For Coke's reports of the conferences of 19 and 20 May at which these slight changes in the petition were worked out, see: (1) CD 1628, 3:467–68, 470–71, 475–77; (2) 3:491, 493–94, 495–96, 499–500, 504–5, 507. For a direct report of the 19 May conference, see CD 1628, 3:482–87.

that the phrase "sovereign power" "flies at" all points made in the petition. Its use in the addition would have the effect on destroying whatever limitations the petition might otherwise have imposed on the king's power of "granting commission[s] for loans" or for martial law and on the king's power to imprison or confine. He then called on the Commons to "[l]ook into all the petitions of former times" and told them that they would find that previous parliaments had "never petitioned for the King's sovereignty, as if the subjects would save it." "Let every man meddle with that which belongs to him," he said. "Shall we claim our right [to] talk of 'sovereign power'? It was never seen, neither is it a parliamentary way." He also objected to the Lords' saving for the king sovereign power, first, because it was "not fit" that "there should be a 'sovereign power' above acts of parliaments, . . . in respect of the extent of it," and, second, because "it is against all parliamentary courses." "I know the prerogative is part of the law," he said, "but 'sovereign power' is no parliament word in my opinion. It weakens Magna Carta and all other statutes, for they are absolute and without any saving of sovereign power; and shall we now add it, we shall weaken the foundations of law, and then the building must needs fall." "Take heed what we yield unto," Coke warned. "Yet once I found that Magna Carta had a saving, which in reasonable construction might have been borne, but take heed [lest?] what the subject yields will forever be gone." The Confirmatio Cartarum of Edward I, he said, had had a saving for the ancient aids, and "[t]his saving made this statute to be of no force." The king's servants "found that [back]door; and then the statute of de tallagio non concedendo had to close it." This example showed, he said, that "Magna Carta is such a fellow as he will have no saving." "If we grant this addition," he said, "we do [use?] that [which] was never the language of Parliament, 'sovereign power'. We do not speak of sovereign 'prerogative' but 'power'." "By implication we give a sovereign power above all these laws. Power in law is taken for a power with force. What is meant here God only knows. It is repugnant to our petition, that is a petition of right grounded on acts of Parliament." Coke then declared, "We must not admit of it; and to qualify it, it is impossible. Let us hold our privileges according to the law. That power that is above this is not fit for the King and people to have it disputed further. I had rather for my part have the prerogative acted and myself to lie under it, than to have it disputed with. When it was [disputed] in former times it ever bred ill spirits." In conclusion, he moved "to tell the Lords that this [addition] extends to all 4 [branches of the petition]" and erected "a power over all when laws have settled them."[187]

187. For Coke's speech, see *CD 1628*, 3:494–95, 497, 502–3, 505, 506–7.

After further debate, in which no one supported the addition, the Commons informed the Lords that they would not even debate the matter with them.[188] The Lords, however, were not yet ready to abandon the addition and tried to rebut the Commons's arguments against it at a conference on 21 May. Their efforts were unsuccessful,[189] but they still managed to concoct another compromise plan. They proposed on the twenty-third that a joint committee of both Houses "see if by protestation, manifestation, or declaration, or any other way there might be any reconciliation touching this great business of his Majesty."[190] When the Commons debated this proposal on the twenty-fourth, Wentworth and Seymour saw some good in it,[191] but most members, including Coke, opposed it. Coke argued that the proposal was utterly inappropriate, because it was obviously aimed at producing something like the addition, even though the Lords had never satisfactorily answered the Commons's reasons against that proposed text. As "[f]or protestations, manifestations, declarations [or whatever]," he said, "I shall never assent to them." In his opinion, the House should now ask if the Lords approved of the petition or not. If they did, then no further accommodation needed to be considered. If they did not, then the petition "must sleep," unless the Lords could persuade the Commons to make some change in it. The addition, he insisted, provided no basis for any such agreement, because it "wounded" "the fundamental laws."[192]

The Commons then voted to reject the proposal for a joint committee,[193] and when this vote was reported to the upper house, the Lords abandoned further attempts to secure the Commons's assent to any accommodation. Instead, they passed their own declaration on 26 May, stating that their "intention" was "not to lessen or impeach any thing which by the oath of supremacy" they had "sworn to assist and defend."[194] They then voted unanimously to join in the petition and to inform the Commons of their vote at a conference.[195] Opening his report of this conference with the words "I am almost dead for joy," Coke said that the Lords "in omnibus, agreed with us, and stood upon no alterations but those which were already granted." The Lords now awaited the

---

188. Ibid., 3:495. For Coke's report of the conference at which the Commons made this point to the Lords, see CD 1628, 3:512–13, 515–16, 517–18, 520, 522–23.
189. For Noy's report of this conference, see CD 1628, 3:527, 539, 549. For Coke's speech following Noy's report, see CD 1628, 3:531, 541, 545, 546, 550–51.
190. Ibid., 3:595; cf. 599, 604.
191. For references to reports of these speeches, see CD 1628, 3:591–92.
192. Ibid., 3:598, 600, 602–603, 604.
193. Ibid., 3:594, 598.
194. Cobbett, PH, 2, col. 371.
195. LD 1621–1628, p. 205.

lower house's approval of the petition, after which they would "move the King for a speedy hearing."[196] The Commons quickly approved the amended petition after three quick readings, and the fourth stage of their proceedings came to a close.[197]

The last stage began on 27 May as the Commons finally confronted the problem of how to proceed with the petition so that it would have the force of a law, but would not be subject to the king's veto. They made a start at solving it by appointing a select committee to determine how the petition should be sent to the Lords and how it should be answered by the king.[198] Coke soon reported, however, that this committee had reached "no positive resolution of anything" and therefore referred the whole matter back to the House.[199] Nevertheless, in the debate that followed, Coke gave one of the fullest and clearest statements as to how the House should proceed with the petition. He first said that if he could go "the strongest way" with it, he "would have it endorsed" and go to the Lords "as a bill"; but he then maintained that the Commons should not now employ this procedure. He explained that they had previously resolved to proceed by petition of right, and not by bill, because it was "a middle way" that would not directly contravene the king's indirect order against proceeding with anything but a "bare" bill. If they were now to proceed by bill, he argued, they would be reversing a decision on the basis of which all of their recent proceedings had rested. Moreover, if they were to proceed by a petition of right, and not by bill, their act would still have legal force and be of record. He conceded that when the question of how they should proceed was "first in agitation," he had said that "the way of petition was not equivalent to [the way of] a law" and that "this way" would not lead to something with the force of an act of Parliament. Now, however, he had come to the view that a petition passed by both Houses of Parliament would, in fact, have the force of a statute, and that was why he had "begged of God that the Lords might join us." "[F]or whatsoever the Lords' house and this House at any time have agreed upon," he claimed, "no judge ever went against it. And when the judges in former times doubted of the law, they went to the Parliament, and there resolutions were given to which they were bound." If the judges now dared to oppose such joint resolutions, he said, "let me speak no more."

Having established or argued that a petition of right, approved by

196. *CD 1628*, 3:611, 614, 618–19, 620.
197. On 26 and 27 May. See *CD 1628*, 3:611 and 623.
198. Ibid., 3:623.
199. Ibid., 3:624, 626, 630, 632.

both houses, would have binding legal force, Coke then turned to the questions of how it should be sent to the Lords and how it should be presented to the king. The first of these questions he simply dismissed by saying that the Commons had already "possessed the Lords" with the petition. As for presenting it to the king, he said that he was "utterly against going to Whitehall" and having the Speaker present it there, because this was "no Whitehall case," and to present the petition there would not be a "parliamentary way." Instead, he proposed, first, that the lord keeper or some other member of the upper house deliver the petition to the king in Parliament; and, second, that the king also give his assent to it in full Parliament. Then, he said, he would have the petition "exemplified under the Great Seal" and would "leave it to my child as his greatest inheritance."[200]

Without further debate, the Commons made two orders: that Coke deliver the petition to the Lords for transmission to the king; and that the Lords be "acquainted with the desire of this House that his Majesty would be pleased to make his answer to this petition in full Parliament, and that his Majesty be moved to that purpose."[201] Coke then took the petition to the Lords, calling it "a true exposition of the Great Charter,"[202] and the Lords then assented to it[203] and had it presented to the king.[204] On 2 June, the Commons were asked to come to the upper house, where Charles I was ready to answer the petition. After brief speeches by the king and lord keeper, the petition was read and then answered by the king: "The King willeth that right be done according to the laws and customs of the realm; and that the statutes be put in due execution, that the subject may have no just cause of complaint of any wrong, or oppression, contrary to their just rights and liberties, to the preservation whereof he holds himself in conscience as well obliged as of his just prerogative."[205] This was obviously not the sort of answer that the Commons had expected, and upon returning to their own house, they quickly adjourned.[206]

On 3 June, the reading of the king's answer to the Commons was followed by a long silence. Eliot then moved for a two-day postponement of debate. No one seconded his motion or even spoke. He then presented a long catalogue of the Commons's grievances that clearly constituted an attack on Buckingham, even though the duke was never named, and

200. For Coke's speech, see CD 1628, 3:624, 628–29, 630, 632–33, 634.
201. Ibid., 3:624.
202. Ibid., 3:624, 629, 630, 633.
203. LJ, 3:826.
204. Ibid., 3:827.
205. CD 1628, 4:52–53, 54, 55, 55–56.
206. Ibid., 4:54.

then concluded by saying that the times called for a remonstrance.²⁰⁷ After a few other members had indicated their cautious support for Eliot's views,²⁰⁸ Coke firmly supported his proposal for a remonstrance. "If I did think that the King were truly informed of the true cause of our dishonors and disasters," he said, "I would leave this remonstrance. But he knows not the true cause which we know, and some of us feel." He then urged the House to "join in an humble [and "true"] remonstrance" to the king, while "leaving the remedy to him for [later?] time and other circumstances." "Let us fly to him as our refuge," he said; for "we are now in a miserable condition." After suggesting that the remonstrance include several points that he had made in the parliament of 1625 about the management of royal finances, he said, a bit mysteriously, that if the Commons were now to aid the king in such matters, their action would "give wings to the Parliament" and might procure them not only thanks from the king, but also "a better answer" to their petition than they had yet received. "I will deal plainly with you," he said. "[W]e have not yet so full an answer [to our petition] as I hope we shall, neither do I yet like it." In conclusion, he expressed his support for a remonstrance, "so as it be with all duty and humility."²⁰⁹ On 4 June, Charles I responded to this debate in the Commons by informing them that his answer to the petition was "full of justice and grace," that he intended to abide by it "without further change or alteration," and that they were to entertain no new matter but simply to bring to "a happy conclusion" what they had begun.²¹⁰ In response, the Commons, led by John Pym, speeded up their proceedings against Manwaring, which they had revived some time before.²¹¹ This action further provoked the king, who informed them on the fifth that he still intended to dissolve Parliament in a few days and that he now "required" them to "enter not into, or proceed with any new business, which may spend greater time, or which may lay any scandal or aspersion upon the state, government, or ministers thereof."²¹² The House then went into committee to discuss the message and "to consider what is fit to be done for the safety of the kingdom." It was also ordered that no one was to leave the House "upon pain of going to the Tower."²¹³

Very early in the committee's debate, Coke observed that the Commons had proceeded with unprecedented "moderation and duty" in view of the fact that "such a violation of the liberties of the subject" had taken

207. Ibid., 4:60–62, 68–69, 72–73, 77–78.
208. See CD 1628, 4:65–67.
209. Ibid., 4:67, 75, 78.
210. Ibid., 4:86.
211. Ibid., 4:90, 101–2.
212. Ibid., 4:113.
213. Ibid., 4:114.

place, and he said that they were now suffering for having done so. God was punishing them, he said, "because we have hoodwinked ourselves and have not spoken plainly." Coke urged the Commons to take "to heart" the maxim that "[w]hosoever violates laws does not hurt certain citizens but goes about to overthrow the whole commonwealth"; and he then called the king's latest message "the greatest violation" of the laws "that ever was, for in former times," Parliament had often "complained of" ministers of state and sought and received redress for all of the grievances of the sort that Eliot had attacked the day before. To prove his point, he asked rhetorically, "In the 50[th year] of Edward [III's reign], were they afraid to name any man that had offended? John of Gaunt, Duke of Lancaster, the King's own son, was he not accused and sent to the Tower? Latimer and others? Are we now to be afraid how we shall answer it to our country?" Under Henry IV, he continued, Parliament had complained that members of the council "mewed up the King and dissuaded him from the common good" and had had them "removed from the King." Under Edward III and Richard II, he claimed "the Parliament moderated the King's prerogative," and had taken similar actions under Henry IV. After asserting that the Commons had "records enough" to support them, he asked, "Why are we now required from that way we were in [when the king's message had arrived]? Why may we not now name those that are the cause of all our evils?" "Whatsoever has or shall grow to abuse," he declared, "this House ever had power to speak of it, and until we do so God will not bless us, nor go out with our armies."

Coke finally arrived at his main point. "Because men have been named," he said, "I will name a man, the Duke of Buckingham." "I will not stick to name [him]," he asserted, for "[h]e is the grievance of grievances," and "the cause of all our miseries." "We cannot for his sake go out with honor, nor come home with honor," he said; and after repeating his claim that Buckingham was "the grievance of grievances," he declared: "I am the first to tell you so this day and I shall never repent it, for you will find that all that is amiss will reflect on him." "Let us tell the King so," he argued, and while they had other grievances to complain about, they ought to complain of the duke "before any others." Then, returning to the subject of the king's recent message, he noted that it contained the phrase "'The King requires.'" "I do not believe," he said, that "the King said so, but rather that it was the information of the man I named before." In conclusion, he argued that it was not fit to go to the Lords about these matters, as some had suggested, because the Commons's liberties were "now impeached," and the Lords were "not participant with" the Commons's liberties. Now, it was "[f]it to repair to the King."[214]

After long debate, the committee appointed a subcommittee to draft a declaration to the king concerning their proceedings during the entire parliament, as well as the recent attack on their liberties contained in the royal message of 5 June.[215] Because the subcommittee was also to list the Commons's principal grievances and "the cause of them," Selden made a point of saying that its members must not set down "a cause general, but the cause, whose name we ought not to decline: the Duke of Buckingham." Coke also insisted that the remonstrance name the duke as the "chief and principal cause" of their grievances.[216] Reports of this attack on Buckingham obviously worried the king, for he quickly backed down from his intransigent position of the fifth. On 6 June he informed the Commons that he had not intended his previous message to bar them "from what has been your right, but only to avoid all scandal on his counsel and actions past."[217] Nevertheless, despite this royal attempt at conciliation, the Commons continued to deliberate about a remonstrance on the true state of the kingdom in a debate to which Coke contributed a long speech on religious abuses.[218]

On 7 June, several members of the Lords decided that because the king was now eager to avoid an attack on Buckingham and to get a parliamentary grant of supply, it was time to press for a further answer to the petition. At a conference held later that day, the lord keeper informed the Commons that the Lords thought it fit "to make an humble suit to his Majesty for a clear and satisfactory answer to the Petition of Right . . . and desire you will join with them."[219] The Commons quickly voted to grant the Lords's desire, and the king immediately agreed to appear before both houses in a few hours. At four o'clock Charles came before the Lords and Commons, and after the reading of the petition he gave the answer: "Soit droit fait comme est desire."[220] When the Commons returned to their own House, Coke told them that this new answer was the

214. Ibid., 4:115, 119, 124, 129–30, 132.

215. Ibid., 4:131. Prior to the appointment of the subcommittee, Coke made another speech in which he referred to the Protestation of 1621 (see *CD 1628*, 4:116, 121, 126, 130, 132–33).

216. Ibid., 4:131.

217. Ibid., 4:138.

218. For an outline of the debate, see *CD 1628*, 4:135–37. For Coke's speech, see *CD 1628*, 4:143–44, 156, 163, 167, 169, 173. For other brief speeches that Coke made in this same debate, see: (1) *CD 1628*, 4:163; (2) 4:146, 164; (3) 4:146; and (4) 4:168.

219. Ibid., 4:193.

220. Ibid., 4:178. For a note on the king's second answer to the petition, see *CD 1628*, 4:148 n. 8.

best possible one. He said that while he had believed that the king's "meaning was at first to give us as absolute and real an answer as now," he had not actually done so. He then admitted, "I would not find fault with the last answer, had I so much wit in my head, till I was sure whether we should have a better [answer] or no. [Because] [i]n a doubtful thing interpretation goes always for the King." He could now tell the House, however, that the king's new answer was much better than his previous one; and since it contained "no doubtfulness nor shadow of ambiguity," the Commons were now "free" and had successfully concluded the main part of their proceedings on the Petition of Right.[221]

221. Ibid., 4:182, 185, 190, 193.

Eight

Epilogue

With the delivery of the second royal answer to the Petition of Right on 7 June 1628, Coke's parliamentary career effectively came to an end. During the next several weeks prior to Parliament's adjournment on 26 June, he continued to participate in the Commons's debates and took a particular interest in securing the enrollment of the petition[1] and in protesting the king's collection of tonnage and poundage.[2] But his speeches on these subjects were anticlimactic once a satisfactory answer had been given to the petition, and he did not see fit to return to the House of Commons for the session of 1629. His failure to take part in this next parliamentary session has never been satisfactorily explained, but in the absence of direct evidence bearing on this point, it can reasonably be attributed to his advancing age and to his desire to complete his *Institutes*. His decision not to return to Parliament may also have indicated his conviction that the formal acceptance in Parliament of the principles expressed in the Petition of Right constituted a suitable conclusion to his active political life, even though he may have known of the king's attempts to undermine the legal and political force of the petition.[3]

Coke's declaration that he would leave the petition to his child as his "greatest inheritance" reflects his taste for ponderous yet homely legal metaphors, but it probably expressed his sincere beliefs. Although he must have taken satisfaction in knowing that his heir's inheritance would far exceed the one that he himself had received more than fifty years earlier, he had come to believe that such inheritances could be protected and maintained only through the reaffirmation of those legal principles that constituted the "inheritances" of English subjects. During his last years in Parliament, he had come to regard the power of an untrustworthy and ungodly royal court as the greatest "grievance of the commonwealth" and to believe that this grievance could not be remedied unless Parliament were to give formal legal expression to certain fundamental "liberties of the subject." He had become convinced that the underlying causes of the abuses that he had attacked during the early 1620s were

1. See: (1) CD *1628*, 4:369; (2) 4:362, 365, 366, 370; (3) 4:390, 394, 397, 399, 400.
2. See: (1) CD *1628*, 4:447–48, 455, 457, 461–62; (2) 4:449.
3. On these efforts, see Foster, "Printing the Petition of Right"; and Berkowitz, *Selden*, chap. 10, pp. 112–13 and nn. 512–14.

to be found at court and that attempts to eliminate them would be futile, unless certain basic constitutional principles were formally re-affirmed.

The changes that took place during the 1620s in Coke's political attitudes and in his way of accounting for the existence of evil in the English commonwealth were thus related to the processes by which a host of specific conflicts within post-Reformation English society be-came transformed into an incipient clash between groups that espoused conflicting ideologies. Coke was not responsible, of course, for effecting this transformation, but he played an important role in the process by which it came about. He was more successful than almost any other figure of his era in identifying the grievances of a certain segment of English society, in portraying these grievances as the grievances of the commonwealth as a whole, and in justifying and legitimating the actions by which members of the House of Commons tried to purge the realm of these grievances. Coke did not live to sit in the Long Parliament, and if he had, he might well have opposed its actions. But in his final years in Parliament, he had helped to create the rhetorical and constitutional framework for the actions of this later, revolutionary parliament by ef-fectively translating the dissatisfactions of particular segments of English society into more abstract, and seemingly universal, terms of modern constitutional discourse.

Appendixes
Bibliography
Index

Appendix A

Legislative Committees on Which Coke Served in 1621, 1624, 1625, and 1628

1621

"An Act for Limitations of Actions, and for Avoiding of Suits in Law" (*CJ*, 1:511).

"An Act against Certain Troublesome Persons, Commonly Called Relators, Informers, and Promoters" (*CJ*, 1:523).

"The Bill for the Sabbath" (*CJ*, 1:523).

"An Act to Suppress the Taking of Tithes for Fishing Voyages" (*CJ*, 1:527).

"An Act of Explanation of a Branch of a Statute in the Third [Year of King James, concerning Recusants]" (*CJ*, 1:534).

"An Act to Enable the Most Excellent Prince Charles to Make Leases of Lands, Parcel of His Highness' Duchy of Cornwall" (*CJ*, 1:534).

"An Act for the General Quiet of the Subject against All Pretences of Concealments Whatsoever" (*CJ*, 1:534).

"An Act for the Free Trade and Traffick of Welsh Cloths . . . " (*CJ*, 1:534).

"An Act for the Restraint of Abuses, in Levying Debts for Common Persons, in the Name, and by Prerogative, of the King" (*CJ*, 1:540).

"An Act for Making the Arms of This Kingdom More Serviceable in Time to Come" (*CJ*, 1:544).

"An Act for the Grant of Two Entire Subsidies, Granted by the Temporality" (*CJ*, 1:544).

"An Act Prohibiting the Importation of Corn" (*CJ*, 1:544–45).

"An Act concerning Bankrupts" (*CJ*, 1:551).

"An Act concerning Monopolies" (*CJ*, 1:553–54).

"An Act for Avoiding the Returns of Insufficient Jurors" (*CJ*, 1:582).

"An Act against Secret Offices, and Inquisitions to Be Taken on His Majesty's Behalf to the Prejudice of His Subjects" (*CJ*, 1:597).

"An Act for the Further Reformation of Jeofails" (*CJ*, 1:602).

"An Act concerning Fees in Courts of Justice" (*CJ*, 1:606).

"'An Act for Better Securing of the Subjects' against Wrongful Imprisonment, Contrary to Magna Charta" (*CJ*, 1:609–10).

"The Bill for Sea-marks and Mariners" (*CJ*, 1:611).

"An Act concerning 'Sutton's Hospital' " (*CJ*, 1:612).

"An Act for Probate of Suggestions in Cases of Prohibition" (*CJ*, 1:622).

"A Private Act for John Mohu " (*CJ*, 1:623).

"An Act for the Abbreviation of Michaelmas Term" (*CJ*, 1:641).

"An Act for the Restitution of the Necessary Use of Writs of *Ad quod Damnum*, or Commission, or Commissions in Nature of the Same" (*CJ*, 1:641).

"[An Act to Make] Ministers, and other Spiritual Persons, [Capable of Leases of]

Lands, for the Behoof of Their Wives [and Children]" (*CJ*, 1:642).
"An Act against Scandalous and Unworthy Ministers" (*CJ*, 1:643).
"An Act for the Election of Knights, Citizens, and Burgesses, to Serve in Parliament" (*CJ*, 1:649–50).

1624

"An Act concerning Probate of Suggestions in Cases of Prohibition" (*CJ*, 1:671, 716).
"An Act for the General Quiet of the Subject against All Pretenses of Concealment Whatsoever" (*CJ*, 1:673, 717).
"An Act for the Explanation of a Branch of a Statute, Made in the Third Year of the King's Majesty's Reign in England, Entitled, An Act for the Better Discovering and Repressing of Popish Recusants" (*CJ*, 1:673, 718).
"An Act concerning Monopolies, and Dispensation with Penal Laws, and the Forefeitures Thereof " (*CJ*, 1:674, 719).
"An Act for the Ease in the Obtaining of License[s] of Alienation, and in the Pleading of Alienations with License, or of Pardons of Alienations without License, in the Court of Exchequer or Elsewhere" (*CJ*, 1:678, 719).
"An Act against the Exportation of Wool, Woolfells, Fullers Earth and Fulling Clay" (*CJ*, 1:678, 730).
"An Act against Secret Offices, and Inquisitions; to be Taken in His Majesty's Behalf, to the Prejudice of His Subjects" (*CJ*, 1:679, 731).
"An Act for the Continuance of a Former Statute, Made 4° *Jac.* Intituled, An Act for the True Making of Woolen Cloth" (*CJ*, 1:679, 730).
"An Act to Enable the Most Excellent Prince Charles to Make Leases of Lands, Parcel of His Highness' Duchy of Cornwall" (*CJ*, 1:680, 731).
"An Act for the Better Securing of the Subjects from Wrongful Imprisonment, and Deprivation of the Trades and Occupations, Contrary to the 29th Chapter of the Statute of Magna Charta" (*CJ*, 1:680, 731).
"An Act to Prevent the Abuses, in Procuring . . . Process, and Supersedeas for Good Behaviour [*sic*]" (*CJ*, 1:680).
"An Act for Avoiding of Vexatious Delays, Caused by Removing Actions and Suits out of Inferior Courts" (*CJ*, 1:680, 731).
"An Act Confirming the Sale of Certain Lands Sold by Sir Edward Heron" (*CJ*, 1:681, 730).
"An Act for Making the Estates of Attainted Persons Liable to Payment of Their Just Debts" (*CJ*, 1:681, 732).
"An Act for the Relief of Patentees, Tenants, and Farmers, of Crown Land and Duchy Land" (*CJ*, 1:681, 732).
"An Act for the Confirmation of the Foundation of the Hospital of King James, Founded in Charter-House, in the County of Middlesex, at the Humble Petition, and Costs and Charges, of Thos. Sutton, Esquire, and of the Possession Thereof " (*CJ*, 1:685, 736).
"An Act for the Sale of the Land of Thomas Cope, the Father, and Thomas Cope, the Son" (*CJ*, 1:737).
"An Act for the Freer Liberty of Fishing, and Fishing Voyages, to Be Made and Performed in the Sea-Coasts and Place of Newfoundland, Virginia, New England, and other the Sea-Coasts and Parts of America" (*CJ*, 1:686, 736).
"An Act for the Abbreviation of Michaelmas Term" (*CJ*, 1:686, 736).

"An Act for Reversing a Decree, [Procured] Indirectly and by Corruption" (*CJ*, 1:688).

"An Act for the Making of the River Thames Navigable to Oxford" (*CJ*, 1:744).

"An Act for the Further Description of a Bankrupt" (*CJ*, 1:745).

"An Act concerning Anwell River" (*CJ*, 1:745).

"An Act to Make Ministers Capable of Leases . . . " (*CJ*, 1:746).

"An Act to Abolish all Trials by Battle, in All Writs of Right" (*CJ*, 1:746).

"An Act to Enable the Lady Alice Dudley to Confirm the Manor of Killingworth to the Prince His Highness" (*CJ*, 1:747).

"An Act to Avoid the Exactions of Fees of Customs Comptrollers" (*CJ*, 1:747).

"An Act against Depopulation, and Converting of Arable into Pasture" (*CJ*, 1:748).

"An Act against Abuses in Levying of Debts for Common Persons, under the Name and Prerogative of the King" (*CJ*, 1:748).

"An Act Concerning the New Erecting and Ordering of Inns." (*CJ*, 1:751).

"An Act concerning Ostlers and Innholders" (*CJ*, 1:751).

"[An Act concerning] Butter and Cheese" (*CJ*, 1:753).

"An Act for the Prostrating of Weirs upon the River Wye" (*CJ*, 1:753).

"An Act against Such as Shall Levy Any Fine, [or] suffer Any Recovery [under the Name of Another]" (*CJ*, 1:754).

"Viscount Mountacue, His Bill" (*CJ*, 1:755).

"An Act to Make Sale of the Lands of Sir Anthony Aucher, Sir Roger James, and John Wroth" (*CJ*, 1:757).

"An Act for Restitution in Blood of Carew Raleigh, Son of Sir Walter Raleigh, Attainted of High Treason" (*CJ*, 1:758).

"An Act for the Inning or Gaining of the Earith and Plumsted Marshes" (*CJ*, 1:762).

"An Act for Establishing of Three Lectures in Divinity" (*CJ*, 1:762).

"An Act to Prevent Simony in Colleges and Halls" (*CJ*, 1:762).

"A Bill . . . for Bennister" (*CJ*, 1:766).

"An Act for the Naturalising of Philip Jacobson of London, Merchant" (*CJ*, 1:767).

"An Act for Relief of Creditors against Such as Die in Execution" (*CJ*, 1:769).

"An Act concerning the Apothecaries" (*CJ*, 1:772).

"An Act to Prevent Great Charge and Expense, that Divers are Put Into, by Laying Actions of Debt, and Other Actions, in London and Middlesex" (*CJ* 1:772).

"An Act concerning the Ancient Revenue of the Crown, of 2d. upon a Chaldron of Sea-coals sold, in the Port of Newcastle upon Tyne" (*CJ*, 1:693, 778).

"An Act for the Relief of Felt-Makers of London, against a Decree in Chancery against One Warwick" (*CJ*, 1:695).

"An Act for the More Speedy Sealing of Original Writs" (*CJ*, 1:695, 778).

"An Act for Avoiding a Decree concerning One Morgan" (*CJ*, 1:695).

"An Act for Making Void Certain Letters Patent, Granted to Sir Henry Heron, for the Sole Packing and Drying of Fish . . . " (*CJ*, 1:691, 783).

"A Private Act for 'Jesse Glover'" (*CJ*, 1:700, 785).

"An Act against the Transportation of Iron Ordnance" (*CJ*, 1:702, 787).

"An Act against Receiving of any Secret Pensions from Any Prince or State" (*CJ*, 1:703, 787).

1625

"An Act for Punishing of Divers Abuses Committed on the Lord's Day . . . Called Sunday" (*CJ*, 1:800).

"An Act to Enable the King's Majesty to Make Leases of Lands, Parcel of His Highness' Duchy of Cornwall, or Annexed to the Same" (*CJ*, 1:801).

"An Act to Repeal So Much of the Statute, Made in the 21st Year of the Reign of . . . Henry the VIIIth, *cap.* 13°, as doth Restrain Spiritual Persons to Take Farms" (*CJ*, 1:808).

"The Bill for the Quiet of Ecclesiastical Persons, and the Preservation of the Right of Patrons" (*CJ*, 1:809).

"The Bill against Simony" (*CJ*, 1:809).

1628

"An Act to Restrain the Passing or Sending of [Any] to Be Popishly Bred Beyond the Seas" (*CJ*, 1:874).

"An Act concerning the Searching and Sealing of Divers Stuffs, Commonly Called New Draperies" (*CJ*, 1:877).

"An Act to Avoid Suspicion of Injustice in any Member of the Commons House of Parliament" (*CJ*, 1:877).

"An Act to Avoid Suspicion of Misdemeanour in Any Member of the Commons House of Parliament" (*CJ*, 1:877).

"An Act for the Better Continuance of Peace and Unity in Church and Commonwealth" (*CJ*, 1:879).

"An Act for the Establishing and Confirming of the Foundation of the Hospital of King James, Founded in Charter-House, in the County of Middlesex, at the Humble Petition, and at the Only Cost and Charges of Tho. Sutton, Esqu., and of the Possession Thereof" (*CJ*, 1:880).

"An Act for the Mitigation of the Sentence of the Greater Excommunication, and for Preserving of Ecclesiastical Jurisdiction" (*CJ*, 1:882–83).

"An Act for the Better Supressing of Unlicensed Alehouse Keepers" (*CJ*, 1:884).

"An Act for the Maintenance and Increase of Shipping and Navigation, and for Freer Liberty of Fishing and Fishing Voyages to be Made in and upon the Seas and Sea-coasts, and Places of Newfound-land, Virginia, New England, and Other the Seas, Sea-coasts, and Parts of America" (*CJ*, 1:884).

"A Bill for the Repeal and Continuance of Statutes" (*CJ*, 1:885).

"An Act for the Better Ordering of the Office of Clerk of the Market, and Reformation of False Weights and Measures" (*CJ*, 1:885).

"An Act for Explanation of a Branch of a Statute Made in the Third Year of the Reign of Our Late Sovereign Lord King James, Intituled, An Act for the Better Discovering and Repressing of Popish Recusants" (*CJ*, 1:887).

"An Act for the Naturalizing of Sir Ro. Dyell . . . and of George Kirke" (*CJ*, 1:888).

"An Act for the Getting of Salt-peter, and for the Furnishing of the Realm with Great Store, and at Easier Prices Than Heretofore" (*CJ*, 1:888).

"An Act concerning Liberties of Parliament" (*CJ*, 1:889).

"A Private Act for the Right Honourable Dutton Lord Gerrard" (*CJ*, 1:893).

"An Act for the Better Maintenance of the Ministry" (*CJ*, 1:893).

"An Act for a Better Allowance of Preaching Curates, and to Redress the Neglect of Preaching and Catechizing" (*CJ*, 1:895).

"An Act against Begging of Forfeitures before Attainder" (*CJ*, 1:898).

"A Private Act for Sir Thomas Nevyll and His family" (*CJ*, 1:898).

"An Act for Exempting the Counties of Gloucester, Worcester, Hereford, and Salopp., and the Cities of Gloucester, and Worcester, and of the Counties Thereof, from the Jurisdiction of the Lord President [of the Council of the Marches in Wales]" (*CJ*, 1:900).

"A Private Act for the Earl of Arundell" (*CJ*, 1:910).

"An Act for the Establishing of the Estates of the Tenants of Bromfield and Yales, in the County of Denbighe" (*CJ*, 1:913).

Appendix B

Coke's Experience with Economic Affairs Prior to 1621

Throughout much of his long career, Coke was frequently involved in the process of economic administration. For example, while serving successively as solicitor general, attorney general, chief justice of the Commons Pleas, chief justice of the King's Bench, and treasury commissioner, he had regularly taken part in decisions concerning royal finances. He often gave advice on the management of crown lands,[1] and he also dealt with various other issues bearing on royal finances. In 1601 he wrote a memorandum on how the queen's revenues could be managed so as to allow her to pay off her debts;[2] and sometime prior to 1606, he collaborated with Sir John Popham in drawing up a plan for the abolition of feudal tenures, which they claimed would increase James I's revenues by £100,000 per year.[3] Throughout James I's reign, Coke played an important part in managing the revenues of Queen Ann of Denmark,[4] and in September 1615 he was an active participant in an important Privy Council debate on royal finances.[5] Coke's competence in dealing with financial matters, moreover, did not go unrecognized. He was regarded as a leading candidate for the office of lord treasurer after Salisbury's death in 1612[6] and after the fall of the duke of Suffolk in 1618;[7] and while serving for several years on the treasury commission,[8] he was praised for his expertise even by Bacon.[9]

During these same decades, Coke must also have become well acquainted with the affairs of various London companies while acting in the capacities of private counsel, administrative arbitrator, or legal officer of the crown. His continuing connection with the Drapers' Company, for example, is clearly documented. In 1595, the company retained him as their counsel and used his services

---

1. See *CSPD, 1591–94*, pp. 489, 495; *CSPD, 1595–97*, pp. 140, 316, 320, 328–29, 386, 392–93, 430; *CSPD, 1598–1601*, pp. 377, 520, 522; *CSPD, 1603–10*, pp. 46, 61, 361, 560.

2. *CSPD, 1601–3*, p. 140.

3. See F. C. Dietz, *English Public Finance, 1558–1641*, p. 131.

4. *CSPD, 1603–10*, p. 106; *CSPD, 1611–18*, pp. 349–56, 609; *CSPD, 1619–23*, pp. 6, 171; *HMC, 4th Report* [Earl de la Warr], p. 302; Dietz, *English Public Finance*, p. 163.

5. *CSPD, 1611–18*, p. 310; Willson, *Privy Councillors*, pp. 36–37, 271 n. 4; Prestwich, *Cranfield*, pp. 180–81; Gardiner, *History*, 2:364–66; Bacon, *Works*, 12:194–206.

6. *HMC, Downshire*, 3:306, 412; *CSPD, 1611–18*, p. 216.

7. *CSPD, 1611–18*, pp. 482–83, 566, 581; Prestwich, *Cranfield*, pp. 192–93, 198; Bacon, *Works*, 12:252.

8. Dietz, *English Public Finance*, pp. 171–72; Gardiner, *History*, 3:189; Prestwich, *Cranfield*, p. 220.

9. Bacon, *Works*, 12:378–79; cf. Prestwich, *Cranfield*, p. 220.

when it prepared to defend its right to have its own printer in 1596.[10] In 1610 the company again retained Coke when it was contesting the decision of the city of London to impose taxes on livery companies to pay for Irish lands.[11] In the meantime Coke was also involved in the affairs of other London companies. In 1608 he was requested to give an opinion about a dispute that had arisen over the new charter of the Cutlers' Company.[12] In 1614 he served as an arbitrator in a dispute between the mayor and aldermen of London, on the one hand, and the Cooks' Company, on the other, about the Cooks' new charter;[13] and in 1619 he was one of the privy councillors assigned to settle a dispute between the Stationers' Company and two men who had recently been granted a printing monopoly.[14] Coke's position as a judge, moreover, requried that he often involve himself in the affairs of such companies, since the statute 19 Henry VII, *c.* 7 provided that all ordinances of any guild or craft had to be ratified by the chancellor, the lord treasurer, the two chief justices, or the justices of assize;[15] and pursuant to this act, he ratified the ordinances of the Merchant Taylors, the Salters, Sadlers,[16] and presumably other companies.

The extent of Coke's involvement in the details of economic administration is best illustrated, however, by his long association with the Privy Council's efforts to oversee and regulate various aspects of English economic activity.[17] Long before he became an official member of the council in 1613, that body was frequently calling on him to investigate economic problems and to serve as an arbitrator in disputes concerning economic organization. Among the economic issues that Elizabeth's council ordered him to investigate were a complaint by the Company of Woolmen in London;[18] a dispute over a Cornish tin mine;[19] a complaint by the city of Kingston upon Hull about marketing practices in the "north parts";[20] a dispute about the making of vinegar;[21] complaints against the

10. A. H. Johnson, *The History of the Worshipful Company of Drapers of London*, 2:170 n. 5, 170–71.

11. Johnson, *Drapers*, 3:24.

12. Charles Welch, *History of the Cutlers' Company of London*, pp. 198–201.

13. Frank Taverner Phillips, *A History of the Worshipful Company of Cooks, London*, pp. 34–35; and Frank Taverner Phillips, *A Second History of the Worshipful Company of Cooks, London*, p. 22.

14. William A. Jackson, *Records of the Court of the Stationers' Company, 1602 to 1640*, pp. xvii–xviii.

15. See Holdsworth, *History*, 4:323, and n. 1.

16. See Charles M. Clode, *The Early History of the Guild of Merchant Taylors*, pp. 268–69, 340–41; [Charles M. Clode], *Memorials of the Guild of Merchant Taylors*, pp. 201–2; Harry Lennox Hopkinson, *Report on the Ancient Records in the Possession of the Guild of Merchant Taylors*, p. 32; J. Steven Watson, *A History of the Salters Company*, p. 57; and J. W. Sherwell, *The History of the Guild of Sadlers of the City of London*, p. 51 and n. 1. Coke also witnessed the charter of the Cordwainers (see C. H. Waterland Mander, *A Descriptive and Historical Account of the Guild of Cordwainers of the City of London*, p. 183).

17. For references to works on the role of the Elizabethan and early Stuart Privy Council in economic administration, see chap. 4, fn. 10.

18. *APC, 1592–93*, pp. 294–95.

19. Ibid., pp. 228–29.

20. Ibid., p. 8; *APC, 1597–98*, p. 544.

21. *APC, 1595–96*, pp. 485–86.

train oil monopoly;[22] disputes over the making of sail cloth in Suffolk;[23] an information in the Exchequer against the Company of Brewers;[24] a dispute over the privileges of the borough of Coventry;[25] a complaint by the butchers of Norwich;[26] a project for draining the Fens;[27] a dispute arising over the manufacturing activities of the Dutch congregation in Canterbury;[28] a dispute over the making of aquavitae and vinegar;[29] a dispute between London and Newcastle;[30] complaints about the manufacture of false dice;[31] a dispute about market rights at Scarborough;[32] a plan for new coins for the East India Company;[33] a question about new privileges to be issued to the town of Berwick upon Tweed;[34] the seizure of English cloth carried into Scotland;[35] the transportation of undressed cloth out of the realm;[36] and measures to be taken against rogues and vagabonds.[37]

No registers survive for the period between 1602 and 1613, but when they resume, they show Coke playing an even more active role in economic administration. Among the miscellaneous topics that he dealt with between 1613 and 1621 were a dispute arising out of the activities of the commissioners of the sewers in the counties of Northampton, Cambridge, Huntingdon, Lincoln, Norfolk, and the Isle of Ely;[38] a complaint by the justices of the peace of Wiltshire against abuses of common informers;[39] and complaints about abuses in the granting of writs of protection against creditors in the County Palatine of Chester.[40] During this same period, Coke was also ordered by the council to investigate many other economic problems that are closely connected with the issues raised in parliamentary debates of the early 1620s. Most of these concerned one or more of the following three topics: local trade and manufacturing, foreign trade, and the organization of the wool and cloth trades. The disputed questions concerning internal trade and manufacturing that he investigated during this eight-year period included a dispute about the manufacturing activities of the Dutch congregation of Norwich;[41] the dispute about the new charter of the Cooks' Company;[42] the dispute between the Apothecaries and the Grocers;[43] a dispute

22. *APC, 1596–97*, p. 426.
23. *APC, 1597*, pp. 17–18, 186–87.
24. Ibid., pp. 97–98.
25. *APC, 1597–98*, p. 178.
26. Ibid., p. 545.
27. *APC, 1598–99*, p. 323.
28. Ibid., pp. 646–47, 737.
29. *APC, 1599–1600*, p. 132.
30. Ibid., pp. 425–28.
31. Ibid., pp. 614–15.
32. *APC, 1600–1601*, p. 6.
33. Ibid., p. 77
34. *APC, 1601*, pp. 10 ff.
35. Ibid., p. 365.
36. Ibid., p. 489.
37. Ibid., pp. 503–4.
38. *APC, 1618–19*, pp. 291–92.
39. *APC, 1619–21*, pp. 42, 128–29.
40. Ibid., p. 211.
41. *APC, 1613–14*, pp. 90–91, 280–81, 292–94, 355–60.
42. Ibid., pp. 445, 591–93; *APC, 1615–16*, p. 130.
43. Ibid., pp. 450–51.

about the making of glass;[44] a dispute about the making of salt;[45] a dispute between the Pinmakers and the Haberdashers;[46] a dispute between the "hoastmen trading for coals" and the king's patentees for the maintenance of light house at Wintertonness;[47] a plan for the levying of money in arrears for the repair of seabreakers between the towns of Great Yarmouth and Happsborough, co. Norfolk;[48] complaints against two patents, one restraining the importation of gold and silver thread, the other barring the importation of gold and silver foliate;[49] a petition from a London merchant asking for the power to search and seal all sacks of hops;[50] a complaint by the mayor and commonalty of Bristol against a new charter procured by the Bristol Bakers;[51] and abuses in the licensing of butchers and poulterers.[52]

During this same period, questions concerning foreign trade also came under Coke's scrutiny, as the council ordered him to investigate a complaint by the Silkweavers' Company about the importation of silk by merchant strangers;[53] a dispute between the London merchants trading to France and merchants from the outports;[54] a dispute between the merchants trading to Russia and the lord admiral about whale fishing;[55] complaints by members of the Levant Company about Dutch competition;[56] a dispute between the Merchants of the Staple and East India Company;[57] various miscellaneous complaints by the Muscovy Company;[58] complaints by West Country merchants about the Spanish Company's new charter;[59] a dispute between London and Bristol merchants trading to the Levant;[60] a petition by the Eastland Company;[61] an investigation of the patent granted to one Captain Harcourt for the plantation in Guiana;[62] a petition by the Cinque Ports about the decay of trade and merchandizing in those towns;[63] a dispute between the mayor, burgesses, and Society of Merchants of Hull, on the one hand, and divers other merchants "free of the Company of Merchant Adventurers," on the other, about trade into Gascony and the Low Countries;[64] similar disputes in Kingston upon Hull about the exportation of lead to Germany and the Low Countries;[65] disputes about the organization of the Russia Com-

---

44. Ibid., pp. 269, 545–46.
45. *APC, 1615–16*, pp. 7, 9, 17.
46. Ibid., pp. 590–91; *APC, 1618–19*, pp. 272, 279–80; *APC, 1619–21*, pp. 6, 162.
47. *APC, 1618–19*, p. 285.
48. Ibid., p. 300.
49. *APC, 1619–21*, pp. 252, 283.
50. Ibid., pp. 167–68.
51. Ibid., p. 49.
52. *APC, 1618–19*, p. 378.
53. *APC, 1613–14*, pp. 307–9.
54. Ibid., pp. 247–48.
55. Ibid., pp. 262–63; *APC, 1618–19*, p. 105.
56. *APC, 1615–16*, p. 98.
57. *APC, 1616–17*, p. 345.
58. Ibid., pp. 344, 346.
59. Ibid., pp. 350, 353.
60. *APC, 1618–19*, pp. 48, 70.
61. Ibid., pp. 260–61, 290–91.
62. Ibid., pp. 398–400.
63. Ibid., pp. 442–43.
64. Ibid., pp. 482–83.
65. *APC, 1619–21*, pp. 90–91.

pany;[66] complaints about the transportation of iron ordnance;[67] various disputes involving the French merchants;[68] and a plan for drawing more silver into the king's mint.[69]

Finally, during this same period, Coke was called upon to investigate many matters concerning the wool and cloth trades: petitions from woolgrowers about legal restraints imposed on their right to sell to all persons;[70] a complaint by the Merchant Adventurers against interlopers in the cloth trade;[71] a complaint by Edward Misselden about defective cloth sent to him by a clothier in Wiltshire;[72] a complaint by the woolgrowers of Cumberland, Westmorland, and Northumberland;[73] a complaint from the clothmakers and clothier-merchants of Totnes, co. Devon, about the customs demanded for overlength kersies;[74] a complaint by the Merchant Adventurers of Newcastle upon Tyne;[75] a dispute between the Merchant Adventurers and the justices of the peace of Somerset about the trade of "blues";[76] a petition from the worsted weavers of Norwich;[77] a complaint by eighty poor clothiers in Suffolk and Essex;[78] and complaints from Cornwall about informations in the Exchequer on the statute 5 & 6 Edw. VI, c. 7.[79]

The most notable example of Coke's involvement with economic administration in this period and the only one that historians have discussed is his support of the Cockayne Project.[80] In March 1613, Coke was added to a committee instructed to investigate the project.[81] He was retained on a new committee appointed shortly afterwards[82] for the same purpose, and, along with its other members, requested the Levant Company's opinion of the project in a letter written in July.[83] On 18 December Coke reported to the Privy Council on the committee's progress.[84] After presenting three arguments against the validity of the charter of the Merchant Adventurers,[85] he then expressed his strong support

66. Ibid., p. 157.
67. Ibid., pp. 316–17.
68. Ibid., pp. 131, 152, 174–75.
69. Ibid., p. 141.
70. APC, 1615–16, pp. 536, 564–65.
71. APC, 1618–19, pp. 1–2.
72. Ibid., p. 42.
73. Ibid., pp. 148, 445.
74. Ibid., pp. 212–13.
75. Ibid., pp. 122, 136–7.
76. Ibid., pp. 194–5.
77. Ibid., p. 316.
78. APC, 1619–21, pp. 79–80.
79. Ibid., pp. 227–28.
80. For the most detailed discussion of the Cockayne Project, see Friis, *Alderman Cockayne's Project*, pp. 224–381. For a more recent treatment, see Supple, *Commercial Crisis*, esp. pp. 33–51.
81. CSPD, 1611–18, p. 176; Friis, *Alderman Cockayne's Project*, pp. 240–41. According to Friis, nothing is known of this committee's work.
82. Friis, *Alderman Cockayne's Project*, p. 241.
83. Ibid., p. 242 and n. 4.
84. Ibid., p. 244; APC, 1613–14, pp. 303–4. The account of this committee meeting in the council registers is supplemented by notes taken at the meeting by Sir Julius Caesar (Caesar Papers, British Museum, Add. MS. 14027, ff. 261–62). These notes are printed in Friis, *Alderman Cockayne's Project*, pp. 458–60.
85. Friis, *Alderman Cockayne's Project*, pp. 245–46, 458–59. Caesar's notes of Coke's speech contain the following passage:

for the Cockayne Project,[86] and in a meeting of the council held on 4 July 1614, he again argued for the project.[87]

There is, then, little doubt that Coke was originally a supporter of the Cockayne Project. Not until 1616, according to Friis, did he turn against it;[88] and, Friis suggests, his support of the project may help to explain his appointment to the Privy Council during the period when the project was under discussion.[89] Nevertheless, the conclusions about Coke's views on trade and economic policy that may be inferred from his support of the project are far from clear. Friis suggests that his support for it reflected his narrow, legalistic outlook. He was, she says, "unaffected by all the arguments against the project, . . . blind to everything save the fact that several statutes rendered the exportation of undressed cloths illegal."[90] Friis also believes, however, that Coke supported "free trade"[91] and thus concludes that he later opposed the project because he saw that "the new company [had] developed into something quite different from what he had imagined and no less objectionable to him than the old company."[92] On the other hand, Menna Prestwich suggests that Coke's support of the project indicates that he did not support "free trade."[93] Malament claims that Coke supported the

---

All companies which hinder the general trade of England are revocable by the law of England, as void.
9 E. 3. cap. 2.
18 E. 3. cap. 5.
25 E. 3. cap. 2.   for the maintenance of public trade
12. H. 7. cap. 6.
Order may not bar a man of his birthright.
The King's statute against the Spanish Company 3 Jacobi cap. 3.
Darcy's case Mich. 3 Jacobi, touching the monopoly of playing cards.
[any?]thing granted to a hundred is a monopoly if the rest prohibited.
—Whatsoever is granted to any of the hinderance of trade, is void in law. [Friis, *Alderman Cockayne's Project*, p. 459]

86. Ibid., pp. 246–47, 459. Friis says that Coke's "arguments when discussing the convenience of the measure were less weighty than his legal refutation of the privileges of the Merchant Adventurers" (p. 459). Nevertheless, his remarks are of interest because of their close similarity to arguments he made in the Parliament of 1621:

In matter of conveniency.
2 things principally considerable.
1. the maintenance of the clothier.
2. The maintenance of the merchant.
Of things transportable the cloth of England is nine parts of 10.
3 or 400 thousand lib. a year must be provided for the buying of cloth yearly.
Some have undertaken to take the cloth made off the hands of the clothiers. [Friis, *Alderman Cockayne's Project*, p. 459]

87. Friis, *Alderman Cockayne's Project*, pp. 260–61.
88. Ibid., pp. 292–93. See also Prestwich, *Cranfield*, p. 175.
89. Friis, *Alderman Cockayne's Project*, p. 244. See also Prestwich, *Cranfield*, p. 168 and n. 3.
90. Friis, *Alderman Cockayne's Project*, p. 261.
91. Ibid., pp. 156, 246, 267. Coke was, Friis writes, "an opponent of every sort of organization of an exclusive character" (p. 246), and it was to Coke's influence that she ascribes the insertion of a clause upholding the principle of free trade in a proclamation issued on 23 July 1614, prohibiting the export of undyed or undressed cloths (p. 267).
92. Ibid., p. 292.
93. Prestwich writes, "When skepticism [about the project] was shown by so many

project "[i]n the hope of aiding the unemployed clothiers and of increasing the revenue of the State by eliminating the need to import finished cloth,"[94] and she maintains that these goals were consistent with his "protectionist bias"[95] and his firm opposition to "*laissez-faire* notions with regard to foreign commerce."[96] Malament is correct when she argues that Coke's support of the Cockayne Project reveals beliefs antithetical to laissez-faire notions. But she is probably mistaken in attributing a "protectionist bias" to Coke, because he did not consistently espouse "protectionist" policies.

---

councillors, Coke's enthusiasm is difficult to account for. He had on the Bench condemned monopolies, but if in attacking the Merchant Adventurers he retains his reputation as the advocate of economic liberalism, yet by supporting Cockayne he was merely substituting one monopoly ring for another. He was guilty of blinkered thinking at the least, if he did not recognize this" (*Cranfield*, p. 168).

94. Malament, "Coke," p. 1331.
95. Ibid., p. 1330, n. 48.
96. Ibid., pp. 1329–30.

Appendix C

The Bankruptcy Act of 1624

In a debate on the cloth trade on 14 February 1621, six reasons were given for the "great fall of wools and clothing," of which the second was "the great number of bankrupts that deceitfully and fraudulently breaks to the overthrow of divers clothiers," and "it was propounded to make some strict law for punishing such bankrupts and to help the creditor to his debts."[1] On 1 March Sir Francis Crane preferred "a bill for the further description of a bankrupt and for relieving of . . . creditors and for inflicting corporal punishment on bankrupts in some cases,"[2] but the bill was not debated until 24 May,[3] when Solicitor Heath reported it back from committee.[4] Both Sir Edward Mountagu and Sir Henry Poole wished to have the bill amended. Mountagu proposed that the bill extend to landlords as well as to businessmen,[5] and Poole wanted the bill to extend to aliens and strangers.[6]

After several other members had spoken to the bill,[7] Coke rose.[8] He complained that bankrupts had overthrown many merchants,[9] and that they often borrowed money when they knew that they were about to go bankrupt.[10] Adrian, he declared, had ordered that bankrupts be whipped to death.[11] Such a penalty, Coke thought, was just;[12] but he said that he disliked "laws written in blood,"[13] and that bankrupts should be subjected to corporal punishment only in a few extreme cases.[14] Coke then turned his attention to the amendment proposed by Poole. Poole had wanted to include both aliens and strangers in the bill, whereas another speaker, Keightley, had wanted both left out.[15] Coke now proposed that

1. CD 1621, 5:457.
2. CD 1621, 2:162; 5:266 n. 1; CJ, 1:532. For a brief of the bill, see CD 1621, 7:104.
3. The bill was given a first reading on 5 March (CD 1621, 2:162). It was read for a second time and committed on 13 March (CD 1621, 2:211); and on 26 March it was reported and recommitted (CD 1621, 2:267). A committee meeting for the bill was scheduled on 30 April (CD 1621, 2:331) and again on 5 May (CJ, 1:609).
4. CD 1621, 3:296; 2:385; 4:366; 5:175–76; 5:382; 6:166. For amendments made by the committee, see CD 1621, 4:366; and 5:175–76.
5. CD 1621, 3:296; 2:385; 4:366; 5:176; P&D, 1:95. The bill extended "only to such bankrupts as seek their living by buying and selling" (CD 1621, 7:104).
6. CD 1621, 3:296; 2:385; 4:366; 5:176; P&D, 1:95–96.
7. Mr. Keightley, Heath, Perrott, and Towerson. See CD 1621, 3:296; 2:385; 4:366.
8. CD 1621, 2:385; 3:296; 5:176; P&D, 1:96.
9. CD 1621, 2:385.
10. Ibid., 3:296.
11. Ibid., 5:176; 3:296.
12. Ibid., 5:176.
13. Ibid., 3:296.
14. Ibid., 5:176.
15. Ibid., 2:385; 3:296.

aliens be left out of the bill, just as they had been in two previous bankruptcy bills,[16] "but for the denizen," he said, "whom the King's patent makes free to have benefit by the laws, I desire he may be beloved by this law."[17]

The House voted to recommit the bill.[18] On 30 May Heath again reported it back to the House, and it was ordered to be engrossed.[19] It never received a third reading in the Commons in 1621, but it was quickly revived in the parliament of 1624. On 29 April Mr. Lowther reported it from committee with several amendments and a proviso.[20] The proviso was to this effect: that "if the debtor, after 5 proclamations and 3 summons under the hand of the commissioners, did absent himself six months," he could be charged with a felony.[21] Coke spoke against the proviso and also moved that the bill be amended so as to provide that the bankrupt be allowed to have counsel and to examine witnesses.[22] The House rejected the proviso but also rejected Coke's proposed amendment, and it ordered that the bill be engrossed.[23] The Commons passed the bill on 3 May[24] and sent it up to the Lords, where it also passed. It was enacted as 21 *Jac.* I, *c.* 19.[25]

16. 34 and 35 *Hen.* VIII, *c.* 4 and 13 *Eliz.*, *c.* 7.
17. *CD 1621*, 3:296.
18. Ibid., 4:366–67.
19. Ibid., 6:182; *CJ*, 1:632.
20. *CJ*, 1:694; Pym, 1624, f. 83v; Holland, 1624, I, f. 60.
21. Pym, 1624, f. 83v. See also Nicholas, 1624, f. 182v.
22. Holland, 1624, I, f. 60.
23. *CJ*, 1:694.
24. Ibid., 1:696.
25. *SR*, 4, pt. 2, pp. 1227–9.

Bibliography

PRIMARY SOURCES

Note: Annotated transcripts of all parliamentary sources noted here, except Hawarde's diary for 1621 and 1624 and Pym's diary for 1625, were made available to me at the Yale Center for Parliamentary History, Sterling Library, Yale University. Copies of the original manuscripts of Hawarde's diary and Pym's diary for 1625 were also made available to me at the Yale Center for Parliamentary History.

THE PARLIAMENT OF 1621

House of Commons

Commons Debates, 1621. Edited by Wallace Notestein, Frances Helen Relf, and Hartley Simpson. 7 vols. New Haven, 1935.

Hawarde, John, M.P. for Bletchingley, Surr. Proceedings of the House of Commons, 20 Nov.–19 Dec., 1621. Unnumbered MS., Wiltshire Record Office (deposited by the Marquess of Ailesbury).

Journals of the House of Commons, 1547–1714. 17 vols. Vol. 1, pp. 507–669. London, 1803.

Proceedings and Debates of the House of Commons in 1620 and 1621. Collected by a Member of that House [Edward Nicholas]. Edited by T. Tyrwhitt. 2 vols. Oxford, 1776.

House of Lords

"The Hastings Journal of the Parliament of 1621." Edited by Lady de Villiers. *Camden Miscellany,* vol. 20. Camden Society, 3d series, vol. 83. London, 1953.

"A Journal by Lord Montagu of the Proceedings in the House of Lords, 20 Nov.–19 Dec., 1621." *Historical Manuscripts Commission. Report on the Manuscripts of the Duke of Buccleuch & Queensbury . . . ,* vol. 3, pp. 222–23. London, 1926.

Journals of the House of Lords, 1578–1714. Vol. 3, pp. 3–204. London, 1846.

Notes of the Debates in the House of Lords . . . 1621. Edited by S. R. Gardiner. Camden Society, 1st series, vol. 103. London, 1870.

Notes of the Debates in the House of Lords . . . 1621, 1625, 1628. Edited by Frances H. Relf. Camden Society, 3d series, vol. 42. London, 1929.

"Notes of Speeches and Proceedings in the House of Lords, 1610–1621." *Historical Manuscripts Commission. Report on the Manuscripts of the Late Reginald Rawden Hastings . . . ,* vol. 4, pp. 286–90. London, 1947.

THE PARLIAMENT OF 1624

House of Commons

Anonymous. Proceedings in the House of Commons, 19–24 Feb., 1624. MS. Rawlinson D. 732, Bodleian Library, Oxford University.

D'Ewes, Sir Simonds. Proceedings in the House of Commons, 12 Feb.–29 May, 1624. Compiled from the Journals of the House of Commons and from unidentified private diaries and separates. Harleian MS. 159, British Museum, London.

Dyott, Richard, M.P. for Stafford. Proceedings in the House of Commons, 5–15 March and 20 Apr.–29 May, 1624. MS. D 661/11/1/2, Staffordshire Record Office (deposited by the Dyott family).

Erle, Sir Walter, M.P. for Poole, Dors. Proceedings in the House of Commons, 19 Feb.–29 May, 1624. Add. MS. 19597, British Museum, London.

Hawarde, John, M.P. for Bletchingley, Surr. Proceedings in the House of Commons, 12 Feb.–29 May, 1624. Unnumbered MS., Wiltshire Record Office (deposited by the Marquess of Ailesbury).

Holland, Sir Thomas, M.P. for Norfolk. Proceedings in the House of Commons, 25 Feb.–9 April. MS. Tanner 392, Bodleian Library, Oxford University.

Holland, Sir Thomas. M.P. for Norfolk. Proceedings in the House of Commons, 10 Apr.–15 May, 1624. MS. Rawlinson D.1100, Bodleian Library, Oxford University.

Holles, John, M.P. for East Retford, Notts. Proceedings in the House of Commons, 23 Feb.–19 May, 1624. Harl. MS. 6383, British Museum, London.

Horne, Robert. Proceedings in the House of Commons, 19 Feb.–29 May, 1624. Compiled from separates and newsletters. MS. Rawlinson B. 151, Bodleian Library, Oxford University.

Jervoise, Sir Thomas, M.P. for Whitchurch, Hants. Proceedings in the House of Commons, 23 Feb.–28 Apr. 1624. Unnumbered MS., Hampshire Record Office (deposited by the Jervoise family).

Journals of the House of Commons, vol. 1, pp. 670–715.

Journals of the House of Commons, vol. 1, pp. 715–98 (another version).

Nethersole, Sir Francis, M.P. for Corfe Castle, Dors. Parliamentary newsletters to Sir Dudley Carleton, 1624. P.R.O., S.P. 81/30 (German); S.P. 14/161–5, 167 *passim*.

Nicholas, Edward, M.P. for Winchilsea. Proceedings in the House of Commons, 19 Feb.–29 May, 1624. P.R.O., S.P. 14/166.

Pym, John, M.P. for Tavistock, Devon. Proceedings in the House of Commons, 19 Feb.–7 May, 1624. Finch-Hatton MS. 50, Northampton Record Office (deposited by the Earl of Winchilsea).

Pym, John. Fragment of the Pym diary, 23–26 Feb., 1624. Harleian MS. 6799, British Museum, London.

Rich, Sir Nathaniel, M.P. for Harwich, Essex. Proceedings in the House of Commons, 23 Feb.–6 Mar., 1624. Add. MS. 46191, British Museum, London.

Spring, Sir William, M.P. for Suffolk. Proceedings in the House of Commons, 19 Feb.–27 May, 1624. MS. English 980, Houghton Library, Harvard University (frequently cited as the Gurney diary).

Wright, John, Clerk of the House of Commons. Third Version of the Commons Journal, 12–25 Feb., 1624. Braye MS. 73, House of Lords Record Office, London.

House of Lords

"A Journal by Lord Montagu of the Proceeding in the House of Lords, 12 Feb.–
29 May, 1624." In *HMC, Buccleuch*, vol. 3, pp. 228–45.
Journals of the House of Lords, vol. 3, pp. 205–430.
Notes of the Debates in the House of Lords . . . 1624 and 1626. Edited by S. R.
Gardiner. Camden Society, 2d series, vol. 24. London, 1879.

THE PARLIAMENT OF 1625

House of Commons

Anonymous. Proceedings in the House of Commons, 18 June–11 Jul., 1–12
Aug., 1625. Add. MS. 48091, British Museum, London.
Debates in the House of Commons in 1625 . . . Edited by S. R. Gardiner. Camden
Society, 2d series, vol. 6. London, 1873.
"Draft Journal of the House of Commons, 21 June–8 Jul., 1625." Edited by M.
F. Bond. In *The Manuscripts of the House of Lords*, new series, vol. 11, *Ad-
denda, 1514–1714*, pp. 177–207. London, 1962.
Eliot, Sir John. *Negotium Posterorum, by Sir John Eliot*. Edited by A. B. Grosart.
2 vols. London, 1881.
Pym, John, M.P. for Tavistock, Devon. Proceedings in the House of Commons,
1625. Add. MS. 26639, British Museum, London.

House of Lords

"A Journal by Lord Montagu of Proceedings in the House of Lords, 1–12 Aug.,
1625." In *HMC, Buccleuch*, vol. 3, pp. 247–52.
Journals of the House of Lords, vol. 3, pp. 431–89.
Notes of the Debates in the House of Lords . . . 1621, 1625, 1628. Edited by
Frances H. Relf. Camden Society, 3d series, vol. 42. London, 1929.

THE PARLIAMENT OF 1628

House of Commons

Commons Debates, 1628. Edited by Robert C. Johnson, Mary Frear Keeler,
Maija Jansson Cole, and William B. Bidwell. 3 vols. New Haven, 1977.
Further volumes to appear.
Journals of the House of Commons, vol. 1, pp. 872–920.

House of Lords

Journals of the House of Lords, vol. 3, pp. 685–881.
Notes of the Debates in the House of Lords . . . 1621, 1625, 1628. Edited by
Frances H. Relf. Camden Society, 3d series, vol. 42. London, 1929.

OTHER PARLIAMENTARY SOURCES

Bowyer, Robert. *The Parliamentary Diary of Robert Bowyer, 1606–1607*. Edited
by D. H. Willson. Minneapolis, 1931.
[Cobbett, William.] *The Parliamentary History of England, from the Early Period
to the Year 1803 . . .* 36 vols. London, 1806–20.
Commons Debates for 1629. Edited by Wallace Notestein and France H. Relf.
Minneapolis, 1921.

A Complete Collection of State Trials . . . Edited by [W. Cobbett and] T. B. Howell. Vols. 1–3. London, 1809–16.

D'Ewes, Sir Simonds. *The Journal of Sir Simonds D'Ewes from the Beginning of the Long Parliament to the Opening of the Trial of the Earl of Strafford.* Edited by Wallace Notestein. New Haven, 1932.

The Parliamentary or Constitutional History of England. 24 vols. London, 1751–61.

Proceedings in Parliament, 1610. Edited by Elizabeth Read Foster. 2 vols. New Haven, 1966.

Return of the Name of Every Member of the Lower House of the Parliaments of England, Scotland and Ireland . . . *1213–1874.* Parliamentary Papers, vol. 72, parts 1–3. London, 1878.

Rushworth, John. *Historical Collections of Private Passages of State, Weighty Matters in Law, Remarkable Proceedings in Five Parliaments.* 4 parts in 7 vols. London, 1759–61.

The Statutes of the Realm. 5 vols. in 6. 1810–28. Reprint ed. London, 1963.

Coke's Principal Writings

(Only the editions cited in this work are noted here. For discussions of Coke's writings, see the works cited in footnote 41 of chap. 1)

The First part of the Institutes of the Laws of England; or, A Commentary Upon Littleton. 19th ed. 2 vols. London, 1832.

The Second Part of the Institutes of the Laws of England, Containing the Exposition of Many Ancient and Other Statutes. London, 1797.

The Third Part of the Institutes of the Laws of England: Concerning High Treason, and Other Pleas of the Crown, and Criminal Causes. London, 1797.

The Fourth Part of the Institutes of the Laws of England: Concerning the Jurisdiction of Courts. London, 1809.

The Reports of Sir Edward Coke, Knt. in English, in Thirteen Parts Complete . . . Dublin, 1793.

"Sir Edward Coke's 'Vade Mecum' [selections]." In *Collectanea Topographica et Genealogica,* vol. 6 (London, 1840), pp. 108–22.

Other Primary Sources

Acts of the Privy Council of England. 1542–1604. Edited by John Roche Dasent. 32 vols. London, 1890–1902.

Acts of the Privy Council of England. 1613–31. 13 vols. London, 1921–64.

Bacon, Francis. *The Works of Sir Francis Bacon.* Edited by James Spedding, R. L. Ellis, and D. D. Heath. 12 vols. London, 1864–69.

Brooke, Sir Robert. *La Graunde Abridgement.* London, 1573.

Bulstrode, Edward. *The Second Part of the Reports of Edward Bulstrode* . . . 2d ed. 1688. Rpt. in *The English Reports,* vol. 70, King's Bench Division, 9, pp. 909–1193. Containing Yelverton; Hobart; Davies (Ireland); Ley; Calthorpe; Bulstrode, 1 and 2. London, 1907.

Calendars of State Papers, Domestic Series, for the Reigns of Edward VI, Mary, Elizabeth, and James I. Edited by Mary Anne Everett Green et al. 12 vols. London, 1856–72.

Calendars of State Papers, Domestic Series. 1603–1704. 81 vols. London, 1857–.

Calendars of State Venice. Edited by H. F. Brown and A. B. Hinds. vols. 10–38 (1603–75). London, 1900–.

Chamberlain, John. *The Letters of John Chamberlain*. Edited by Norman Egbert McClure. 2 vols. Philadelphia, 1939.

Discourse of the Common Weal of this Realm of England. Edited by Elizabeth Lamond. Cambridge, England, 1893.

A *Discourse of the Commonweal of this Realm of England. Attributed to Sir Thomas Smith*. Edited by Mary Dewar. Folger Documents of Tudor and Stuart Civilization. Charlottesville, 1969.

Glanville, John. *Reports of Certain Cases Determined and Adjudged by the Commons in Parliament in the Twenty-first and Twenty-second Years of the Reign of King James the First* . . . London, 1775.

Harrison, William. *The Desription of England*. Edited by Georges Edelen. The Folger Shakespeare Library. Ithaca, N.Y., 1968.

Hawarde, John. *Les Reports del Cases in Camera Stellata*. Edited by W. P. Baildon. London, 1894.

Historical Manuscripts Commission.

> *Calendar of the Manuscripts of the* . . . *Marquis of Salisbury* . . . 18 vols. London, 1883–1940.

> *Third Report of the Royal Commission on Historical Manuscripts*. London, 1872.

> *Fourth Report of the Royal Commission on Historical Manuscripts*. London, 1874.

> *Fifth Report of the Royal Commission on Historical Manuscripts*. London, 1876.

> *Sixth Report of the Royal Commission on Historical Manuscripts*. London, 1877.

> *Seventh Report of the Royal Commission on Historical Manuscripts*. London, 1879.

> *Ninth Report of the Royal Commission on Historical Manuscripts*. London, 1883–84.

> *Tenth Report of the Royal Commission on Historical Manuscripts*. London, 1885.

> *Eleventh Report of the Royal Commission on Historical Manuscripts*. London, 1887–88.

> *Twelfth Report of the Royal Commission on Historical Manuscripts*. London, 1891.

> *Twelfth Report. Appendix, Part 7. The Manuscripts of S. H. Le Fleming, Esq., Rydal Hall*. London, 1890.

> *Report on the Manuscripts of the Duke of Buccleuch and Queensbury* . . . vol. 1. London, 1899.

> *Supplementary Report on the Manuscripts of the Earl of Mar & Kellie* . . . Edited by the Rev. Henry Paton, M.A. London, 1930.

Hobbes, Thomas. *A Dialogue between a Philosopher and a Student of the Common Laws of England*. Edited by Joseph Cropsey. Chicago, 1971.

Lambarde, William. *Archeion*. Edited by C. H. McIlwain and P. L. Ward. Cambridge, Mass. 1957.

Malynes, Gerard de. *The Centre of the Circle of Commerce* . . . London, 1623.

Malynes, Gerard de. *Consuetudo, vel, Lex mercatoria, or, The Ancient Law Merchant*. 1622; new ed., London, 1636.

Malynes, Gerard de. *The Maintenance of Free Trade* . . . London, 1622.
Malynes, Gerard de. *A Treatise of the Canker of England's Commonwealth* . . . London, 1601/02.
Misselden, Edward. *The Circle of Commerce* . . . London, 1623.
Misselden, Edward. *Free Trade* . . . London, 1622.
Moore, Sir Francis. *Cases Collect* [sic] *and Report* [sic] *per Sir Fra. Moore* . . . 2d ed. 1688. Rpt. in *The English Reports*, vol. 72, King's Bench Division, 1, pp. 397–997. Containing Bellewe, Keilwey, and Moore. London, 1907.
Mun, Thomas. *A Discourse of Trade* . . . London, 1621.
Mun, Thomas. *England's Treasure by Forraign trade* . . . London, 1644.
Noy, William. *Reports and Cases in the time of Queen Elizabeth, King James, and King Charles* . . . 2d ed. corrected and amended. 1669. Rpt. in *The English Reports*, vol. 74, King's Bench Division, 3, pp. 972–1141. Containing Leonard, vols. 1–4; Owen; and Noy. London, 1907.
The Political Works of James I. Edited by C. H. McIlwain. Cambridge, Mass., 1918.
Rotuli Parliamentorum; ut et petitiones, et placita in Parliamento . . . 6 vols. n.p., n.d.
Select Cases in Star Chamber. Edited by I. S. Leadam. The Publications of the Selden Society, vol. 15. London, 1910.
Select Charters of Trading Companies, A.D. 1530–1707. Edited by Cecil T. Carr. The Publications of the Selden Society, vol. 28. London, 1913.
Whitelocke, Sir James. *Liber Familicus of Sir James Whitelocke*. Edited by J. Bruce. Camden Society, 1st series, vol. 70. London, 1858.
Wentworth Papers, 1597–1628. Edited by J. P. Cooper. Camden Society, 4th series, vol. 12. London, 1973.
Wilbraham, Roger. "The Journal of Roger Wilbraham." Edited by Harold Spencer Scott. *Camden Miscellany*, no. 10. Camden Society, 3d series, vol. 4. London, 1902.
Wilson, Thomas. "The State of England, Anno Dom. 1600." Edited by F. J. Fisher. *Camden Miscellany*, no. 16. Camden Society, 2d series, vol. 2. London, 1936.
Yonge, Walter. *Diary of Walter Yonge*. Edited by G. Roberts. Camden Society, 1st series, vol. 41, London, 1848.

SECONDARY SOURCES

Abbott, L. W. *Law Reporting in England, 1845–1585*. London, 1973.
Adair, E. R. "The Petition of Right." *History* 5 (1921): 99–103.
Alexander, Michael Van Cleave. *Charles I's Lord Treasurer: Sir Richard Weston, Earl of Portland, 1577–1635*. Foreword by A. L. Rowse. Chapel Hill, N.C., 1975.
Anderson, C. B. "Ministerial Responsibility in the 1620s." *Journal of Modern History* 34 (1962): 381–89.
Ashton, Robert. *The Crown and the Money Market, 1603–1640*. Oxford, 1960.
———. "Jacobean Free Trade Again." *Past and Present* 43 (1969): 151–57.
———. "The Parliamentary Agitation for Free Trade in the Opening Years of the Reign of James I." *Past and Present* 38 (1967): 40–55.
Aubrey, John. *Aubrey's Brief Lives*. Edited by Oliver Lawson Dick. 2d ed. London, 1950.

Aumann, Francis Robert. "Lord Coke: The Compleat Student of the Common Law." *Kentucky Law Journal* 17 (1930): 64–69. .

Aylmer, G. E. *The King's Servants: The Civil Service of Charles I, 1625–1642.* New York, 1961.

———. *The Struggle for the Constitution, 1603–1689: England in the Seventeenth Century.* London, 1963.

Baker, J. H. "Coke's Note-Books and the Sources of his *Reports.*" *Cambridge Law Journal* 30 (1972): 59–86.

———. "The Common Lawyers and the Chancery." *Irish Jurist*, n.s. 9 (1969): 368–92.

———. "Counsellors and Barristers." *Cambridge Law Journal* 27 (1969): 204–29.

———. *An Introduction to English Legal History.* London, 1971.

———. "New Light on Slade's Case." *Cambridge Law Journal* 29 (1971): 51–67, 213–36.

———. "The Status of Barristers." *Law Quarterly Review* 85 (1969): 336–38.

Ball, J. N. "The Impeachment of the Duke of Buckingham in the Parliament of 1626." In *Mélanges Antonio Marongiu*, pp. 35–48. Studies Presented to the International Commission for the History of Representative and Parliamentary Institutions, *Études* 34. Palermo, 1967.

———. "The Parliamentary Career of Sir John Eliot, 1624–1629." Ph.D. dissertation, University of Cambridge, 1953.

———. "The Petition of Right in the English Parliament of 1628." In *Album É[mile] Lousse*, vol. 4, pp. 43–64. Louvain, 1964.

———. "Sir John Eliot at the Oxford Parliament, 1625." *Bulletin of the Institute of Historical Research* 27 (1965): 127–48.

Barrett, C. R. B. *The History of the Society of Apothecaries of London.* London, 1905.

Bell, H. E. *An Introduction to the History and Records of the Court of Wards and Liveries.* Cambridge Studies in English Legal History. Cambridge, England, 1953.

Beller, E. A. "The Thirty Years War." In *The New Cambridge Modern History*, vol. 4, *The Decline of Spain and the Thirty Years War, 1609–48/59*, edited by J. P. Cooper, pp. 306–58. Cambridge, England, 1970.

Beresford, Maurice W. "The Common Informer, the Penal Statutes, and Economic Regulation." *Economic History Review*, 2d ser. 10 (1957): 221–38.

———. "Habitation versus Improvement: The Debate on Enclosure by Agreement." In *Essays in the Economic and Social History of Tudor and Stuart England in Honour of R. H. Tawney*, edited by F. J. Fisher, pp. 40–69. Cambridge, 1961.

Berger, Raoul. "*Doctor Bonham's Case*: Statutory Interpretation or Constitutional Theory?" *University of Pennsylvania Law Review* 117 (1969): 521–45.

Berkowitz, David S. "Parliamentary History, American Style." *American Journal of Legal History* 16 (1972): 260–73.

———. "Reason of State in England and the Petition of Right, 1603–1629." In *Staatsräson: Studien zur Geschichte eines politischen Begriffs*, edited by Roman Schnur, pp. 165–212. Berlin, 1975.

———. *Scholar in Politics: The Life and Times of John Selden*, forthcoming.

Boudin, L. B. "Lord Coke and the American Doctrine of Judicial Power." *New York University Law Review* 6 (1928–29): 233–46.

Bowden, Peter J. *The Wool Trade in Tudor and Stuart England*. London, 1962.
Bowen, Catherine Drinker. *The Lion and the Throne: The Life and Times of Sir Edward Coke, 1552–1634*. Boston, 1957.
Boynton, Lindsay. "Billeting: The Example of the Isle of Wight." *English Historical Review* 74 (1959): 23–40.
————. "Martial Law and the Petition of Right." *English Historical Review* 79 (1964): 255–84.
Brailsford, H. N. *The Levellers and the English Revolution*. Edited by Christopher Hill. Stanford, 1961.
Breslow, Martin Arthur. *A Mirror of England: English Puritan Views of Foreign Nations, 1618–1640*. Harvard Historical Studies, vol. 84. Cambridge, Mass., 1970.
Brook, Christopher, and Sharp, Keven. "History, English Law, and the Renaissance." *Past and Present* 72 (1976): 133–42.
Burch, Charles Newell. "The Rivals [: Coke and Bacon]." *Virginia Law Review* 14 (1928): 507–25.
Campbell, Lord John. *The Lives of the Chief Justices of England*. 4 vols. New York, 1874.
Caraman, Philip. *Henry Garnet, 1555–1606, and The Gunpowder Plot*. New York, 1964.
Cheyney, Edward P. *History of England from the Defeat of the Armada to the Death of Elizabeth*. 2 vols. London, 1914–26.
Christianson, Paul. "The Causes of the English Revolution: A Reappraisal." *Journal of British Studies* 15 (1976): 40–75.
————. "The Peers, the People, and Parliamentary Management in the First Six Months of the Long Parliament." *Journal of Modern History* 49 (1977): 575–99.
Clifton, Robin. "Fear of Popery." In *Origins of the English Civil War*, edited by Conrad Russell. pp. 144–67. New York, 1973.
————. "The Popular Fear of Catholics during the English Revolution." *Past and Present* 52 (1971): 23–55.
Clode, Charles M. *The Early History of the Guild of Merchant Taylors . . . In two parts*. London, 1888–89.
[Clode, Charles M.] *Memorials of the Guild of Merchant Taylors . . . London*, 1875.
Cockburn, J. S. *A History of the English Assizes, 1558–1714*. Cambridge Studies in English Legal History. London, 1972.
Coke, Dorothea. *The Last Elizabethan: Sir John Coke, 1563–1644*. London, 1937.
Colbourn, H. Trevor. *The Lamp of Experience: Whig History and the Intellectual Origins of the American Revolution*. 1965. Reprint. New York, 1974.
Cole, Charles Woolsey. *Colbert and a Century of French Mercantilism*. 2 vols. New York, 1939.
Cole, Maija Jansson, and Gray, Charles M. "Bowdler's Case: The Intestate Bastard." Typescript.
Coleman, D. C. "Eli Heckscher and the Idea of Mercantilism." *Scandinavian Economic History Review* 10 (1957): 3–25; reprinted in *Revisions in Mercantilism*, edited by D. C. Coleman, pp. 92–117. London, 1969.
————. ed. *Revisions in Mercantilism*. Debates in Economic History. Edited by Peter Mathias. London, 1969.

Cooper, J. P. "Economic Regulation and the Cloth Industry in Seventeenth-Century England." *Transactions of the Royal Historical Society*, 5th ser. 20 (1970): 73–99.

———. "The Fall of the Stuart Monarchy." In *The New Cambridge Modern History*, vol. 4, *The Decline of Spain and the Thirty Years War, 1609–48/59*, edited by J. P. Cooper, pp. 531–84. Cambridge, England, 1970.

———. "The Fortune of Thomas Wentworth, Earl of Strafford." *Economic History Review*, 2d ser. 2 (1958): 227–48.

Corfield, Penelope. "Economic Issues and Ideologies." In *Origins of the English Civil War*, edited by Conrad Russell, pp. 197–218. New York, 1973.

Cotterell, Mary. "Interregnum Law Reform: The Hale Commission of 1652." *English Historical Review* 83 (1968): 689–704.

Davies, Margaret Gay. *The Enforcement of English Apprenticeship: A Study in Applied Mercantilism, 1563–1642*. Harvard Economic Studies, vol. 97. Cambridge, Mass., 1956.

Davies, D. Seaborne. "Further Light on the Case of Monopolies." *Law Quarterly Review* 48 (1932): 394–414.

Davies, Godfrey, *The Early Stuarts, 1603–1660*. The Oxford History of England, vol. 9. 2d ed. Oxford, 1959.

Dawson, John P. "Coke and Ellesmere Disinterred: The Attack on Chancery in 1616." *Illinois Law Review* 36 (1941): 127–52.

———. *A History of Lay Judges*. Cambridge, Mass., 1960.

de Smith, S. A. "The Prerogative Writs." *Cambridge Law Journal* 11 (1951): 40–56.

Dictionary of National Biography, s.v. "Coke, Sir Edward."

Dietz, F. C. *English Public Finance, 1558–1641*. New York, 1932.

Donald, M. B. *Elizabethan Monopolies: The History of the Company of Mineral and Battery Works from 1565 to 1604*. London, 1961.

Elton, G. R. *"The Body of the Whole Realm": Parliament and Representation in Medieval and Tudor England*. Charlottesville, 1969.

———. "A High Road to Civil War?" In *From the Renaissance to the Counter-Reformation: Essays in Honor of Garrett Mattingly*, edited by Charles H. Carter, pp. 325–44. New York, 1965.

———. "Informing for Profit: A Sidelight on Tudor Methods of Law Enforcement." *Cambridge Historical Journal* 11 (1954): 149–67.

———. *Reform and Renewal: Thomas Cromwell and the Common Weal*. Cambridge, England, 1973.

———. "Reform by Statute: Thomas Starkey's *Dialogue* and Thomas Cromwell's 'Policy'." *Proceedings of the British Academy* 54 (1968): 165–88.

———. "Studying the History of Parliament." *British Studies Monitor* 2 (1971): 4–14.

———. *The Tudor Constitution: Documents and Commentary*. Cambridge, England, 1962.

———. "Tudor Government: The Points of Contact." *Transactions of the Royal Historical Society*, 5th ser. 24 (1974): 183–200; 25 (1975): 195–211; and 26 (1976): 211–28.

Eusden, John Dykstra. *Puritans, Lawyers, and Politics in Early Seventeenth-Century England*. Yale Studies in Religious Education, vol. 23. New Haven, 1958.

Farnell, James E. "The Social and Intellectual Basis of London's Role in the English Civil Wars." *Journal of Modern History* 49 (1977): 641–60.

Ferguson, Arthur B. *The Articulate Citizen and the English Renaissance.* Durham, N.C., 1965.

Finley, M. I. "The Ancestral Constitution." In *The Use and Abuse of History,* by M. I. Finley, pp. 35–59. New York, 1975.

Fisher, F. J. "London's Export Trade in the Early Seventeenth Century." *Economic History Review* 2d ser. 3 (1950): 151–61.

Flemion, J. S. "The Dissolution of the Parliament of 1626: A Re-evaluation." *English Historical Review* 87 (1972): 784–90.

———. "Slow Process, Due Process, and the High Court of Parliament." *Historical Journal* 17 (1974): 3–16.

———. "The Struggle for the Petition of Right in the House of Lords: The Study of an Opposition Victory." *Journal of Modern History* 45 (1973): 193–210.

Forster, John. *Sir John Eliot: A Biography, 1590–1632.* 2 vols. London, 1864.

Foss, Edward. *The Judges of England.* 9 vols. London, 1848–64.

Foster, Elizabeth Read. *The Painful Labour of Mr. Elsyng.* Transactions of the American Philosophical Society, n.s., vol. 62, pt. 8 (1972). Philadelphia, 1972.

———. "Petitions and the Petition of Right." *Journal of British Studies* 14 (1974): 21–45.

———. "Printing the Petition of Right." *Huntingdon Library Quarterly* 28 (1974): 81–84.

———. "The Procedure against Patents and Monopolies, 1621–24." In *Conflict in Stuart England: Essays in Honour of Wallace Notestein,* edited by W. A. Aiken and B. D. Henning, pp. 59–85. London, 1960.

Frank, Joseph. *The Levellers: A History of the Writings of Three Seventeenth-Century Social Democrats: John Lilburne, Richard Overton, and William Walwyn.* Cambridge, Mass., 1955.

Friis, Astrid. *Alderman Cockayne's Project and the Cloth Trade: The Commercial Policy of England in Its Main Aspects, 1603–1625.* Copenhagen, 1927.

Fuller, Thomas. *The History of the Worthies of England.* Edited by P. A. Nuttall. 3 vols. London, 1840.

Fussner, F. Smith. *The Historical Revolution: English Historical Writing and Thought, 1580–1640.* New York, 1962.

Gardiner, Samuel R. *History of England from the Accession of James I to the Outbreak of the Civil War, 1603–1642.* 10 vols. New York, 1908.

Gest, Charles Marshall. "The Writings of Sir Edward Coke." *Yale Law Journal* 18 (1909): 504–32.

Gleason, J. H. *The Justice of the Peace in England 1558 to 1640: A Later Eirenarcha.* Oxford, 1969.

Glen, Garrard. "Edward Coke and Law Restatement." *Virginia Law Review* 17 (1931): 447–60.

Gordon, J. W. *Monopolies by Patents.* London, 1897.

Gough, J. W. *Fundamental Law in English Constitutional History.* 2d ed. Oxford, 1961.

———. *The Rise of the Entrepreneur.* London, 1969.

Gould, J. D. "Cloth Exports, 1600–1640." *Economic History Review,* 2d ser. 24 (1971): 249–52.

———. "The Crisis in the Export Trade, 1586–1587." *English Historical Review* 70 (1956): 212–22.

————. "The Date of *England's Treasure by Forraign Trade*." *Journal of Economic History* 15 (1955): 160–61.

————. "The Trade Crisis of the Early 1620s and English Economic Thought." *Journal of Economic History* 15 (1955): 121–33.

————. "The Trade Depression of the Early 1620s." *Economic History Review*, 2d ser. 7 (1954): 81–90.

Gras, Norman Scott Brien. *The Early English Customs System: A Documentary Study of the Institutional and Economic History of the Customs from the Thirteenth to the Sixteenth Centuries*. Harvard Economic Studies, vol. 18. Cambridge, Mass., 1918.

Gray, Charles M. "Bonham's Case Revisited." *Proceedings of the American Philosophical Society* 116 (1972): 35–58.

————. "The Boundaries of the Equitable Function." *American Journal of Legal History* 20 (1976): 192–226.

————. *Copyhold, Equity, and the Common Law*. Harvard Historical Monographs, no. 53. Cambridge, Mass., 1963.

————. "Introduction." In Sir Matthew Hale, *The History of the Common Law of England*, edited by Charles M. Gray, pp. xi–xxxviii. Chicago, 1971.

————. "Reason, Authority, and Imagination: The Jurisprudence of Sir Edward Coke." Typescript.

Greene, Douglas G. "The Court of the Marshalsea in Late Tudor and Stuart England." *American Journal of Legal History* (1976): 267–81.

Gruenfelder, John K. "The Electoral Patronage of Sir Thomas Wentworth, Earl of Stafford, 1614–1640." *Journal of Modern History* 49 (1977): 557–74.

————. "The Lord Wardens and Elections, 1604–1628." *Journal of British Studies* 16 (1976): 1–23.

Hall, Hubert. *A History of the Customs Revenue in England: from the Earliest Times to the Year 1827 . . .* 2 vols. in 1. Cheap Edition. London, 1892.

Hanson, Donald W. *From Kingdom to Commonwealth: The Development of Civic Consciousness in English Political Thought*. Harvard Political Studies. Cambridge, Mass., 1970.

Harding, Alan. *A Social History of English Law*. Baltimore, 1971.

Harrison, G. B. *The Life and Death of Robert Devereux, Earl of Essex*. New York, 1937.

Hassall, W. O., ed. *A Catalogue of the Library of Sir Edward Coke*. Preface by Samuel E. Thorne. New Haven, 1950.

Heaton, Herbert. "Heckscher on Mercantilism." *Journal of Political Economy* 45 (1937): 370–93.

Heckscher, Eli. *Mercantilism*. Authorized Translation by Mendel Shapiro. Revised ed. Edited by E. F. Soderlund. 2 vols. 1955. Reprint. London, 1962.

Henderson, Edith G. *Foundations of English Administrative Law: Certiorari and Mandamus in the Seventeenth Century*. Publications of the Ames Foundation. Cambridge, Mass., 1963.

Hexter, J. H. "Parliament under the Lens." *British Studies Monitor* 3 (1972): 4–15.

————. "Power Struggle, Parliament, and Liberty in Early Stuart England." *Journal of Modern History* 50 (1978): 1–50.

Hill, Christopher. *Economic Problems of the Church from Archbishop Whitgift to the Long Parliament*. Oxford, 1956.

————. *Intellectual Origins of the English Revolution*. Oxford, 1965.

————. "The Norman Yoke." In *Puritanism and Revolution: Studies in Interpretation of the English Revolution of the Seventeenth Century*, by Christopher Hill, pp. 50–122, 1958. Reprint. New York, 1964.

————. "Recent Interpretations of the English Civil War." In *Puritanism and Revolution: Studies in Interpretation of the English Revolution of the Seventeenth Century*, by Christopher Hill, pp. 3–31. 1958. Reprint. New York, 1964.

————. "William Perkins and the Poor." In *Puritanism and Revolution: Studies in Interpretation of the English Revolution of the Seventeenth Century*, by Christopher Hill, pp. 215–38. 1958. Reprint. New York, 1964.

Hinton, R. W. K. *The Eastland Trade and the Common Weal in the Seventeenth Century*. Cambridge, England, 1959.

Hirst, Derek. "Elections and the Privileges of the House of Commons in the Early Seventeenth Century: Confrontation or Compromise?" *Historical Journal* 18 (1975): 851–62.

————. *The Representative of the People?: Voters and Voting in England under the Early Stuarts*. Cambridge, England, 1975.

————. "Unanimity in the Commons, Aristocratic Intrigues, and the Origins of the Civil War." *Journal of Modern History* 50 (1978): 51–71.

Holdsworth, Sir William. *A History of English Law*. 16 vols. Vol. 1. 7th ed. 1956. Reprint. London, 1969. Vol. 4. 3d ed. 1945. Reprint. London, 1966. Vol. 5. 3d ed. 1945. Reprint. London, 1966. Vol. 7. 2d ed. 1937. Reprint. London, 1966.

————. "The Influence of Coke on the Development of English Law." In *Essays in Legal History*, edited by Paul Vinogradoff, pp. 297–311. Oxford, 1914.

————. "Sir Edward Coke." *Cambridge Law Journal* 5 (1935): 332–46.

————. "Sir Edward Coke." In *Some Makers of English Law*, by William Holdsworth, pp. 111–32. The Tagore Lectures, 1937–38. 1938. Reprint. Cambridge, England, 1966.

Hopkinson, Harry Lennox. *Report on the Ancient Records in the Possession of the Guild of Merchant Taylors . . .* London, 1915.

Horwitz, Morton J. *The Transformation of American Law, 1780–1860*. Studies in Legal History. Cambridge, Mass., 1977.

Hulme, E. Wyndham. "The History of the Patent System under the Prerogative and at Common Law." *Law Quarterly Review* 12 (1896): 141–54.

Hulme, Harold. "The Leadership of Sir John Eliot in the Parliament of 1626." *Journal of Modern History* 4 (1932): 361–86.

————. *The Life of Sir John Eliot, 1592 to 1632: Struggle for Parliamentary Freedom*. London, 1957.

————. "Opinion in the House of Commons on the Proposed Petition of Right," *English Historical Review* 50 (1935): 302–6.

————. "The Winning of Freedom of Speech by the House of Commons." *American Historical Review* 61 (1956): 825–53.

Hurstfield, Joel. "Political Corruption in Modern England: The Historian's Problem." In *Freedom, Corruption and Government in Elizabethan England*, by Joel Hurstfield, pp. 137–62. Cambridge, Mass., 1973.

————. "The Political Morality of Early Stuart Statesmen." In *Freedom, Corruption and Government in Elizabethan England*, by Joel Hurstfield. pp. 183–96. Cambridge, Mass., 1973.

————. *The Queen's Wards: Wardship and Marriage under Elizabeth I*. London, 1958.

Ives, E. W. "The Common Lawyers in Pre-Reformation England." *Transactions of the Royal Historical Society*, 5th ser. 18 (1968): 145–73.
———. "The Reputation of Common Lawyers in English Society." *Birmingham Historical Journal* 7 (1960): 130–42.
———. "Social Change and the Law." In *The English Revolution, 1600–1660*, edited by E. W. Ives, pp. 115–30. London, 1968.
Jackson, William A. *Records of the Court of the Stationers' Company: 1602–1640*. Bibliography Society. 2 vols. London, 1930–57.
James, Charles Warburton. *Chief Justice Coke: His Family and Descendants at Holkham*. London, 1929.
Jenks, Edward. "The Prerogative Writs." *Yale Law Journal* 32 (1923): 523–34.
Johnson, A. H. *The History of the Worshipful Company of the Drapers of London . . .* 3 vols. Oxford, 1914.
Johnson, Cuthbert William. *The Life of Sir Edward Coke*. 2 vols. London, 1837.
Johnson, Robert C. "Parliamentary Diaries of the Early Stuart Period." *Bulletin of the Institute of Historical Research* 44 (1971): 293–300.
Jones, W. J. "The Crown and the Courts in England, 1603–1625." In *The Reign of James VI and I*, edited by Alan G. R. Smith, pp. 177–94. 1973. Reprint. London, 1977.
———. *The Elizabethan Court of Chancery*. Oxford, 1967.
———. "Ellesmere and Politics, 1603–1617." In *Early Stuart Studies: Essays in Honor of David Harris Willson*, edited by Howard S. Reinmuth, pp. 11–63. Minneapolis, 1970.
———. *Politics and the Bench*. New York, 1971.
Jones, Whitney R. D. *The Tudor Commonwealth, 1529–1559 . . .* London, 1970.
Judson, Margaret. *The Crisis of the Constitution: An Essay in Constitutional and Political Thought in England, 1603–1645*. New Brunswick, 1949.
Keir, David L. *Constitutional History of Modern Britain since 1485*. 9th ed. London, 1969.
Kelley, Donald R. "History, English Law, and the Renaissance." *Past and Present* 65 (1974): 24–51.
———. "A Rejoinder." *Past and Present* 72 (1976): 143–46.
Kenyon, J. P. *The Stuart Constitution, 1603–1688: Documents and Commentary*. Cambridge, England, 1966.
Kerridge, Eric. *Agrarian Problems in the Sixteenth Century and After*. Historical Problems: Studies and Documents. Edited by G. R. Elton. Vol. 6. New York, 1969.
Kishlansky, Mark. "The Emergence of Adversary Politics in the Long Parliament." *Journal of Modern History* 49 (1977): 617–40.
Kitching, C. J. "The Quest for Concealed Lands in the Reign of Elizabeth." *Transactions of the Royal Historical Society* 5th ser. 24 (1974): 63–78.
Knafla, Louis A. *Law and Politics in Jacobean England: The Tracts of Lord Chancellor Ellesmere*. Cambridge Studies in English Legal History. London, 1977.
Kocher, Paul H. "Francis Bacon on the Science of Jurisprudence." *Journal of the History of Ideas* 18 (1957): 3–26.
Kuehn, George W. "Coke's Cawdrey *Treatise* 'Of the King's Ecclesiastical Laws' and Persons's *Answer*, 1605–1609." Typescript.
Lacey, Robert. *Sir Walter Raleigh*. New York, 1974.

Levack, Brian P. *The Civil Lawyers in England: A Political Study*. Oxford, 1973.

Lewis, John Underwood. "Coke's Theory of Artificial Reason." *Law Quarterly Review* 84 (1968): 330–42.

Lipson, E[phraim]. *The Economic History of England*. Vols. 2 and 3, *The Age of Mercantilism*. 6th ed. 1956. Reprint. London, 1964.

Little, David. *Religion, Order, and Law: A Study in Pre-Revolutionary England*. New York, 1969.

Lucke, H. K. "Slade's Case and the Origin of the Common Counts." *Law Quarterly Review* 81 (1965–66): 422–45, 539–61; 82 (1966): 81–96.

Lyon, Hastings, and Block, Herman. *Edward Coke: Oracle of the Law*. Boston, 1929.

MacCaffrey, Wallace T. "Place and Patronage in Elizabethan Politics." In *Elizabethan Government and Society: Essays Presented to Sir John Neale*, edited by Stanley T. Bindoff, Joel Hurstfield, and Charles H. Williams, pp. 95–116. London, 1961.

McIlwain, Charles Howard. *Constitutionalism, Ancient and Modern*. Rev. ed. Ithaca, N.Y., 1947.

———. *The High Court of Parliament and its Supremacy*. New Haven, 1910.

MacKay, R. A. "Coke—Parliamentary Sovereignty or the Supremacy of Law?" *Michigan Law Review* 22 (1924): 215–47.

Mackinnon, Sir Frank Douglas. "Sir Edward Coke." *Law Quarterly Review* 51 (1935): 289–98.

Maitland, Frederic William. *The Constitutional History of England*. Cambridge, England, 1908.

Malament, Barbara. "The 'Economic Liberalism' of Sir Edward Coke." *Yale Law Journal* 76 (1967): 1321–58.

Mander, C. H. Waterland. *A Descriptive and Historical Account of the Guild of Cordwainers of the City of London*. [London], 1931.

Marcham, Frederick G. *A Constitutional History of Modern England, 1485 to the Present*. New York, 1960.

Marwil, Jonathan. *The Trials of Counsel: Francis Bacon in 1621*. Detroit, 1976.

Mason, R. Hindry. *The History of Norfolk*. London, 1884.

Mendenhall, T. C. *The Shrewsbury Drapers and the Welsh Wool Trade in the Sixteenth and Seventeenth Centuries*. London, 1953.

Milsom, S. F. C. *Historical Foundations of the Common Law*. London, 1967.

Mitchell, Williams M. *The Rise of the Revolutionary Party in the English House of Commons, 1603–1629*. New York, 1957.

Moir, Thomas L. *The Addled Parliament of 1614*. Oxford, 1958.

Mosse, George L. *The Struggle for Sovereignty in England: From the Reign of Queen Elizabeth to the Petition of Right*. 1950. Reprint. New York, 1968.

Mullett, Charles F. "Coke and the American Revolution." *Economica* 12 (1932): 457–71.

Neale, J. E. *Elizabeth I and Her Parliaments, 1559–1581*. 1956. Reprint. New York, 1966.

———. *Elizabeth I and Her Parliaments, 1584–1601*. 1958. Reprint. New York, 1966.

———. *The Elizabethan House of Commons*. Rev. ed. Harmondsworth, 1963.

Nef, J. U. *Industry and Government in France and England, 1540–1640*. 1940. Reprint. Ithaca, N.Y., 1957.

———. *The Rise of the British Coal Industry*. 2 vols. London, 1932.

Niehaus, Charles R. "The Issue of Law Reform in the Puritan Revolution." Ph.D. dissertation, Harvard University, 1957.

Notestein, Wallace. *The House of Commons, 1604–1610.* New Haven, 1971.

——. "The Winning of the Initiative by the House of Commons." British Academy Lecture, 1924. Reprinted in *Studies in History: British Academy Lectures,* selected and introduced by Lucy S. Sutherland, pp. 145–203. London, 1966.

Nourse, G. B. "Law Reform under the Commonwealth and Protectorate." *Law Quarterly Review* 75 (1959): 512–29.

Ogilvie, Sir Charles. *The King's Government and the Common Law, 1471–1641.* Oxford, 1958.

Parkinson, C. Northcote. *The Gunpowder Treason and Plot.* London, 1976.

Phillips, Frank Taverner. *A History of the Worshipful Company of Cooks, London.* London, 1932.

Plucknett, T. F. T. "Bonham's Case and Judicial Review." *Harvard Law Review,* 40 (1926–27): 30–70.

——. *A Concise History of the Common Law.* 5th ed. Boston, 1956.

——. "The Genesis of Coke's Reports." *Cornell Law Quarterly* 17 (1942): 190–213.

——. "Some Proposed Legislation of Henry VIII." *Transactions of the Royal Historical Society,* 4th ser. 19 (1936): 119–44.

Pocock, J. G. A. *The Ancient Constitution and the Feudal Law: English Historical Thought in the Seventeenth Century.* 1957. Reprint. New York, 1967.

Ponko, Vincent, Jr. *The Privy Council and the Spirit of Elizabethan Economic Management, 1558–1603.* Transactions of the American Philosophical Society, n.s. 58, pt. 4 (1968). Philadelphia, 1968.

Powicke, F. M. *The Thirteenth Century, 1216–1307.* The Oxford History of England, vol. 4. 2d ed. Oxford, 1962.

Prall, Stuart E. *The Agitation for Law Reform during the Puritan Revoution, 1640–1660.* The Hague, 1966.

——. "Chancery Reform and the Puritan Revolution." *American Journal of Legal History* 6 (1962): 28–44.

Prest, Wilfred. *The Inns of Court under Elizabeth and the Early Stuarts, 1590–1640.* Totowa, N.J., 1972.

Prestwich, Menna. *Cranfield: Politics and Profits under the Early Stuarts: The Career of Lionel Cranfield, Earl of Middlesex.* Oxford, 1966.

——. "English Politics and Administration, 1603–1625." In *The Reign of James VI and I,* edited by Alan G. R. Smith, pp. 160–76. 1973. Reprint. London, 1977.

Price, William Hyde. *The English Patents of Monopoly.* Harvard Economic Studies, no. 1. Cambridge, Mass., 1913.

Rabb, Theodore K. "Francis Bacon and the Reform of Society." In *Action and Conviction in Early Modern Europe: Essays in Memory of E. H. Harbison,* edited by Theodore K. Rabb and Jerrold E. Seigel, pp. 169–93. Princeton, 1969.

——. "Free Trade and the Gentry in the Parliament of 1604." *Past and Present* 40 (1968): 165–73.

——. "Parliament and Society in Early Stuart England: The Legacy of Wallace Notestein." *American Historical Review* 77 (1972): 705–14.

————. "Sir Edwin Sandys in the Parliament of 1604." *American Historical Review* 69 (1964): 646–70.

Ramsay, G. D. *The Wiltshire Woollen Industry in the Sixteenth and Seventeenth Centuries.* 2d ed. London, 1965.

Randall, Charles H., Jr. "Sir Edward Coke and the Privilege against Self-Incrimination." *South Carolina Law Quarterly* 8 (1956): 417–53.

Read, Conyers. *Lord Burghley and Queen Elizabeth.* London, 1960.

Reid, Rachel R. *The King's Council in the North.* London, 1921.

Relf, Frances Helen. *The Petition of Right.* University of Minnesota Studies in the Social Sciences, vol. 8. Minneapolis, 1917.

Rex, Millicent Barton. *University Representation in England, 1604–1690.* Preface by R. L. Schuyler. Études préséntées à la Commission Internationale pour l'histoire des Assemblées d'États, vol. 15. New York, 1954.

Roberts, Clayton. "The Earl of Bedford and the Coming of the English Revolution." *Journal of Modern History* 49 (1977): 600–16.

————. *The Growth of Responsible Government in Stuart England.* Cambridge, England, 1966.

Ruigh, Robert E. *The Parliament of 1624: Politics and Foreign Policy.* Harvard Historical Studies, no. 87. Cambridge, Mass., 1971.

Russell, Conrad. *The Crisis of Parliaments: English History, 1509–1660.* The Shorter Oxford History of the Modern World, edited by J. M. Roberts. London, 1971.

————. "The Examination of Mr. Mallory after the Parliament of 1621." *Bulletin of the Institute of Historical Research* 50 (1977): 125–32.

————. "The Foreign Policy Debate in the House of Commons in 1621." *Historical Journal* 20 (1977): 289–309.

————. "Parliament and the King's Finances." In *The Origins of the English Civil War,* edited by Conrad Russell, pp.91–116. New York, 1973.

————. "Parliamentary History in Perspective, 1604–1629." *History* 61 (1976): 1–27.

————. ed. *The Origins of the English Civil War.* New York, 1973.

Schwoerer, Lois G. *"No Standing Armies!" The Anti-Military Ideology in Seventeenth-Century England.* Baltimore, 1974.

Seaver, Paul S. *The Puritan Lectureships: The Politics of Religious Dissent, 1560–1662.* Stanford, 1970.

Shapiro, Barbara. "Codification of the Law in Seventeenth-Century England." *Wisconsin Law Review,* no. 2 (1974): 428–65.

————. "Law Reform in Seventeenth-Century England." *American Journal of Legal History* 19 (1975): 280–312.

Sherwell, J. W. *The History of the Guild of Sadlers of the City of London.* 3d and rev. ed. by Lt. Col. K. S. Laurie. N.p., 1956.

Simon, The Rt. Hon. Sir Jocelyn. "Dr. Cowell." *Cambridge Law Journal* 26 (1968): 260–72.

Simpson, A. W. B. *A History of the Common Law of Contract: The Rise of the Action of Assumpsit.* Oxford, 1975.

————. *An Introduction to the History of the Land Law.* Oxford, 1961.

————. "The Place of Slade's Case in the History of Contract." *Law Quarterly Review* 74 (1958): 381–96.

Smith, A. Hassell. *County and Court: Government and Politics in Norfolk, 1558–1603.* Oxford, 1974.

Smith, Alan G. R., ed. *The Reign of James VI and I.* 1973. Reprint. London, 1977.

Smith, Goldwin. "The Reform of the Laws of England, 1640–1660." *University of Toronto Quarterly* 10 (1941): 469–81.

Snapp, H. F. "The Impeachment of Roger Manwaring." *Huntingdon Library Quarterly* 30 (1967): 217–32.

Snow, Vernon F. "The Arundel Case, 1626." *Historian* 26 (1964): 323–49.

————. *Essex the Rebel: The Life of Robert Devereaux, The Third Earl of Essex, 1591–1646.* Lincoln, Neb., 1970.

Spielman, D. C. "Impeachments and the Parliamentary Opposition in England, 1621–1641." Ph.D. dissertation, University of Wisconsin, 1959.

Stephen, H. L. "The Trial of Sir Walter Ralegh." *Transactions of the Royal Historical Society*, 4th ser. 2 (1919): 172–87.

Stephens, W. B. "The Cloth Exports of the Provincial Ports, 1600–1640." *Economic History Review*, 2d ser. 22 (1969): 228–48.

————. "Further Observations on English Cloth Exports, 1600–1640." *Economic History Review*, 2d ser. 24 (1971): 253–57.

Stone, Lawrence. *The Causes of the English Revolution, 1529–1642.* New York, 1972.

————. *The Crisis of the Aristocracy, 1558–1641.* Oxford, 1965.

————. "Elizabethan Overseas Trade." *Economic History Review*, 2d ser. 1 (1949): 30–58.

————. *Family and Fortune: Studies in Aristocratic Finance in the Sixteenth and Seventeenth Centuries.* Oxford, 1973.

————. "The Fruits of Office: The Case of Sir Robert Cecil, First Earl of Salisbury." In *Essays in the Economic and Social History of Tudor and Stuart England in Honour of R. H. Tawney,* edited by F. J. Fisher, pp. 89–116. London, 1961.

Supple, B. E. *Commercial Crisis and Change in England, 1600–1642: A Study in the Instability of a Mercantile Economy.* Cambridge Studies in Economic History. Cambridge, England, 1964.

————. "Thomas Mun and the Commercial Crisis, 1623." *Bulletin of the Institute of Historical Research* 28 (1954): 91–94.

Tanner, J. R. *Constitutional Documents of the Reign of James I, 1603–1625.* 1930. Reprint. Cambridge, England, 1960.

————. *English Constitutional Conflicts of the Seventeenth Century, 1603–1689.* 1928. Reprint. Cambridge, England, 1961.

Taswell-Langmead, Thomas P. *English Constitutional History from the Teutonic Conquest to the Present Time.* 11th ed. Edited by T. F. T. Plucknett. Boston, Mass., 1960.

Tawney, R. H. *Business and Politics under James I: Lionel Cranfield as Merchant and Minister.* Cambridge, England, 1958.

————. , and Power, Eileen. *Tudor Economic Documents.* 3 vols. London, 1924.

Thirsk, Joan, and Cooper, J. P., eds. *Seventeenth-Century Economic Documents.* Oxford, 1972.

Thomas, Keith. *Religion and the Decline of Magic.* 1971. Reprint. London, 1973.

Thompson, Christopher. "The Origins of the Parliamentary Middle Group, 1625–1629." *Transactions of the Royal Historical Society,* 5th ser. 22 (1972): 71–86.

Thorne, Samuel E. "The Constitution and the Courts: A Re-examination of the

Famous Case of Dr. Bonham." *Law Quarterly Review* 54 (1938): 543–52. Reprinted in *The Constitution Reconsidered*, edited by Conyers Read, pp. 15–24. Rev. ed., with a new preface by Richard B. Morris. New York, 1968.

———. "Courts of Record and Sir Edward Coke." *University of Toronto Law Journal* 2 (1937): 24–49.

———. "The Equity of a Statute and Heydon's Case." *Illinois Law Review* 31 (1936): 202–17.

———. "Introduction." In *A Discourse upon the Exposition and Understanding of Statutes*, edited by Samuel E. Thorne, pp. 3–100. San Marino, Calif., 1942.

———. "Praemunire and Sir Edward Coke." *Huntingdon Library Quarterly* 2 (1938): 85–88.

———. *Sir Edward Coke, 1552–1952*. Selden Society Lecture, 17 March 1952. London, 1957.

———. "Tudor Social Transformation and Legal Change." *New York University Law Review* 26 (1951): 10–23.

Tillyard, E. M. W. *The Elizabethan World Picture*. London, 1943.

Tite, Colin G. C. *Impeachment and Parliamentary Judicature in Early Stuart England*. London, 1974.

Tittler, Robert. "Nicholas Bacon and the Reform of the Elizabethan Chancery." *University of Toronto Law Journal* 23 (1973): 383–95.

Trevor-Roper, H. R. "Three Foreigners." In *The Crisis of the Seventeenth Century: Religion, the Reformation and Social Change*, by H. R. Trevor-Roper, pp. 237–93. New York, 1968.

———. *The Gentry, 1540–1640*. Economic History Review, Supplement, no. 1. Cambridge, England, 1953.

Turner, Jesse. "Concerning Divers Notable Stirs between Sir Edward Coke and His Lady." *American Law Review* 51 (1917): 883–903.

Unwin, George. *Industrial Organization in the Sixteenth and Seventeenth Centuries*. 1904. Reprint. London, 1957.

———. "The Merchant Adventurers' Company in the Reign of Elizabeth." In *Studies in Economic History: The Collected Papers of George Unwin*, edited by R. H. Tawney, pp. 133–210. London, 1927.

Upton, A. F. *Sir Arthur Ingram, c. 1565–1642: A Study of the Origins of an English Landed Family*. London, 1961.

Usher, Roland Greene. "James I and Sir Edward Coke." *English Historical Review* 18 (1903): 664–75.

———. *The Reconstruction of the English Church*. 2 vols. New York, 1910.

———. *The Rise and Fall of the High Commission*. Oxford, 1913.

van Eerde, K. S. "The Spanish Match through an English Protestant's Eyes." *Huntingdon Library Quarterly* 32 (1968): 59–75.

Veall, Donald. *The Popular Movement for Law Reform, 1640–1660*. Oxford, 1970.

Wagner, Donald O. "Coke and the Rise of Economic Liberalism." *Economic History Review*, 1st ser. 6 (1935): 30–44.

———. "The Common Law and Free Enterprise: An Early Case of Monopoly." *Economic History Review*, 1st ser. 7 (1937): 217–20.

Wallace, Willard M. *Sir Walter Raleigh*. Princeton, 1959.

Watson, J. Steven. *A History of the Salters Company*. London, 1963.

Welch, Charles. *History of the Cutlers' Company of London . . .* 2 vols. London, 1916–23.

White, Stephen D. "Rev. Colin G. C. Tite: *Impeachment and Parliamentary Judicature in Early Stuart England.*" *Harvard Law Review* 89 (1976): 1934–45.
_____. "Sir Edward Coke in the Parliaments of 1621 and 1624: Parliament, the Law, and the Economy." Ph.D. dissertation, Harvard University, 1972.
Wiener, Carol Z. "The Beleaguered Isle: A Study of Elizabethan and Early Jacobean Anti-Catholicism." *Past and Present* 51 (1971): 27 62.
_____. "Popular Anti-Catholicism in England, 1559–1618." Ph.D. dissertation, Harvard University, 1969.
Willcox, William Bradford. *Gloucestershire: A Study in Local Government, 1590–1640.* New Haven, 1940.
Williamson, H. R. *The Gunpowder Plot.* London, 1951.
Willson, David Harris. *James VI and I.* London, 1956.
_____. *The Privy Councillors in the House of Commons, 1604–1629.* Minneapolis, 1940.
Wilson, Charles. "'Mercantilism': Some Vicissitudes of an Idea." *Economic History Review*, 2d ser. 10 (1957): 181–88.
_____. "Mercantilism." Historical Association, General ser. no. 37. London, 1958.
Winslow, O. E. *Master Roger Williams: A Biography.* New York, 1957.
Woolrych, Humphrey W. *The Life of the Right Honourable Sir Edward Coke Knt.* London, 1826.
Wormuth, F. D. *The Royal Prerogative, 1603–1649: A Study in English Political and Constitutional Ideas.* Ithaca, N.Y., 1939.
Wright, Louis B. *Middle-Class Culture in Elizabethan England.* Chapel Hill, N.C., 1935.
Yale, D. E. C. "Hobbes and Hale on Law, Legislation, and the Sovereign." *Cambridge Law Journal* 31 (1972): 121–56.
Zagorin, Perez. *The Court and the Country: The Beginning of the English Revolution.* 1969. Reprint. New York, 1971.
Zaller, Robert. *The Parliament of 1621: A Study in Constitutional Conflict.* Berkeley, 1971.
Zeeveld, Gordon. *Foundations of Tudor Policy.* Cambridge, Mass., 1948.

Index

175, 180; and royal court, 187, 188–89;
serjeant of, 202, 203; remonstrances,
214; and Petition of Right (1628),
222–36 passim, 242, 245, 247, 248, 251,
252, 254, 259–74 passim; resolutions,
225, 236, 237, 240, 242, 244, 245, 252,
253, 255, 257, 262; journals, 236, 247.
See also Parliament
House of Lords, 3, 5, 6, 28, 37, 42, 53, 57,
58, 64, 182, 257, 272; and legislation,
36, 67, 68–69, 72, 75, 76n, 113n, 128,
129n, 132, 133, 135, 292; and parliamentary judicial proceedings, 117,
142–64 passim, 201, 203, 204;
privileges, 159; and supply, 181–82, 199,
200; and Petition of Right (1628), 216,
223, 225, 236–52 passim, 255, 256,
263–73 passim; royal messages to, 265.
See also Parliament
Howard faction, 6
Huguenots, 189
Hull, merchants of, 287
Hulme, Harold, 179n
Huntingdonshire, 286
Hyde, Sir Lawrence (judge), 215, 216, 233

I

Imports, 95; excessive, 90; French wines,
90, 94; luxuries, 90, 101, 138; cattle, 94,
95, 96–97; tobacco, 95, 96; grain, 95,
97; restraints on, 101, 130, 131. *See also*
Monopolies: on foreign trade; Trade
Impositions, 90, 91, 94, 97, 98, 99, 101,
112, 194, 199, 206, 220; of Merchant
Adventurers Company, 90, 98n, 99, 107;
of corporate towns, 98; "new," 99, 100,
196; on cloth, 102; on malt, 220; on
wine, 220. *See also* Customs; Trade:
overburdening of
Imprisonment, 227–28, 230, 233, 235,
238–39, 258, 261. *See also* Commitment
without cause shown
Inconveniences, 19, 80, 232
Informations, 34, 50, 65n, 138, 288
Informers, 34, 36, 41, 44, 50, 52, 53, 54,
65, 67–69, 113n, 286
Inner Temple, 4
Inns: patent for, 57
Inquisitions post mortem, 64
Inventions, new, 125, 126, 130, 131n, 134,
138–39, 140
Ireland, 9, 90, 96, 97, 113, 198, 210;
grievances of, 166, 170–71
Iron ordnance: patent for, 131, 132; export
of, 138, 288
Iron ore: patent for, 135

J

James VI and I, 5, 23, 27, 58, 67, 143, 172,
177, 189, 197, 210; and Sir Edward
Coke, 6, 7, 8, 167; religious policies, 30,
160; foreign policies, 30, 31, 142, 165,
171, 206, 209; and Parliament, 30, 31,
34, 35–36, 42, 45, 84–85, 142, 166,
173n, 180, 192, 207; and monopolies,
73, 122, 129, 145; and Commons's
privileges, 165, 166, 167, 168, 169, 170,
171, 174, 175, 176–77, 178, 179; and
Dr. Richard Montague, 190, 200, 201;
revenues of, 284
Jefferson, Thomas, 11
John of Gaunt, 204, 205, 212, 272
Judges, 81, 130, 132, 133, 134, 136, 151,
161, 216, 235, 236, 239, 240, 242, 245,
250, 251, 257, 258, 265, 269. *See also*
Corruption: judicial
Judicial notice, 262
Judicial review, 16
Judson, Margaret, 47n
Juries, 32, 50, 51, 55; reform of, 52, 55
Justices. *See* Judges
Justices of Assize, 285
Justices of the peace, 57, 286, 288

K

Keightley, Thomas, 291
Kersies, 288
King's Bench, Court of, 6, 66, 67, 150, 215,
231, 232, 233, 234, 241, 244, 284, 285;
marshal of, 216
"The King's Book." *See* "Book of Bounty"
King's prerogative. *See* Royal prerogative
Kingston upon Hull, 285, 287
Kishlansky, Mark, 28n
Knightley, Winifred (mother of Sir Edward
Coke), 4

L

Laissez-faire, 290. *See also* Freedom of
trade
Lambarde, William, 85n
Lambe, Dr. John, 53
Lancaster, duke of. *See* John of Gaunt
Land registration, 49, 76, 77
La Rochelle, 189
Latimer, William, Lord, 100n, 204, 212,
272
Laud, William (archbishop of Canterbury),
160
Law, 227, 238, 248; codification of, 49, 76,
81; of the land, 227, 248, 249, 254;
ancient, 238, 253; municipal, 248; of
nations, 249; ecclesiastical, 249; of con-

The Author
Stephen D. White is assistant professor of history at Wesleyan University.

The Book
Typeface: Stempel V-I-P Sabon
Design and composition: The University of North Carolina Press
Paper: Sixty pound 1854 by S. D. Warren Company
Binding cloth: Roxite B 53515 by The Holliston Mills, Incorporated
Printer and binder: Braun-Brumfeld, Incorporated

Published by The University of North Carolina Press